Civil War on the
Western Border
1854–1865

Civil War on the
Western Border
1854–1865

by
JAY MONAGHAN

University of Nebraska Press
Lincoln and London

Wm

Copyright 1955 by James Monaghan
All rights reserved
Manufactured in the United States of America

First Bison Book printing: December 1984
2   3   4   5   6   7   8   9   10

Library of Congress Cataloging in Publication Data
Monaghan, Jay, 1891–
  Civil War on the western border, 1854–1865.

  Reprint. Originally published: Boston : Little, Brown,
c1955.
  Includes index.
  1. Southwest, Old—History—Civil War, 1861–1865.
2. Kansas—History—1854–1861. I. Title.
E470.45.M65 1984   973.7   84-11856
ISBN 0-8032-3091-5
ISBN 0-8032-8126-9 (pbk.)

Reprinted by arrangements with Swarthmore College and the
UCSB Foundation (heirs to the estate of Mildred Monaghan).

This edition is reprinted from a copy of the 1955 edition graciously
loaned to the publisher by the Swarthmore College Library.

78-82707

DEDICATED TO THE MEMORY OF LLOYD LEWIS

On a pack trip up Divide Creek the horses got away, and Lloyd enlivened a long hunt with flavorful anecdotes about the five years of Civil War which raged along the Western border before spreading across the nation. These stories and years of companionship with Lloyd were the seed of this book.

Contents

Civil War on the
Western Border
1854–1865

I

A Challenge Accepted

ABRAHAM LINCOLN sat on the edge of his bed talking to Lyle Dickey. The day had been a hard one on the Illinois Circuit. Dickey blinked sleepily at the yellow candle flame, but Lincoln wanted to talk. News of the passage of the Kansas-Nebraska Act by Congress had just been received, and Lincoln's deliberate mind would not rest. He had deserted the hustings for the more lucrative practice of law, but this act aroused his indignation and tempted him to re-enter politics. Dickey fell asleep. Next morning, when he awoke, Lincoln sat propped up in bed still talking as though the conversation had been uninterrupted.

Lincoln had watched excitement grow over the Kansas-Nebraska bill since its introduction on January 4, 1854, by his political antagonist of twenty years' standing, Senator Stephen A. Douglas. The Little Giant, as he was called, had concocted the measure to end political turmoil over slavery, make him the leader of a reunited Democratic Party and, perhaps, President of the United States. His bill's panacea was simple: Quit discriminating against slaveholding pioneers; open all territories to settlers from both North and South, and let them decide by vote whether to exclude or countenance slavery. What could be fairer than that?

Douglas understood the rules of equity better than he did the temper of the American people. He failed, utterly, to foresee that this doctrine of squatter sovereignty would ignite a civil war.

The Little Giant had reached his eminent position by courage and resourcefulness. Confidence gleamed from his tailored clothes and highly polished boots. If the North reproached him for opening Western territories to slavery, he could explain to them that a free economy would triumph over slavery in a fair contest. The concession, therefore, was nominal. Yet, by gaining it, Southerners might feel appeased, and be willing to switch their votes to give the North the terminus of the first railroad to the Pacific. Surely, hardheaded Yankee money-makers would applaud such political logrolling.

Foremost among the bill's proponents in the Senate was David Rice Atchison, a man who, like Douglas, made success a habit, and brooked no interference. He had learned that the doctrine of slavery expansion was a vote-getter in rural Missouri. On this issue he had defeated his rival, Thomas Hart Benton, senior senator, whose German constituents in St. Louis clamored for abolition. Flushed with this victory, Atchison foresaw the opening of all territories to slavery as the best hope of carrying the institution to the Pacific. "We are playing for a mighty stake," he said.

Douglas and Atchison formed an odd team to pull the Kansas-Nebraska bill through Congress. Douglas stood only a fraction over five feet tall, a gamecock and every inch a fighter. Atchison towered above him. He was a florid, sociable man-mountain, fond of horses, hunting, fishing, and liquor. All the Atchisons grew to giant size. One of the six brothers tipped the scales at four hundred pounds before he died. A bit pompous from size and senatorial service, yet full of jokes, David Rice Atchison boasted that he was born in Frogtown, Kentucky — biggest frog in the puddle, sir! Senatorial colleagues had elected him president pro tempore sixteen times.

Atchison epitomized the slave power, and his official position augured well for the Kansas-Nebraska bill's passage. In Washington he lived with two slavocratic nabobs, Senators R. M. Hunter and James Murray Mason. The former was a disciple of Calhoun's, destined to become Secretary of State under the Confederacy. The latter had authored the hated Fugitive Slave Act. Atchison was also close to Secretary of War Jefferson Davis. They had been schoolmates together in Kentucky. Davis, in turn, was intimate with President Franklin Pierce, whose one great ambition for his administration was to re-establish harmony on the slavery issue in the Democratic Party. Like Senator Douglas, he saw the equity in squatter sovereignty and agreed to announce the Kansas-Nebraska bill as an administration measure, thus making the vote on it a test of party regularity.

This was Frank Pierce's first great mistake. Northern Democrats pronounced the opening of any free territory to slavery inexcusable appeasement. In February 1854, while the bill was still being debated in the Senate, a group of liberals met in Ripon, Wisconsin, and resolved — in case it passed — to form a new party pledged against the extension of slavery. The name "Republican" was suggested. Horace Greeley, in his *New York Tribune,* warned: "The attempted passage of this measure is the first great effort of slavery to take American freedom directly by the throat." Hundreds of petitions and memorials of protest flooded the mails to Washington. Mass meetings, antislavery societies, and political conventions sent resolutions. Three thousand and fifty New England clergymen signed a protest. Lincoln, traveling the Illinois Circuit with Lyle Dickey, had realized that this was no summer shower but, instead, a rising tornado of resentment.

In past years, hundreds of people had emigrated to the Pacific annually, but in the spring of 1854, even while the Kansas-Nebraska bill was being debated, the number swelled to thousands — congesting the outfitting towns of St. Joseph, Weston, and Independence, Missouri. All were obviously going to Kansas, not California. As the congressional debates grew vindictive, newspapers reported Ohio River steamboats packed with emigrants from Pennsylvania, Ohio, and Kentucky. The entire country had gone mad about Kansas. Former national excitements over temperance and spirit rapping seemed small by comparison. Political revolution was an ideal of the day, and it was noticeable that Westbound travelers affected the faddish full beard and soft felt hat peculiar to the popular Hungarian revolutionist Louis Kossuth.

Senator Atchison was surprised and shocked by this migration. Strangely enough, he seems to have expected the whole United States to stand back and allow his constituents to pre-empt Kansas. Moreover, his constituents expected the same thing. They were enraged in April when they learned that the Massachusetts legislature had incorporated an emigrant aid society. However, it was late in July — almost two months after the passage of the Kansas-Nebraska bill — before the company was actually organized. New England emigrant aid companies had been helping travelers go West for years, but now the prospect of emigrants with antislavery traditions being sent to Kansas set Senator Atchison's teeth on edge.

The new emigrant aid company was being promoted by a zealot named Eli Thayer, an odd-appearing man with the bald crown of his head gleaming like a snowcap above a timber line of hair and luxuriant black beard.

A correspondent of the *New York Evening Post* said of him: "He may make a place for himself in political history, but he never will be President. He is the vassal of one idea." Grotesque as Thayer appeared, he held an audience as well as or better than Senator Atchison or James Mason, or even the great Senator Douglas himself. The New Englander's long face and solemn expression italicized the droll humor of his words.

Thayer had been a poor farm boy who worked his way through Brown University, class of 1845. While teaching school, young Thayer purchased a five-acre tract known as Goat Hill and from it quarried enough stone to build a castle with serrated towers — "Thayer's Folly" it was called by skeptics. Eli opened a college for women in the building — a daring venture in 1849. To everyone's surprise the institution succeeded amazingly, and "Oread Castle," as he named it, became justly renowned for progressiveness. Prospering financially, Thayer looked to other reforms. The tangled banking situation in Massachusetts interested him for a while. Next the debate over the Kansas-Nebraska bill attracted his attention. Here was a chance to make more money and at the same time extend human freedom. Thayer organized the Massachusetts Emigrant Aid Company and wrote its first constitution. With witty oratory and enthusiasm, he began stumping New England to sell stock. What a chance for speculation in soil more fertile than anything in Massachusetts! He proposed to preempt blocks of land with company funds, send whole villages of settlers to develop farms, and then split the profits with the homesteaders. Thayer insisted that New England institutions be taken to the frontier — schools, sawmills, steam engines. New England's mechanical ability was sure to win Kansas from the "horseback chawbacks" of the border. Stumping the state, he shouted: "The steam engine is a singer, and will sing nothing but freedom. Set it sawing pine logs into boards and it will sing at its work day and night, 'Home of the Free. Home of the Free.' Set it to sawing tough gnarled oak and its song will be, 'Never a slave state! Never a slave state!'"

Thayer boasted that his work was not evangelical. He was not traveling and speaking to draw tears from sentimental women, but to end slavery. New England farmers, shipowners, and mill men, who had seen their proposed laws blocked in Congress for years by the representatives of distant slave owners, understood Thayer's oratory and bought stock in his company. Wealthy Amos A. Lawrence, merchant prince with great spinning interests in New England, invested heavily. His money and Thayer's eloquence made the company.

Senator Atchison realized that he must hurry back to Platte County as soon as the Kansas-Nebraska bill passed, and save his constituents from the threatening money power. American patriots had fought George III, and embattled frontiersmen could yet conquer King Cotton-Bobbin. In the halls of Congress, Atchison rallied his colleagues to force through the law. President Pierce reasserted its importance as a party measure. Victory in the Senate was easy, but it was not until May 22 that the bill passed the House, with wild excitement, by the narrow margin of thirteen votes. Two days later a runaway slave was arrested in Boston, and the nation was impressed again by the depth of popular indignation against any act supporting slavery. The army, the marines, and several regiments of militia restrained protesting rioters until the unfortunate black man was put aboard a vessel which took him back to slavery. On the crest of this excitement, President Pierce signed, on May 30, 1854, the Kansas-Nebraska Act — and lawyer Lincoln, out in Illinois, knew that the die was cast. He would go back into politics.

In Michigan, Senator Zachary Chandler signed a call for all free-state men to assemble in Jackson and organize a new party similar to the one formed in Ripon, Wisconsin. Other states were following suit. Senator William H. Seward of New York, sensing the sincerity of the popular clamor as Lincoln did, declared: "Come then, gentlemen of the slave states: since there is no escaping your challenge, I accept it in behalf of freedom."

Senator Atchison wrote his constituents in Missouri to prepare for the challenge. He had opened the great territory for them. Now let them assert their rights.

Missourians had not waited for the Nebraska bill to pass. Early in the spring they crossed the Big Muddy, staked claims on land still owned by the Indians, organized self-defensive associations to guarantee members' rights, then returned home to work for the summer. These organizations were a traditional extralegal device used by squatters on the frontier for a generation. Other settlers — intent on getting a home at once — stayed on the land, put in a crop, joined no lodge, and were soon classed as abolitionists. Among these were the Cody family with their eight-year-old boy Bill, who from the door of a cabin on Salt Creek saw his first wagon trains, soldiers, buckskin-clad trappers, and Indians — a panorama he remembered all his life.

In June, Senator Atchison returned to his pillared mansion in northwest Missouri. He drove off at once in his buggy, the springs tipping precariously under his weight. At taverns and crossroads he warned his constituents that Boston's Faneuil Hall was coming to rule them.

At Weston, Missouri, he had two ardent supporters named Stringfellow. These little men of the old Virginia school stood scarcely five feet six, but their words carried weight. James H. Stringfellow practiced medicine, served as a pillar of the Methodist Church South, and swung his cane importantly on the main street. He also enjoyed roistering with disreputable characters on the levee, as became a political aspirant. He had a reputation for stirring up trouble and justifying it in his newspaper, the *Squatter Sovereign*. Certainly, he looked forward to an active part in the territorial wrangle. His brother, Benjamin Franklin Stringfellow, was an easy-going man with genial eyes blinking in a cloud of smoke from his ever-present pipe. A lover of fast horses, he was wont to race his buggy team down the dirt road, tossing coins to waving urchins as he whirled by. In the village, he enjoyed sauntering along the street to his favorite chair in front of the hotel. He knew everybody, his business, and the latest whimsical occurrences. By courtesy he was called "General." Senator Atchison, on his political circuit, would draw rein before Stringfellow's rural throne, call a Negro boy to take his horse, and the two would lounge together talking politics for hours.

Less educated but equally as influential was picturesque Milt McGee, at Kansas City landing, the new settlement below Independence. At the age of six, Milt had come from Kentucky with his trapper father. Unschooled and semiliterate, Milt grew to man's strength on the border, blacked his father's eye, and set off to make his fortune in the Rockies. He crossed the plains seven times — with fur traders, with the Great Migration of 1843, with Frémont, and with the gold seekers. Between trips he had taken an active part, with Atchison, in expelling the Mormons from Missouri — a violent procedure which might be used also against Yankee abolitionists. Milt had fought the Comanches in Texas and the Seminole at "Occachubby" — his spelling in his autobiography. At Lassen's Pass in California he had been wounded by Indians. One hand was cupped permanently, but not enough to prevent him from driving a spirited team. Now, at the age of thirty-six, Milt looked like an old man and had settled down as a prosperous trader at the new Kansas City landing. The road from the landing was still barely wide enough for two wagons to pass, but the bluff above it was being excavated for a big hotel and warehouse.

Milt McGee's friend A. G. Boone, grandnephew of the famous pioneer, had profited by an equally adventurous career and now owned a store at Westport, terminus of the Salt Lake City mail-stage line and outfitting point for both the Santa Fe and Oregon trails. Border militiamen usually congregated at his hospitable home and store. A new newspaper in Westport welcomed Kansas settlers who favored the ruling grandees' proslavery sympathies. Boone and McGee, having achieved success through courage and violence, could be counted on to fight abolitionists who threatened their prosperity as they had fought Mormons or Indians out on the plains. Proslavery leaders on the border staked out another city where a bend of the Missouri reached farthest west into "their Kansas." They named it Atchison and pointed out that the river bend made this future city a whole day's travel closer to the Pacific.

Another town, founded within two weeks of the signing of the Kansas-Nebraska Act, was Leavenworth, close to the fort which served as headquarters for the plains army. Here the first settlers pitched four tents and, with a barrel of whiskey and another of water for refreshment, began speculating in town lots.

These towns all promised fortunes for the "home folks" and had commenced building before the first party of Emigrant Aid Company settlers left Boston on July 17, 1854. There were only twenty-nine in the group, yet Senator Atchison feared them like the plague. A few more joined the little party as it moved along, but not many. Small as their number was, this little company included at least two men who would make their mark among the incoming thousands — John Doy and Dan Anthony. Both resented discipline and bondage for themselves or for the Negro. Dan Anthony was the son of a wealthy, independent-minded Quaker who had been suspended for marrying "out of meeting." Reinstated, he was reproved for buttoning his coat contrary to the meeting's rules. Finally, the

Friends expelled him for permitting his children to dance at home — a safer practice, he maintained, than drinking and dancing at the hotel. His son, Dan, and daughter, Susan B. Anthony, both inherited their father's independence and a determination to speak and be heard. Dan's positiveness augured ill for any Missourian who crossed his will. John Doy was less intellectual, but he was obsessed with a desire to operate an underground railroad station helping Negroes to freedom. Kansas seemed ideal for such an adventure.

The Massachusetts party debarked at Kansas City landing on July 28, 1854, to face a hostile and sullen crowd and a notice that a reward of $200 would be paid for the delivery of Eli Thayer into the hands of the "squatters of Kansas Territory."

The emigrants loaded their tents, bedding, and cooking utensils into wagons. They brought a printing press, with the first edition of the *Herald of Freedom* already in print. The editor, irascible but punctiliously truthful George Washington Brown, had been employed by the Emigrant Aid Company for this work in Ohio before joining the party. The little cavalcade drove off along the Santa Fe Trail between walls of sunflowers taller than a man's head. From the wagon seats these Massachusetts emigrants looked across an agricultural Garden of Eden. Far to the north they could see a distant line of trees along the Kaw River. For fifty miles they followed the historic California road which led out to the short-grass country of wild Indians and buffalo. This road had been used for years by explorers, soldiers, Mexican War veterans, fur trappers, and delegations of red men coming with their agents to visit the Great White Father in Washington. Finally the Massachusetts party came to a mound, south of the Kaw, from which they could look out in all directions across the ocean of grass. Here they halted, pitched their tents, and decided to settle. They named the hill Mount Oread for Thayer's castle in Worcester, and the city of their dreams was called Lawrence in honor of their benefactor.

The townsite had been chosen by an advance agent of the company, Charles Robinson — another of those New Englanders. Robinson had crossed the plains to California in 1849, and remembered the charm of this spot. On the Pacific coast he had taken an active part in a squatters' revolt, had been wounded and jailed for a time. Coming home, his ship was wrecked off Lower California, and he held the survivors together until rescued two weeks later. Home again, he studied medicine and became a doctor. When the debates over Kansas began in Congress, Robinson wrote a series of articles in the *Worcester Spy* which attracted the attention of Thayer and Amos A. Lawrence. As a veteran colonist, practicing physician, and forceful idealist, he seemed the right man for Kansas, and they employed him to aid their colonists.

Robinson was a calmer man than Dan Anthony. Older and more experienced, he had seen much violence, yet was essentially a man of learning, tall and solemn, with a thin layer of long hair plastered across his wide, flat-topped, balding head. His beard was close-cropped. One observer described him as looking like a print of John Knox with uplifted finger and perpetual expression of rebuke. His lifelong motto was "Suffer and grow strong."

On the rich land between Mount Oread and the Kaw River the emigrants unpacked their wagons. In the tall grass they noticed claim stakes, and a few Missourians were camped nearby to defend their absent friends' rights. One of them brought a note to the New Englanders giving them half an hour to strike their tents, repack their wagons, move, or suffer the consequences. The emigrants turned to their agent.

Robinson scribbled a reply, warning the proslavery settlers to touch his tents at their own risk. The messenger strode off through the sunflowers, and the free-state men gathered around Robinson, guns ready for action. One man asked the agent, "Will you fire over their heads or to kill if they decide to come?"

"I'd be ashamed to fire at a man and not hit him," replied the impersonification of Calvinism.

Out in the weeds, the proslavery settlers sensed Robinson's determination. Atchison had not told them that these despised city folk would fight. Better wait until the odds were in their favor. One of the claimants was George Washington Clarke, Indian agent appointed by President Pierce on recommendation of the Missouri senator. With such influence in court the Federal government would surely come to the Missourians' rescue.

The second Massachusetts Emigrant Aid party profited by the experiences of the first and departed from New England with studied drama.

The Kansas-Nebraska bill challenged New England, and the Puritans intended to make the most of it. Sixty-seven prospective settlers enrolled. John Greenleaf Whittier, Quaker poet, wrote for them:

> We cross the prairie as of old
> The pilgrims crossed the sea,
> To make the West, as they the East,
> The homestead of the free!

In the Boston railroad station the settlers sang a new hymn, written for a contest conducted by the Emigrant Aid Company. Eight or ten sunbonneted women and children stood in the group. Several men held rifles and all appeared the picture of pioneer determination. The party increased in size as it traveled west. At Worcester, Thayer's home town, the train stopped for a delegation at the station to present the pilgrims with a handsomely bound Bible.

During the summer of 1854, six Emigrant Aid troupes, totaling approximately six hundred people, came out — a mere drop in the flood of emigration pouring into Kansas. The New Englanders settled in Lawrence or plotted new villages nearby, among them Osawatomie, Manhattan, and Topeka. In almost every case they contested the staked claims of absentee Missourians.

The disturbances in Kansas did not differ from what might be expected at any frontier land opening. There was some blustering but not open civil war. Atchison bounced around his Missouri bailiwick in his buggy, agitating the people to defend their rights. The Stringfellows added to the political commotion, but merchants in their own town of Weston protested against driving away good cash customers. With a little forbearance peace could easily have been maintained, but the slavery issue had become bigger than Kansas. Senator Douglas, returning to Chicago in September, noted in cities, towns, and crossroads along the route that his effigy was burning. He heard himself called the "Benedict Arnold of 1854." Lincoln had been correct when he surmised that the Kansas-Nebraska Act would split the Democratic Party. A dark horse might well become the next President of the United States.

In October, Kansas Territory's first governor arrived. His task of organizing the government was difficult, but Pierce had apparently made a good selection for the job. Andrew H. Reeder, lawyer from Easton, Pennsylvania, had taken an active part in politics without holding office. He was enthusiastic about Douglas's popular sovereignty as a solution for the slavery problem and welcomed an opportunity to put it into practice. At Leavenworth the proslavery speculators eyed his side whiskers and false teeth suspiciously, but accepted him as a "Philadelphia gentleman," offered him a share of their prospective land profits, and expected him to co-operate with them in making their town the capital. Reeder did not commit himself. He wanted to see all his "squatter sovereigns" before making a decision, so he hired a carriage and jogged off around his prairie domain. At each cluster of cabins he spoke from a bench, a wagon end, or an upturned dry-goods box. He learned that every community was composed of land speculators, and all hoped to make their site the state capital. Each settlement offered to give the new governor town lots. Reeder left behind him an atmosphere of encouragement. But he began to see the politician's dilemma: nine enemies for every friend gained by patronage.

Reeder returned from his tour with ample proof of the cupidity of free-state as well as proslavery settlers. He also learned that the Missourians planned coming over on the first election day to outvote the newcomers. As governor, he determined that his administration should be just, and he announced that he would allow the franchise only to actual residents. But the territory's organic act did not specify how long a legal voter must reside in the territory, so the Missourians were not discouraged. Next, Reeder decided to sample the temper of the squatters by holding an election only for a territorial delegate to Congress. Let the more important selection of territorial legislators be held after he had time to know the people better.

The day for the first election approached. Atchison, his florid face slightly swollen from age and good living, redoubled his activity. He told his Missouri constituents: "When your peace, your quiet and your property depend upon your action, you can, without an exertion, send five hundred of your young men who will vote in favor of your institutions." His instructions were printed in the *Platte Argus,* and on election day, November 29, 1854, he strapped a bowie knife and revolver around his ample waist and rode across into Kansas with an army of voters. Careful to stay away from polling places himself, he established headquarters out on the prairie and, according to reports, sent his men where most needed to carry the election. He did not vote personally, maintaining that that would have disqualified him at home.

The invaders dared ride as far inland as Lawrence to cast their ballots. Robinson and his New Englanders watched the strangers vote for and elect the proslavery candidate, J. W. Whitfield, a thick-tongued Tennessean who, like Clarke, had been appointed Indian agent in Kansas on recommendation of Senator Atchison. Although some seventeen hundred Missourians were estimated to have invaded the Kansas polls, the settlers accepted the result, admitting that Whitfield would have won even if the election had been fair. Ballot-box stuffing was common enough in American politics. In Nebraska, Iowans had marched across the state line to vote illegally, and their act was accepted. In Louisiana, the ballot boxes had recently been stuffed in the Plaquamine Parish by a steamboatful of voters sent down from New Orleans by Atchison's colleague Senator John Slidell. This was politics — but precedent failed to make it honest, and in Kansas, the challenge between North and South stimulated the whole nation to do something about it.

Violence at the polls had been relatively slight, with only one man killed, but the homicide elicited more than casual interest, for the dead man was proslavery, and the man who killed him was free-state. However, the killer was properly vindicated by Judge Samuel D. Lecompte, easygoing appointee from Maryland, who really cared more about reading the classics on a comfortable seat in the "trotway" of his double log house on the Leavenworth road than he did about frontier brawls. No one objected to this decision, and the possibility of a civil war between the free-state and slavery factions was postponed. But the propagandists on both sides continued to harp on Seward's challenge and the justice and injustice of opening free Kansas to slavery. Moreover, the fall elections of 1854 swept out many of the congressmen who had voted for the Kansas-Nebraska Act. The next Congress would be filled with their successors. These anti-Nebraska men, as they were called, might break the Democratic majority. But the Southerners had not given up hope. The population of Kansas was still far too small for statehood. Perhaps enough settlers might be encouraged to emigrate next summer to maintain the present proslavery victory already achieved out there. The proslavery leaders had asked for a test of stamina between the sections. Give them time!

The contest between the sections stopped temporarily during the cold winter of 1854-1855. Westbound settlers concentrated in St. Louis. Ears wrapped in mufflers and boots in burlap, they ventured out on the windswept levee watching miles of ice-locked steamboats. Three hundred and fifty miles away on the Kansas plains, settlers at Lawrence finished their houses during the bitter months. Cellars could not be dug in the frozen ground, but sawmills puffed their energetic breaths into the sparkling air, singing, as Thayer had prophesied, to the accompaniment of ringing hammers. Shivering Missourians watched and wondered at these ingenious Yankees, their patent apple peelers, their books, their queer houses — no chimney on the outside — their church services in tents with a boy feeding chips into a sheet-iron stove while the wind whistled against the canvas. Most noticeable of all was their insistence on schools — a continual insult to the proslavery culture around them. "If their object is not to offend," one Southerner wrote, "why did they not wait until they had more leisure before they busied themselves about schoolhouses?"

The diligent New Englanders heard the Emigrant Aid Company called ugly names, Thayer's plan of profit damned as Yankee money grabbing. Robinson, always the personification of reproach, wrote Lawrence about it, and the philanthropist insisted that the company be reorganized. Thayer objected, but Lawrence was obdurate. Born to wealth, he cared more for principle than money. So Thayer's idea of paying dividends was discontinued, and contributions became exclusively charitable. Henceforth "aid" would consist of free information and a fifteen per cent reduction in railroad and steamship fares through quantity purchases. No political questions were asked emigrants. Contributors' one concern was to get people into Kansas and let them compare the two forms of society — slave and free. Thayer continued to stump for the organization, neglecting his school, contributing his own funds. Most hamlets in New England learned the sound of his voice and his persuasive assurance that:

> Every colony planted by the Emigrant Aid Society was provided with a church, a school and a steam-engine. Slavery cannot stand before these things. Wherever the steam-engine goes, liberty will prevail. An ordinary dull man, seeing one of these pioneers of freedom going up the Missouri river will say, "There goes a steam-engine." David Rice Atchison seeing it, says, "There goes another damned abolition city into Kansas."

I I

It Looks Very Much Like War: 1855

F OR OVER A YEAR after Lincoln's bedroom decision to re-enter politics, he did not join the new anti-Nebraska party. As he had foreseen, his own Whigs split on the slavery issue, many voting the Know-Nothing ticket — a party opposed to immigration of foreigners. The new Republican Party, pledged to counteract the Kansas bill, was fast becoming national but as yet had no organization in Illinois. Lincoln showed reluctance to join it, although he watched the Democrats beating their own brains against the Kansas wall.

During the winter of 1854–1855, emigrants continued to congregate at Alton and St. Louis — steamboat embarkation points. Many more waited impatiently at home for spring to open the roads and rivers. With time to spare these would-be pioneers fumed to be off, pre-empt claims, and fight for democracy on the plains. In anticipation of the spring rush, Kansas City grew, weedlike, and now numbered three hundred inhabitants. The hotel on the levee under the bluff had been purchased by the Emigrant Aid Company to accommodate all travelers — regardless of politics, the owners were careful to announce. A man named Gaius Jenkins welcomed guests.

Beyond Kansas City, Westport showed even greater prosperity. In addition to the overland-trail business, it now had the Kansas trade. All day and all night hammers tinkled in nine blacksmith shops, one with six forges. The town also boasted sixteen trading houses, four saloons, and two large, three-story brick hotels — a great change in the ten years since Francis Parkman had outfitted for the Oregon Trail here, purchasing a mule from A. G. Boone, a big man of the town then as now.

Across the Kansas border from Westport, Governor Reeder established a temporary capital in the Shawnee Indian Mission Manual Training

School buildings. The Leavenworth speculators construed this as a sure indication that he planned to ignore their town as the permanent site. They began scheming with neighboring Missourians for the removal of the governor from office. Reeder, on his part, had spent the winter studying the Kansas situation. He ordered an election for the territorial legislature on March 30, 1855, and he hoped to forestall wholesale fraud this time. To prevent it, he had taken a census, so he could now estimate the approximate number of legitimate voters, and he threatened to throw out returns which were obviously spurious. The entire territory contained only 8501 white persons with 5128 males, 3373 females. There were also 242 slaves and 151 free Negroes.

Rumors were rife that Senator Atchison planned coming again from Missouri to carry the election. Back in Massachusetts, wealthy Amos A. Lawrence considered that anyone as prominent as Atchison would understand amenities and want to be fair, also. He wrote him a long letter, laying out the North's case, and requesting that the contest, as Seward had proclaimed it, be honorably conducted. He said that there was no truth in the assertion that the New England emigrants were abolitionists, "but," he added significantly, "oppression may make them abolitionists of the most dangerous kind."

Senator Atchison replied respectfully, defending the Missourians as being no more guilty than New Englanders who voted and returned home. He said further that he regarded any man who came to make Kansas a free state as an "abolitionist," and he suggested that Mr. Lawrence with all his wealth might better serve humanity by purchasing some slaves himself instead of stirring up strife. Let him bring them to Kansas. Put them to useful work and take good care of them. Here, at last, Atchison had touched the spot which Lincoln had seen so quickly. Static paternalism — a fixed economy — could never agree with a society bottomed on equality, opportunism, constant enterprise, and competition. The two points of view had become sectional, and politicians across the nation awaited the coming election.

Ice melted in the Western rivers early in March 1855, and steamboats soon began to arrive in Kansas. Rumor of a great invasion of New England settlers, being paid a hundred dollars to come and vote, infuriated the border men. Atchison should have known that this was not so. He had not questioned Amos A. Lawrence's statement to the contrary, but he wanted to win and any measure against those interlopers seemed justified. The local press and orators screamed against Yankee "paupers" — men who owned no slaves — abolitionists, and wealthy Eastern corporations. Everybody was urged to cross the border and vote to save the country. Those unable to go personally were urged to pay for someone who could. Mass meetings assembled in downriver towns halfway across Missouri. At Boonville a tipsy planter stumbled through an audience to the speakers' table and slapped down a thousand dollars. "I've just sold a nigger for that," he said, "and I reckon it's about my share towards cleaning out the dog-gauned Yankees." At Platte City a crowd of some twenty-five hundred to three thousand assembled to organize a Missouri migration to Kansas ahead of the New Englanders. "General" Stringfellow exhorted Missourians to emigrate en masse before Kansas "should become the home of a lawless set of infidels and abolitionists." He assured the people that he had heard "from a reliable source" that Southern states were sending an immense countermigration. "Families," he said, "with all their slaves are making preparations to move as soon as the weather will permit." Until they arrived, the Missourians must hold Kansas and "vote at the point of the bowie-knife and the revolver." Similar meetings were held down the river at Lexington and as far inland as Randolph County in north central Missouri.

As the time for electing territorial legislators approached, many Missouri border counties sent contingents to vote. Steamboats plied back and forth to Atchison and Leavenworth, offering a special round-trip rate. "General" Stringfellow, in a dragoon jacket, led patriots forward. Senator Atchison also crossed, reassuring the timid. He maintained later that he went in the capacity of peacemaker, to counsel against violence — the identical defense given continually by rascally Ned Buntline, the riot rouser of the decade. Bands of men trailed down to the ferries, their wagons loaded with camp supplies. The Reverend Frederick Starr remembered one vehicle with a five-foot pole carrying a whiskey bottle, revolver, bowie knife, powder horn, black flag with skull and crossbones, and a long streamer of glossy hemp. As far away as Waverly, Missouri, successful little Jo Shelby closed his ropewalk and with forty men — some recruited in the Blue Grass — rode to Lawrence to vote. Shelby, Kentucky aristocrat and graduate of Transylvania, was steeped in the romance of Sir Walter Scott and fond of quoting chivalric passages. He soon learned that his short stature gained magnitude on a big horse, that a black plume decorated his hat admirably, and that great exhilaration came from commanding a troop of light-horse. He was fast becoming the wealthiest slave-holder in Missouri. To him, Boston aid societies were anathema. Governor Reeder, in his quarters at Shawnee Mission, watched part of this tousle-headed, tatterdemalion army of voters traipse through town, bristling with firearms and bowie knives.

Lawrence had now become the focal point of all antislavery forces. The most important events in the Kansas war would occur within thirty miles of this New England village. On the night before the election a thousand strangers, with several cannon, halted their wagons in a ravine east of town. Negro fiddlers strolled from fire to fire. The prominent Missouri politician Claibourne Jackson seemed to be in charge. A man of means, Claib Jackson had married in succession the three daughters of Dr. John Sappington, wealthy manufacturer of quinine pills to remedy frontier malaria. Gossips said that the old doctor had told Claib when he came for the third daughter, "I reckon you'll be back next for the old woman." Jackson had been elected twice to the Missouri legislature and was now running for Congress. His followers had had their expenses paid, and they had brought printed ballots with them.

Jackson called a mass meeting around his tent, explained the vague law concerning residence in the territory, and told the assembly that they had as much right to vote in the morning as they would if they had lived in Kansas four or five years. Then he divided his command, holding enough to win the Lawrence election and detailing the others to districts where they might be needed.

In the afternoon the Missourians started home, grumbling that they were no guiltier than the free-staters and vowing to hang Reeder if he did not sanction the election. The final count in Lawrence showed 781 pro-slavery ballots and 253 free-soil, with an estimate of only 369 legitimate voters. Later, a congressional investigating committee reported that 232 of the votes were legal.

Conditions were worse in other districts. In the second, around Bloom-ington, the Claib Jackson men arrived under the command of A. G.

Boone's son-in-law, Samuel J. Jones, stormy postmaster of Westport, Missouri. The polling cabin was immediately surrounded and the judges ordered to resign.

At Leavenworth the voting was questioned by a free-state attorney there, William Phillips, who threatened to have the election returns canceled as fraudulent. A mob seized him, shaved his head, had him tarred, feathered, and auctioned off by a grinning Negro: "How much, gentlemen, for a full-blooded abolitionist, dyed in de wool, tar feathers and all?" The *Parkville Luminary* dared cry out in print against Atchison and his Platte County regulators. A mob destroyed the presses.

Of the 6207 votes cast in the territory, 80 per cent were estimated to be spurious. Only one free-state man was elected — Maryland-born, South Carolina-educated Martin Conway. All the others were proslavery, among them Dr. J. H. Stringfellow, editor of the *Squatter Sovereign*.

After the election, Dr. Charles Robinson led a small band of his followers to Shawnee Mission and asked Governor Reeder to declare the entire election fraudulent. Robinson knew that the governor had been threatened bodily and might be killed for such a decision, but the free-staters offered to serve as a personal bodyguard. Reeder temporized, champing his false teeth. He hesitated to countenance dishonesty, yet knew that President Pierce and the administration press would roar if he made trouble. Besides, he hoped to demonstrate that his panacea of squatter sovereignty would solve the territorial slavery problem. Finally Reeder decided on a halfway course. He would certify all the returns except the most fraudulent ones and in those districts would order a new election.

Robinson jogged back to Lawrence and wrote long letters about his disappointment to influential friends in the East. He warned Thayer:

> It looks very much like war, and I am ready for it and so are our people. Wouldn't it be rich to march an army through the slaveholding States and roll up a *black cloud* that should spread dismay and terror to the ranks of the oppressors?
>
> Cannot your secret society send us 200 Sharps rifles as a loan till this question is settled? Also a couple of field-pieces? If they will do that, I think they will be *well used,* and preserved.

George Washington Deitzler set off for New England to get the guns. Sharps were a new and advanced type of breech-loading rifle. Only some fourteen thousand had been manufactured. The Emigrant Aid Company would always claim that the corporation never bought any Sharps rifles for emigrants to Kansas but admitted that prominent members of the company did purchase guns individually — a questionable admission, for the records of the Sharps Company show purchases by both company and individual members.

Waiting for the guns, the citizens of Lawrence decided to build permanent fortifications. The Emigrant Aid Company began work on a fine concrete hostelry called the Free-State Hotel or Eldridge House, for the lessee, Shalor Eldridge. The roof of the building was constructed with portholes at the top of the walls. Dr. J. H. Stringfellow viewed the military preparations with alarm, urged readers of the *Squatter Sovereign* to retaliate, defied Governor Reeder, and gossips said that he slapped the Chief Executive's face. However that may have been, Reeder determined to give not an inch to these Missouri politicians. He ordered the first session of the legislature to meet in July at Pawnee, a new capital site close beside the Fort Riley army reservation out beyond the tall-grass prairies, on the edge of the great plains — the short-grass country where wagon travelers began to carry "buffalo chips" for firewood and to shoot the shaggy monsters for meat. After publishing this official decree, Governor Reeder boarded the boat for Washington to explain the tangled situation to the President.

At the White House, Reeder learned that Atchison, fresh from the election invasion, had preceded him, told his side of the story, and demanded the governor's removal. President Pierce, as honest as Reeder but considerably weaker in character, seemed impressed, yet he hesitated to dismiss an appointee without a hearing. He understood the constant pressures exerted on an administrator. Territorial governors were always being maligned by groups of speculators or others wanting special privileges. His appointee to Utah was being criticized loudly by the Mormons. Senator Douglas was urging removal of the governor of Minnesota, but accommodating as Pierce wanted to be, he refused to sacrifice a man without cause.

As Reeder listened to the President, he could only surmise what tales Atchison had told him, but he felt confident that his own course of action had been the only one possible. He soon learned that Pierce viewed the situation differently. First, the President said that he had heard nothing but complaints from Kansas. He believed that the Emigrant Aid Company was stirring up all the trouble. Amos A. Lawrence was a distant relative, but Pierce had no sympathy with his activities. Abolitionists were ruining the Democratic Party and might bring on a civil war. Were the proslavery people in Kansas as bad as the abolition press represented? According to information reaching Washington, free-state men had packed the election as fraudulently as the proslavery group. If the election was unfair, why had Reeder accepted part of it? Moreover, proslavery settlers complained that the governor was speculating, said that he favored the abolitionists because they gave him the biggest blocks of town lots. They also accused him of acquiring claims to land still held by Indians. This had been reported by trustworthy George Washington Clarke, Indian Agent — appointee recommended by Senator Atchison. Rascally New Englanders had jumped his claim near Lawrence. The President also had been informed that the governor delayed the legislative election from November 1854 to March 1855, in order that free-state voters might come from Boston — a delay that would make Kansas free soil and hinder unity in his party. According to the President's information, the much maligned Missouri invaders were legitimate settlers who had returned, after voting, to get their families and would have brought them the first time except for the inclement weather. False abolitionist propagandists were making an unwarranted display. Moreover, the fortunate election of slavery sympathizers to the territorial legislature in Kansas had encouraged thousands of Southerners to emigrate there with slaves. These people had their rights. No doubt there were proslavery irregularities, but neither side was lily white. Pierce suggested a face-saving compromise. If Reeder would resign amicably, the President would tender him a comparable job elsewhere, and arrange an exchange of correspondence for publication. In these letters the President would uphold, in theory, Reeder's position in Kansas, thus satisfying the Northern Democrats. At the same time, Reeder's removal should placate the proslavery wing. Pierce even offered to make good Reeder's land speculations, and he hinted diplomatically that it might be dangerous for Reeder to return. Atchison had spoken at some length about the belligerency of the border people.

Reeder listened impatiently, said that he was not personally afraid but that he would resign if a suitable exchange of letters might be agreed upon for publication. Angry and stubborn, he stalked out of the conference. At his hotel, Reeder wrote letters outlining his case and maligning the illegal actions of the proslavery wing. This, of course, was unsatisfactory to the President, and after a few more attempts the matter was dropped. Governor Reeder returned to Kansas, and Franklin Pierce resorted to the old political trick of doing nothing. Perhaps if the territory had been closer, the President might have kept himself better posted and, in view of the overwhelming evidence, backed Reeder's efforts for an honest administration. The Missouri River, however, was a long way from Washington, and other business demanded attention. A week was required for the delivery of a telegram to Kansas and two for a letter. Pierce took up the immediate problems on his desk and thus neglected a great chance to quash one of the major agitations which led to the Civil War.

President Pierce's hope to evade unpleasant publicity proved fatuous. He might have listened, too, to Amos A. Lawrence's prophecy that continued Southern aggression would make "abolitionists of the most dangerous kind." The entire North was aroused by the Kansas usurpation, and eager newspaper reporters hurried to the territory. Foremost among them was James Redpath, correspondent for the *Missouri Democrat,* the *Chicago Press and Tribune* and Horace Greeley's *New York Tribune.* With his father, in Scotland, Redpath had helped compile *Tales and Traditions of the Border* when sixteen years old. In Kansas, at twenty-two, he was credited with coining the term "Border Ruffian," which Greeley gave wide publicity. An erratic, volatile, sentimental chap, dedicated to abolitionism, he was not one to be deterred from reaching a righteous goal by conforming to a strict statement of the truth. In journalism, life, and in love, he specialized in sensationalism. Once he wrote a young lady that he had purchased her novel on his way to the cemetery to commit suicide, began to read it, and decided not to kill himself but devote his life to promoting her book instead. In addition to his connection with the Eastern antislavery newspapers, Redpath soon published a paper of his own in Kansas, the *Crusader of Freedom.*

Other abolitionist writers who arrived in 1855 were Richard J. Hinton and William Phillips — not the lawyer. Both were Scotch-born, like Redpath. All three were in their twenties. Each was determined to take the Declaration of Independence literally and die, if necessary, for freedom of the slave. These youngsters, eager for "copy," reform, and excitement could all be counted on to scratch journalistic matches in the Kansas powderhouse. Freedom of the press, what! The Kansas to which they came almost doubled in population with the spring migration of 1855, totaling fifteen thousand people. The towns were still scattered along the Missouri and in the high-grass prairies.

Among the incoming thousands one odd character yelled "Whoa" and pulled his moccasin-colored horse to a halt in front of the free-state newspaper office in Lawrence. The stranger, dressed in overalls and roundabout, stalked through the doorway and asked the way to "Tecumsey" — twenty miles on up the Kaw. His large prehensile lips denoted fluency and nicotine. His personality seemed peculiarly magnetic, and his expressive eyes followed the full-skirted women tripping along the wooden sidewalks. Obviously, he was putting on an act, for the logical place to ask about the road was at the livery barn. Moreover, he decided to stay in Lawrence, in fact, resided there the rest of his life. In his characteristically confidential manner he told the newspapermen that he wore his rude costume in order to pass through Missouri without being stopped by the Border Ruffians — another obviously untrustworthy statement, for James Henry Lane was a prominent proslavery Democrat and as congressman had voted for the Kansas-Nebraska bill. He was a well-known figure back in Indiana, where he had been lieutenant governor. He had served with credit as a colonel in the Mexican War, but politics was his great interest in life — an interest he inherited from his father. Lane's sisters possessed his aptness for intrigue. In the campaign of 1840, they had almost ruined the presidential candidate, General William Henry Harrison, with their smiles, champagne, and soft music. The aging Indian fighter made himself ridiculous by singing for them songs of love and war at a time when his campaign managers hoped to keep him quiet.

The Grim Chieftain of Kansas, as Lane was soon called, became a controversial figure almost immediately. In all probability he came to Kansas, as did so many other hopeful politicians, to help organize the Democratic Party and rise with it in a new field. Whether he planned to work for a slave or a free Kansas remains a mystery. A colleague in Indiana remembered that Lane vowed, before leaving, to make Kansas free. A colleague in the West remembered Lane's telling him in confidence that he had come at the instigation of Pierce and Douglas, who already foresaw the impossibility of making Kansas a slave state and wanted to organize it as a free Democratic one. Both are hindsight recollections. On arriving in Kansas, Lane announced publicly that he had come to look for a location to raise hemp, and that for working the soil he knew no difference between a Negro and a mule. He deplored the secret shipments of Sharps rifles. Certainly, if Lane did come to Kansas at Pierce's order, to double-cross the governor, Reeder did not know it.

The proslavery, Missouri-controlled legislature convened at Pawnee the first week in July 1855. This new hamlet on the edge of the short-grass country was a hundred and forty miles from the Missouri River. The first settlers had arrived on Christmas Day, 1854, having braved the winter weather that stopped most emigrants. Coming under the auspices of the Emigrant Aid Company, they were spurned by the Missourians, but the army officers in nearby Fort Riley proved friendly in a growling, military way — especially redheaded Captain Nathaniel Lyon, a stanch Democrat who had campaigned for Pierce, but since watching the Border Ruffian aggressors, opposed proslavery men. The snow had drifted twenty feet deep at Pawnee, but the settlers had survived by pitching their tents in a gulch out of the wind.

When the newly elected legislators drove in after a long camping trip across the prairies, they found only a score of houses along a brushy creek in the bottom of a grass-carpeted hollow. One large, two-story stone building had been constructed for a capitol. The governor's mansion was built of hewn logs. Another log house, fifty feet long and sixteen wide, offered hotel accommodations. As the legislators pulled off their saddles and unhooked their teams, they learned that the Fort Riley army officers, as well as Governor Reeder, had been given town lots. Already tired and disgruntled from the overland trip, angry with Reeder for pronouncing some of their election returns fraudulent, they planned to retaliate against the governor at once.

With the legislators came government employees and hangers-on. In Pawnee, they all camped along the creek, many cooking beside their wagons. Horses were picketed on the plains above the hollow, and three times a day legislators, clerks, and lobbyists led the animals down to the creek for a drink. Among the throng strode the Grim Chieftain with his moccasin-colored horse. Jim Lane had visited a rally in Lawrence on June 27, 1855, intent on organizing the Democratic Party in Kansas, but the sparse attendance opened his eyes. Five days later he appeared at Pawnee. From morning until evening he spent his time confidentially buttonholing the assemblymen. At night he slept under a wagon, safe from the hoofs of loose horses. He seemed particularly interested in having the legislature grant him a divorce from the wife who had followed him from Indiana. She was the daughter of distinguished General Arthur St. Clair, president of the Continental Congress, and first governor of the Northwest Territory. Lane's enemies would say later that he had sold all her property, amounting to ten thousand dollars, for the trip to Kansas — and that Mrs. Lane, in desperation, raised money for her return passage by appealing to fellow townsmen, while he was away "politicking." Both allegations were contradicted in Mrs. Lane's later suit for divorce.

Out at Pawnee, on the opening day of the first session, the legislators clumped, in their muddy boots, into the stone capitol. All took their seats, and Reeder, in an upholstered high-backed throne facing the assembly, stood up to read his first message. The windows were open, and the hot breath of July simmered in from the tawny, sun-scorched grass. Perfunctorily the governor asked the lawmakers "to lay aside all the selfish and equivocal motives, to discard all unworthy ends, and in the spirit of justice and charity to each other, with pure hearts, tempered feelings and sober judgments" proceed with the territory's business.

Thus admonished, the solons promptly seated the entire slate of the first election, regardless of the free-state men who had won in the districts where Governor Reeder ordered re-elections. A scraping of feet and thumping on the wooden stairs announced that the honestly elected free-state members were leaving in a huff. Young Martin Conway, the sole recognized free-state legislator, resigned in order to fight the injustice without restraint. As the son of a slaveholder he had learned to hate the institution and the methods used to perpetuate it. His articles for the press, along with Redpath's and Hinton's, would be the basis of the Eastern reading public's knowledge of Kansas politics.

The proslavery legislature, now left to itself, nominated and elected J. H. Stringfellow speaker, then forthwith adjourned to reconvene in the more hospitable atmosphere of the Shawnee Mission on the Missouri border. Reeder promptly vetoed the move, and as promptly the act passed over his veto. The legislature drove off, the governor following. A report of cholera at the fort may have hastened the retreat from Pawnee. Secretary of War Jefferson Davis backed the legislature's action by extending the boundary of the Fort Riley military reservation, thus wiping out the Pawnee settlers' land holdings and adding to the bitterness of tough little Captain Lyon, who dutifully drove the courageous settlers from their houses, and scored another tally to his hatred of slavocrats. Lyon's own messmates complained about his disagreeable manners. He persisted in reading political tracts instead of playing cards. He even argued about religion: fixing cold, unblinking blue eyes on unwilling listeners, he had declared, "I am an infidel, perhaps an atheist. Socrates was nobler than Jesus." Certainly Lyon was a dangerous man to have authority, come civil war.

While the first legislature drove to and from Pawnee, Charles Robinson planned an elaborate demonstration in Lawrence. Ever since the second election, he had been addressing conventions, decrying the illegal Missouri procedure, calling the newly elected legislature "bogus." The grand culmination came on Independence Day. That morning two companies armed with Sharps rifles marched through town to be presented with flags by the citizens. Settlers with claims not recognized by the Lawrence Association looked askance at the military display, listened to a reading of the Declaration of Independence — an endorsement of revolution, but how could they object? Then Dr. Robinson, who had been reared near Bunker Hill, went one step further. To the citizens of Lawrence he delivered a Fourth of July oration worthy of a patriot of the Revolutionary days.

"Let us repudiate all laws enacted by foreign legislative bodies," he said. "So thought and so acted our ancestors, and so let us think and act."

Robinson's remarks were responded to by Samuel N. Wood, a little Hicksite Quaker and a notorious underground railroad conductor from Ohio, who planned to write for Eastern newspapers and claimed a homestead on the California road. As yet, no objectionable state laws had been passed by any "foreign legislative bodies," for the newly elected legislature had not yet set to work. Robinson's demonstration, therefore, was only a protest against the Missouri usurpation of the ballot boxes, and perhaps fear of being overruled on land claims. But already "slavery" was a name around which settlers could rally for their own protection and thus draw sympathy from the entire North.

Down at the Shawnee Mission the legislators set up government in the brick school buildings. Governor Reeder roomed in the American Hotel in nearby Kansas City, while the Harris House in proslavery Westport accommodated many of the lawmakers. Some slept in the mission shed or in the residence of the missionary, a slave-owning divine named Thomas Johnson. At noon the governor and the legislature all ate together in Johnson's house. Governor Reeder feared riding alone from Kansas City to the mission and asked Shalor Eldridge, proprietor of the American Hotel (as well as the Lawrence hostelry) to accompany him to the capital. The two men were joined by Kersey Coates, one of the governor's fellow Pennsylvanians now living in Kansas City. At dinnertime, when the bell rang, Reeder and his friends hurried to the "eating house." The governor seated himself at the head of the table, beckoning to Coates and Eldridge to sit on either side. Before the legislators arrived, Reeder unbuttoned his coat, loosened his belt, and slipped two revolvers to the front, although concealed under the table. Coates and Eldridge followed his example. Soon the legislators crowded in, talking among themselves, sitting down noisily, ignoring the presence of the governor. At the foot of the table the Reverend Thomas Johnson stood up, raised a huge carving knife, and brought it down with a thud. The startled solons turned, then saw that he was only soliciting silence so that he might request divine blessing on the meal.

How long any governor could keep his head above such a turbulent frontier assembly was anybody's guess. Robinson wrote Amos A. Lawrence frequently, and that philanthropist wrote his kinsman President Pierce, that Reeder needed vigorous support from the government to uphold his courageous stand. Pierce demurred, so Lawrence and his friends sent the settlers more "means of defense."

President Pierce, almost desperate now, solved his problem by dismissing the governor — an act of appeasement which encouraged the slave power to demand more. The Atchison wing of the party urged the President to fill the executive chair with Territorial Secretary Daniel Woodson, an attorney from Independence who had marched with invading voters in November 1854. Pierce showed sufficient strength to ignore this pressure, but he still hoped to satisfy everybody and weld the two wings of the party. To replace Reeder, he appointed another half-and-half man. Wilson Shannon appeared to have many advantages over Reeder as governor. He had had years of practical political and diplomatic experience as congressman from Ohio and as minister to Mexico. He knew the frontier, having accompanied a party of forty-niners to California. Most important of all, he was a loyal Democrat, had voted dutifully for the Kansas-Nebraska Act, and all in all seemed ideal to represent the two wings of the party.

Before Shannon's arrival, the Kansas legislature proceeded with its business. First and foremost, it passed a slave code abridging the American rights of freedom of speech and of the press. The death penalty was imposed for helping a slave insurrection by either printed or spoken word. Death or imprisonment could be imposed for expressing an opinion calculated to help a slave escape. A fine of five hundred dollars might be imposed on anyone who refused to help apprehend a fugitive slave. Any person convicted of violating the Fugitive Slave Act or refusing to take an oath to uphold it was disfranchised, and the sheriff was empowered to exclude certain people from jury duty in cases that involved slavery. In addition, all voters were required to take an oath to uphold the obnoxious laws, and no period of residence was specified as necessary for voters. Thus the fraudulent elections were upheld.

It was useless to excuse these laws on the ground that they were similar to those in force in Missouri and other slave states. It was useless to point out that there were not enough slaves in all Kansas to warrant such excitement. These Missourians were working themselves into an emotional state where they would fight and die in defense of an institution that really affected them very little. Obviously the real issue in Kansas was whether a Missouri minority or the "foreign majority" should rule. Both sides were Democrats — one supported by the party's proslavery wing, the other by the free-staters.

The proslavery legislature voted to establish a new capital and promptly speculated in land there. They named the site "Douglas" for the sponsor of the Kansas-Nebraska Act, but soon changed it to "Lecompton" for Judge S. D. Lecompte, the accommodating jurist whose decisions might be invaluable to the clique in power. A. G. Boone was elected vice-president of the Lecompton Town Company. An appropriation of fifty thousand dollars was voted for the proposed buildings.

While these acts were being passed, disgruntled free-state voters assembled in many mass meetings. Between June 8 and August 15, 1855, seven conventions in Lawrence repudiated the legislature.

Robinson's July Fourth speech about revolution was much too radical for most of them. Men liked to complain but hesitated to stage an insurrection. It would be better, surely, to circumvent the proslavery legislature by peacefully electing a general convention to draft a free-state constitution and ask for admission into the Union under it. The only obstacle to this plan was the distrust of the free-state individuals for one another. Midland emigrants disliked Robinson's abolitionists almost as much as the Missouri usurpers. To them the human race was divided into three classes: "Yankees, niggers en white people." Yet they must combine with the codfish aristocrats or submit to the Lecompton machine. Evading the hated New England influence, they convened at Big Springs, a cluster of four or five shake-cabins and a hotel on the California road, halfway between Lawrence and Topeka.

Eastern idealists watched this convention with the same excitement shown over the Kansas-Nebraska Act, but now the budding Republican Party had made it an issue. On July 13, 1855 — anniversary of the adoption of the Northwest Ordinance of 1787, which prohibited slavery north of the Ohio River — the Republicans held state conventions in Ohio, Indiana, Wisconsin, and Vermont. Robinson's associates doubtless wanted to start the party in Kansas, too, but a majority of the disaffected voters were still good Democrats. The Big Springs convention, however, might be a step in the new party's direction.

Lane and Dr. Robinson, the likable Midwestern Satan and the New Englander's Jehovah, ran as rival candidates for delegate to the Big Springs convention — the beginning of an antagonism that would be lifelong and grow more bitter with the years. The two men were different as could be. Robinson was solemn, ministerial, dictatorial, not an organization man. He had never joined a church or a medical society. However, he represented the Emigrant Aid Company, and the Sharps were brought from New England by his man, G. W. Deitzler. Lane had deplored the importation of rifles, admitted that he was a Democrat — friend of Douglas and President Pierce — a "joiner" claiming membership in all organizations and brotherhoods. Robinson's followers called Lane a turncoat, pointed out that he had come to Kansas as a proslavery man, and even intimated that he changed only because the "bogus" legislature failed to grant his divorce.

Lane thrived under the criticism. It gave him notoriety. Voters came to criticize the libertine and fell under the spell of his oratory. One old resident recalled years later: "He talked like none of the others; none of the rest had his husky, rasping, bloodcurdling whisper or that menacing forefinger, or could shriek 'Great God!' on the same day with him." Everyone acknowledged Lane's power over an audience. When the ballots were counted, Lane, instead of Robinson, was elected to represent the radical town of Lawrence at Big Springs.

The free-state men were planning their Big Springs convention when the new governor, Wilson Shannon, came up the river with a Missouri entourage. He was a tall, well-built man, with gray hair and coarse features but pleasant eyes — just the kind of man for a frontier office. The legislature had adjourned at the Shawnee Mission, but an elaborate welcoming assemblage awaited him at Westport. Fluent frontier orators assured the governor that in this recovered Eden, "the morning prayer is heard on every hill, the evening orison is chanted in every valley and glen."

Governor Shannon watched the sunburned faces — hearty, outdoor fellows of the old American stock. Surely they were not so blackhearted as pictured by the revolutionary party preparing to assemble at Big Springs, a day's drive west.

Shannon told the welcoming multitude that he regretted the disposition of some settlers to nullify the laws passed by the legislature. He did not know the laws in question, but if they were unconstitutional, the courts should pronounce against them. To do otherwise was revolution — in short, treason.

At Big Springs the free-state men assembled on September 5, 1855, knowing that the governor, the legally recognized legislature, and the judges appointed by the President were against them. So far, the United

States Army had taken no part in the civil strife. Last spring it had marched out on the plains under the Southern sympathizer General William S. Harney to chastise the Sioux at Ash Hollow. It would come back with the winds of winter. Until then the settlers might hold their own against the Missourians, but the ugly charge of treason troubled them.

A hundred delegates assembled at the Big Springs cabins, and at least three hundred spectators came with them, including Ex-Governor Reeder — his trunk packed and his boat and train schedule prepared for the trip back to Pennsylvania. The delegates hailed Reeder everywhere he went, asked him to talk. In a formal speech he urged them to protect their rights "with the steady arm and sure eye" — Robinson's plea for revolution.

The assemblage greeted this call for violence with a great cheer, but the resolutions they passed would have suited an old-line Democrat. To these settlers "free state" did not mean abolition, but only the right to rule themselves without interference from the Missouri machine. The quicker Shannon and Frank Pierce learned this, the better it would be for them.

The free-state settlers determined to go ahead with their revolution — to organize a government of their own regardless of the one already functioning, and to draft a free-state constitution under which Kansas might be admitted to the Union. Lane and Robinson were both elected to take part in this movement, but the New Englander had become strangely conservative of late. He had received a letter from Amos A. Lawrence warning him to beware of treason and allow no one to fire the Sharps rifles at United States troops. Lane, on the other hand, had noted the popular demonstration in favor of violence, and as chairman of the executive committee of the new government he issued scrip to pay delegates' expenses — a sly step, surely, toward holding their interest in the revolution's success.

The free-state constitutional convention assembled at Topeka in October. Lane, always seeking notoriety, challenged to a duel Grosvenor P. Lowrey, secretary to Ex-Governor Reeder. The Grim Chieftain alleged that Lowrey had falsely accused him of improper relations with his wife. Robinson and others tried to smooth over the misunderstanding. What would the Eastern idealists say? Think of the philanthropists who were supporting the free-state movement! Lane did not care. Easterners were not backing him. The duel must be held as arranged. On the morning scheduled for the fight, Lane addressed the convention with a philippic on patriotism and the importance of Kansas. His audience watched the speaker and the clock. As the hands moved toward the fatal hour, the Grim Chieftain closed his address with a flourish, picked up his hat, and, throwing his cloak around his shoulders, stalked dramatically from the building.

I I I

The Wakarusa War

THE EXTRALEGAL Topeka constitutional convention adjourned on November 11, 1855. Lane credited himself, forever after, with being first to plan the free-state organization and to draft its platform. Robinson always maintained that the idea was his. How Lane settled his duel without fighting, yet with satisfaction to all, remains vague. Certainly he did not stop the whispering about his sexual irregularities, but his dramatics kept the prairie boys amused and inspired — two emotions Dr. Robinson could not arouse.

The so-called Topeka Movement was treated with contempt by Governor Shannon. A seasoned politician, as well as a California forty-niner who understood vigilantes, he had come to Kansas to straighten out a crooked situation for President Pierce. On the day he arrived in Kansas, Shannon learned about a free-state men's secret organization for the protection of their land claims, which was fully as unwarranted as the Missourians' self-defensive associations. A member of the society had just come to town as a fugitive, claiming that his life had been threatened for disclosing some of the secrets. He had killed his assailant, Samuel Collins, and wanted protection in the proslavery ranks.

Shannon saw, at once, that the two communities, free-state and slave, could not coexist. Fugitives would continually dodge from one to the other. As governor, he would, of course, support the recognized legislature and make people submit to its laws. To demonstrate his position, he presided at a Leavenworth "law and order" meeting, but even so, the proslavery faction did not feel secure. They realized only too well that the majority of settlers were behind the Topeka government, that the South must send more homemakers or the North would win Kansas. The Missouri politicians continued to prepare pleas for circulation in Southern newspapers.

United States Senator Robert Toombs, of Georgia, hearkened to the call and attended a meeting in Columbus to organize and send settlers. Accepting a pamphlet by Stringfellow as gospel, he told constituents that slaves could raise hemp, tobacco, wheat, and corn as profitably in Kansas as they could raise cotton. In adjoining Missouri, the number so engaged had doubled in a decade. Other speakers pointed out that only one dollar need be contributed for each slave owned in the fifteen Southern states to equal the sum raised by the Emigrant Aid Company. Let the South assess itself and surpass the New Englanders.

In Alabama, Thomas J. Orme attempted unsuccessfully to raise men and money. A more enterprising Alabaman, Major Jefferson Buford, also campaigned for recruits. Buford, a lawyer and planter at Eufaula, had had military experience in the Seminole war. He proposed to open recruiting offices in the Carolinas, Georgia, Alabama, Mississippi, and Louisiana. To begin the financing of the project, he sold forty of his own plantation slaves. "I am not rich," he announced, "and have found no money, but have made what little I possess — have four small children of tender age to support, and, with less at stake than thousands of others, am only battling for our common section, against a powerful, untiring, fanatical enemy, who, fighting as he thinks for humanity, is in fact bringing degradation, desolation and woe to our beloved South." For every fifty dollars contributed to his worthy cause Buford agreed to take one emigrant to Kansas, passage free, keep him a year, and give him forty acres of land — a more generous offer than the New England company made. Surely the South would respond and beat the Yankees. All that was now necessary for the slave sympathizers was to hold the status quo. The Southern emigrants, when they arrived, would vindicate President Pierce, and Governor Shannon's immediate troubles, and quash the Boston zealots. The free-state men's persistence in issuing scrip for money, guaranteeing land claims, recording deeds, and ignoring the duly established courts and justices of the peace was revolution, but a solid majority of proslavery voters from the South would settle it.

Serious trouble came sooner than Shannon expected. Ten miles south of Lawrence, in the timber area, property lines were difficult to determine. A free-state squatter, Charles Dow, disputed the line claimed by proslavery Franklin Coleman, a man of property who had come out from Kansas

City. A free-state neighbor, Jacob Branson, helped Dow drive Coleman off the land in question. Later in the day, as Dow walked from a nearby blacksmith shop, he met Coleman on the road. What passed between them is not known, but Dow's body was found thirty yards beyond the meeting place, his back riddled with shotgun slugs — Coleman's ammunition.

This murder of a free-state man by a proslavery settler created more excitement than the killing of the proslavery man by the free-state settler last November. The intervening months had taught free-state men to hate all proslavery Missourians. Moreover, Eastern philanthropists promised to back free-state resistance. To avenge Dow's death they grabbed their guns and threatened vengeance. Coleman and his proslavery neighbors — some fifteen families — packed their wagons and whipped away to the Shawnee Mission, determined to get help and return to their homes. News of the murder was carried by spurring riders to other free-state communities. A hundred men congregated at the fateful scene. Only two of them from Lawrence — Sam N. Wood, the little Ohio Quaker who had responded to Robinson's belligerent Fourth of July speech, and Sam F. Tappan, correspondent for the *Boston Journal* and *New York Times*. These young newspaper reporters had come to make news as well as report it.

Lane had just issued a formal Thanksgiving proclamation in the name of the Topeka government, and the crowd felt confident of protection under its authority. Assembled along the road, they passed resolutions of condolence to Dow's family, and vowed to bring the murderer to justice. Many of the group wanted to burn all vacated proslavery settlers' cabins in the neighborhood. Sam Wood spoke out against this, but after dark three homes crackled up in flames.

Meanwhile, at the mission, the proslavery refugees appealed to the law for protection. Coleman obtained an order for Branson's arrest, alleging that the fellow had threatened personal vengeance, must be restrained and bonded to keep the peace. The new sheriff of Douglas County, Samuel J. Jones, set off in the night, with Coleman as guide, to serve the process. Having succeeded as leader of an election mob near Bloomington in the preceding March, this violent and courageous son-in-law of A. G. Boone determined to have his new office of sheriff properly respected. Time had come to assert proslavery authority in the Lawrence free-state community! Sheriff Jones, with a nine-man posse, drew rein at Branson's cabin sometime after midnight. The sheriff dismounted and knocked. Mrs. Branson peeped out and asked the men their business. Jones pushed in, pointed a seven-shooter at her husband, and ordered him to get up. Branson rolled sullenly out of bed, pulled on his trousers, struggled into his coat, took his tattered straw hat from its peg, and padded barefoot into the night. The posse had no horse for him to ride, but someone led up a saddleless mule, which he mounted. Arrogant now, Jones started along the road to Lawrence, but news of the arrest traveled ahead of him. At Blanton's Crossing of the Wakarusa, fives miles from town, a mob stood in the road. Armed with Sharps rifles, squirrel guns, and rocks, they stopped the sheriff, rescued Branson, and threatened to lynch Coleman. Jones swore furious retaliation against them all, including the radical town of Lawrence, and clattered off in the dark.

Tappan and Wood, both members of the mob again, realized that trouble was imminent. With a few friends, they set off to warn the people of Lawrence. They went first to the home of their fellow abolitionist, Dr. Robinson, on Mount Oread. Dawn was breaking as the doctor came sleepily to the door, listened to their story, then told them to go down the hill, call a mass meeting of citizens for eight o'clock that morning. He would dress and be present.

At the appointed time, Robinson walked into the assemblage. None of his fiery July Fourth oratory illuminated his solemn, studious face this morning. Indeed, since receiving that warning letter from Amos A. Lawrence, he had become a cautious man. Robinson explained that the people of Lawrence might have to suffer for something done by outsiders. The entire town would be blamed. He proposed that they all disclaim implication of any kind, but arm themselves and protect their property from plunderers. If any violence occurred, let the Missourians be the aggressors.

Meantime, Sheriff Jones had arrived in Franklin, a proslavery hamlet on the Wakarusa only three miles from Lawrence. Before going to bed, he sent a messenger to Governor Shannon announcing that his authority had been flouted, his prisoner rescued, and Coleman threatened with lynching. The militia must be called out to maintain peace. Three thousand men would be needed.

Shannon's duty seemed clear. He had heard much about the domineering free-state men. He would show them that law and order had come.

As governor, he issued a call for the militia. To his amazement only a handful responded. Obviously, the majority of the citizens were free-state! His friends explained that the territorial guard was as yet unorganized. The notorious Daniel Woodson, secretary of the territory, sent a call for Missouri's Platte County Rifles to come at once. He ended the appeal with: "Do not implicate the governor, whatever you do."

Shannon should have realized the true state of affairs now, but having taken the side of the "bogus" government, he did what weak men — average men, perhaps — always do. He tried to rectify his mistake by getting himself deeper into the injustice. He appealed to the Federal troops at Fort Leavenworth. By coincidence, Colonel Edwin V. Sumner was in command there. His superior — aristocratic, handsome, proslavery General Harney — had gone on a trip to Europe with his wealthy St. Louis wife. Sumner had been ordered to spend the winter at Fort Laramie, but had risked court-martial by coming back rather than lose his horses by starvation on the distant plains. The colonel was called "Old Bull Sumner" by his men because he removed his upper teeth and bellowed before leading a charge. Sumner, like fiery little Captain Lyon at Fort Riley, was an antislavery man. He refused to send soldiers to the governor unless ordered to do so from Washington. Shannon wired the President. However, before a satisfactory reply was received, a Missouri "army" of fifteen hundred men straggled across the border toward Lawrence. Two wagonloads of guns came from as far away as Jefferson City, the Missouri capital. Seven cannon were brought from the Federal arsenal at Liberty, Missouri. Long, lean, and likable Hiram Bledsoe marched a company from Lexington, Missouri, trundling a Mexican War cannon said to have been cast from Chihuahua church bells. Missouri's hero, Alexander W. Doniphan, had captured several at Sacramento and distributed them as war relics in the river towns. For years Bledsoe had been firing this ancient gun at Fourth of July celebrations. From Waverly, Missouri, young Jo Shelby rode in again — with fighting men, not voters, this time. Senator Atchison came again also, as peacemaker, he claimed, to keep the Missourians under control and to counsel forbearance — a plausible but unconvincing defense. Free-state settlers watched the enemy muster at Franklin on the Wakarusa, three miles from Lawrence, and pitch their tents.

No man in Lawrence had any experience in military command except

Jim Lane, but Robinson succeeded in being elected "major general" with Lane second in command. The Grim Chieftain took over at once, ordered the men drilled, and set them to work constructing five blockhouses. Supplies were purchased in stores and paid for in scrip, increasing still more the free-state men's interest in their revolutionary government. Night and day, men worked in details of fifty, shoveling, hewing, and hammering. They could hear cannon being fired in practice on the Wakarusa. Pickets at Lawrence tested their own marksmanship by shooting at floating logs in the river, until ordered to save powder for the fight ahead. Over two hundred volunteer defenders came from outlying settlements. One wagon, hauled by a skeleton of a horse, contained seven tall, angular giants, each holding a pole surmounted by a bayonet. A pistol and short navy sword protruded from each man's belt. The strangers were named Brown — old John and his boys from Osawatomie Creek. This sudden influx of volunteers taxed the town's food supplies. The enemy, holding the roads to the Missouri, appropriated incoming groceries, guns, and ammunition. Cattle belonging to free-state settlers on the prairie furnished the invaders with much-needed meat.

For the first time now, Kansas and Missouri armies faced one another, both with cannon peeping over fortifications — the beginning of a civil war that would last until 1865. On December 2, 1855, Mrs. Hannah Anderson Ropes, who had recently come from Boston with two children — a son, eighteen, and daughter, eleven — wrote her sister-in-law: "Now I must tell you, we are in the midst of most serious preparations for *defensive war*. It is a week today since the rumor first reached Lawrence, that it is to be destroyed. Everybody is armed and everybody sleeps with their arms about them and clothes on."

Mrs. Ropes had partitioned a corner of her room for her son and another soldier. A second rifleman slept, under a buffalo robe, in the attic. "I am getting quite used to fire arms," she continued. "They all give me charge whenever they get in, at whatever hour, to be sure and call them if I hear the *call drum* — Our cabin is on the outskirts of the town, and quite in view of the prairie over which the Missourians must come. You can imagine how many times I listen while the weary men sleep, and how often I take a peep off to see if they are coming in upon us in the night time. Several tribes of Indians have sent in word that they will stand by us. . . ."

The balmy December weather turned suddenly cold, with wind and biting snow. Farmer volunteers remembered warm beds in their distant cabins. One man complained, as he shoveled frozen dirt, "We had all better be at home fixing up for winter than fooling our time away here." Grumbling became contagious. "General" Lane, riding around to inspect the work, noted the disaffection. He dismounted and sprang upon the nearest embankment. The men put down their picks and shovels to watch him. Lane began to speak in a soft tone. In a minute the street was full of men. As the audience grew, so did Lane's ardor. One listener reported:

> He became afire with eloquence. Off went his large, circular military cloak, next his hat, soon his coat, as he saw his appeal was telling; then his vest followed . . . and his necktie was soon lying with his other clothing upon the ground, his shirt was unbuttoned down the front, while shouts and cheers of applause went up from the men.
>
> Next his shirt-sleeves were unbuttoned and rolled above his elbows, and as he paced, like some wild animal, rapidly back and forth on the embankment, with the perspiration standing in great beads upon his face, notwithstanding it was a sharp December day, he poured forth a stream of eloquence. . . .

What Lane said and what he advocated will remain a disputed point between those who agreed or disagreed with him later. Did Lane merely want to keep the men from deserting, or did he try to precipitate an immediate attack on the entrenched enemy? Some maintained that an aggressive detail was preparing for a sortie on the Wakarusa at midnight, but Robinson, the top commander, learned about it and countermanded the order. If so, this added more bitterness to the growing jealousy between Robinson and Lane, the New Englander and the Midwesterner.

A few men in Lawrence hoped to forestall hostilities by a last-minute appeal to the governor. After midnight, two rode off to the Shawnee Mission. They were stopped at the Wakarusa, then allowed to pass. Next morning they called on the governor. He had heard about the proposed resistance to his administration, and was determined to have his authority respected. The peace envoys — one of them G. P. Lowrey — urged the governor to come and see the true situation for himself. A thousand embattled farmers could not be altogether wrong. Shannon called peremptorily for his two-horse buggy. "I shall go to Lawrence," he said, "and insist upon the people agreeing to obey the laws and delivering up their Sharps rifles." The messengers reminded Shannon that the citizens of Lawrence had resisted no laws, and if he thought that they would give up the time-honored American right of bearing arms, he had better not risk his own neck by trying to stop them.

Shannon wanted to be fair. He bundled himself in a greatcoat and with A. G. Boone, the wealthy trader, as his companion, settled in the back seat of the buggy. Lurching over the frozen roads across the prairie, black and desolate from fires, the travelers learned about the first casualty of the "war." Only yesterday, as the free-state emissaries had ridden out, three of the farmer volunteers — a young man named Thomas Barber, his brother, and brother-in-law — had decided to go home. If they had listened to Lane's oratory, it had not influenced them. On the California road they saw a Missouri patrol and turned off into the high prairie grass, galloping away.

The patrol was in charge of "Major" George W. Clarke, notorious Indian agent who had suffered from the actions of the Lawrence claim association. To him the three horsemen looked suspicious. With two companions, he galloped after them, called a halt, and ordered the boys back to his patrol. The free-staters argued, refused to go, and spurred their horses forward. A few shots were exchanged. A patroller said later that he knew one of the abolitionists was hit. He saw "fur fly from his old great coat." Barber's own companions believed no one hurt, until Thomas muttered, as they galloped along, "My God! I am a murdered man!" Then he slipped from the saddle as his brother reached to catch him. Clarke, leader of the patrol, was always blamed for the killing.

A riderless horse trotted into Barber's barnyard with reins trailing. The womenfolk comforted themselves with the hope that the animal had got loose in town, but before dark the men came and took them all to Lawrence, where Barber's body was laid out.

Governor Shannon listened to the story and, of course, regretted it — but this could hardly be called war. However, when he arrived on the Wakarusa, he saw the army of noisy, carousing men clamoring for an attack on the village three miles beyond. He could not help noticing that these rowdies were Missourians, assembled to fight Kansans.

The executive party drove on through their lines and across the prairie to Lawrence, where they were formally halted by a sentry and conducted to the revolutionary chieftains, Robinson and Lane. Shannon stepped stiffly out of the carriage. Here was a diplomatic mission more delicate than anything he had attempted as minister to Mexico!

The free-state "generals" greeted the travelers cordially, warmed them with wine, and suggested that the governor speak to the townspeople in the Eldridge House. An upper room had been arranged for the meeting. The famous portholed building was still unfinished but, like the free-state hotel in Kansas City, was shaping up into one of the finest in the West. These New Englanders built magnificently.

Curious women in Lawrence watched the newcomers enter the hotel and pick their way through kegs of nails, buckets of mortar, and piles of lumber. They noticed the governor's red face and steel-gray hair, his rusty black frock coat buttoned tightly around his thickset body. Beside him strode the tall and handsome Colonel Boone — a gracious gentleman of the old school who looked, acted, and dressed the part. "Hard to believe, isn't it, that he led an expedition of mountain men to the Rockies only last year!"

The two envoys climbed the stairs. In the upper hall they passed the body of Barber, lying, in farm clothes, on a table. The young widow sobbed audibly in an adjoining room. Mrs. Robinson heard Boone say to the governor, "I did not expect this."

At the meeting, the governor listened intently to the free-state men's side of the difficulty. He could find no concerted effort on the part of the citizens to thwart an arrest in their town, but obviously they were determined to defend their homes from an attack by Missourians. The scales fell from Shannon's eyes at last. Those ruffians yonder, across the prairie, could never justify their whiskey threats to sack this town. But what should he do? How could he induce them to go home? The governor asked Robinson and Lane to accompany him, under a flag of truce, to the enemy lines and tell the men there what they had told him.

Back on the Wakarusa the "army" assembled for a parley and after listening to the governor and his companions, agreed to go back to Missouri. Then Shannon returned to Lawrence and signed a "treaty" with the free-state "generals": they agreeing not to resist the execution of any *legal* process, the governor agreeing not to call on residents of any other state to aid in the execution of the laws — weasel words, for both agreements depended on definitions of terms. At best, the "treaty" was nothing but a stay of immediate hostilities. However, both sides had saved face and could report success. Neither reckoned with wily Jim Lane, who held a card in his sleeve to play against the governor at the first opportunity.

Another storm lowered, and the Missourians on the Wakarusa showed no sign of striking their tents. Were they, or were they not, going home? During the evening the Lawrence people congregated in the hotel again. Sentries still patrolled the town. Mrs. Ropes noticed that the governor appeared nervous, distinctly unhappy. He kept looking out the window into the driving storm. The Missourians were angry, he said, because he had interfered in the interests of peace. They had objected to his coming back to Lawrence from their camp and, in their anger, might rush the town and lynch him. This fear gave Lane an opportunity to play his hidden card.

A messenger came to the distraught governor stating that armed men were approaching the town. Would he give the people of Lawrence permission in writing to repel the invaders? The governor paused a moment and scratched his coarse gray hair. Here was a pretty state of affairs. He had come to enforce submission to the Missouri militia and was now asked to acknowledge sovereignty to the free-state outlaws. However, with his own life endangered, it seemed best to authorize the people of Lawrence to protect him. He signed the paper.

Before morning, Shannon learned that no attack had come. He asked for the suppression of his signed statement, but it was too late. Multiple copies had been given to the ambitious young journalists, and stories of Shannon's capitulation were far on their way toward Eastern newspapers. The governor, in a great huff, wrote a long letter to President Pierce, claiming that he had been deceived, tricked, had not read the whole paper he signed in the urgency of the moment — all the excuses usually manufactured by a weak man with a strong imagination. Some said later that Lane got the governor drunk before the signing, and became pretty well intoxicated himself. Others maintained that the Grim Chieftain drank from a different and less potent bottle. As Lane never drank, it seems more likely that Shannon was the prey of his natural inclination to be swayed by the company around him.

Thus the Wakarusa War ended with the killing of Barber. Free-staters, as well as proslavery men, packed their wagons to go home, firebrands on both sides sputtering. In Lawrence, tall, angular John Brown, with Puritan strength in his deeply lined face, mounted a dry-goods box to denounce the "treaty." His blue-gray eyes glowed with unworldly intensity as he castigated the base surrender of a principle that could be upheld only by shedding blood. Bystanders helped him down before the speech was well started. Old Brown had come to Kansas in October to live with his sons, one of whom had taken a minor part in the Big Springs meeting. The "old man" — he was fifty-five — had become conspicuously belligerent during the siege, and was in the little party that wanted to attack the enemy at midnight. He returned to his sons' homesteads smoldering with resentment.

On December 15, 1855, the people assembled again to vote on the now much-discussed Topeka Constitution, and on the same day Barber was buried with state formality. His body had been held nine days for this event. Lane and Robinson, by slow steps, had changed places. Robinson was now thoroughly conservative, but Lane was becoming more and more radical. The Grim Chieftain had watched the Western men rally to Reeder's revolutionary talk at Big Springs last fall and to his own oratory on the Lawrence embankments. Still a good Democrat, a national Democrat, he had tired of moderation. In his best stump manner he reminded the audience, "You still retain the rifles you know so well how to use. The ladies — God bless them! — are still among us, to encourage manly and chivalric deeds."

The dramatic scene was followed by a vote on the Topeka Constitution, which ratified it by a safe majority, disclosing without doubt the will of the Kansas settlers. Now let Douglas and Pierce demonstrate their sincerity by approving squatter sovereignty!

Thus, by New Year's Day, 1856, the free-state settlers had triumphed in a two-year struggle, suffering surprisingly few fatalities — probably three all told. Several emigrants had been manhandled but not killed, notably William Phillips, attorney at Leavenworth, and Reverend Pardee Butler, an itinerant abolition preacher at Atchison. However, the South had hardly started to send colonizers. Let Buford's men come. The final test of strength and resourcefulness between the sections would be part and parcel of the presidential election of 1856.

I V

The Crime Against Kansas

COLONEL EDWIN V. SUMNER watched the Kansas winter of 1855–1856 through the frosted windows of Fort Leavenworth — the worst blizzard on record, killing plains cattle by thousands as far south as Texas. In Missouri towns, more freight accumulated than usual, for the spring overland trade was to be augmented by the biggest Kansas rush yet known. Old Bull Sumner disliked the prospect of summer police duty among political partisans. The stress of regular army jealousy over promotion was bad enough without adding the strain of civil politics. Sumner was already in trouble with General Harney for disobeying orders on the plains last fall, and he would have to restrain his own antislavery assertions. That fanatic Captain Lyon, out at Fort Riley, was getting a bad reputation. Mess-hall gossips said that he would "foam at the mouth" in arguments with fellow officers over slavery.

The prejudices of other officers in Sumner's department were harder to fathom. The Virginian Lieutenant Colonel Joseph E. Johnston was sure to be a proslavery Harney man. So was brand-new Lieutenant J. E. B. Stuart, just arrived from West Point. A dashing horseman, bearded to the eyes like a Cossack, he had swept the daughter of literary Lieutenant Colonel Philip St. George Cooke completely off her feet, satin slippers, crinoline and all. The happy bridegroom waited, like Sumner, for spring. A conventional young man with a reputation for being religious and — paradoxically — combative, he scuffled at every opportunity with officers his age. Soldiers on parade stepped briskly to his shrill metallic commands. He loved to train things — horses or men — and was said to pet his favorite mount even more than his bride. The animal followed him around like a dog. Jeb Stuart wanted to fight Indians, but he was not averse to putting free-soil settlers in their place.

The officers could keep informed on the growing political friction around them by reading five local newspapers — two proslavery and three free-state. Few of them did so, however, but all understood that both factions were oiling their guns for the decisive struggle that was coming after the second winter of agitation and preparation.

In January 1856, the free-state rebels held their election for legislators to the illegal Topeka government. Few disturbances were reported at the polls except along the river where proslavery Missouri settlers tried to stop all voting. In a skirmish at Easton on election night a proslavery man was killed. Next day the so-called Kickapoo Rangers waylaid R. P. Brown, a drawling Kentucky free-stater, recently back from the defense of Lawrence in the Wakarusa War, and arrested him for murdering the proslavery man. Someone chopped the accused man's head open with a hatchet. His tormented body was tossed into a wagon and hauled across the snow-swept plains. "I am very cold," he moaned. The vindictive tormentors spit tobacco juice in his gashes, saying, "Anything would make a damned abolitionist feel better." At his cabin, the still-living body was dumped out with the curt words to his wife, "Here's Brown." At least, this was the story the free-state newspaper reporters sent East, and it was widely copied.

When the ballots were counted, the entire free-state ticket was found elected, including abolitionist Robinson for "governor" — a notable new trend in Kansas politics, for most of the legislators elected were Democrats, very different from the New England radicals. Obviously, the settlers now associated political injustice with slavery and voted accordingly — a prejudice expressed as early as the Big Springs convention.

The proslavery press denounced this plebiscite. Stringfellow's *Squatter Sovereign* and the *Kickapoo Pioneer* urged the people to hang and shoot every "black and poisonous" abolitionist.

In Washington, President Pierce worried about the revolution's growth, the failure of his administration to cope with the critical situation. Two objectives always loomed in his mind above other considerations — his own renomination for the presidency in the spring, and the preservation of the Democratic Party. He sent for Governor Shannon, on leave in Ohio, and the two conferred confidentially. Diplomat Shannon agreed with the President better than had Reeder. Certainly the Kansas elections had been fraudulent, but they had been accepted, and the Atchison group would not surrender now. If the administration reversed itself at this late date, the party might lose its Southern Wing. Pierce felt confident that most Kansans wanted peace. With that restored — even by force — the people would surely submit and be happy, but so long as violence continued, the national Democratic administration was under constant fire from the new so-called Republicans. Peace, peace and harmony, Pierce reiterated, peace and prosperity, rather than majority rule — the dictator's choice — were his objectives.

To enforce peace and the recognized laws, President Pierce offered Shannon the United States Army, and the governor returned to Kansas. On March 4, 1856, the Topeka legislature met and approved a memorial, addressed to Congress, seeking admission of Kansas as a state under the new constitution. Lane and Robinson set off for Washington with hope in their hearts and the document in their pockets — Robinson to work with the anti-Nebraska Republicans, Lane with the old-line Democrats. Here, at last, was a chance for the President to end the Kansas trouble and prove the sincerity of his belief in squatter sovereignty.

The United States House of Representatives, with its anti-Nebraska majority, voted to accept the free-state organic act. Then Lane turned to the Senate, which was controlled by the administration. Astutely, the Grim Chieftain consulted ancient Lewis Cass, veteran Democratic senator who had originated the doctrine of squatter sovereignty. Cass and Lane had both voted for the Kansas-Nebraska bill, and now, in all fairness, wanted Kansas admitted under a free-state constitution, since the squatters willed it. Cass agreed to introduce an enabling act. Republican William H. Seward, the challenger of the South, spoke on April 9, 1856, for immediate acceptance.

Senator Douglas objected. He strode out on his short legs, Websterian forehead wrinkled with emotion, to defend the administration and make one more attempt to hold the Democratic Party together. Many objections to an enabling act at this time could be made. Kansas had insufficient population for statehood. Let the much-publicized Southern aid companies send their emigrants to Kansas and then follow the will of the squatters — valid objections, certainly more justifiable than Pierce's discharge of Reeder to appease the Atchison faction. However, Douglas went one step further. He questioned the memorial's genuineness. Slapping the document with the back of his pudgy hand, he accused Lane of bringing a partially forged document.

A vote was taken on the Kansas memorial, and the state was denied admission under the Topeka Constitution. Lane immediately challenged Senator Douglas to a duel, which Douglas declined as coming from one of inferior station. Lane was deeply insulted and when the Grim Chieftain resolved to get even with a man, he usually succeeded.

The thwarted House of Representatives resolved to send a committee of investigation to Kansas and learn the truth. Speaker Nathaniel Banks, Jr., appointed John Sherman, Ohio Republican whose brother William Tecumseh was in the army out in Oregon; Mordecai Oliver, elderly Whig from the Missouri border, who did not want to serve; and William Howard, Republican from Michigan — surely no committee to save the Democratic Party. The three men, with clerks and secretaries, started to Kansas, while Lane toured the Eastern states criticizing the administration's actions — a Democrat flaying the Democrats. As he and a dozen other speakers were lecturing, the congressional committee arrived at Kansas City landing in April 1856. They loaded their carpetbags in a hack and drove up the hill to the booming village of Westport. All about them the streets were lined with wagons. In pens on every side hundreds of horses, mules, and cattle stamped in the hot mud, switching tails at myriads of flies. Under long sheds the committeemen saw glowing forges, heard hammers ringing on anvils, smelled burning hoofs.

Sherman had brought along his wife. He pointed out to her the picturesque drovers in broad hats, flannel shirts, homespun trousers tucked in cowhide boots, knives and pistols at their belts. No wonder democracy functioned awkwardly among such individualistic barbarians! Here were Indians, half-bloods, Mexicans, and Americans, "as rough a set of men of mixed color, tribe and nativity as could be found anywhere in the world," Sherman said.

The committee drove first to Lecompton, a cluster of rude frame and log buildings around an unfinished "capitol." Lodging houses were crowded, with ten or fifteen men sleeping in a single room. The most commodious and best patronized place in town was a barroom. The committee clerks were set to work copying records pertinent to their investigation. John Sherman and his wife drove on to Lawrence, eight miles away. They found this little New England village very different from the frontier capital — neat as Boston Common, but fortified with redoubts and block-houses.

Other members of the committee soon arrived and had hardly sat down to take testimony before the long-heralded emigrants from Dixie disembarked at Kansas City. A rising young newspaperman in Westport, Henry Clay Pate, had toured the South last winter and reported that settlers were coming "by thousands." Pate hoped to retrieve his fortune with an anti-abolitionist journal, the *Border Star*. He had failed with an anti-Catholic Know-Nothing paper in Cincinnati in 1853. Milt McGee read Pate's glowing account of the impending migration and began work on a hotel — as fine as the Kansas City free-state hostelry — to accommodate "Southern gentlemen."

The first big contingent consisted of four hundred, all on one boat — the much-touted Jefferson Buford party. Pate described them in his newspaper as mechanics, physicians, lawyers, and civil engineers. Southern towns had celebrated their departure with patriotic speeches, and a subscription had been raised to purchase Holy Scriptures for each man. The Alabama group all wore white silk badges inscribed *Bibles — not Rifles*. They embarked at New Orleans. At Cairo, Illinois, where the steamboat stopped to unload iron rails for the new Illinois Central Railroad, a reporter described the emigrants as "the most despicable ruffians and cut-throats." Another antislavery paper delighted in announcing that Buford's strong box had been broken open and $5000 stolen, presumably by his own patriots. Most of the men enlisted in Alabama and South Carolina. Fifty came from Georgia, one from Illinois, and one from Boston. At Kansas City they marched off the boat waving the state flags of Alabama and South Carolina along with banners inscribed KANSAS THE OUTPOST and SUPREMACY OF THE WHITE RACE. Were these Southern states invading a United States territory as Missouri had done repeatedly?

In military array, Budford's men marched up the hill and across to Westport to be welcomed at the Harris House, opposite Boone's store. A crowd had waited since eight in the morning. Henry Clay Pate opened the meeting with his best Southern oratory. He welcomed the "army" as fellow Georgians come to settle in Lawrence and "beard the lion in his den." Pate followed this quotation from Sir Walter Scott with a discussion of the constitutionality of secession. He ended by crying: "Should this arm ever fail to lift itself in defense of the Union when menaced, let God strike it with palsy terrible as the curse of Ananias and Sapphira! But if Kansas is to be kept out of the Union because of slavery in her Constitution, the Union, instead of being an instrument of justice, is an instrument of injustice, and therefore a nullity."

Then J. W. Whitfield, the proslavery Indian agent who had been elected territorial representative to Congress, made a few spirited and amusing remarks in his thick-tongued Tennessee drawl. Next, Major Buford was presented with a fine horse and saddle. He accepted the gift, stated that his men had come to help fill the territory peaceably and hoped to buy several hundred horses — a remark that must have made Milt McGee rub his cupped hand expectantly.

The congressional investigating committee now in Lawrence read about the reception. They also noted that the newcomers did not take up homesteads or even get employment over at Lecompton, where plenty of work was available on the new capitol buildings. Free-state men complained that their taxes were paying for that work, and they did not intend to tolerate it much longer. Then proslavery Judge S. D. Lecompte put a stop to possible subversiveness by issuing subpoenas for Robinson, Reeder, Lane, and others — including Dan Anthony at Leavenworth — to appear before a grand jury on charges of treason. True, these men had all participated in forming the Topeka government regardless of the Lecompton government, but heretofore treason had been defined as bearing arms to overthrow the government, and this the free-state men had been careful to avoid. It was thought, with some reason, that the subpoenas were not for the purpose of getting indictments but to scare the leaders out of the country before they testified at the committee of inquiry hearings. John Sherman talked over the ugly situation with Robinson and urged him to leave the territory as soon as possible, but to take a copy of the committee's findings with him for delivery to Nathaniel Banks, speaker of the House.

The free-state "governor" and his wife promptly left for the river and boarded a steamboat. Snugly ensconced in a stateroom, the couple were reading themselves to sleep when the vessel docked at Lexington, Missouri. They heard the ship's clerk remonstrating with a noisy crowd at the gangplank. Then many feet scuffled along the deck, and the sheriff knocked at their stateroom with a warrant. He explained, through the door, that the complaint charged Robinson with escaping from an indictment for treason.

Mrs. Robinson's face hardened. A woman of more than usual physical courage, her strong nose betokened aggressiveness and her slightly protruding lower lip stubbornness. "They will kill you if you go," she whispered, "and you may as well make a stand here."

The "governor" reached for his pistol — a feeble weapon against a mob. Then, with fatalistic resignation equal to his wife's emotional fury, he said that he would surrender. Dressing quickly, he stepped out and went with the sheriff, who sent him back a prisoner to Lecompton. Mrs. Robinson continued the voyage, taking all the incriminating testimony so far collected by the committee. She planned to visit her family in New England, where many zealots would be interested in her experience. On her way, she would stop and see the Democratic governor of Ohio, Salmon P. Chase, who as senator had dared defy the President when the Kansas-Nebraska bill was made a party measure. She would also offer her services as a lecturer on any platform where her story might help the cause of freedom. In Illinois a convention was being planned to organize the Republican Party. She might talk there. Abraham Lincoln, Whig politician, was said to be much interested in the proceedings.

The proposed treason arrests had not stopped with Robinson's flight. "Senator" Reeder, the ex-governor, resisted — peaceably — an arrest by United States Deputy Marshal William F. Fain. The crowd hooted and Deputy Fain stalked away without his prisoner. Shortly thereafter, Sheriff Jones with three deputies arrested Samuel Wood, the Hicksite Quaker accused of abetting the rescue of Jacob Branson five months before. A few young men in Lawrence mobbed the four officers and liberated their friend. Next day — Sunday, April 20, 1856 — Jones returned with a ten-man posse. On the street he met and attempted to arrest Sam Tappan. Church services had just ended, and the posse found themselves surrounded by a hooting, groaning congregation. The ten men decided to return to Lecompton without any prisoners. Jones was thoroughly aroused. He now had a good case against the townsmen of

Lawrence for resisting territorial laws. Appealing to Governor Shannon, he was given a detail of United States dragoons in charge of Lieutenant James McIntosh, and with these he returned on April 23. However, all the culprits had disappeared.

That night the soldiers encamped on a vacant lot northeast of the Eldridge House. Sheriff Jones lodged with Lieutenant McIntosh and popped in and out of the tent officiously. A crowd gathered to watch him. At dusk a few bystanders began to pelt him with eggs. Jones stepped to a water barrel to sponge his clothes, when a bullet set the water splashing. He darted back into the tent. "I believe that was intended for me," he said, examining a hole in his trousers. "That *was* intended for me," he concluded.

Lieutenant McIntosh threw back the tent flap and strode out. He walked across to the crowd and mingled with it. Charlie Lenhardt, a printer on the *Herald of Freedom,* peered in the door of the illuminated tent and saw Jones sitting on a cot. Charlie withdrew in the dark, and a few moments later another shot flashed and Jones toppled over. Soldiers, running out to investigate, stumbled over the guy ropes, and the would-be murderer escaped.

Charlie Lenhardt admitted throwing the eggs and shooting into the barrel but denied the second shot. Moreover, Jones's wound was questionable. He was taken hurriedly back to Lecompton. Dr. Stringfellow refused to let people interview the wounded man, and he was soon in the saddle again. The *Squatter Sovereign* screamed for vengeance: "We are now in favor of leveling Lawrence and chastising the traitors there congregated, should it result in the total destruction of the Union."

The congressional investigating committee moved on to Leavenworth and then to Westport in time to witness a new invasion of Missourians. Sheriff Jones had cried for help, and the United States Marshal at Lecompton, Israel B. Donaldson, had issued a proclamation calling all law-abiding citizens to muster and help enforce the laws. The call was answered, as it had been in the past, by Missourians, and the investigating committee watched them stream through town by hundreds to enforce Kansas laws. Squatter sovereignty indeed! With this last evidence of illegal administration — of a dictatorial machine assuming authority in the name of the people — the congressmen boarded the boat for home.

Ex-Governor Reeder, in Lawrence, realized that he would soon be arrested for treason. In disguise he slipped quietly from town and, with Gaius Jenkins, traveled fifty miles of prairie to Kansas City, arriving the day of Donaldson's proclamation. The Eldridge brothers gave the fugitives accommodations at the American Hotel, cautioning them to stay in their rooms, and to beware of dangerous guests lodged across the hall. Soon other refugees straggled in — George W. Deitzler, the man Robinson had sent East for arms, and George W. Brown, noisy *Herald of Freedom* editor. One day Reeder watched from his window as a mob under Milt McGee and Henry Clay Pate invaded the hotel and dragged out the man they believed to be George W. Brown. The fellow was saved from lynching only by identifying himself as a different and innocent Brown.

The Eldridges realized that they could not shelter free-state men indefinitely, especially while the Missouri militiamen arrived daily to join the muster. George W. Brown and Gaius Jenkins both tried to escape but were captured. Milt McGee sent them to Lecompton as prisoners in charge of one of his slaves. The number of "traitors" imprisoned up there with Robinson was growing apace. Reeder, hoping to go East, still lurked in his hotel room.

Back in Lawrence, excitement, despair, and confusion reigned as the proslavery militia marched to the Wakarusa, pitched tents, and built a blockhouse. All the free-state leaders were in jail, hiding or — like Lane — lecturing back East. Independent free-state scouts ventured out on the prairie to investigate the military preparations, and two of them were reported shot. There was no doubt about the seriousness of the crisis. In Leavenworth, James Redpath, eager always to precipitate a war over slavery, wrote the *Chicago Tribune*: "There will in all probability be a battle in a day or two between the men of the North and the minions of the Slave Power in Kansas."

The forthcoming "battle" was watched by Eastern editors, as each new development came from the prairie reporters. Lecturers on Kansas drew crowded houses. "Senator" Lane, speaking in Indiana, was reported to be in imminent danger of arrest for treason. The excitement reached Washington, where congressmen sweltered in ninety degrees of humid heat. Waving palm-leaf fans, they speculated on possible candidates for President. The Democrats were convening in Cincinnati the following week to select nominees, and Pierce's failure on the Western border would be an important factor in their decision. Then, to augment the growing tension, Senator Sumner of Massachusetts announced that he intended to deliver some official remarks in the Senate on the crime against Kansas.

On May 19, 1856, with the proslavery army encircling Lawrence, and delegates preparing to assemble for the Cincinnati convention, Sumner pushed back his upholstered chair in the Senate and rose to deliver his address. He wore a light sack coat and white pantaloons, suitable for the sultry weather. He glanced up at the packed galleries. Alongside the congressmen from the House who had come over to listen sat antislavery Joshua Giddings and proslavery Alexander H. Stephens. Old-line Democrat Frank Blair and Whig-machine boss Thurlow Weed, both now antislavery, were also interested spectators.

Sumner haughtily surveyed the encircling senators. He tossed back his leonine locks from his shoulders and, in a restrained but rumbling voice, reviewed the administration's illegal actions in Kansas. He gave no credence to the President's complaint about New England agitators. He recounted how Senator Atchison had led voters from Missouri to Kansas in November 1854, and in March and October 1855, with bowie knives and banners flying.

Senator Sumner described the Kickapoo Rangers' method of regulating elections. He referred to R. P. Brown, whose head had been hacked for resisting, and the dumping of his freezing body out of a wagon at his cabin door. Conscientious settlers, Sumner said, were exposed to perpetual assault by murderous robbers from Missouri, "hirelings, picked from the drunken spew and vomit of an uneasy civilization — in the form of men."

Protests at such language echoed across the gallery. The president of the Senate pounded for order; Senator Douglas, writing busily at his seat, appeared not to hear. Sumner waited for silence. Then the lion in him roared again, this time at the senator from South Carolina, Andrew Pickens Butler, who had advocated the forced disarmament of free-state men. Butler had lived in Washington with Atchison, Mason, and Hunter. Sumner snarled at him with biting sarcasm:

The senator from South Carolina has read many books of chivalry, and believes himself a chivalrous knight, with sentiments of honor and courage. Of course he has chosen a mistress to whom he has made vows, and who, though ugly to others, is always lovely to him; though polluted in the sight of the world, is chaste in his sight. I mean the harlot slavery.

Another protest sputtered across the gallery. Sumner flung his head back contemptuously and turned on the diligent Douglas. He ridiculed the Little Giant's objection to the Topeka Constitution, censured him for calling Lane a forger. Peace could be had, he said, by letting the majority rule in Kansas, not by forcing a government on them.

Senator Douglas replied to Sumner with equal vindictiveness. Such language as Sumner used, he said, might "provoke some of us to kick him as we would a dog."

Somebody was provoked to kick Sumner, truly enough. Representative Preston S. Brooks of South Carolina, a relative of Butler's, was known as an inoffensive man. He had spoken and voted for the Kansas-Nebraska bill and had contributed to Buford's emigrant aid plan, but he had sat aloof in the recent violent demonstrations in Congress. He had even introduced a resolution against carrying concealed weapons on the floor. Brooks was a large, handsome man, tall as Sumner, with black hair, bright eyes, and fashionably careless in dress. Rumbling with resentment, he skulked around the Capitol, waiting for a chance to horsewhip the Massachusetts senator. Two days after Sumner's speech, but before full news of the sacking of Lawrence had come, Brooks entered the Senate chamber after adjournment and stepped to Sumner's desk, raised his gutta-percha cane, and flailed the senator's bowed head. Sumner tried to rise, found himself wedged under the desk, and soon fell bleeding and unconscious in the aisle — another example of Southern lawlessness to shock the North.

Brooks winced under the storm of protest, the comparison of his brutality with Border Ruffianism. He resigned his seat but was immediately re-elected. Southerners sent him dozens of gold-headed canes, endorsing his viciousness and thus permitting the North to point with truth at the effect of slavery on Southern society. In a state of high excitement the Democratic delegates left for Cincinnati to nominate a new President. As they took their seats, details came to them about the sacking of Lawrence.

The proslavery "army" had been ostensibly a posse under the direction of United States Marshal Donaldson and Sheriff Samuel Jones. Governor Shannon was conspicuously absent. As a representative of President Pierce on the eve of a convention in which he hoped to be renominated, Shannon wished to make no false step. The "army" encamped, as they had in December 1855, along the Wakarusa, four miles from town. The Eldridge brothers, businessmen as well as politicians, feared the destruction of their expensive furnishings in the Emigrant Aid Company's hotel. They drove over to the enemy lines to tell the commanders that they would personally aid in serving any legal warrants which the officers might have, if their property were spared. Colonel Harry Titus, a new man who had been discussed in the Lawrence papers as a Florida pirate, announced emphatically that the newspaper presses in town would have to be destroyed to satisfy the boys from South Carolina. Titus was a large, handsome man with a commanding presence and the clear skin common to one increasing in weight. A man of means, he affected the Missourians' homespun dress, loud talk, and knife flourishing. The Eldridges returned to town, fearing trouble. On Massachusetts Street, the crisis was discussed, and the frightened citizens, with no leader to advise them, decided to continue the old policy of nonresistance preached by their imprisoned "Governor" Robinson.

Early on the morning of May 21, 1856, the citizens of Lawrence saw horsemen in military array on Mount Oread. The rising sun shone on the grim barrels of cannon pointed toward the city. Red banners flapped in the wind against the green slope. Far to the south, companies could be seen marching along the California road, wheeling to the right, coming to reinforce the "soldiers" on the hill. Soon a few scouts walked into town, looked around for possible resistance. Reassured by the citizens, they walked out again. Then United States Deputy Marshal W. F. Fain rode down the street with a posse in shirt sleeves. He deputized six Lawrence citizens, among them the Eldridge brothers, to help make arrests. G. W. Smith, G. W. Deitzler and others were apprehended for treason, and the citizens made no protest. The Eldridges then invited the United States officers to dinner in the Free-State Hotel, and everything seemed to be progressing peaceably.

At three o'clock in the afternoon Sheriff Jones clattered into town. He arrested Jacob Branson, who had evaded him since the Barber affair, and

still there was no opposition. Then the sheriff ordered his men in line before the Free-State Hotel, and called on Samuel C. Pomeroy, reputed agent
of the Emigrant Aid Company, to surrender all arms and the village cannon. Pomeroy offered to wheel out the cannon but said the Sharps rifles
were private property over which neither he nor the Emigrant Aid Company had any jurisdiction.

This was unsatisfactory, so the "army" marched into town with fixed
bayonets. General William P. Richardson, of the territorial militia, was
ostensibly in command. At the head of regiments and companies rode all
the notorious Border Ruffians. With one of the first battalions came
George W. Clarke, Indian agent and alleged murderer of Barber. With
other units rode dignified A. G. Boone, the Westport merchant. Ex-
Senator Atchison led the Platte County (Missouri) Rifles. Dr. J. H.
Stringfellow, the editor, rode with the Kickapoo Rangers, apparently una-
shamed of Brown's murder. Then came Henry Clay Pate, editor of the
Border Star, with colors presented his company by the females of Westport. Dark, handsome, and romantic filibuster Titus rode with Buford's
men. Ladies adored his complexion, but on horseback his increasing girth
showed disadvantageously. Friends wished him luck with the grandiose
saloon and gambling establishment he planned for Kansas City.

A galaxy of unknown Southerners brought up the rear. Over the column
floated Buford's flags — the state banners of South Carolina and Alabama,
the others inscribed SOUTHERN RIGHTS, SUPREMACY OF THE WHITE RACE and
KANSAS THE OUTPOST. One was striped black and white. Another had a tiger
in place of the Union.

The army advanced with military caution, halting every three hundred
yards to support a battery of artillery which unlimbered for action while
others advanced. At the Free-State Hotel all guns were trained on the
hostelry and the army halted. The Eldridges repeated their pleas to save
their property. Sheriff Jones gruffly drew out his watch and allowed them
until 5 P.M. — two hours — to remove their furnishings.

Waiting, watch in hand, the officers assigned two companies to destroy
the Herald of Freedom and Kansas Free State presses. A three-hundred-
volume library fluttered out the windows. Type was shoveled into wagons
and hauled to the river. Newspaper files were tossed into the Kansas wind.
The free-state cannon were surrendered, as Pomeroy had promised. Then

the invaders formed in a hollow square before the hotel. David Rice Atchison mounted one of the surrendered guns and harangued the men with senatorial gusto.

The text of Atchison's speech is controversial. The incendiary free-state reporters quoted him as saying: "Boys, this day I am a Kickapoo Ranger, by God! This day we have entered Lawrence with 'Southern Rights' inscribed upon our banner. . . . If one man or woman dare stand before you, blow them [*sic*] to hell with a chunk of cold lead." Atchison's defenders maintain that he spoke conciliatorily, hoping to restrain the men from undue violence. Perhaps, but it is difficult to justify his being on the ground at all. Furthermore, he seems to have knelt unsteadily beside the cannon and aimed it at the hotel — a three-story structure eighty feet wide — and ordered "Fire." The ball whistled over the entire building and thumped into a distant hill where women had congregated for safety. This marksmanship from the old sportsman led many to conclude that the former president of the United States Senate had indulged too freely from the hotel cellar. Perhaps his unsteadiness was only fatigue, for at forty-nine years of age Atchison was unable to stand the long rides he had when younger, but the *Boston Evening Telegraph* announced maliciously that, in Missouri, Atchison was known as "Staggering Davy."

Later shots pounded the building but were unable to wreck the concrete walls. Finally, two kegs of powder were rolled in the doorway. A slow match of lard and powder was laid out to a safe distance and ignited. The flame sputtered toward the building, disappeared inside, and a few moments later great clouds of smoke belched from the windows. But still the walls stood firm. Finally, stock paper from the newspaper offices was brought and set on fire, thus gutting the hotel.

As flames licked out the window, Sheriff Jones stood up in his stirrups before his men and shouted less fluently than Atchison: "Gentlemen, this is the happiest day of my life. I determined to make the fanatics bow before me in the dust and kiss the territorial laws. I have done it, by G-d. You are now dismissed."

General looting began at once. The men, completely out of hand, raided the stores and caroused along the wooden sidewalks with satin vests buttoned over red flannel shirts, silk curtain cords holding up butternut pantaloons. Bags of canned goods were tied to saddles for the long trip home.

Somebody found and looted Ex-Governor Reeder's trunk. According to gossip, Dr. Stringfellow, presiding officer of the legislature, walked into Paul R. Brooks's store and took two boxes of cigars, saying: "Well, boys, I guess this is all the booty I want."

After dark, the invaders rode away, some to their homes in Lecompton, others to encampments around Mount Oread. Next morning "General" Atchison sent a messenger into Lawrence for permission to march his men down Massachusetts Street to the ferry, where he hoped to cross the Kaw and thus go home by the shortest route. No objections were raised, and the townsmen watched from windows and sidewalks as the "army" passed, solemnly as a funeral procession, cannon rumbling ahead and in the rear. Atchison, on his big horse, seemed to be dejected. Was he suffering from "the morning after," or did his bowed head indicate remorse over opening the armed conflict between slavery and freedom — not only opening it, but missing the first shot!

V

I Went to Take Old Brown
and Old Brown Took Me

THE SACKING of Lawrence frightened property owners in Kansas City. Townsmen warned the Eldridges to sell the interest they had acquired in the American Hotel there, lest it be destroyed and thus give the community a bad name. The brothers realized that they could not keep Ex-Governor Reeder hidden any longer. They asked Kersey Coates, the successful Pennsylvanian, to arrange with a steamship captain to stop for a passenger at a wharf six miles below town. Then a suit of workman's clothes was purchased for Reeder. The ex-governor shaved off his distinctive side whiskers. Mr. and Mrs. Edward Eldridge took his heavy valise between them, walked out the front door, and crossed the levee to a waiting skiff. The disguised ex-governor came down the stairs later, clay pipe in mouth, ax in hand. In the street a mob was gathering to hear a speaker blast the abolitionists. Reeder listened for a few minutes, then picked up his ax and walked to the skiff where his valise was waiting. The oarsman shoved off and the ex-governor escaped.

Details of the capture of Robinson, the escape of Reeder, and the sack of Lawrence were on everybody's lips as a convention of the leading politicians in Illinois assembled on May 29, 1856, to organize the Republican Party in Illinois and work with the national organization. Surely the time was ripe for a new organization to fight established tyranny. Abraham Lincoln, Whig leader in the state, had been loath to leave his party. Yet he had shown interest in this convention from the first. Bloomington was selected for the meeting — a suitable place, centrally located and reasonably close to Chicago. The town was antislavery in sympathy, had organized emigrant parties for Kansas, and was accustomed to abolition meetings, but this one would be unusual, for two much-publicized Kansas refugees were to speak.

At the appointed time, Andrew H. Reeder stepped out on a balcony and told the multitude about disguising himself in order to escape. His hair still showed the dye. Indoors, Mrs. Charles Robinson spoke with sweet determination in her eyes and a shawl over the broad lace collar on her sloping shoulders. At the opportune time, Lincoln stood up and delivered the speech that would go down in history as his greatest — his "lost speech," which so moved reporters that they threw down their pencils and took no notes. Surely, Reeder and Mrs. Robinson had found a sympathetic advocate.

The Democratic national convention in Cincinnati followed almost immediately. Delegates came with full realization of the dangerous growth of the Republican Party — especially the addition of the powerful state of Illinois. President Pierce's supporters still blamed Kansas disturbances on Northern agitators and fanatic pressmen — writers who incited settlers to resist the laws. The Lawrence raid, with its property damage, was dismissed by them as mostly propaganda. But before the convention was called to order, telegrams told of a horrible massacre of proslavery settlers on Pottawatomie Creek — no propaganda this time.

The outrage had started at Palmyra, where John Brown, Jr., was encamped with two companies of riflemen coming to the relief of Lawrence. On the morning of May 22, 1856, the riflemen had learned that they were too late. Lawrence had been sacked and the Free-State Hotel burned. The men rested all day in the shade of their wagons discussing the raid. As they talked, H. H. Williams rode into camp reporting that proslavery men were evicting free-state settlers at Osawatomie or Dutch Henry's Crossing of the Pottawatomie. Old John Brown — tall, spare, dressed in soiled clothes and a tattered straw hat — called his boys together and talked to them earnestly. He had wanted to fight the proslavery Missourians when they surrounded Lawrence last winter, but had been stopped. Now his people's homes on the Pottawatomie were threatened by the miscreants. Time had come for revenge.

Brown's boys and a few others began sharpening their cutlasses on a grindstone. Early on the afternoon of May 23, Old Brown, four sons, a son-in-law, and two others started in a wagon for Dutch Henry's Crossing, amid cheers from the two companies. Down the road they passed a traveler, James Blood, whom Brown had met in the Wakarusa War. The grim old man talked with him a few minutes and on leaving said, "We are on a secret mission — don't speak of meeting us."

Two days later, excited riders brought word that five proslavery men had been called out of their cabins during the night and killed with cutlasses. Three of the deceased were a father and two minor sons. The fourth was a bullying member of the proslavery legislature, the fifth a settler notorious for frightening free-state homesteaders. Of the five, only one could read or write. Unconfirmed gossip excused the murders on the ground that one of the dead men had raped a free-state settler's daughter — political propaganda of the worst kind, no doubt.

No matter how vicious the free-soil settlers might be, President Pierce was destined to suffer for the inability of his administration to maintain order. Resentment against him grew as the delegates caucused in Cincinnati. Surely a new man must be selected to win — especially since these upstart Republicans had added the great and growing state of Illinois to their organization, and planned to hold their first national convention on June 17, 1856.

The Democratic convention was called to order on June 2. Ghastly details of the Pottawatomie massacre had arrived now. The assassins had hidden all day in the woods near Dutch Henry's Crossing to select the settlers to be killed. Agreeing finally on a roster, the men set off late at night, cutlasses swinging from their belts. At the home of the first victim they knocked. No response! All was silent, but the men thought they heard a rifle cocked, so decided to move on. At the next three cabins they were more successful. Doomed men were called out by name, led a short way down the road and sabered to death — a quiet method of slaughter. One was shot in the face, powder smoke burning his skin. An innocent traveler taken from Dutch Henry's cabin was spared, but found dead some days later, probably assassinated to shut his mouth in case of a trial. The murderers rode away on the dead men's horses.

After the night's work, Brown asked the Lord's blessing at breakfast — as was his custom — raising to heaven gnarled hands stained with the dried blood of his victims. Intelligent free-state men shuddered over the possible consequence of his fanaticism, at the same time admitting that the old zealot would have been at home in the Old Testament armies of Israel which put to the sword the cities of Canaan.

Henry Clay Pate's Westport Sharpshooters were breaking camp at Franklin when word of the Pottawatomie massacre was received. Here was an opportunity for patriotic service. Pate announced grandly, for publication, that he would capture the old rascal. His men struck their tents, loaded their wagons, and the company started south. Along the way they "requisitioned" supplies, as needed, from pioneer stores. At Prairie City six foragers, intent on fun and groceries, rushed the handful of cabins. One had blacked his face; another wore chicken feathers in his hat. All had forgotten that the day was Sunday. They did not notice the large number of horses and buggies hitched along the fence until it was too late. Divine services were being held in one of the cabins, and the congregation stormed out the doors and windows, waving guns. The raiders with the blackened face and chicken-feather headpiece were captured. The rest dashed away to safety.

Old Brown learned that Pate's posse was coming. Volunteers came quickly to reinforce his handful, and he mustered twenty-eight men — among them the Viennese August Bondi, another of those foreigners who would fight and die if need be for the Declaration of Independence. With these, John Brown went to meet Pate, and found him encamped, with his wagons, near the Santa Fe road, three quarters of a mile from the village of Black Jack. A timbered gulch crossed the prairie behind the camp. Brown distributed his men in the brush and on June 2 — day of the Democratic convention — opened fire. The bombardment lasted two or three hours, then Pate sent over a flag of truce. The bearer stated that Pate was a United States deputy in search of persons for whom writs had been issued. Brown insisted that the "deputy" surrender unconditionally.

Pate asked for fifteen minutes to consider. Brown refused. The click of cocking rifles rippled along the edge of the gulch. Pate handed over his sword, surrendering twenty-three men — among them a brother of Milt McGee's. Brown moved them, their horses, and wagons, to his own camp at Middle Creek. "I had no alternative but to submit or to run and be shot," Pate reported to the *Missouri Republican*. "I went to take Old Brown, and Old Brown took me."

The capture of Pate caused wide publicity, and vengeful Missourians rallied at Westport and Independence. At Lexington, wealthy young Jo Shelby, who had just returned from Lawrence, wheeled his troop and started back. Other companies mustered in Jackson, Johnson, Clay, Platte, Ray, Saline, and Carrol counties.

To defend Brown, the Lawrence Stubbs shouldered arms and swung down the road to Black Jack. On other roads came the Bloomington Rifles, the Blue Mound Infantry, Wakarusa Boys, the Prairie City Company — about a hundred and fifteen men in all.

Governor Shannon was desperate. He knew the Democratic convention was in session in Cincinnati and that he, as well as Pierce, would be blamed for all the turmoil. On June 4 he issued a proclamation ordering all armed and illegal organizations to disperse, then cautioned Colonel Sumner to see that it was obeyed. With two companies of regulars the colonel approached the woods where Brown's men were bivouacked. The Bull of the Woods was engaged, at last, in the police work he detested. A messenger from Brown met him in the dusty road with a request for a conference.

"Tell him I make no terms with lawless men," Sumner replied. There was no question in his mind about his military duty. Then Old Brown himself stepped into the road and beckoned the soldiers back through the brush to his camp. The prisoners were called out and told that they were free. Henry Clay Pate bounded up on a log and began to speak.

"I don't want to hear a word from you, sir," Sumner snapped. "You have no business here. The governor told me so." The colonel then ordered both prisoners and captors to disperse and go home. Brown's party protested. They explained that several hundred men were marching in from Missouri to kill them all, in fact were only two miles away.

Colonel Sumner was not one to leave the men helpless. He sent, at once, for reinforcements for his own troops, then rode to the invaders' lines, ordering them all to go home. Captain Jo Shelby, still glorying in military activity, reported that Sumner had come with twenty-five hundred men from Leavenworth and "drove me clear out of the territory" — the beginning of a hatred of the Federal Army that would lead to exciting days.

Neither the free-state nor the Missouri army had supplies, and they returned home, plundering along the way. Everyone learned how easy it was to live by looting. Brown, with his men, continued to skulk in the brush.

Before Pate's capture and release were known in the East, the Democratic convention adjourned in Cincinnati. Franklin Pierce had been repudiated and James Buchanan chosen for the nominee. He was a lifelong Democrat and a Northerner, "sensible about slavery." Moreover, he had been absent from the country during the recent quarrels over Kansas within the party. Thus, he cherished no old grudges and should attract conservative votes, North and South.

President Pierce, with seven months yet to serve, held doggedly to his own policy, wiring Shannon to "maintain the laws firmly and impartially." However, the Atchison-Stringfellow faction, having been appeased constantly by the administration, planted cannon along the Missouri River to stop steamboats. "Colonel" Buford assigned his followers on border patrols. Mobs of "law and order men" boarded incoming vessels when they docked at Lexington, Kansas City, and Leavenworth, questioning passengers about their politics and taking weapons from freestate men. Confiscated goods were stored in the giant warehouses of Russell and Majors, overland freighters whose annual profits were just beginning to enter the $300,000 bracket. David Rice Atchison moved across the river to camp with the Kickapoo Rangers, to laugh, drink, and caper among their tents. People said that the great man might change his residence permanently and re-enter politics in Kansas.

Governor Shannon watched this growing aggression with mounting disapproval. His party and his President had sanctioned the proslavery government, yet apologized for the sack of Lawrence. He knew that Pierce wanted the Lecompton government to succeed harmoniously if possible, by force if necessary. Regardless of the popular will, the Topeka legislature, scheduled to meet July 4, 1856, must not convene. Governor Shannon ordered Colonel Sumner to be at Topeka and stop the meeting. Then he boarded a steamboat for St. Louis to be out of the territory at the time.

News had already come West concerning the Republican national convention, which assembled in Philadelphia on June 17. Kansas had been the main topic of conversation, and the Democratic failure promised to be the big issue of the coming campaign. John Sherman attended, fresh from his congressional investigation duties. So did Shalor Eldridge, with details about the destruction of the Free-State Hotel. Martin Conway, the slim, red-headed boy-orator with South Carolina accent, who had resigned from the "bogus" legislature, nominated John C. Frémont for President after an impassioned oration. The Pathfinder's name promised popular appeal. As son-in-law of Thomas Hart Benton, who was the old enemy of David Rice Atchison, Frémont should attract free-state Democrats. "Governor" Robinson had endorsed the choice from jail, recalling their California experiences. Abraham Lincoln had been suggested for the vice-presidency but was defeated by William L. Dayton of New Jersey.

The lists were thus prepared for the contest between the old established Democrats and the new Republicans, with all eyes looking sideways at Kansas. Could things be straightened out there before the November elections? Governor Shannon, as has been said, thought it better to be out of the territory when the Topeka legislature convened. Colonel Sumner, obeying orders, marched five companies of dragoons and two pieces of artillery to the edge of town on July 3. He camped in the weeds a short distance off the road. With him came proslavery Lieutenant Governor Woodson, elderly and easygoing Marshal Israel B. Donaldson, and young Jeb Stuart, with his trick horse and a contempt for free-state mudsills. The soldiers learned that two companies of free-state men had been drilling with fife and drum in town — not for resistance, but merely for a proposed Fourth of July celebration, citizens assured them. Genial old Donaldson fanned himself with his ragged straw hat. He knew that these pacific declarations from free-staters had been deceiving.

On the morning of the Fourth, Topeka was crowded with men, women, and children — families of the legislators and curious onlookers. Old Brown was reported to have a small band of riflemen in the nearby sunflowers.

Members of the Senate and House sauntered into the building proudly named Constitution Hall. With squealing fifes the companies marched up and down the dirt streets, halting to ground arms, rest, then shoulder and march again. A tall, limber man of forty-five or fifty walked in from the army camp, coat off and vest open in the heat. His jeans flapped about dusty boots. His iron-gray whiskers were topped by a very dirty straw hat.

"That's Marshal Donaldson," people said. James Redpath's dispatch to the *Chicago Tribune* reported him to have "imbecile looking eyes."

Donaldson walked up the steps to Constitution Hall and down the aisle, where the solons congregated slowly. He handed a paper to the presiding officer stating that it was a proclamation from the President of the United States and from the governor of Kansas ordering them not to convene. The dignitary called the members present to order. Someone moved that the proclamation be read. This was done and complete silence followed, except for the thud of Donaldson's boots as he strode back up the aisle. Out in the brilliant sunshine again, he put on his battered straw hat and walked down the road to Sumner's tent. "There will be a fight," he reported.

Colonel Sumner waited until almost noon. Then he ordered his men to mount and they rode to town. The free-state battalion stood in martial array before Constitution Hall, receiving banners from the ladies inscribed, OUR LIVES FOR OUR RIGHTS. Colonel Sumner halted and watched grimly from his saddle. No observer reported him as removing his upper teeth, so an attack was not imminent. The citizens concluded the ceremony undisturbed. The free-state companies marched away, and the dragoons occupied the town square. Cannon were unlimbered. Sumner ordered slow matches lighted. Then he swung from his horse and walked stiffly — he was fifty-nine — into the hall, sword sheathed at his side. In the House chamber a clerk was calling the roll as he entered. Sumner walked to the desk and waited until the clerk finished and announced "no quorum."

Colonel Sumner was stumped. How does the military disperse a government that does not meet? He waited as the roll was called again. Only seventeen answered — still no quorum. The speaker ordered the sergeant at arms to go out in the heat and bring members known to be in town. Sumner waited no longer. He announced that he had been assigned the unpleasant duty of disbanding the legislature. "God knows I have no party feeling in the matter, and will have none so long as I hold my present position in Kansas."

The solons rose dutifully and walked from the room. Colonel Sumner then went to the Senate chamber, found them not in session, and told those present not to convene. Then he turned and left the building, well aware that he had made history in what might be a big way. As Sumner walked down the steps, William Phillips, correspondent for the *New York Herald*, said to him, with Scotch brogue, "Colonel, you have robbed Oliver Cromwell of his laurels."

Sumner walked slowly to his horse, mounted, and led his battalion out of town. People hurrahed the solemn man who had done an unpleasant duty. Someone diverted the shouting to "Three cheers for Frémont" and "Three groans for Pierce." The crowd responded, free-state Democrats shouting — without realizing it — for the new Republican Party. And this was exactly what was happening all through Kansas.

Both President Pierce and Secretary of War Jefferson Davis denied ordering the dispersal of the Topeka legislature. They had only sanctioned use of the army to disperse persons combining for insurrection, they maintained. However, Colonel Sumner was soon replaced — a graceful disciplinary gesture — but his command was given to Pulsifer F. Smith, a Pennsylvanian with known Southern sympathies. True, he was a virtual invalid, so dashing Jeb Stuart and other hotbloods were sure to put free-state settlers in their place.

At last everything had gone in favor of the slave power. The free-state leaders were all imprisoned or driven from the territory; the ports of entry were all blockaded, and the Topeka government had been officially dispersed However, two things remained to be reckoned with: In the coming election the entire nation would vote on the Kansas issue, and that man Jim Lane was back East talking as he had never talked before.

V I

Lane's Army of the North

JAMES HENRY LANE strode up and down Chicago's wooden sidewalks with a scowl on his rugged face. A great problem weighed down his eloquent mind. He was as slow as Lincoln had been to renounce his party allegiance and join the Republicans. Scheduled to speak at the Bloomington convention, along with Ex-Governor Reeder and Mrs. Robinson, Lane had not attended, but he had now heard all about the impassioned meeting and Lincoln's "lost speech." He decided to address a Chicago rally with his best oratory.

The Metropolitan Hall failed to hold the crowd, so Lane and his accompanying orators moved to the north steps of the courthouse. The multitude below them was excited about reports of Missouri cannon turning back fellow Chicagoans bound for Kansas. Was a corrupt administration to be allowed to usurp the public domain without opposition, or should Chicago send gunboats to open the Missouri River? Lane was allegedly a fugitive charged with treason in this political imbroglio. Surely he was a man worth hearing.

The Grim Chieftain began calmly enough by eulogizing the new territory, by describing the opportunities for settlers there. His platform magnetism electrified the throng. Kansas, he said, was not the home of despised "Massachusetts Yankees" as so many Missourians claimed. Instead it had been settled by Midwesterners, like themselves, shackled out there now under the tyranny of slavocrats. Nine tenths of the Kansas homesteaders, he said, came from Illinois, Indiana, and Ohio.

Lane could control an audience's every emotion. Like a musical director with an orchestra, he could draw out laughter, scorn, anger, tears, wild enthusiasm. Remembering now that he was talking to Illinoisans, he lauded his own patriotic record in the Mexican War. He told how, at Buena Vista, he had sat on his horse beside the great and lamented Illinois General J. J. Hardin, and the present candidate for governor of the state, William H. Bissell — a former Democrat nominated at the recent Bloomington convention. That, indeed, was a glorious day, Lane said, and "It did not occur to me [then] that I should be indicted for treason because I loved liberty better than slavery."

Lane paused, let his words sink into the minds of his audience. Then he held up a copy of the Kansas statutes, ruffled the printed sheets, identified them carefully so there would be no mistake, opened the leaves at the recently enacted fugitive code. Carefully he read the penalty for helping a slave to escape from its master, then snapped the pages together with dramatic finality and summarized the act:

> If a person kidnaps a white child the utmost penalty is six months in jail — if a "nigger" baby, the penalty is death. . . . To kidnap a white child into slavery, six months in jail — to kidnap a "nigger" into freedom, death!

This law, Lane reminded the people, was chargeable to the present incumbent of the White House. The violent deaths of the men who had protested it were all chargeable to the Democratic President. Unpleasant as it was to admit, Lane confessed that he, as presidential elector in Indiana, had cast his ballot for the author of these outrages. Thus, Frank Pierce was a creature of his own hands, but now — Lane paused and a hush fell across the people packed in the street — "Now," Lane screamed with a wild gesture of his arms, "before God, and his people, I arraign Frank Pierce as a murderer."

More than once Lane had stood before a mob keen for his death and, within half an hour, had instilled into them a frenzy to do his bidding, but never had he thrilled an audience like this one. At midnight he asked contributions for establishing freedom in Kansas. The audience surged forward. Workmen emptied their pockets; sailors tossed in their cash, widows their mites, boys their savings. People without money offered to march in Lane's army of supporters and make Kansas free. With empty pockets and brimming hearts they stormed away through the streets of Chicago, singing the "Star-Spangled Banner" and the "Marseillaise" —

time indeed for revolution against a government that thwarted the people's will with cannon. The editor of the *Chicago Tribune,* Dr. Charles Ray, who had recently joined the staff to fight slavery, prophesied that the meeting would inaugurate a new era in history.

Lane continued his lecture tour, traveling East, where he set community after community aflame with his eloquence. A dozen other orators did likewise, distributing pamphlet abstracts from the slave code, extolling the virtues of Frémont, and urging emigrants to travel by a northern route to the territory. Various state "Kansas societies" had combined into a National Kansas Committee, and $200,000 had been raised to help defray emigrants' overland expenses. Massachusetts alone offered $80,000 and sent supplies. A company of "Rifle Christians" left New Haven, Connecticut, armed with Sharps as well as Bibles. One cheering contingent left Milwaukee. Chicago became the usual outfitting place whence parties left by train, their covered wagons on flatcars to be unloaded at Iowa railheads for the final leg of the journey.

Emigrants, careful to make no political declarations, could still go by the usual routes and slip through the Missouri blockade, but Lane's Army of the North had become a part of the presidential campaign — a marching symbol of Free Soil, Free Men, and Frémont, an army of protest against encroaching slave-power dictatorship. The final test had come. So far, the North had contributed the most money and the most settlers. Now it was also prepared to meet Southern violence with the most violence. And if, by chance, the proslavery border boys desired to match their horse-stealing skill with the Eastern immigrants', this challenge would be accepted, too.

Lane had no official command over the National Kansas Committee's parties, but he rode along with them. Eastern newspapers reported his progress. On July 1, 1856, the *New York Weekly Times* reported him to be at Council Bluffs with a thousand belligerent buffalo hunters, all eager to "make tyrants tremble." A letter from Indianola, Iowa, reported him passing through the country with a hundred and fifty men, stopping to make speeches at every hamlet and wagon camp. With no authority Lane issued high-sounding military commissions and marked the prairie with cairns — Lane's chimneys — to guide later parties. The National Kansas Committee wondered at this authority, sent out investigators to inquire about Lane's reputation in Kansas. They learned that he represented the lawless element and that the United States Army was waiting at the state line to stop him and all armed parties. The committee asked Lane to leave the train, lest the entire emigration be discredited.

Down in Kansas the free-state settlers also learned about the United States Army's vigilance on the border. Hotheads talked about marching out to strike the army in the rear and thus open the way for Lane's Army of the North. Others, preferring the old nonresistance procedure, sent a letter to Lane urging him not to stir up violence by bringing in an armed force. Samuel Walker was selected to carry the message and he rode off on imprisoned "Governor" Robinson's horse at the head of a small party. If anyone had influence over Lane it was Walker — a Midwesterner, like Lane, and an abolitionist, like Robinson. Walker was a small man, slightly crippled for life with "hip-disease." He had come to Kansas with the spring breakup in 1855. In a sleet storm his nine-year-old daughter had jumped from his wagon, slipped, and been run over, breaking her leg in two places. A proslavery Baptist preacher had refused to let her be carried into his house. Henceforth, Walker's hatred of slavery became fanatic. Like others, he pre-empted a claim which conflicted with a proslavery settler's. Gangs had stopped more than once at his cabin to beat or threaten to kill him unless he moved. To hide his identity Walker trained his children to treat him like a stranger when travelers stopped at the house.

In addition to human enemies Walker was plagued by hunger during his first winter in Kansas. Desperate for food, he went to Lane's cabin in Lawrence, begging work. Lane had neither work, money, nor supplies, but he gave Walker an order for eleven dollars. With this, and soup made from wild peas and native herbs, the cripple's family survived. It was beside the point that Lane never paid the eleven dollars. Mere money meant nothing to him. More than once he drew cash himself from a merchant, stating that he had funds on deposit in an Eastern bank. Weeks later, when the merchant showed Lane the order, returned with the notation "Depositor Unknown," the Grim Chieftain replied casually that there must be some mistake and turned away, intent on more important matters.

Walker felt great loyalty for Lane and had "enlisted" under him to help repel raiding Missourians. Certainly Lane would heed his request not to bring in an invading army.

On the ride north, Walker overtook Old John Brown, trekking across the prairie with a little party of his own, eager to meet the Army of the North and lead it back to victory or death. The two parties rode on together. They found Lane near Nebraska City in Dr. Blanchard's house, grim, disconsolate, almost in tears. He had just been requested by the National Kansas Committee to leave the "army." Walker handed him the letter from the free-state conservatives, watched him read and then sit with bowed head, tears glistening on his beard. Finally, Lane looked up and said, "Walker, if you say the people of Kansas don't want me, it's all right, and I'll blow my brains out. I can never go back to the states and look the people in the face and tell them that as soon as I had got these Kansas friends of mine fairly into danger I had to abandon them. I can't do it. No matter what I say in my defense no one will believe it. I'll blow my brains out and end the thing right here."

Walker had come north to stop the invasion, not to see his hero commit suicide.

"General," Walker told him, "the people of Kansas would rather have you than all the party at Nebraska City. I have fifteen good boys that are my own. If you will put yourself under my orders, I'll take you through all right." Lane's eyes brightened. Dr. Blanchard disguised him for the ride, and Mrs. Blanchard brought some old clothes. Silver nitrate was sponged on Lane's grizzly beard to blacken it — all to no effect. Lane looked more like himself in the old clothes than he did in the new ones he had worn on Eastern lecture platforms. After dark they set off — Walker, his men, and Old Brown's party — some thirty in all. The Grim Chieftain had not been deterred even by Sam Walker! Instead, Walker, who had gone to stop him, became his stanchest supporter.

Recent rains had flooded the prairie streams and a constant downpour drenched the riders, but they splashed along until dawn, then stopped to graze the horses. The men lay down in their wet clothes to sleep, but Lane soon roused them, restless to be on his way. "Captain" Walker got up at once and limped around, poking the drowsy figures. He found Old Brown dozing with his back against a tree, a gun across his knees. Walker twitched the old man's arm. Brown leaped to his feet and fired, burning a hole in Walker's coat. The "captain" never forgot that lesson and said later, "Old Brown always seemed most wakeful when he was asleep."

Spurring across the sodden prairies, the men covered a hundred and fifty miles in thirty hours, but horses and riders continually dropped behind exhausted. Only six remained when the party reached the Kaw River ferry late on the second night. The boat was on the south bank and the ferryman had gone to Topeka. The men whipped their mounts into the stream. Walker's horse alone had the strength to cross. Lane and Charlie Stratton abandoned their horses, swam to the south shore, and strode, dripping, into the darkened town. The three men got a bite to eat — the first since leaving Nebraska City. Lane wrote a dramatic note announcing his triumphal arrival with the Army of the North and offered to release the treason prisoners at Lecompton by attacking Federal troops if necessary. Then, on fresh horses, the three set off in the midnight rain for Lawrence, passing south of the proslavery capital. Walker, almost exhausted, fell from his horse three times in twenty miles. Fatigue aggravated the old "hip-disease." At his cabin, only seven miles from Lawrence, he gave up. Lane left him with instructions to raise his minutemen and await orders. Two miles beyond, Stratton quit, and Lane rode into Lawrence alone at 3 A.M. By 8 o'clock in the morning of August 11, 1856, he was on the streets talking as casually as though he had never been away.

Excited people told Lane that Lawrence was blockaded. The proslavery men had established three forts — Franklin, Saunders, and Titus — and were stopping all supply wagons on the roads. The town would be starved out. A week ago a little party had crept out to Franklin and fired all night at the fortifications — a blockhouse with the hotel in one wing and the post office in the other. The free-staters had killed one man and wounded others but, at dawn, came back discouraged. A party was out there now preparing another attack. Lane did not wait for more details but rode off through the hot, damp sunflowers toward the hamlet.

The new attack lasted three hours, and Lane's participation is apocryphal — depending on the politics of the witnesses reporting. One thing is sure: the siege was successful, being terminated by a load of burning hay wheeled toward the buildings. The approaching flames dispersed the defenders, and the postmaster's wife surrendered an empty structure.

The victors came back to Lawrence in high spirits, trundling a cannon they called Old Sacramento, one of the battery which Doniphan's men had hauled for a thousand miles across the Mexican deserts. Lane made much of the gun's capture and of the surrender of Fort Franklin as the first victory of his Army of the North, although no man who crossed with him was present. Nevertheless, the retreating enemy believed him and spread the word that Lane had come with his indomitable horde.

The next proslavery stronghold of importance was Fort Saunders on Washington Creek, southwest of Lawrence — a building twenty-five feet square and two stories high, with rows of loopholes on both levels. A hundred men in this blockhouse might stand off a thousand. The victors of Franklin — Lane surely among them now — marched out to investigate this citadel. "Major" David S. Hoyt, of the free-state forces, volunteered to go ahead and learn the number of defenders. Perhaps the fort was invulnerable. Friends tried to dissuade Hoyt from such a fool's errand, but he persisted, reminding them that he was a Mason. Brothers of the order in the enemy camp would protect him from harm. Hoyt's corpse was picked up outside the fort — two balls through his body and one, a *coup de grâce,* through his head. Tracks in the dirt road showed that he had left the fort with an escort who shot him and took his horse.

This news came to Lawrence as a company of Illinois emigrants under "Colonel" Harvey marched into town — the first of Lane's Army of the North. Harvey had succeeded as a saloonkeeper in Chicago, now owned considerable property, and craved action in Kansas. United States soldiers had not found the guns his men concealed under sacks of seed in their wagons and had let the alley cats pass. On arrival in Lawrence, Colonel Harvey learned that the free-state settlers were congregating out on the prairie to get revenge for the death of Hoyt. He ordered his men to stop unpacking and join them at once.

Down the dirt road, Harvey found the motley crew. Old Brown was there with his hearty boys. Walker had his minutemen, horse and foot. Harvey looked them all over and urged an immediate attack. Lane objected — better display Hoyt's body, call for more recruits, and indulge in proper oratory. Thus, with much speaking, some five hundred men assembled. Then, Lane ordered each volunteer to prepare a straw man, thus doubling the apparent size of his "army." Men, with the dummies, climbed into wagons, and all drove toward Fort Saunders with much fanfare, Lane sending word ahead to the defenders that he was coming with the Army of the North.

The defenders of Fort Saunders counted the heads in the long line of wagons. Estimating the enemy as twelve hundred strong, they fled, leaving forty guns, three kegs of powder, and Hoyt's horse. Lane took full credit for the victory, ordered a parade, and refreshed the troops with another speech. Then he formally turned the command to "Captain" Walker, wheeled his horse and galloped away with half a dozen followers. When he was next heard from, he was back in Nebraska.

Dumfounded, Walker ordered the brigade disbanded. Various companies rode off with their leaders, Walker's going to his claim near Fort Titus on the California road. Next morning the Topeka-Lecompton-Lawrence stage drew rein at Walker's cabin. The driver beckoned to the "captain" and whispered, "I've got Titus's wife and two children in the stage. If you want to get the damned scoundrel, now is your time."

Titus's new and gleaming pillared mansion stood only three miles away. What a chance to retaliate on the ruffians who had invaded his cabin threatening to thrash him! Walker ordered all his men with horses to saddle and follow him. Footmen were instructed to bring Old Sacramento. Down the road, Walker's horsemen met Colonel Harvey. The Chicagoans had fought a night skirmish with Titus's men, and had killed one of them, but the rest had retreated over there. Harvey waved in the direction of dark clouds gathering over Fort Titus — a storm coming sure. The two leaders planned an attack, as the storm brewed. Old Brown appeared out of the tall weeds with his hard-eyed boys. They, too, were looking for Colonel Titus.

The over-all command was given to Samuel Walker. He divided the men into squads of ten and deployed them around Titus's buildings, warning each to prevent any of the proslavery men from escaping to the United States soldiers encamped in nearby Lecompton. At a given signal the free-state men opened fire from behind trees, outhouses, and the barn, shouting gleefully as frightened figures ran from their tents to the shelter of Titus's blockhouse.

The bombardment lasted several hours with casualties on both sides. Walker himself was knocked down, with several buckshot in the chest, but continued to give orders. Finally, Old Sacramento rumbled in. Cannon balls, melted from type destroyed in Lawrence last May, were rammed down her throat. "Here comes a new edition of the *Herald of Freedom*," men shouted, as the big gun belched at the buildings. The storm clouds were getting darker, and Walker sent for a load of hay — the old persuader — to set on fire before the rain came. The burning wagon rolled toward the blockhouse and a white flag appeared. Twenty-seven disheveled men slouched into the yard. Six remained inside, too badly wounded to move. Titus himself stood in the doorway, his heavy-set figure ragged and blood-smeared from gashes on his head, face, and shoulder.

A dozen rifles pointed in his direction, the hammers clicking ominously. Walker ordered the guns down, limped forward, took the miserable man's sword, and entered the building, where a poster on the wall announced a reward of five hundred dollars for his own head "off or on his shoulders."

The wounded men were carried out as prisoners. Harvey's men loaded Titus's tents in their wagons for their own use. Then the pillared mansion was set on fire, and the men marched merrily down the California road in a drizzling rain. One wounded man, left on the second floor, burned to death. A Negro belonging to Titus joined the throng chuckling, "Massa Titus wanted six abolitionists for breakfast! Yah! Yah! Gorra Massy! guess he get his belly full dis mo'nin'."

At the Walker cabin, Sam's wife stormed out to give the victorious commander a tongue-lashing for sparing Titus's life, threatening not to live with him until the villain was executed. She and her little ones had suffered too much at Titus's hands to feel any sympathy for him.

Walker grinned sheepishly and marched on. Never before had the free-state men achieved such victories — three in rapid succession, Franklin on August 11, Saunders on the fifteenth, and Fort Titus on the sixteenth. All hail Lane's Army of the North, whether or not many men from it had taken part!

United States soldiers had heard the firing from their encampment outside Lecompton, but paid no attention. The deaths of three men, the wounding of half a dozen more, and the capture of Titus could not be completely overlooked, however. On August 17, Governor Shannon drove into Lawrence to make a treaty of peace — strange recognition! Twice now, he had met the free-state men as belligerents on an equal footing with the administration. The terms were simple: prisoners held on both sides to be liberated; Old Sacramento to be sent back to Lecompton; the free-state cannon, taken from Lawrence in May, to be returned. When all arrangements were concluded, Shannon attempted to address the citizens of Lawrence — not the old crowd of free-state men he had seen in December but arrogant newcomers from the Lane trail, many of them Harvey's Chicago toughs. Shouts and waving guns prevented the governor from being heard until Walker jumped on his horse and with drawn pistols restored order.

The ordeal ended, Shannon went home across the quiet prairie, musing about the sudden increase of lawless free-state men in Lawrence. Things looked very dark ahead. At Lecompton he stepped down from his carriage, walked into his new executive residence, and sat down at his desk. He wrote to the department commander that the situation was "dangerous and critical." Eight hundred desperate men in Lawrence seemed determined to come to Lecompton and destroy the capital. Shannon blotted the paper with a sprinkling of sand, then dipped his pen in ink to write another letter — this one to Franklin Pierce, tendering a formal resignation as governor of Kansas. In the mail his letter passed another from the President dismissing him.

Daniel Woodson became acting governor once more, and immediately took the Missourians' part, as he had always done. Gangs of proslavery settlers rode nightly on errands of revenge. Within two days seven cabins — including Sam Walker's — were burned to balance accounts for Titus's home. Atchison and Stringfellow had already called a meeting at Kansas City, urging all friends of law and order "who are not prepared to see their friends butchered, to be themselves driven from their homes, to rally instantly to the rescue." A mass meeting at Lexington, Missouri, voted men and guns "to kill the damned Abolitionists or drive them from the territory." The *Weston Argus* announced that Lane and his Army of the North had destroyed Franklin, also a Georgia hamlet on the Marais des Cygnes, and was now battering at Lecompton — "Civil War has begun." The *Mobile Tribune* printed a letter from Kansas imploring the South to send reinforcements. "Bring each of you a double-barrel gun, a brace of Colts revolvers and a trusty knife." The *Weekly Mississippian* announced: "Lane is already in the territory with his marauders and

2000 more men are on the northern boundary waiting to enter." The *Chicago Tribune* asserted: "Kansas is now in a state of open war. . . . It is not a war in which the interests of Kansas are alone at stake, but the cause of freedom in the whole country." The editor urged men to go or finance others to go. The Massachusetts State Kansas Committee purchased two hundred carbines and sent them for John Brown to sell to reliable settlers. Propagandists urged the North not to wait for the November elections but send aid "now-today."

The Missourians aroused the border with a broadside stating, in bold-faced type, that Lane with "3000 lawless abolitionists" was planning to attack Lexington, Independence, Westport, and New Santa Fe. Missouri militiamen reached for their double-barreled guns and traipsed out to the rallying ground. Acting Governor Woodson called out the militia and accepted Missourians, as he had in the Wakarusa War, officially calling them Kansas volunteers. "Let the watchword be 'extermination total and complete,'" he crowed.

The disorders were reported to President Pierce by General Pulsifer Smith, with an enclosure of Woodson's proclamation and the additional information that the Missouri militia were in the field. Something must be done or the two states would be in open war. Pierce laid down the immediate problems on his desk and appointed a new governor for Kansas — John W. Geary, an ideal choice if there ever was one. Geary stood six feet, five and a half inches tall, a majestic figure who had distinguished himself in the Mexican War by leading the charge for Chapultepec. He understood the frontier, knew how to deal with border outlaws and vigilance committees, having been first mayor of San Francisco. Moreover, Geary was a Pennsylvanian by birth. He understood both sides of the sectional controversy, had employed slaves in his Virginia mines, yet had helped bring California into the Union as a free state. Furthermore, Geary possessed the courage to make a decision. Surely he would not blow hot and cold according to his company, as Shannon had done. The President promised to continue the full co-operation of the army and, most important, to placate the free-soil opposition, he would release the "treason" prisoners — at least on bail — until duly tried. This was a big concession, for the President blamed the Kansas trouble on New England agitators like Robinson.

With these promises, Geary hoped to launch his administration on an even keel. Then the antiadministration majority in Congress ruffled the water before he took the helm. Lane's Army of the North seemed to be turning the tide in favor of the antislavery party. Why permit the United States Army to check them and reinstate the proslavery dictatorship? Better tie the new governor's hands and let the squatters be sovereign. The House tacked an amendment on the army appropriation bill to prevent the military from upholding the Lecompton laws in Kansas. Let the proslavery Senate agree to that amendment or have no funds for the army! The Senate refused, and taunts shuttled back and forth between the factions. Next, to show that they meant business, the majority in the House adjourned, leaving the army with insufficient financial support.

President Pierce was caught. The nation could not live without an army. Other areas besides Kansas needed the military. On the plains, Cheyenne bubbled with revolt, vigilantes in California defied the authorities, and a boundary dispute with Britain in Oregon might entail the show of force before proper adjustment. President Pierce immediately called a special session and laid the dire predicament before Congress. Would the nation's entire existence be sacrificed on the Kansas altar? Jim Lane was reported to be just north of the Kansas line, with a second division of his "army," waiting for the failure of the army bill. Did the House, on due deliberation, want civil war out there? A majority decided in the negative, the army appropriation bill passed, and Geary set off to his new post.

As the new governor traveled west, the militia which Woodson had called to the colors entered Kansas in two columns under command of Ex-Senator Atchison, "General" Stringfellow, and the Honorable John W. Reid, a Missouri legislator. Reid, a six-foot giant weighing two hundred pounds, had distinguished himself under Doniphan at Sacramento and now held a claim two miles west of the Shawnee Mission, where he had built a fine two-story log house with puncheon floors and trotway boarded up as an entrance hall. A third column, of a hundred and fifty men, under the command of Ex-Indian Agent George Washington Clarke, marched out of Fort Scott — the principal town in southeast Kansas, only recently abandoned as an army post. Reid and Clarke both marched toward Osawatomie — infamous lair of Old John Brown. Atchison hoped to destroy the "Boston abolition town" of Lawrence. Of the three, Clarke's column marched first, but the free-state settlers in southeast Kansas rallied under James Montgomery, a small, black-bearded "Campbellite" preacher who had come to Kansas from Ohio, via Kentucky and Missouri, and hated slavery. He had made a name for himself locally by daring to oppose fraudulent elections. On August 25, 1856, Montgomery's men overtook Clarke's during a noon rest at Middle Creek, nine miles from Osawatomie, and opened fire. Thoroughly surprised, the proslavery partisans fled, leaving their baggage, most of their horses, boots, coats, vests, hats, two wounded men, a dinner already cooked, and a flag inscribed, VICTORY OR DEATH.

The gleeful free-state men collected the loot and returned to their homesteads — all but Montgomery. He crossed into Missouri disguised as an unemployed schoolteacher, got a job, taught two weeks, compiled a list of Clarke's men, and disappeared. In the next few months, he waylaid twenty of the raiders, taking their money, weapons, and horses.

While Clarke's invasion was breaking up in panic, the columns under Atchison and Reid advanced arrogantly. Reid commanded two hundred and fifty men and one cannon. Beside him, as guide, rode the Reverend Martin White, chaplain of the Lecompton legislature. He had been expelled from Osawatomie on account of his proslavery beliefs. Jogging south and west along the dirt road, the little column met Frederick Brown, son of Old John. The minister recognized the hated free-stater and shot him down, leaving his body in the roadside gutter. Reid ordered the column to spur ahead and surprise the town.

Old Brown, with little warning, mustered forty-one defenders, posted them behind trees and a stone fence along the Marais des Cygnes Creek. When the enemy approached, Brown's men opened fire and held the invaders for over an hour, the giant form of "General" Reid booming threats of awful vengeance as soon as his six-pounder arrived.

Finally the gun trundled down the road, was unlimbered, and balls blasted holes in the stone fence. Reid ordered a charge. His men rushed forward, powder horns flapping against butternut shirts. Over the wall they scampered and found it vacated. The enemy had retreated. One man remembered seeing Old Brown crossing the Marais des Cygnes with his linen duster floating out behind.

The exulting victors cheered, shook hands, tossed wool hats into the sky, and passed around the bottle. Some returned to Missouri in high spirits. Others rode on to Osawatomie and burned four or five free-state houses there.

Atchison's column, the largest of the three, marched straight for Lawrence. As by magic, Lane appeared from across the horizon, rallying men from farms and shops — among them wild young James Butler Hickok, who had been working with wagon trains on the Santa Fe Trail. A native of northern Illinois, "Wild Bill's" sympathies were naturally free-state, but extravagant clothes and soft glances from under sunbonnets interested more than politics, even more than the growth of his new, silky, long-horn mustache. Most important of all to him was the opportunity to display his rare skill with a pistol.

Lane's volunteers met Atchison's on Bull Creek, fifteen miles north of Osawatomie. Both sides skirmished and retreated — Lane to Lawrence, Atchison to Missouri. Newspapers across the North crowed about the Grim Chieftain's military valor.

As these three engagements were being fought, the stream of independent overland parties continued to arrive in Kansas with rifles concealed among their plows. Lane's men marched back from Bull Creek to find many newcomers fresh from the trail and eager to kill slaveholders. The Grim Chieftain decided that the time had come to capture Lecompton and end the proslavery government — at least get back the prisoners who had not been returned under the last treaty.

A plan of attack was agreed upon: Lane to lead one column out the California road and attack from the south; Colonel Harvey to cross the Kaw and invest Lecompton from the north. According to this agreement the Chicagoan marched up the north bank on September 4 and took position in the trees at the ferry, thus cutting off a retreat from the capital. All night long the Illinoisans lay on their arms in a sticky rain, waiting for Lane to begin the action across the river. Finally, a milky-pale dawn illuminated the eastern sky. Harvey's city toughs watched the sleeping hamlet stir, men trudging out to milk cows and lead horses to the river for a drink — but nowhere could they see Lane's men. An hour passed. The summer sun peeped over the horizon, striking diamond brilliance from the raindrops on grass and leaves — but still no Lane. The men complained. They were hungry, hot, and wet. Colonel Harvey ordered them back to Lawrence, learned that Lane had marched twelve hours late and now stood before the proslavery capital. To hell with such a fellow!

As Harvey brooded, Lane's battalion, with Walker second in command, deployed along the ridge south of Lecompton. The men scattered behind trees, in fence corners and weed thickets. Old Brown strode grimly with his boys, and "Wild Bill" Hickok, a veteran now, stood by to watch the fun. Two cannon were wheeled into place overlooking Lecompton. Flankers reported citizens barricading themselves in the unfinished capitol. Others, with the militia, crowded across the ferry — some swimming — but no Harvey lay concealed to stop their passage.

In the United States Army camp at the edge of town, Lieutenant Colonel Philip St. George Cooke ordered bugles to blow "Boots and Saddles." Lieutenant Colonel Joseph E. Johnston and Captain H. H. Sibley both watched the dragoons swing into their saddles. Colonel Cooke instructed the sergeant to count off a detail, and with it he rode out to investigate the hostile lines. Lane saw them coming, dismounted, took a private's rifle and stood in ranks, undistinguishable among hundreds of armed men.

Cooke followed the dirt road to the top of the low ridge and found himself at the flank of sixty horsemen. He recognized Walker in command and called, "What in hell are you doing here?"

"We are after our prisoners and our rights," Walker replied, reining his horse toward the lieutenant colonel.

Cooke looked at the invaders' determined faces. He saw other detachments on other hills around Lecompton. "How many men have you?" he asked.

"About four hundred foot and two hundred horseback," Walker said.

"Well, I have six hundred men and six cannon, and you can't fight here — except with me." Evidently the United States Army was pledged to protect the capital.

"I don't care a damn how many men you have," Walker said. "We are going to have our prisoners, or a big fight!" The little fellow showed plenty of spunk today, with the courage and assurance of a major general. Would the fortunes of life ever put him in such an exalted position?

Cooke knew citizen soldiers. He had watched Illinois frontiersmen in the Black Hawk War and the Mormon Battalion in the Southwest. Such troops might fight bravely or run in panic. "Don't make a fool of yourself, Walker," he said. "You can't fight here. Show me to General Lane."

Walker replied that Lane was not in command. If the lieutenant colonel wished to confer with the leaders, however, he would call a council of war. Walker turned in his saddle and gave instructions to his aides. Soon the officers trotted up the hill and sat on their horses in a circle around the lieutenant colonel.

"You have made a most unfortunate move for yourselves," Cooke told them. "The Missourians, you know, have gone and the militia have nearly gone, having commenced crossing yesterday to my knowledge. As to the prisoners, whilst [Cooke liked literary language and was writing a book on his Western adventures] I will make no *terms* with you, I can *inform* you that they were promised to be released yesterday morning."

The assembled horsemen asked for particulars and, as Cooke replied, a United States deputy marshal rode into the circle demanding the arrest of Walker and Lane.

"Go to hell," Cooke snapped at him, "or rather go back to your camp." The marshal, "white as a cloth," replied shamefacedly that he dared not. Every tree, stump, and rock on the way was topped by a gun pointed at him, and the hammers were cocked. Walker agreed to escort the man out of his lines and to order the "army" dispersed if the prisoners were given up at once. With this, Lieutenant Colonel Cooke galloped back to town. He met Jones, greatly excited. The sheriff wanted Lane arrested, even if the deputy did not. Cooke, happy to have averted hostilities, said that he would help with no arrests this night. Then, recalling his military instruction to act under the governor's orders, he took Acting Governor Woodson to one side and said, "If you want him arrested, write your requisition, but I think, on reflection, you will hardly make it."

Woodson understood the meaning of Cooke's statement. He, too, had seen the determined men surrounding the capital and decided to let sleeping lions alone. The three weeks he had been in office had stirred up sufficient violence already.

V I I

Geary Takes Command

FOUR DAYS after Sam Walker had stood firm before the United States Army, Governor John W. Geary steamed up the Missouri to administer a situation that had ruined his two predecessors. The vessel was loaded with bearded Border Ruffians clumping along the decks in rough boots with knife handles peeping from the tops, pistols thrust precariously in broad belts. At Lexington, Missouri, a belligerent crowd in gaudy red and blue shirts embroidered with hearts and eagles stood on the dock. At Kansas City landing, the crowd was greater still. A hack on the levee had both sides painted in flaming capitals: BORDER RUFFIAN. Loafers shouted that a Missouri "army" was assembling at Westport to retaliate for the siege of Lecompton. Everywhere the governor looked, he saw men enjoying the indolent life of a soldier.

Striding down the gangplank at Leavenworth, the governor found the town in the hands of proslavery outlaws — fantastic fellows with weatherbeaten hat brims pinned up in front or on one side with a cockade, star, or eagle. Chicken, turkey, or goose feathers in the crowns made some hats resemble Indian war bonnets. Lawyer William Phillips had been lynched recently. A man of courage, he had dared come back after being tarred, feathered, and sold at auction for protesting the fraudulent election.

Outside Leavenworth, the road Geary must take to the capital was reported to be infested with armed robbers who thought nothing of killing a traveler for his horse. Before venturing on it, Geary wrote a long letter to United States Secretary of State William L. Marcy describing the chaos. Most of the bona fide settlers on both sides, he reported, sincerely wished peace, but ambitious scoundrels incited the lawless elements for their own profit. Already, he said, it was plain to him that the partisan militia had aggravated the situation. More Federal troops were needed.

On the morning of September 10, 1856, Governor Geary set off for Lecompton with a military escort — a resolute man determined to govern. Along the road he noticed deserted cabins, charred chimneys, broken fences, and was told that many settlers had returned East. Others had fled for security among the reservation Indians. Once he spied a distant group of people. The picket who rode over to investigate reported them to be free-state refugees, huddled together for mutual protection.

At Lecompton, Geary stepped down from his carriage, bold and confident. Rowdies in the street resembled gold-rush forty-niners. Geary knew the breed. In a crude board building he established headquarters, and things began to hum. The militia and all other armed bands were ordered to disperse. He saw to it that the treason prisoners were released on bail and asked for the removal of Judge Lecompte, "General" Clarke, and elderly Marshal Donaldson — the three hated Federal officials. He refused to accept the services of a volunteer company offered by Henry Clay Pate, who had just arrived from a recruiting trip to Virginia. Boldly, he told one and all that he had come to serve no clique nor faction. "Mark my word," Sam Walker told him, "you'll take the underground railroad out of Kansas in six months."

Tall, experienced, and impressive, Geary thought not. Border Ruffians looked no bigger to him than Californians. "I'll show you," he retorted, striking the table with his fist, "and all the d—— rascals that I'm governor of Kansas. The administration is behind me."

Governor Geary had not reckoned with the proslavery forces. Fearing for their reign, they plotted at once to give Geary a dose of Shannon and Reeder medicine. They had forced the President of the United States to back down before. They would do so again. Robinson, released from jail, had been back in Lawrence just four days, when several thousand Missourians under the command of Atchison were reported to be marching towards the town — militia disbanded "in a horn!"

Citizens quaked before the report. Robinson had had no time to organize his followers and Lane's whereabouts were unknown — probably in Nebraska guiding incoming emigrants. Old acquaintances had learned new tricks and many of them were out of town on raids with wild bands like Harvey's, stealing horses and pillaging travelers. Old Brown stalked the streets, unafraid of the approaching "army" and advising all who would listen, "Keep cool and fire low." Robinson was at his wit's end. He had known Geary in California and decided to appeal to him for protection. To insure getting the message through, he dispatched three couriers by three different routes. One of the riders, H. A. W. Tabor, was an adventurous young man with big ideas who intended to keep going west to the Rockies if he failed to make a fortune in Kansas.

Governor Geary received the messages late at night. Being a man of action, he aroused Lieutenant Colonel Cooke and the two set off with four hundred dragoons and four cannon at two o'clock on the morning of September 13, 1856. At dawn they drove into Lawrence, found the village demoralized as reported — but crowded with roistering men. Inadequate barricades obstructed two streets. The wrecked hotel's smoky wall had been converted into a fort. Lieutenant Colonel Cooke sniffed contemptuously. Soldiers asked curiously about Jim Lane and were told by grinning loafers that he had gone to California "with a cannon under each arm."

"Governor" Robinson invited Governor Geary to a conference. The Kansan's house had been burned down by the pillagers in May, and he was practically a stranger in his own town among the hundreds of newcomers who had flocked down the Lane Trail during his imprisonment. Robinson either did not know, or did not care to say, that many of these were Harvey's "thieves" just in from a rich raid, having stolen a goodly number of horses and supplies from the Russell and Majors depot. (Waddell joined the firm in 1857.) The transportation firm was considered fair game, since its Leavenworth warehouse had been opened for storage of equipment taken from free-state emigrants. Governor Geary had seen these "thieves" in the distance as he drove from Leavenworth to Lecompton and had mistaken them for refugees. As the two governors watched the motley assemblage in the Lawrence streets, Robinson excused their possession of arms as necessary to ward off the impending invasion of Border Ruffians, only four miles away. He failed to add, if he knew, that a town committee was at that moment planning distribution of Harvey's loot as a civic bonus.

Geary accepted Robinson's explanation, admitting that Americans of spirit would protect their property. This was a new attitude for an administration governor. The balding personification of John Knox looked curiously at Geary's giant military figure, his bold staring eyes, full beard and delicate pointed nose. Could this man be representing the President? Certainly Frank Pierce must have changed his policy. First, treason prisoners had been released, and now the people were recognized as having the right to defend themselves from Missourians. Perhaps the November elections were behind it all. Did the Democrats fear losing their free-soil Northern wing more than the slave power? In any event, Robinson saw plainly that Geary did not want Lawrence destroyed. But he was unprepared for the next turn of events. As the conference terminated, travelers announced that Atchison's army was marching back to Missouri. Had peace come?

Governor Geary's determined administration had succeeded admirably — so it seemed. He called a mass meeting of the Lawrence citizens, reminded them of his proclamation ordering both parties to lay down their arms, promised to make the enemy obey it, and hoped that all would return "to their peaceful fields and benches in this fair and blooming land of opportunity." Then the imposing man stepped into his carriage and drove with the dragoons back to Lecompton.

Twenty-four hours later scouts dashed into Lawrence stating that Atchison's army had not dispersed, as reported, but had wheeled and was marching once more toward their city. Governor Geary whipped back in his carriage, this time going to the proslavery encampment. He found a real army of twenty-seven hundred men, well-organized, and commanded by red-faced Atchison, Territorial Representative Whitfield, Indian Agent George W. Clarke, and the grandiose Colonel Titus, his wounds bandaged. The entourage included Judge Sterling Cato and Sheriff Sam Jones, the former presumably to issue warrants and the latter to serve them, thereby proving the proslavery government's sovereignty.

Governor Geary asked the leading officers to meet with him in the cool room of a nearby clapboard house in Franklin. Here Atchison explained that their errand was peaceful. They had come only to apprehend an "organized band of murderers and robbers said to be under the command of Lane, who have plundered and butchered large numbers of our fellow-citizens." Atchison said that his only purpose was to overpower the band and drive it from the territory — a revealing admission!

Governor Geary told him that he had just visited Lawrence. Lane and his band were not there, and destruction of the village would only aggravate matters. As a good Democrat, he wished to remind good Democrats that an attack on Lawrence might cost them the November election. He was fresh from Washington as a representative of the President and knew the wishes of the administration. Let the Missourians go home, and he, Governor Geary, would take care of the abolitionists.

These positive words from a military man backed by the President had their effect. Atchison ordered his men to their homes saying: "He [Geary] promised us all we wanted." Thus Lawrence was spared, and old John Brown disappeared in the sunflowers — a dangerous place for him!

Governor Geary drove back to Lecompton behind Atchison's Kickapoo Rangers. The experience turned him against the proslavery party in Kansas. Jogging along the dirt road, between walls of weeds, the governor noticed that every house had been freshly pillaged by the Missourians ahead of him. At one, he talked to a dying man, writhing by his gate, great sweat drops of pain on his forehead. The victim gasped his name, David C. Buffum, and said he had been working his field as the rangers passed. They spied his good horses and came in. Buffum begged to keep his property, said that he was a cripple supporting an aged father, a deaf and dumb brother, and two sisters all dependent on him for a living, and the horses were all he had. One of the rangers replied that he was a "God d----d abolitionist," and shot him in the stomach, unhooked the horses and led them away. The governor was familiar with battle and sudden death but not with murder of this kind by members of his own party.

He arrived in Lecompton to find a detail of dragoons with a recently captured contingent of Lane's and Harvey's men, caught raiding the proslavery village of Hickory Point. These disheveled and bleary-eyed men might well have changed the governor's mind about guilt for all the violence in the territory, but he could not forget the haunting words of Buffum. He ordered the immediate arrest of that farmer's murderer. A culprit was brought in, and Judge Lecompte — not dismissed, as Geary hoped — released him on a bond signed by Sheriff Jones, who was known to have not a dollar's worth of property.

The enraged governor investigated further. He examined the circumstances behind other arrests and discovered a jail full of free-state men, held on trivial or trumped-up charges. Perhaps this excused the retaliatory depredations of the notorious Jim Lane.

Had Governor Geary known all that was occurring behind his back, the death of Buffum might not have influenced him so strongly. He did not know that on the day he arrived in Lecompton to assume office Jim Lane had ridden out of Lawrence to meet James Redpath, the journalistic showman, who admitted frankly that he was bringing a company to hasten a civil war. On the way Lane found many horses belonging to proslavery men. He decided to confiscate them for the cause. Good horses brought high prices in Nebraska and Iowa. With money in his pockets, Lane greeted the three or four hundred overland travelers who rumbled westward daily toward Kansas. He gave them instructions about the road ahead, described the best camping places, and reminded everyone to vote in November for Frémont and thus make Kansas a free state.

Wagon men flocked to his rallies at Nebraska City and over the river at Tabor, Iowa. Always sensational, Lane announced next that he had been challenged to fight a duel "by two aged men" who hoped to end the war in Kansas by sacrificing their lives, if necessary. Let the fate of slavery in the territory be settled on the field of honor, and thus stop the future shedding of innocent blood. Lane pronounced this a good idea and suggested an even better counterproposition. Why not leave the old men out of it and let him, James Henry Lane, and David Rice Atchison, each pick a hundred men to fight before twelve United States senators and twelve members of the House?

Thus, with many guffaws, the trial by combat ended in a farce, and when a newspaper in Nebraska City — edited by J. Sterling Morton — attacked Lane, his followers threatened to sack the office. Lane saw this as another opportunity of the kind he loved. He called for "a conciliatory meeting." The crowd came armed — free-state partisans and proslavery Missourians eager to give Lane his deserts. The Grim Chieftain looked them over, a contemplative scowl on his expressive face. Then he commenced to speak. He thanked the Missourians for coming, complimented their civic interest in the few remarks he hoped to make, claimed to have had intimate friends in Missouri, said he had fought in the Mexican War beside the illustrious Doniphan, a brother in arms to many in the audience, no doubt. Were Doniphan present today, Lane continued, he would be much moved by this meeting to restore harmony and good will between Americans of opposing factions. Then Lane reminded the audience that he belonged to their political party, believing in the principles of Andy Jackson. Yes, he was proud of it, but as a good Democrat — and not a Frank Pierce Democrat — he believed in letting slavery alone where it now was (Frémont's Republican doctrine), but not extending it into the territories. Would the audience consider an experience he had once suffered in the South and then judge for themselves if they wanted slavery in Kansas? Some years ago, Lane said, he and a young carpenter had gone to a sugar plantation seeking work. They asked the proprietor if he wanted any carpentering done? The slave owner looked them over, hooked his thumbs in the armholes of his vest and sneered, "I bought two carpenters yesterday."

"Great God," Lane boomed, "if such men are buying carpenters, machinists, engineers, how soon will they sell you and me in their marts of human merchandise?"

The Missourians looked at one another's calloused hands. They liked this fellow Lane. After all, free-state emigrants might be good for the country.

Among the wagon trains rumbling into Kansas rode most of the militant free-state men who had fled the territory. The stubby Scotsman, Richard J. Hinton, was reported to be leading a party of five hundred footmen armed by the Boston humanitarian, Theodore Parker. Shalor W. Eldridge, the free-state hotel man, led still another wagon train with Samuel C. Pomeroy, the Emigrant Aid Company's agent. Both had witnessed the May raid on Lawrence and gloried in the retribution rolling across the prairies. Other young men with the wagons were John Kagi and Richard Realf, zealots barely out of their teens, eager to participate in some wild attempt to free the slaves. Kagi was the earnest son of Austrian emigrants, Realf a handsome boy-poet recently arrived from Britain. James Redpath, the journalist, brought a hundred and thirty men, Old Brown another battalion of fighters.

A United States patrol on the Kansas border searched all wagons for arms. Trains without women were particularly suspect. Wily emigrants smuggled their weapons through beneath sacks of grain, plows, and spinning wheels. A noteworthy party of three wagons led by nineteen-year-old

Preston Plumb brought a brass twelve-pounder, 250 boxes of Colt revolvers, 250 bowie knives, and 20,000 rounds of ammunition. With him came Samuel F. Tappan, rescuer of Branson from Sheriff Jones, and prominent in most Kansas shooting affairs since. Plumb was a slim, freckle-faced youth, flat-chested and with a bad cough. He had serious, pouting lips, a self-important bearing, and a nervous habit of tossing his head as though to throw back a lock of hair. By trade a newspaper printer, he planned a great future for himself in politics and constantly sought an audience. When talking to any individual, he watched to see if others were listening and raised his voice for them to hear. On the trip west he joined the men's amusements with a patronizing air, and at every opportunity discoursed on politics. He was sure that Kansas tyranny had dimmed Buchanan's prospects in the November election and gloried in being part of a grand crusade against a dictatorial government.

Sam Tappan had brought along a copy of Whittier's poems, and he walked ahead of the wagons, singing with Plumb:

> We cross the prairie as of old
> The pilgrims crossed the sea.

Plumb could not sing a note but made plenty of noise striding along, coatless and in high-heeled boots, tossing the imaginary lock of hair out of his eyes.

Plumb's wagons succeeded in crossing the border with the artillery unde-tected, but after reaching Topeka, Plumb learned that Geary's military heel had crushed out violent protest. The war was over, so Plumb rode south, where he founded the town of Mariposa, named for his beloved Frémont's California estate. He planned to stay on the fringe of civiliza-tion until after the November election, then ride west of Fort Riley, live in the open, hunt buffalo, and overcome his tendency to tuberculosis. In case he learned to be a good marksman, he might add a military career to his political ambitions.

Geary had restored peace by upholding the proslavery government and at the same time remorselessly preventing the persecution of free-state men. He had diverted the turbulent energies of both Walker and Titus by commissioning the homespun free-stater and the jaunty becaped cava-lier in his state troops. He had even connived to have Old Brown leave

Kansas without arresting him. Thus, as the national election day approached, Geary could announce to a watching world: "Peace now reigns."

With Kansas quiet at last, Buchanan won the election over Frémont, and secession was postponed another four years. However, the victory was narrow, and Buchanan would be a minority President. The Know-Nothing or antiforeign party had polled more votes than the antislavery Republicans, but the Democrats had definitely lost popular favor, although they did carry the pivotal state of Pennsylvania by an overwhelming majority in spite of vigorous opposition by Ex-Governor Reeder.

Pierce's failure in Kansas had been due to faulty administration. Buchanan was an older man with much more diplomatic experience. He would inherit a bad muddle but might have the character to straighten it out. In the meantime, Pierce had almost four months to serve. Admittedly, the free-staters dominated Kansas. Proslavery leaders had wanted a contest, had tried to win Kansas by violence and had lost. Colonel Titus realized that his usefulness was gone and he embarked on a new adventure. President Pierce had recently recognized filibuster William Walker as dictator of Nicaragua. Titus decided to raise a company and join him. Central America seemed more attractive to a freebooter now than Kansas. He offered to release all political prisoners who would go with him. Titus left Kansas in an artificial blaze of glorious entertainments at the Planters House in Leavenworth and the Gillis House in Kansas City.

The Kansas which Buchanan would inherit differed from the Kansas which had given Pierce so much trouble. In 1857 over a hundred thousand emigrants arrived in the territory — most of them from Ohio, next from Missouri. The tremendous increase in population started an unprecedented boom in land values. The bitter proslavery town of Leavenworth became free-state, and a lot which had cost $8 sold for $2000 within six months. Judge Samuel D. Lecompte paid $1900 for a squatter's right to a claim on land still owned by the Indians. In addition to the money made by speculation, the overland freighting business continued to boom. Military posts out on the plains must be supplied. A campaign against the Cheyenne was being outfitted, and a gigantic expedition — to cost at least $6,000,000 — was being planned against Mormons, who were as recalcitrant as the Topeka Kansans had ever been. Russell, Majors and Waddell now had 20,000 work cattle and 2000 wagons, together with all the men necessary for such a business. Positive Dan Anthony, who had come with the first Emigrant Aid party, started a newspaper in Leavenworth. Tom Ewing, a young lawyer, looking for a location for himself and his brother-in-law, William Tecumseh Sherman, decided that Leavenworth was the place. "Everything is with the Squatters," Ewing wrote his wife, "Governor, Army officers, soldiers and all — even the speculators have gone in with them and become identified in interest."

Leavenworth was not the only bonanza burgeoning in Kansas. Special trains of twenty-five and thirty cars brought emigrants from the Middle West to all the embarking docks — freemen all, with no slaves. A macadam road was built through the mud from Kansas City landing to Westport, and the leaders of that proslavery town passed resolutions welcoming newcomers regardless of their politics.

Victory for the free-state faction seemed assured at last. All that was left of the Atchison machine sat in the legislature, and they could easily be deposed at the next election. With this favorable prospect "Governor" Robinson resigned from the Topeka government, giving the document to Geary. Everything was now in order for the establishment of peace and a rule of the majority in Kansas. But when the legislature convened in January, 1857, for its second and last session, instead of bowing to the will of the people, they passed a bill for a convention to draft a state constitution to be sent to Congress for approval without ratification by the Kansas voters. Thus the proslavery clique might impose its machine permanently against the will of the majority.

Geary protested, and the assembly passed the act over his veto. The executive and the lawmakers were now public antagonists, with no hope of compromise. Rowdies threatened Geary's life. He applied to Fort Leavenworth for troops and learned that none were available, all too busy preparing for the spring campaign. Was this true, or had Geary been deserted by the national administration? At midnight Captain Sam Walker was aroused by a knock. The bepistoled governor came in. "I'm going to Washington," he said, "and I'll straighten things out."

At the White House, Governor Geary found his fears confirmed. The administration did not want justice. Kansas must be controlled by the Atchison machine. The slave power demanded it. President Pierce criticized Geary pointedly for certain exaggerated statements he had made about the injustice of Lecompte's decisions — about the incarceration of men on trumped-up charges. There was nothing left for Geary but to resign — the third Democratic governor who would not truckle with injustices demanded by the slave interests. His resignation became effective on March 4, 1857, the day Buchanan took office. Let the new President start with a clean slate on the Western border.

VIII

Buchanan Tries His Hand

JAMES BUCHANAN was thirteen years older than President Pierce. His experience with men and affairs was exceptional. He had been a United States senator, Secretary of State under James K. Polk, and minister to both Russia and Great Britain. Like Pierce, he lamented the widening sectional chasm over slavery and hoped that his administration might be the one to reunite the Democratic Party. He had been a personal friend of Andy Jackson's and counted on holding the allegiance of Old Hickory's admirers both North and South. In short, he looked back for old remedies instead of ahead for new ones. A nervous affliction made his head twitch slightly, but his general health seemed sufficiently robust for the task before him.

Buchanan was by no means sure that the antislavery movement would spread, that the Southern wing of the party must submit. Out in Missouri, next door to Kansas, the trend seemed to be in favor of slavery. Both Missouri's new senators had been elected by proslavery, antiforeign majorities opposed to the Thomas Hart Benton group. Moreover, Buchanan had reason to believe that the Supreme Court of the United States would solve the slavery question in Kansas by a decision in the case of Dred Scott, a Negro who claimed freedom because his master had removed him to free soil.

For governor of Kansas, Buchanan appointed Robert J. Walker, a little whiffet of a man with lifelong Democratic Party allegiance and big constructive ideas. Born in western Pennsylvania, Walker had made and lost a fortune in the South, and had served as senator from Tennessee. He knew the frontier South, had sat in the gallery when Sumner delivered his oration on the crime against Kansas, and had read in the papers about the successive failures of Reeder, Shannon, and Geary. He considered the appointment a doubtful honor and refused to accept it until promised by President Buchanan and the Senate leader, Stephen A. Douglas, that a majority of the people in Kansas would be allowed to determine their own institutions.

The hopeful little governor began his administration by publishing an eight-column inaugural address recognizing the Lecompton government and prophesying great prosperity for everyone in the booming territory, even hinting the possibility of railroad subsidies. On the slavery question he hedged. Like Douglas, he would not insult the Southerners by saying that the institution was wrong. Instead, he hoped to reconcile both wings by saying that the Kansas climate was not suited to slave labor. In short, he was willing, as Douglas was, to see slavery abolished, but he was unwilling to call it wrong. Lincoln, on the other hand, was willing to protect slavery where it was established but insisted that it be admitted wrong — a fine distinction but one that men would fight about. The Kansas governor was promptly dubbed "Isothermal" Walker by the Republican press, which wanted a more outspoken opinion.

In Washington, President Buchanan's cabinet read Walker's inaugural address with suspicion and disfavor. They had expected a special pleader for their proslavery interests, an adroit justification of the tyranny necessary to fix slavery on Kansas. Here was Buchanan's opportunity to reverse Pierce's subserviency and show his own force of character, but instead he agreed diplomatically with his official family. A change might be dangerous. This was typical of Buchanan.

Governor Walker, depending on the promise of Buchanan and Douglas that the majority be allowed to rule, urged the free-state people to vote for candidates to the Lecompton legislature, gain the majority of seats due them, and thus make Kansas legally a free state. He threatened to meet any further resistance with the United States Army. Under this combined promise and threat the free-state settlers voted. Missourians feared to cross the border as they had in previous elections. They knew too well that James Henry Lane could call out his clan from every corncrib and wheat shock. One chawback who had had his fill of marching into Kansas said, "They have got a cannon over there, some Yankee invention, I suppose, that they load by putting the balls in a hopper, the same as a miller puts grain in a hopper, to grind." But the Missouri faction was not whipped. Instead of invading the polls this year, they tried to win by another ruse. Sufficient ballot boxes were stuffed to keep the majority proslavery. Some frauds were blatant. A precinct with six houses returned 1628 votes. A poll book in another area contained names copied from the city directory of Cincinnati.

Governor Walker, true to his word, threw out the questionable returns. Henry Clay Pate's *Border Star* complained that worse frauds had been committed by free-state men. To pad their majority, he claimed, ballots had been cast by "bloomers and children," "hump-backed hirelings," and "two woolly-headed, flat-nosed, thick-lipped negroes. . . . It is hard to conceive the Anglo-Saxon race could stoop so low." Contemptuously ignoring the governor's decision, Judge Cato issued a mandamus for the issuance of certificates of election in the suspected precincts. Sheriff Jones, one of the disqualified candidates, demanded his "paper" at pistol's point.

Governor Walker, outraged at this lawlessness, loaded his own "pepper-box" and with the territorial secretary, Frederick P. Stanton, stamped into all the drinking dives in Lecompton. At card tables and along the bars, he tongue-lashed the politicians. Giant Geary had never shown more courage and energy than this sickly little whiffet.

Complete free-state victory seemed to have been won at last, but the proslavery machine had not forgotten its last line of defense. The delegates sitting in the constitutional convention were members of the old Atchison organization. They could and probably would draft a proslavery constitution and ask to have Kansas admitted under it without popular approval. Geary had objected to this and was removed by President Pierce. Would Buchanan act in the same manner? Already he seemed more firmly in the grasp of the slave power than Pierce had been. Surely he would compel Walker to acquiesce or quit.

The little governor had proved himself as stubborn and righteous as Reeder. President Buchanan had promised him that the majority must rule in Kansas, and he in turn had promised the Kansans an opporutnity to vote on their own constitution. When he saw what the constitutional convention planned, Walker called a special session of the newly elected legislature, with its free-state majority, to convene and, if they thought best, pass an act for a plebiscite on the constitution. The slave power would not tolerate this, and President Buchanan recalled Walker from office — the fourth governor to be removed by executives who put appeasement above principle. Pacifier Buchanan wanted peace in Kansas but, like Pierce, he wanted only a proslavery, one-party peace.

The President's apparent connivance in this subterfuge to thwart majority rule set the Republican press on fire. Flames of protest crackled across the continent. Something must be done. A sly solution to appease both parties was suggested. The remedy was said to come from Senator Douglas, reputed to be the best straddler of the decade. The plan, if his, was simple. Let the people vote on the constitution "with slavery" or "without slavery." Thus, in either case, the proslavery machine's organic act would be accepted without popular approval, and the Democrats would maintain an advantage in Kansas. Senator R. M. T. Hunter, Atchison's old roommate in Washington, published two elaborate arguments justifying this procedure, but the subterfuge succeeded only in convincing the North that the slave power had no intention of playing fair.

Jim Lane spoke openly about leading a party of regulators to Lecompton to break up the deliberations, but never did so. The convention finally adjourned, brazenly agreeing to send the constitution direct to Congress for approval, submitting only the slavery clause to the people. Lane set off behind his moccasin-colored horse to harangue mass meetings against the Lecompton fraud. He urged lynching every member of the convention unless something was done.

Frederick P. Stanton, the acting governor since Walker had left, feared a repetition of the vigilante lawlessness which had disgraced California, and ordered the special session of the legislature to meet on December 7, 1857. Thus the free-state majority came into power at last.

On the opening day of the legislature Jim Lane marched into town with the Lawrence Cornet Band and nine hundred celebrants on foot, on horseback and in carriages. George Deitzler, procurer of Sharps rifles, was elected speaker of the House. Lane was made major general of the territorial militia. In the midst of great gaiety a delegation arrived from southeast Kansas. They represented themselves as free-state settlers whose claims had been jumped by proslavery men, and they wanted Jim Lane to help them. The Grim Chieftain, expansive with new authority, dispatched subordinate "Generals" William Phillips, the stubby Scotsman, and tall, slim Preston Plumb with suitable commands. Then the major general himself followed to direct operations on the front, perhaps to enlist the entire free-state population to evict all proslavery claimants.

Phillips and Plumb both rode south with their political ambitions and the men assigned to them. The former ranked high in the state's free-soil party since authoring a book on Kansas as well as several articles in the *New York Tribune*. Plumb had just returned from hunting buffalo on the plains, his health improved, his freckles more pronounced; so, also, was his peculiar habit of peeping from under an imaginary lock of hair toward an upper corner of the ceiling and tossing back his head before speaking. Maturity was accentuating his purposeful expression and the serious pout on his meditative lips. Already he was called the "Good Bishop," and he walked the earth with a stove poker for a spine. Now at last he could demonstrate military aptitude that would inevitably lead to political preferment.

The southeast Kansas to which the "army" marched had not changed like the rest of the territory. No river transportation enabled hundreds of Eastern emigrants to float to these vast prairies. From Kansas City south to the Indian country a horseman could ride from Missouri to Kansas at any place, without hindrance. The abandoned military post at Fort Scott served as capital, county seat, and place of publication for the *Southern Kansan* — a defender of the proslavery interests. Most of the settlers were Missourians. Some had been driven from northern claims by free-state settlers and had taken new homesteads in these congenial surroundings. A few of Buford's legion who had been unable to beg their way back to Alabama also settled here.

The present trouble was an outgrowth of last year's feud between factions under little, black-haired, Campbellite preacher James Montgomery and the ex-Indian agent George W. Clarke, one of the dispossessed north Kansans who had moved south. Montgomery's followers maintained that Federal Judge Williams, at Fort Scott, invariably ruled against free-state men's claims. Like Lecompte, up in north Kansas, "Fiddling Williams" was an easygoing fellow of the old school, popular with backwoodsmen. He liked to play, sing, and dance with the youngest of them, yet took his position seriously. It was a standing joke that he never charged a jury without managing some way to tell them that he had been chief justice of

Iowa for forty years and in all that time had never seen a more intelligent panel than the one before him.

Montgomery's partisans, noting the free-state success in north Kansas, decided to ignore Williams's decisions, organize a self-protective association and court of their own. Armed and determined, they resisted a United States marshal who came to break up their organization. Jim Lane had been educated with three years of this kind of revolution. People prophesied that he would sweep southeast Kansas with fire and sword. They did not know George Washington Clarke and his proud, vindictive, backwoods aristocrats. Late in December a rider dashed into Lawrence, after a forced ride of a hundred miles in twenty hours. He brought startling news. Lane was making a stand near Sugar Mount before a large body of well-organized Missourians. The border war seemed to be starting all over again.

In desperation over the interminable Kansas imbroglio, President Buchanan turned to James W. Denver, his Indian Commissioner, who happened to be in the territory. Denver was a Californian, having served as state senator there. He had known Kansas before there was a Kansas, knew David Rice Atchison personally, and understood extralegal vigilante organizations and how to deal with them. Taking the oath of governor on December 21, 1857, he announced that he would continue his predecessor's policy. He ordered United States dragoons to disperse the state "army" under Lane and also Clarke's regulators. The Grim Chieftain returned to Lawrence furious. What right had the slave power's governor to interfere with the squatters' right to maintain order with their own miltia? Lane had challenged Douglas for accusing him of forging part of the Topeka constitution. Now he sent an insulting letter to Governor Denver. Then Lane called his supporters to a midnight meeting to await a challenge from the governor. Lane told his friends that as the challenged party, he could choose the weapons, and he had decided on rifles. Owning a special Sharps target gun — the only one in Kansas — he felt confident that he would kill Denver.

Lane notified Sheriff Sam Walker not to stop the fight. Walker had fallen heir to Jones's badge since the governmental turnover. He knew Jim Lane's furious instability, having faced him in another serious crisis

in Nebraska in 1856. Sheriff Walker disregarded Lane's instructions and
drove over to Lecompton to see Denver and prevent the challenge. The
big governor laughed about Lane's letter and scorned the idea of a duel.
He was much too busy. Kansas was booming. Contractors were buying
thousands of oxen and mules for the Utah Expedition, which had stalled
in the mountains. All available men were being hired. More important
still were reports of the discovery of gold in western Kansas — out in the
Rockies. Fall Leaf, the Delaware, a noted guide, had brought back from
an expedition with the soldiers gold nuggets tied in a rag. He was a well-
to-do Indian cattle owner whose quaint English could usually be depended
upon for accuracy, and he maintained that the gold had come from the
South Platte. This discovery might start an exodus of the turbulent border
spirits and thus end the factional fighting. Already, some of the active
young men in Lawrence were outfitting a wagon train. If the powers in
Washington would let Kansans alone, the trouble might stop of its own
accord.

President Buchanan with his proslavery cabinet did not intend to let
Kansas solve its own problem. He was determined to placate the slave
power and recommended that Kansas be admitted under the Lecompton
constitution. His own party newspapers in the North protested this injustice. The Democratic stalwart Stephen A. Douglas had supported the
President from the beginning, but now saw that his own seat was in
danger if he submitted longer. He had championed squatter sovereignty
as a solution of the slavery issue. Like an attorney defending a client, he
had extolled the good points in this doctrine and probed the weak spots in
the territory's case for the Topeka constitution — even to the point of being challenged to a duel by Jim Lane. But now the people's will was evi-
dent. Douglas refused to follow the President farther.

The quarrel in Washington gave new hope to the proslavery group in
southern Kansas. By April 1858, Fort Scott had become a haven of intrigue. Settlers who had sold goods here to the soldiers now operated stores
in the abandoned buildings. Two hotels housed the slave and free factions.
At night partisans rode out to plunder settlers belonging to the opposing
faction and returned to make merry in town. Times were never so gay nor
so dangerous in the days when the army was stationed here. Many of the
townsmen remembered Harney, Sumner, and Joe Johnston, but most

vividly of all Nathaniel Lyon, the intense disciplinarian who had marched delinquent soldiers bareheaded across the parade ground with honey in their hair and barrels over their shoulders to prevent them from brushing away the flies.

A new leader of the proslavery settlers had appeared in the Fort Scott area recently. Handsome, wealthy Charles A. Hambleton came from Georgia, with his brothers, at the suggestion of Milt McGee. Charles's father had contributed a thousand dollars to the Southern Emigrant Aid Company and had bidden his sons Godspeed. In Georgia the proud Hambleton clan was notorious for violence. Charles had been shot three times in a feud, and he came to Kansas with an abiding hatred of "abolitionists." His substantial log house with suitable slave quarters and stockaded corral, in southeast Kansas, became headquarters for proslavery partisans until Montgomery and his followers drove them all from their claims.

In Missouri the refugees rallied around Charles Hambleton, and on May 19, 1858, they rode back into Kansas with seventeen Missouri allies to revenge themselves by what became known as the Marais des Cygnes Massacre. New leaves unrolling on trees and underbrush screened their approach. Spring beauties carpeted the woods and wild apple blossoms illuminated the hillsides. The determined riders jogged silently into the free-state community of Blooming Grove. A man with the euphonious name of Seth Belch operated the log-cabin store which served as center of this loose settlement. The Southerners dismounted, stamped in the open door, disarmed the customers, and bound their hands. Outside, a two-horse wagon emerged from the woods, coming down the road toward them. This, too, was captured. Then Hambleton took from his pocket a list of victims and called their names. Riders galloped to the doomed men's cabins. A blacksmith on the list saved his life by resisting, shotgun in hand. Eleven others, taken from their fields or dooryards, were driven down the road like livestock ahead of the horsemen. At a gulch draining into the Marais des Cygnes the riders herded the footmen off the road and lined them up before a firing squad.

"Gentlemen," one of the free-state victims said defiantly, "if you are going to shoot, take good aim."

"Ready," Hambleton commanded, but before he gave the order to fire, one of the Missourians lowered his gun. "I'll have nothing to do with such a piece of business as this."

Hambleton drew his pistol and, waving menacingly, shouted: "Fire." A volley rang out and the eleven men crumpled to the ground — four dead, six wounded, one unhurt but pretending death. Hambleton strode among the bodies, turning them over with his boot. A man struggled in pain, and Hambleton put his pistol to his head, fired, missed the brain and shot through the cheeks, almost severing the base of the tongue — but the man lived. Other raiders began rifling the stricken men's pockets, leaving them inside out. Then the men mounted their horses and galloped away, separating in order to leave no trails in the soft spring woods.

To revenge this outrage, Montgomery raided north, taking supplies from frontier stores within fifteen miles of Lecompton. Lane called out the militia around Lawrence and Topeka and started south to help Montgomery. Let Denver interfere if he could. One battalion of free-staters marched into Missouri and at West Point demanded the privilege of searching for Hambleton men. The townsmen, claiming innocence, submitted meekly — but no one was found.

Back in Massachusetts, the Marais des Cygnes Massacre wrung from the heart of John Greenleaf Whittier another of those poems, more deadly to the slave cause than Sharps rifles. Describing, in metered pathos, the return of the victims' bodies to homes "yet warm with their lives," he announced to the world that "on the lintels of Kansas, that blood shall not dry."

> Henceforth to the sunset,
>   Unchecked on her way,
> Shall liberty follow
>   The march of the day.

In reply to the rising emotionalism in the Republican Party, President Buchanan doggedly continued to court the slave power. He was determined to admit Kansas under the Lecompton constitution and proposed to buy the Kansans' consent with a block of public land large enough to make the Sovereign Squats' mouths water. But the Kansans, thoroughly angry with his administration and encouraged by Eastern humanitarians, turned down the bribe. Federal authority was openly flouted in southeast

Kansas. Slave owners, or even political supporters of Buchanan, risked their lives whenever they crossed the Missouri border. Conditions became so bad, Governor Denver decided to go himself with a party into southeast Kansas and re-establish law and order.

At country stores and roadside clearings Denver talked with settlers. He asked about their troubles. Dirt farmers pushed their straw hats back on perspiring heads and told him, "I owe this farm to Montgomery. Yes, sir! I figger on votin' him into the legislature sometime."

One day, as the executive carriages rocked along the country road, a black-bearded man rode up and jogged along beside the governor. He was pale and nervous. At times he bowed over his saddle coughing, but he looked Denver straight in the eye and admitted that he was James Montgomery. The governor made no attempt to detain him. Settlers seemed to approve Montgomery's acts, and would certainly prevent his arrest.

Montgomery was not the only disturbing problem in southern Kansas. Governor Denver learned that John Brown had come back, steely eyes glittering with renewed zeal. Rumor said he was accompanied by Richard Realf, J. H. Kagi, and the Viennese August Bondi, who had served the old warrior during the capture of Henry Clay Pate. The presence of these revolutionists was enough to disturb any administrator. Obviously, they had reassembled for some purpose greater than making Kansas a free state, for that was now assured. In all probability they were bent on raiding into Missouri to liberate slaves, horses, and silver spoons from unsuspecting planters. To make things worse, these robbers were being financed by wealthy philanthropists in New England who sincerely believed in abolition. More significant still, the violent practices of Brown, Montgomery, and Jim Lane were unquestionably approved by a great many of the Kansas voters, and in a democracy the people were supposed to rule. Governor Denver drove back to Lecompton a wiser and more perplexed man.

The Kansas capital to which Denver returned was agog with new problems. A few of the gold seekers had straggled back, some discouraged but others with samples of unmistakable "dust." The exciting news was being printed across the nation. Next spring would surely witness a gold rush. Already a town named Denver had been platted at the edge of the mountains, and the governor sent proper officials to establish and administer a new county there. Obviously, the old feud could not go on with such an influx of new men, new interests, new problems. Even "General" Atchison, visiting Leavenworth, told reporters that he had retired from public life and henceforth would devote himself exclusively to his farm and livestock — or could he! Then, to cap it all, the governor learned that Jim Lane, too, was out of circulation. Sheriff Walker held him for murder.

He'll Trouble Them More
When His Coffin's Nailed Down

ALBERT RICHARDSON, British correspondent, was lounging in the *Herald of Freedom* office in Lawrence on June 3, 1858, when someone outside shouted, "Jim Lane has killed Gaius Jenkins and a mob has gathered around his house to hang him." Looking out a window, the newsman saw people closing their offices, barring shutters, before they joined the crowd. Richardson stepped across the sidewalk, mingled with the curiosity seekers and hurried with them toward Lane's house. Breathless boys and grim-faced men with pistols in their belts joined the throng, asking for details, telling all they knew. Lane and Jenkins had quarreled for months over a claim boundary. The Midwestern faction had backed Lane. New Englanders, headed by Robinson, had naturally sided with Jenkins. He had been employed by the Emigrant Company to manage the American Hotel in Kansas City during the turbulent year of 1854. In 1856 he had been arrested for treason and imprisoned at Lecompton, like other free-state patriots. During the claim dispute with Lane he had tried to evict the Grim Chieftain and once, in Lane's absence, occupied his cabin. Lane complained that the New Englander had plowed the ground where his daughter lay buried, leaving no sign of the marker. In speech after speech to the drinking, laughing boys, Lane had minimized Jenkins's patriotic sacrifice and set his listeners roaring with frontier glee about Jenkins's being taken a prisoner to Lecompton by Milt McGee's "nigger."

All these stories were familiar to the mob surging up the road. Men believed or disbelieved them according to their factional prejudices. At Lane's cabin they stopped, mingling with the people already there. From

Jenkins's house, across the field, shrill screams of grief could be heard — the harrowing voices of women and children. Spectators who had been present during the fight pointed to the broken fence. Gaius and a few friends had come through there this morning. He had a bucket in one hand and a gun in the other. As he strode toward the well to draw some water, Jim Lane stepped out of his house with a rifle and ordered him to turn back. Someone in Jenkins's party fired, hitting Lane in the knee. The Grim Chieftain shot Jenkins in the body, killing him. He lay over there in his house now with the mourning women and children. Lane had struggled back through his door and lay wounded under the care of his weeping wife. She had remarried him after getting a divorce.

The crowd stood uncertain, talking angrily, wanting to do something, but lacking leadership. Among them strode Ex-Sheriff Jones, ready now to ally himself with the New Englanders to get revenge on Lane. "Lynch him," Jones shouted.

Sheriff Walker heard the shrill cry and walked up to Jones. "Be careful how you recommend hanging," he said. "These people are a good deal excited already, and if they hang anybody it will be very likely to begin with you." Jones realized that he might serve as a sacrifice for the mob's fury and slipped away. Then Walker knocked at Lane's house, helped him to a carriage, and drove to the jail.

A grand jury found no indictment against the Grim Chieftain, but the killing hurt him politically, especially with church people. The *Leaven-worth Times* quipped: "It seems that Gen. Lane's leg would have to be cut off. Well, in that case, he will, as a candidate, stump it all the better." But Lane shunned political gatherings. Instead he let himself be reconverted into the Methodist Church in several different Kansas towns, though with only partial sincerity, it seems, for a tavern keeper at Baldwin City was heard to admonish a boy leading a team to the creek, "Don't water them horses below where they baptized Jim Lane."

With the approach of cold weather, Lane ventured back to the hustings, claiming always that he was a converted Christian. In platform speeches he would boom: "They say that Jim Lane is a blasphemer. Why he never used profane language in his whole life. Yes, once. At the battle of Buena Vista when he looked across at the enemy's threatening ranks of tasseled lancers, he turned to his mid-western farm boys and said, 'Charge on 'em, God d--n 'em! charge on 'em.' "

Before long, Lane used the Jenkins homicide to his own advantage and on more than one occasion defended himself on the platform by asking: "And they say Jim Lane is a murderer, yes a murderer! What are the facts? When the noble women of Lawrence were endeavoring to establish a public library, what did Jim Lane do? He took his old claybank horse out of the field where he was plowing to raise a little corn for his family, and sold that horse for $37.50 and gave the money to those noble women and yet, great God, they say Jim Lane is a murderer."

The Grim Chieftain completely recouped his old-time popularity during the winter of 1858, but the gold rush had taken some of the zest from politics. Life along the border had been revolutionized by the hundred thousand people who were buying supplies and equipment for the mountains. Merchants had never known such prosperity — much better for them than town-lot speculation. Gold discoveries crowded politics from the newspapers. In addition to suggestions about camp gear and jumping-off places, sixteen guide books were printed to aid overland travelers — one by Redpath and Hinton, who could seldom be diverted from the antislavery crusade. Even Tom Ewing, Sherman's partner in Leavenworth, set aside the practice of law for writing.

Only in southeast Kansas was life unaffected by the Pikes Peak rush. There the endless squabble over land claims, G. W. Clarke's aggressions, and Montgomery's retaliation continued, with Old Brown and his revolutionists lurking in the woods. Fiddling Williams still administered justice unacceptable to the free-state men, and when he committed two of them to jail in Fort Scott, Montgomery rallied seventy-five rescuers — the largest "army" he had yet commanded. Sam Wood, the Quaker boy who had helped rescue Branson before the Wakarusa War, enlisted a troop of vigilantes and rode all the way from Lawrence to join Montgomery. Another party led by Preston Plumb trotted in from Emporia. Old John Brown joined the rendezvous with his followers, intent on action. No more moderation for him! The old fury asked for the top command and promised to lay Fort Scott in ashes. Montgomery spoke against such extremes, said that he had called the rally merely to release the prisoners held by Judge Williams's court. He wanted no property destroyed and no one hurt. The crowd voted in favor of Montgomery, and Old Brown stalked out of the meeting, but his revolutionary supporters remained. The mob marched quickly over to Fort Scott and captured it after a short skirmish. One pro-slavery defender was killed, and J. H. Kagi of Brown's company was wounded.

Old Brown, a wild bull smelling blood, determined to outdo the Montgomery partisans. Financed by Easterners for a crusade, he must show results. The time had come for the tide to turn, for Kansas to begin invading Missouri. Brown organized two little columns and secretly marched across the Missouri state line on December 20, 1858, raided several plantations, and came out with eleven slaves, some good horses, and other property. One slave owner had been killed. Brown started north with his fugitives in an ox wagon. Governor R. M. Stewart, of Missouri, appealed to Governor Denver and also to President Buchanan. The President offered a reward of $250 for Brown, and Brown printed handbills offering a reward of $.25 for Buchanan. Grinning grimly, he disappeared with his ox team and his Negro fugitives into the maze of prairie roads meandering northward through the tall dry weeds.

Governor Stewart put a $3000 reward on Brown's head, but no one arrested him. There had been trouble recently in the river towns with slave catchers suspected of kidnapping free Negroes to sell back into slavery. Leavenworth had effervesced with indignation when some white men were caught trying to abduct a Negro barber, Charles Fisher — threatening him, through the transom above his door, to come out quietly and submit or be shot down. An infuriated mob surged through the streets. Innocent proslavery residents barricaded themselves in a public building, and Democrats in outlying settlements oiled their guns for defensive war. Free-state men held a gigantic rally with Mark Delahay, Lincoln's kinsman, presiding. Dan Anthony spoke as his Quaker father and reforming sister would have approved. Fearlessly he announced that he had "always held it to be his duty to say whatever his conscience told him was right and in all places and at all times." Then he unscabbed all the old sores Kansans had suffered from Missourians, from the illegal voting and the murder of R. P. Brown by the Kickapoo Rangers to the recent Marais des Cygnes Massacre. He added that he had been shot at several times for merely daring to express his opinions.

A week later Lane was cheered to the echo when he stated at a gigantic reception: "If you must choose between kidnapping a man into slavery or kidnapping him into freedom, in God's name kidnap him into freedom."

One thing was very certain. Few, if any, individuals in Kansas were going to lift a saddle to arrest Old Brown and his party. A fifteen-man posse deputized by the United States marshal in Atchison rode out after him and came back with nothing but a report that Brown had a bodyguard of sixty sharpshooters. Several bands of infuriated Missourians crossed on ferries to scour the Kansas roads. They failed to find Brown, but one party of horsemen brought in an "underground railroad train" conducted by Dr. John Doy — the same who had come with Dan Anthony and the first emigrants sent by the New England company. The entire "train," including thirteen fugitive Negroes, were taken to Missouri without warrant, the blacks put back into slavery, the whites jailed for trial. There was little question about their guilt and probable conviction, but what right had Missourians to arrest Kansans on their own soil and take them back across the river for trial! Obviously the Kansas-Missouri feud was far from settled and would loom as big in the election of 1860 as in 1856. With this in prospect, Republicans in Kansas decided to organize their party there. An attempt in 1858 had failed but the time seemed auspicious now.

Osawatomie was selected for the convention, to be held May 18, 1859. The scene of Old Brown's early notoriety seemed suitable, surely, for emotionalizing the wrongs perpetrated by the Democrats in Kansas. Horace Greeley offered to take part in the convention as he traveled west for the *New York Tribune* to visit Pikes Peak, Salt Lake City, and the Pacific. Abraham Lincoln wrote Mark Delahay on May 14, 1859, that law practice kept him from attending, but he hoped the delegates would stand firm on the national party's platform against extending or nationalizing slavery.

In Kansas most of the free-state men were still Democrats interested in land claims and political positions in the government which the Missouri machine had usurped. They had accepted support and sympathy from Eastern antislavery interests, but they were not abolitionists, and Horace Greeley's advanced doctrines might excite a convention of Kansans into hysteria. The political leaders assembling at Osawatomie wondered how they might keep the great editor from talking without offending him.

As Horace Greeley traveled west, his talent for sensing news distracted him for a time from the political convention ahead. Upriver steamboats were crowded with prospectors eager to find gold and little concerned about slavery. They stopped in Kansas only long enough to purchase flour, bacon, and other supplies. The first telegraph from the East reached Leavenworth that year, and an overland stage had been established to the mountains. This wheeled luxury brought occasional trappers in buckskins and moccasins to stare and be stared at in the river towns. Bags of gold were unloaded for onlookers to "heft" and guess their weight and value. Horace Greeley momentarily forgot the part he was to play in the Republican convention and jotted down notes about the magnitude of Russell, Majors and Waddell's overland transportation enterprise. He had seen big business in the mills of New England, and in the harbors of New York, but nothing like this. For Eastern readers he wrote:

> Such acres of wagons! Such pyramids of extra axletrees! Such herds of oxen! Such regiments of drivers and other employees! No one who does not see can realize how vast a business this is, nor how immense its outlay as well as income. I presume the great firm has at this hour two millions of dollars invested in stock, mainly oxen, mules, and wagons. (Last year they employed six thousand teamsters and worked 45,000 oxen.)

Here were craftsmen of a new order, men in a great corporation, who took unusual individual pride in their humble jobs. Drivers of eight and ten ox yokes gloried in the symmetry of their animals and their matching colors — all black, all white, or all spotted. Boys on caparisoned horses carried messages to the wagon bosses. Young Bill Cody was so employed. These elaborate wagon trains rocked off across the horizon to a new world, while Greeley found himself in still a different universe when he arrived at the village of Osawatomie, where a thousand delegates crowded the lodging-houses, and camped in the groves or beside their carriages.

The politicians at Osawatomie met Horace Greeley cordially. The situation was a delicate one. How could they tell the editor of the *New York Tribune* that these people were not so radical in their views about slavery as the Easterners who had been supporting them? A sly ruse finally solved the dilemma. Greeley was treated to a grand parade in his honor with the marchers wearing *Tribunes* in their hats. He was requested to address an open-air meeting, and thus, having been given a major role, he was art-fully excluded from the policy-forming committees and the tedium of practical organization.

Thus the radical and conservative free-state men united in the Republican Party after five years of squabbling over the best method of resisting Missouri usurpation. Robinson and Lane, the New England abolitionist and the Midwestern pragmatist, still eyed each other with familiar hatred. United in the same party now, they could be counted on in every crisis to pull in opposite directions. Then in July the distressing news came to Kansas that John Doy and his accomplices had been sentenced to the penitentiary in Missouri. But before they were incarcerated, people were electrified to learn that a band of Kansans had crossed the river and liberated all of them. If Missourians could invade Kansas, why not Kansans invade Missouri?

At first, John Brown was credited with coming back from Canada for the daring rescue. Already he had become a fabulous figure, but this time other zealots planned and executed the raid. Proudly they posed for photographs — guns, cutlasses, and all. Let abolitionists sing their praises and display their pictures in homes and offices!

Mysterious Old Brown turned up in October 1859, not in Kansas but at Harpers Ferry, Virginia, where, with Kansas-trained followers, he tried to foment a Negro insurrection and was promptly surrounded by marines under Colonel Robert E. Lee and Lieutenant Jeb Stuart, now serving in Virginia. Struck down with bayonets and sabers, Old Brown was dragged to the office of the arsenal superintendent. Virginia's political leaders, Governor Wise and Atchison's former roommate, James Mason, hurried out to interview the prisoner, with newsmen recording every word. "Why did you do this?" "Who put up the money?" "Who sent you here?" came from a half dozen voices. Jeb Stuart recognized the wounded man as Osawatomie Brown and asked, "Did you go out to Kansas under the auspices of the Emigrant Aid Society?"

"No, sir," the battered and bleeding zealot replied from the floor. "I went out under the auspices of John Brown and nobody else."

Senator Mason looked down at the prostrate figure curiously. "How do you justify your acts?" he asked.

"I think, my friend, you [slaveholders] are guilty of a great wrong against God and humanity — I say it without wishing to be offensive — and it would be perfectly right in anyone to interfere with you so far as to free those you willfully and wickedly hold in bondage. I do not say this insultingly."

"I understand that," Mason said.

"I think I did right," Brown continued, "and that others will do right to interfere with you at any time and all times. I hold that the Golden Rule, 'do unto others as you would that others should do unto you,' applies to all who would help others to gain their liberty."

"But you don't believe in the Bible," youthful Jeb Stuart interposed.

"Certainly I do." The stricken man looked with calm dignity at the bearded acolyte of religion and light horse.

"The wages of sin are death," announced the stentorian youth in his soldier suit.

Old Brown, lying on the threshold of immortality, kept his eyes on the upstart lieutenant who prided himself as being the personification of Virginia chivalry. "I would not have said that," Brown replied, "if you had been a prisoner and wounded in my hands."

Governor Wise was counseled to commit John Brown to an asylum instead of hanging. Sufficient affidavits about the old man's past actions and family history warranted such action. But Governor Wise, after watching Brown intently, had to admit that the old man's wits were as sharp as his inquisitors'. Besides, a great cry for Brown's life arose from the South, and the weapons captured from his men were Sharps rifles — undoubtedly the ones sent by the Emigrant Aid Company to Kansas in spite of the old man's insistence on sole responsibility. Many Northern humanitarians — Eli Thayer, Gerritt Smith, and others — realized that they might be personally implicated along with Brown.

The Republican press deplored Brown's lawlessness, but Greeley's *Tribune* adroitly channeled the event into his party's benefit. "Kansas deeds, Kansas experiences, Kansas discipline created John Brown," the readers were told. "Revenge rocked his cradle, disciplined his arm, and nerved his soul." The man to blame for the blood spilled by Brown, the account continued, was Franklin Pierce, who had snarled the national fabric with his appeasement.

An immediate search was made for all John Brown accomplices not captured at Harpers Ferry. Gerritt Smith suffered temporary insanity. His wealth, great as it was, would not protect him from a charge of treason if the Democrats could get the evidence. In Kansas, Brown's earlier acquaintances were interrogated for clues and — most amusing — Milt McGee was arrested and imprisoned because, a known partisan, he happened to be on the railroad train near Harpers Ferry. Henry Clay Pate, having abandoned his newspaper to practice law in Westport, left for New York to lecture in Cooper Institute on his personal acquaintance with Brown and his experiences as a prisoner under him. The *Louisville Journal* scoffed: "We presume the Democrats have secured the living ass to kick the abolitionists' dead lion."

The lecture was a failure. Even New York was not prepared for a man who could modestly introduce himself by saying, "I'm the son of a b— you've heard so much about." In March, Pate was back in Missouri preparing to move. While there, he sold his Negro, invested in town lots, mortgaged them, and started East after arranging with the black boy to run away and join him. On April 21, 1860, he wrote Colonel A. G. Boone, who had been commissioned by Buchanan to treat with the Cheyenne and Arapaho around Denver, "I am truly glad to hear that the brothers are kind in their feelings toward me, for really all the sin I have committed is in making debts I was unable to meet, but intend to pay."

John Brown's raid embarrassed conservative Kansans, but Redpath and Lane extolled his heroism. Dr. Robinson testified against Brown's reputation and his Kansas activities. Lane publicly called Robinson a perjurer. Admirers sent Redpath a sword, which the journalist accepted, announcing that other raids similar to Brown's were being prepared. Journalist Richard J. Hinton, James Montgomery, and several members of the Doy party plotted to release Brown's accomplices from jail. Dan Anthony contributed money for the enterprise. Charlie Lenhardt got a job as prison guard to aid an escape from the inside. Montgomery traveled East to Virginia, looked over the ground, and pronounced a rescue impossible. Planters in southern Missouri were sure that black-bearded Montgomery planned to strike next at them instead. Enterprising slave dealers hurried through the border counties, buying Negroes at bargain prices to be sold for a good profit down south.

The legality of the death penalty for Brown's act could not be questioned but affidavits concerning his sanity continued to pour into the governor's office. Should or should not the old man be committed to an asylum, and his abolitionist supporters to ridicule? Governor Wise, hoping for harmony as much as Buchanan ever did, decided to appease Southern demands for vengeance and thus unwittingly gave Ralph Waldo Emerson an opportunity to say that the scaffold might be glorious like the cross. Moderates everywhere saw the folly of the governor's decision, but Wise obeyed the letter of the law and stubbornly refused to reverse himself. The final decree excited a dirt farmer in Kansas, J. S. Reader, to stop cornhusking and scrawl in his diary:

> Old Brown
>   John Brown
>   Osawatomie Brown
> He'll trouble them more when his Coffin's nailed down!

X

The Election of Abraham Lincoln

THE SPRING AND SUMMER of 1860 opened with a financial depression in Kansas. Leavenworth suffered especially from overexpansion. Many people closed their houses, packed their belongings, and returned East "to visit the wife's folks." More adventurous ones went West to the mines. In April the monotonous prospect was broken by the first Pony Express to California — a hazardous mail service started from St. Joseph by the giant firm of Russell, Majors and Waddell. Mr. Majors and other prominent individuals spoke at the celebration to "see off" the first elaborately dressed rider. Mayor M. Jeff Thompson placed a specially prepared mailbag on a prancing race mare, and she cantered to the ferry amid appreciative applause. On the boat, crossing the Missouri, the jockey changed to workday clothes for the ride ahead.

Mayor Thompson was a lank and colorful Virginian with Yankee mechanical ingenuity and a love of deadly weapons, which indicated that in case of civil war he might side with the picturesque Southern blades. Certainly he would be more at home with Missouri Robin Hoods in their imaginary Sherwood Forest than with the transplanted Germans in south St. Louis who had become a power, in state politics, on the abolition or Kansas side of the national controversy.

The Pony Express and complaints about the depression tinged Western discussions of the presidential election of 1860. Hot, dry weather burned crops, adding to the enforced idleness and dissatisfaction. Several groups of unemployed Kansans tried to support themselves by appeals to New England philanthropists for guns and supplies to fight slaveholders — a standard routine which had been much too successful in past years. James Montgomery resorted to it again, asking now for money to establish a Republican newspaper.

Across the border, Governor Stewart supplied guns for the Missourians to arm themselves as local militia. Kansans complained that the "pukes" were being armed by the state to invade Kansas, and they called on Montgomery again for protection. Thus Kansas and Missouri prepared for open war. A new man named Jennison had appeared in the free-state ranks. Swivel-eyed, a natty dresser, more a city slicker than a backwoodsman, he was nevertheless trusted by Montgomery. The two leaders organized vigilante companies throughout southeast Kansas and claimed to be the core of the Republican Party there.

The Republican national convention was scheduled to meet in Chicago in May. The Missouri Republicans, a minority residing in the eastern part of the state, favored admitting Kansas into the Union, and hoped to nominate Edward Bates of St. Louis for President. Frank Blair had organized the party in Missouri. He was a stern-faced man, fond of his dry joke. A drooping mustache and long goatee made him look the part of a Southern planter. He had been reared a Democrat. His father, old Frank Blair, had gained wealth and great national influence under Andy Jackson. Father and son knew instinctively all angles of the political game.

St. Louis was considered to be the largest foreign city in the United States. German refugees from the unsuccessful revolutions of 1830 and 1848 had immigrated there by thousands, attracted by the propaganda of Gottfried Duden. Frank Blair had cultivated a friendship with their spokesman, Henry Boernstein, a trained Austrian soldier, university graduate, playwright, and editor of a German newspaper, the powerful *Anzeiger des Westens*. Recent riots against foreigners, led by Ned Buntline for the Know-Nothing Party, had done much to unite the Germans in a solid voting bloc — important both in the election of 1860 and more important in case war followed it.

At the Chicago convention the Missouri delegates found themselves outmaneuvered. Lincoln won the nomination, but they came back to St. Louis with the prospect of two cabinet posts — one for Bates and the other for Blair's brother Montgomery, of Maryland. In case Lincoln was elected — which seemed likely — Kansas would certainly be in a top-drawer position, with the Western men holding the key.

The Democrats split themselves in half by nominating two candidates, squatter sovereign Douglas and unconditional proslavery John C. Breckinridge. All candidates opened headquarters in St. Louis — Douglas in the Berthold mansion at Fifth and Pine streets. Frank Blair, knowing that the Republicans were a minority, organized companies of Wide-Awakes — young ward politicians who attended all meetings in military formation and saw to it that speakers were not interrupted. Many of the Germans, who had been Democrats since coming to America, joined the new party. Rich slaveowners who feared the Republicans as abolitionists and had found no protection for their property in Douglas's middle-of-the-road squatter sovereignty, would probably vote for Breckinridge. But the November ballot amazed all pollsters. Lincoln proved a negative factor, winning but ten per cent of the Missouri vote. He carried only Gasconade County and St. Louis — Boernstein's Germans. In the Border Ruffian areas, his vote was practically nil, except in Kansas City where eighty bold Republicans formed in column of two's under Kersey Coates, the Pennsylvanian who had volunteered as bodyguard for Governor Reeder at the Shawnee Mission. Locking arms, the determined Republicans marched to the polls, demanded Lincoln ballots, and waited to see them deposited in the ballot box instead of the wastebasket.

The only contest in Missouri was between Douglas and Bell — both pro-Union candidates who wanted to evade the slavery issue. Douglas won by the narrowest of margins — one tenth of one per cent. Obviously, the people were Unionists, and in case of war might be expected to fight against secession, but the two United States senators, James Green and Trusten Polk, were both proslavery. David Rice Atchison still maintained that he was out of politics. The new governor and lieutenant governor, Claibourne Jackson and Thomas C. Reynolds, were elected on the Douglas ticket and should oppose secession, but both men were anti-North by inheritance and association.

Much-married Claib Jackson had invaded Kansas with his army of voters, and now he would be the legitimate commander in chief of the Missouri militia. The lieutenant governor, a short, chubby chap of forty with dark eyes and refined features, claimed to have been born and reared in South Carolina, but his enemies said that he was a Jew from Prague. Highly educated in the classics, he read Latin, Greek, and Hebrew, spoke French, German, and Spanish fluently. He had served as ad interim chargé d'affaires in Spain and preferred international to local politics. Yet he owed his present position to his skill in combining the Atchison proslavery forces against Thomas Hart Benton's St. Louis Germans. Moreover, Reynolds had seen enough of the gracious South Carolina atmosphere of black servants and gentlemanly leisure to admire it greatly. Several times he had acquitted himself with distinction on the field of honor. In a crisis, both Jackson and Reynolds might readily deliver Missouri to the Confederacy.

After the election the Southern states began to secede. On the Western border Democratic politicians stirred up resentment with false statements which were believed by partisans. Lincoln was reported to have endorsed John Brown's raid. Boston millionaires were said to be financing Montgomery to hire horse and "nigger" thieves. Montgomery and his city slicker, Jennison, were reported to be operating a ring of "desperate jayhawkers" engaged in regular robbing. Stolen mounts were recognized up in Iowa, and jocular people said that the pedigree of every good horse was "out of Missouri by Jennison." Witnesses claiming to be familiar with this traffic fled to Kansas City with stories about being driven out of the country for knowing too much. As soon as Lincoln was inaugurated, they said, these outlaws would begin butchering all proslavery men. Wasn't ex-preacher Montgomery quoting the Bible, as Brown had done, to justify the killing of slaveholders?

Missourians appealed to their neighbors in Arkansas and to the civilized nations in Indian Territory to join with them in common defense against the freebooters. At Little Rock, newspaperman Albert Pike became eloquent, as only he could, about aggression against Southern rights. Boston-born, Pike had been compelled by poverty to leave Harvard. Rumor said his first job, as a schoolteacher, had been terminated by an indictment for cruelty in beating a student. He had moved West, was now wealthy and respected, with an international literary reputation. Christopher North, editor of *Blackwood's Magazine* in Edinburgh, had commended his style, and Ned Buntline, when enlisting the nation's talent for a Western magazine, had got contributions from his pen. A versatile man, Pike had perfected himself in the law, had recently won a $140,000 suit for the Creek Indians, and therefore had great influence with them. In case of war he might be able to guide the Five Nations on a new kind of warpath into Kansas.

The propaganda, the fears, the threats of invasion and murder received renewed impetus when Judge Williams abandoned his court at Fort Scott and fled to Missouri, complaining that he could not convict a horse or "nigger" thief while Montgomery's men were in the country. In the court's absence both factions administered their own kind of justice, hanging four men — two proslavery and two free-state. All settlers were intimidated by bands of night riders, who claimed to be free-state or proslavery according to the politics of any man who owned a good horse or a cupboard full of victuals.

Governor Samuel Medary, who had succeeded Denver, drove down from Lecompton to investigate in person. Missouri's Governor Stewart, nearing the end of his administration, called out the militia, this time in force. Men went from St. Louis and Jefferson City, wearing state badges on their civilian clothes. They boarded trains and steamboats, off at last on a real campaign to learn the rudiments of war that might be their life for years to come. And all this, three months before Lincoln took office.

On December 10, 1860, as the militia columns converged in southwest Missouri, a party of Kansans raided the plantation of wealthy Morgan Walker, up in the central part of the state, seven miles from Independence. Walker owned two thousand acres of land, a hundred horses and mules, and thirty slaves. Shortly before the raid a stranger warned neighbors — in the absence of the owner — to be on guard, Montgomery was coming. The informer said that he would be a member of the gang but wanted to betray it because Montgomery had killed his brother.

Walker's neighbors stationed themselves with loaded shotguns in a harness room and behind a loom at one end of Walker's porch. Soon after dark the robbers appeared as scheduled. Three leaders, including the informer, walked across the porch and knocked at the door. Invited in, they warmed themselves at the fire and told their errand. They wanted the slaves, horses, and cash. Morgan Walker had just returned from Independence. He asked if the slaves had been consulted. Told that they had, he meekly directed the robbers to their quarters. Two of the men then walked out on the porch. The informer remained, presumably to keep the people in the house under guard. As the two other men stepped off the porch, red flashes spit from behind the loom. Both fell — one dead, the other wounded. The latter called for help. A companion appeared from the dark and dragged him away. No one knew the number of raiders lurking in the gloom or dared venture out to investigate.

The robbers, as frightened as the planters, fled with the wagon they had brought to transport the slaves. The wounded man and his lone companion hid in the nearby woods for a day or two. Hunger added to their mental and physical suffering. A slave, hunting hogs, stumbled upon their camp and was promised his freedom if he would bring them food and horses. He agreed readily enough — yes, sah — and hurried away to report them to his master. The planters came with shotguns and killed them both.

Newspapers cried to heaven about this last "Montgomery outrage," but the true leader turned out to be the informer, a border ne'er-do-well who had once taught school, but recently found bigger profits in dodging back and forth across the state line, stealing a horse or two on each trip. He posed as a free-state man in Kansas and a proslavery man in Missouri. In Lawrence he was known as Charles Hart, a loafer around the ferry, wrestling, drinking, picking up a dollar now and then on a horse or foot race along the sand bars. At the ferry, where everyone stopped, an inconspicuous loafer could easily estimate the value of a traveler's load and see how much money he put back in his jeans after paying the bill. Some unsolved holdups along the road may have been Charles Hart's work. As a gambler he had followed wagon trains to Pikes Peak, playing cards around the campfires. His real name was not Hart but Quantrill, and for the Morgan Walker escapade he had enlisted a party of earnest Quakers — natural abolitionists — who had been deeply influenced by Pardee Butler's abolition sermons. Quantrill's reason for leading these innocents to their deaths remains conjectural. He knew that he could not continue his dual role indefinitely and seems to have sought a spectacular entry into the good graces of the slaveholding planters. Obviously much of the outlawry attributed to Montgomery may have been committed by others, but certainly not all of it.

This was the condition on the Kansas-Missouri border as Lincoln cleared his Springfield office to go to Washington, and Governor Stewart arranged for his successor in Missouri. Frank Blair's brother Montgomery wrote the President-elect an invitation to stay in his Washington home prior to inauguration. These Blairs planned close co-operation with the new administration, and Frank's one great interest was to make Missouri a free state.

Jim Lane also hoped to "lay pipe" to the new Executive Mansion and offered to furnish Lincoln with a bodyguard of frontier Kansans to escort him from Springfield to Washington, Sharps rifles on their shoulders, bowie knives in their belts. Why not! Hadn't the wrongs done Bleeding Kansas been the big issue which elected him?

The picturesque display did not appeal to Lincoln. He preferred to have his little party accompanied by two venerable United States soldiers, Major David Hunter, with mustache dyed like his wig, and Colonel E. V. Sumner, the silver-haired Bull of the Woods, happy now to be done forever with the policing of free-state settlers. Neither would finish the trip with their charge. At Buffalo, New York, Hunter broke his collarbone in the crowd which pressed around the Rail Splitter. At Harrisburg, Pennsylvania, Sumner was left behind. Lincoln's managers had decided that the President-elect must proceed to Washington secretly and thus foil a reported plot for his assassination. Sumner objected. The Bull of the Woods would see his master through. No arguments convinced him otherwise. That evening, after a banquet at the Jones House, Lincoln walked out the front door and down the street with the dutiful old colonel respectfully behind him. Someone tapped Sumner on the shoulder. He turned to see what was wanted and when next he looked ahead, Lincoln was gone. A telegram from Washington in the morning reported the President-elect's safe arrival. But this is ahead of the Kansas-Missouri story.

On December 31, 1860, Claibourne Jackson took the oath of office in Jefferson City, Missouri. Retiring Governor Stewart, in a farewell message, discussed the five years of undeclared war west of the Missouri and deplored the fact that it was growing into a national conflict. Then Claib Jackson delivered his inaugural address before the assembly. A man in his middle fifties, with an extensive experience in state politics and diversified matrimony, he had been elected to lead the state through the approaching thunderheads. The legislature watched his erect and dignified figure, his deeply lined face and long hair. Lieutenant Governor Reynolds, peering through little gold-rim spectacles above his close-cropped beard, showed no sign of superiority or annoyance at the mispronunciations from his less educated chief.

Jackson's message differed only by a shade from his predecessor's, yet that shade was significant. The incoming governor did not suggest secession along with the other states dropping from the Union, but he did recommend "standing by them" — whatever that meant. He also said that the North had already dissolved the Union by nullifying the Fugitive Slave Act, the old cliché which Henry Clay Pate and others had used in 1856. Frankly, Jackson offered a working compromise — the general government must agree to protect slavery as an institution. This, of course, was the core of the Civil War dispute and Jackson, the Douglas Democrat, had now taken the Southern Breckinridge radical side. Douglas had advocated the institution's protection by local laws only.

Jackson's speech was received with prolonged applause, encouraging, surely, to an executive who might lead his state into the Confederacy. He promptly recommended a reorganization of the state militia and an election to a convention to consider secession.

In St. Louis, Frank Blair watched these belligerent enactments and converted his political Wide-Awake boys into military companies with himself colonel of a regiment. Secret drills were held in halls where the sawdust muffled marching feet. From the East wealthy John M. Forbes, the railroad magnate who had helped finance the Hannibal and St. Joe, sent money for the purchase of arms. German gymnastic societies which had assumed semimilitary status in self-defense against Ned Buntline's anti-foreigner riots joined to form another regiment. Boernstein opened his opera house for their meetings and became colonel. A little redhead, Franz Sigel, entered eagerly into the warlike preparations. He taught mathematics and history at the German-American Institute in St. Louis and was reputed to have commanded thirty thousand revolutionists in the recent European uprisings. The Flying Dutchman, as this feverish little man was called, soon rallied another regiment. Being interested in a beer hall, German recruits were reported as saying, "Py tam! . . . Mit Sigel . . . you pays not'ing for your lager" — all aspersions, no doubt, for Sigel did not drink beer. To Americans this diminutive blond in gold spectacles and scraggly beard under which his jaw muscles worked nervously seemed insignificant, but the Germans evidently held him in high esteem.

Southern sympathizers retaliated against these military preparations by organizing minutemen. They established headquarters in the Berthold mansion, Douglas's political headquarters, thus giving the appearance that the Union Democrats were behind him.

On February 6, 1861, a weather-beaten little man in a captain's thread-bare uniform arrived in St. Louis from Fort Riley with his company of bronzed and stolid regulars. Nathaniel Lyon's deep-set blue eyes burned with hatred for Missouri Border Ruffians. His experience in Kansas had turned him from a supporter of Frank Pierce to a fanatic abolitionist. At long last he was to have an opportunity to strike for freedom. The slender, bony, red-bearded officer called at once on Frank Blair, listened to the plans for perfecting a citizens' military organization, offered to inspect the gymnastic companies and make suggestions for drill. Only two days ago the secessionist congress had met in Montgomery to organize a Confeder-acy. Lyon realized that the United States arsenal, on the river in south St. Louis, held sufficient munitions to control the state, should Governor Jack-son get his hands on it. The little captain suggested that its brick walls be fortified against mob attack, but his immediate superior, Major Peter V. Hagner, objected.

Lyon suspected disloyalty but could do nothing except tell Blair, who had neither authority nor influence prior to Lincoln's inauguration. In the meantime, as a practical politician, Blair exerted every effort to help elect pro-Union members to the convention which was to consider secession. He knew that the last election showed a large majority of Missourians to be Douglas Democrats — Unionists with or without slavery — and not Re-publicans. His problem was to win as many as possible from this middle group. Claib Jackson, of course, with all the power of the state government behind him, hoped also to win a majority of these same people. David Rice Atchison, despite earlier declarations, re-entered politics as elder states-man, to help the pro-Southerners.

A spirited campaign between Blair and Jackson followed, but when the ballots were counted, both were disappointed. As in the November elec-tion, a large majority of the constitutional delegates — seventy-one per cent to be exact — came in on the Union ticket, only nineteen per cent for secession. Sterling Price was elected presiding officer. M. Jeff Thompson failed to become secretary — too many strong Union men against him, he complained, as his steamboat chugged back to St. Joe. His irrepressible, beaming countenance still glowed with hope, however, for a second glori-ous revolution like the one in 1776.

On March 4, 1861, Lincoln took the oath of office in Washington, and on the same day a Confederate flag was raised over the Berthold mansion in St. Louis — futile arrogance, for the convention seated in the Mercantile Library Hall voted against secession, although it agreed to reconvene at Jefferson City on July 22, 1861. Until then Missouri seemed safe in the Union, unless Governor Jackson dared precipitate some aggression.

In the meantime, Kansas had entered the Union as a free state. President Buchanan signed the admission bill on January 29, 1861, admitting tardily that the trend he had fought was inevitable.

Jim Lane's ambition had always been to sit in the United States Senate. His chance had come at last! The first legislature would elect the first senators, and Lane hurried back from an Eastern speaking tour to campaign for men who would promise to support him. The Grim Chieftain had associated in one way or another in all the vicarious Kansas governments — the Pawnee legislature, the Big Springs convention, the Topeka Movement, which had elicited his duel challenge to Douglas. His name was the best known in all Kansas, but he had no money for his campaign — a usual condition — and, what was worse, he had many influential enemies. Redpath had once agreed to write a campaign biography of him but was estranged by the Grim Chieftain's attempt to seduce his wife. The Robinson faction also combined against Lane, as did friends of the lamented Gaius Jenkins. On the other hand, Dan Anthony, in Leavenworth, promised to support his candidacy.

Lane financed his campaign by defending petty criminal cases and by borrowing odd sums from acquaintances. He had a cunning way of opening men's purses. One bitter cold day in Lawrence he was stopped on Massachusetts Street by a creditor seeking payment. Lane, shivering in his shabby sealskin coat, made excuses. His little son ran up, barefoot, and stood with one foot pressed for warmth against the calf of the other leg. "Mr. Garvey," Lane said, with a sidelong glance at the urchin, "do you suppose that, if I had two dollars in the world, I would pay you before I bought that boy a pair of shoes?"

Garvey pulled off his glove, reached a shivering hand into his pocket, and handed Lane additional cash. The Grim Chieftain was a genius always!

With twenty borrowed dollars, Lane opened political headquarters in Topeka. Enemies tried to have him evicted for nonpayment of rent. Lane taunted them. He would "move into a store box on the avenue," he said with his tragic voice, "and get ahead of the hounds" — a happy reference. The mob enjoyed allusions to "propertied dogs." Later, when the only paper supporting him in Lawrence threatened to shut up shop unless money could be raised to pay the printers, Lane walked thirty-five miles to Leavenworth, through a blizzard, and aroused Delahay at midnight with a scheme for raising $500 — and got it.

Through all this, Lane blasted viciously at political opponents, accusing them of corruption, and secretly promising lucrative posts to his own supporters. Robinson was a candidate for governor. Lane reminded voters that the Robinson faction had collected "war damages" in newly authorized state bonds, some $97,000 in all, including $24,000 for Robinson personally, and $10,000 for the widow of Gaius Jenkins. In a speech at Leavenworth, Lane sneered:

> I have said that name [Robinson] should not profane my lips or disgrace my pen. I regard him as the Benedict Arnold of his age, and pray God that he may feel the just indignation of an outraged people; but if the resurrection horn should reach the dark abyss of crime into which he has plunged himself, may he not rise with perjury on his lips or Kansas bonds in his pockets.

Aiming next at Stephen A. Douglas, Lane reminded voters that the Little Giant had refused to accept his challenge on account of their difference in station. "You owe it to yourselves and to me," he shouted now, "to put me where I can make him fish up that paper."

Dr. Robinson won the governorship, but Lane counted enough of his men in the legislature to elect him to the Senate. Full of hope but taking no chances, Lane reminded them all of their obligation to him for campaign services. Day and night he strode up and down the streets, buttonholing solons on the way to the assembly hall, in the vestibule, in dining rooms, washrooms, bedrooms, exacting from each a pledge and a repledge of support. Some assemblymen fled to the hazel thickets along the Kaw for privacy. Others crept into haylofts for a night's rest, but Lane found their hiding places.

His persistence paid and in April 1861, James Henry Lane was elected to the United States Senate, boasting later that of the fifty-six legislators who supported him forty-five wore shoulder straps — "Doesn't Jim Lane look out for his friends?" Bankrupt but triumphant, the Grim Chieftain laid aside his calfskin vest and sealskin coat so familiar to Kansas audiences, boarded up the small slab-sided cabin on the bare lot he called home, and borrowing money for a broadcloth suit, set off for Washington. Lincoln had been President for approximately six weeks when the Grim Chieftain arrived with his coterie of fellow politicians and newsmen. War clouds frowned blackly over Virginia. Rebels were reported concentrating to take the Federal arsenal at Harpers Ferry, and also the navy yard at Gosport. Washington seethed with hysterical rumors — the White House to be burned, the President assassinated! Senator Lane sprang heroically into the breach. He organized his followers and other Kansans in Washington into what he called the Frontier Guard. Armed with Sharps rifles and cutlasses, they marched to the Executive Mansion and bivouacked in the East Room, Lane with a brand-new sword given him by Colonel Hunter, who was still suffering from his broken collarbone. At midnight on April 18, 1861, the President and Secretary of War appeared in the door. The guard lined up for review. Dan Anthony, Thomas Ewing, Jr., Samuel Pomeroy, and J. A. Cody stood with others in the ranks. Captain Jim Lane, with a dramatic scowl on his face, stalked before the detachment. If we must have war, let men from the Western border start it here!

X I

Lyon Shows Missouri

AFTER Lincoln's inauguration Captain Lyon's authority increased perceptibly, thanks to grim Frank Blair. An effort to sidetrack the redheaded regular on court-martial duty in Leavenworth was scotched. Then in mid-April news of the firing on Fort Sumter set St. Louis trembling on the verge of madness. Pro-Union and secession factions unmasked. Plots, counterplots, treason, hysteria shook the streets, the levees, and the spring leaves unfolding in the parks. Lincoln called on the states for seventy-five thousand volunteers, and Governor Jackson replied that Missouri would not furnish a single man "to subjugate her sister states of the South." The governor appealed to Missourians to "rise then, and drive out ignominiously the invaders who have dared desecrate the soil which your labors have made fruitful, and which is consecrated by your homes." He immediately ordered a special session of the legislature, and mobilized the militia. Envoys were dispatched to Jeff Davis for artillery to enable the people to capture the St. Louis arsenal.

The German regiments, already partly trained, ignored Jackson's defiance and offered to fill Lincoln's quota. Before a reply was received, the distressing news came downriver that the United States arsenal at Liberty, across from Kansas City, had been taken by a mob. M. Jeff Thompson was organizing a battalion of rebels at St. Joseph. Ex-Senator Green's brother was equipping a regiment north of the Missouri, and a dozen other bands of partisans were drilling.

The only safeguard to Federal authority in Missouri was now the St. Louis arsenal. The department commander, aristocratic General Harney, intimate with the weathy slave owners, seemed as reluctant as Major Hagner had been to fortify it and defend national prestige. Captain Lyon, with no authority to act, consulted Blair. Something must be done. A brilliant West Point lieutenant, John M. Schofield, was in town on leave of absence to teach at Washington University. He knew army drill and paper work. Why not commission him to enlist volunteers? Blair agreed and the young man started working, but General Harney refused to arm the recruits from government stores. Was the department commander plotting treason?

Frank Blair stroked his sandy mustache. Delay would lose the arsenal and, with it, the state. He prepared a telegram explaining the emergency to the War Department. Then, to evade military censorship of the wires, he sent the message from a station across the Mississippi in Illinois, addressed to the governor of Pennsylvania. Shortly thereafter, Harney left for Washington to confer with the authorities. Lyon and Blair were now supreme.

Lyon immediately shipped all excess arms in the arsenal to safety in Illinois, and accepted into United States service the volunteer regiments under Colonels Blair, Boernstein, and Sigel. He urged others to be formed.

On May 2, 1861, the special session of the Missouri legislature convened at Jefferson City. Next day the proslavery militia mustered at Lindell Grove in St. Louis. General D. M. Frost, who had commanded the state troops on the Missouri border last winter, was in charge. He was a West Pointer, having graduated three years after Nathaniel Lyon. Like Lyon, he had ranked near the top of his class, but he had not remained in the service. Instead he had resigned to go into active politics and had served as state senator in Missouri. His sympathies, like Claib Jackson's, were for the South, and he named the militia encampment Camp Jackson. The regimental streets were given the names of prominent Confederates — "Davis Avenue," "Beauregard Street," and so on.

The surplus arms had been shipped from the arsenal, but Lyon feared the state's military display. He called a council with his volunteer officers on May 7, 1861. Carefully closing the door to prevent eavesdropping, Lyon walked nervously up and down the floor. "We must take Camp Jackson," he said, "and we must take it at once." Contradictory orders might come back with Harney any moment now.

Tradition says that Lyon drove next day to the rebel camp, heavily veiled and in a woman's dress, a pistol under a basket of eggs ostensibly for sale — unlikely surely, for Lyon's spies knew all that was necessary about Lindell Grove, and his rough red beard could not be disguised by any veil. The night of May 8, 1861, a ship docked at St. Louis with heavy boxes marked "marble" which turned out to be mortars and siege guns from Jeff Davis. If there had been any question about Frost's intentions, there could be none now. But still he pleaded innocence and sent a messenger to Lyon on the morning of May 10, 1861, asking for an explanation of rumors that his militia were to be attacked by United States troops.

Before reaching the arsenal, the courier met Lyon riding at the head of his brigade toward Camp Jackson. Streets, doorways, windows, housetops were black with people watching the four regiments of pasty-faced volunteers who marched well under their German officers. A battalion of bronzed regulars trudged behind Colonel T. W. Sweeney, grizzled Mexican War veteran with an empty sleeve pinned in the opening of his coat.

The regiments deployed in battle line around Lindell Grove. Then Lyon handed his reply to the courier and watched him canter off among the tents. A crowd of civilians gathered behind Lyon's soldiers, among them William Tecumseh Sherman, who, after dabbling unsuccessfully with the legal profession in his brother-in-law's Leavenworth office, was now president of a street railway in St. Louis. Also in the crowd stood Ulysses S. Grant, mustering officer for the governor of Illinois, on vacation for a few days' rest from his duties in Belleville.

As the crowd waited for a reply from Lyon's note, they heard three cheers among the tents. One-armed Sweeney thought this meant fight, and he ordered his battalion to move their cartridge boxes to the front of their belts. A few minutes later the courier appeared. Lyon took the message and read it. General Frost begged time to consider. Lyon flattened the message on the pommel of his saddle and scribbled a reply. The general must surrender in ten minutes or the Federal troops would open fire.

The courier galloped away and soon returned. "Sweeney," Lyon said, reading the second note, "they surrender."

Rough little Lyon swung to the ground from his horse and was immediately kicked in the stomach by an aide's mount. Writhing on the ground, Lyon ordered the details of the capitulation. Acute pain could not divert the furious intensity of this commander's mind. Colonel Sigel was also *hors de combat.* His horse had slipped and fallen on the paved street, hurting the German's leg. A doctor ran forward with a bandage and Sigel soon joined his regiment in a carriage. The disability of the two commanders caused some delay. Blair formed his regiment in single files on opposite sides of the street. The disarmed prisoners — a thousand of them — marched in between, and the long column started for the arsenal. A mob stood along the sidewalks shouting, "Damn the Dutch" and "Hurray for Jeff Davis." Clods and stones pelted the soldiers. A drunken man tried to push through the file to the captives. A file closer shoved him back, down an embankment. The man turned and fired a pistol, wounding an officer. Boernstein ordered his men to return the fire. Redcoats had done the same in Boston Common and a Revolution followed!

Disturbances occurred at other places on the line of march with sporadic shooting. Sherman admitted, in his memoirs, running for his life to escape flying bullets. In all, twenty-eight people were killed, one a babe in arms, and many more were wounded. Fifteen were shot down in one place. The column passed along Olive Street amid the banging of shutters. At the arsenal the prisoners were packed into cramped quarters for the night, but assured that they would be properly paroled in the morning.

Through the midnight streets a roaring mob shouted, "To the *Democrat* office" (the Republican paper) and "Down with the *Anzeiger des Westens*" — a cry the antiforeign American Party under Ned Buntline had used against these same Germans in 1852. The mayor ordered all saloons closed. Ex-Governor Sterling Price addressed a crowd in front of the Planters House, vehemently arraigning the "military despotism." In the morning he boarded a train for Jefferson City, where he found the legislature in a furor of excitement.

Sitting in special session, they had been notified about the capture of Camp Jackson. Wildly indignant, they passed a special military bill, gave the governor dictatorial power, appropriated ten thousand dollars to encourage Indians in the territory to retaliate against Kansans. One million dollars was authorized to be borrowed from banks and another million to be raised by bonds for a state army. Truculent members returned from recesses with guns and bowie knives, leaning them against their desks and along the assembly chamber walls. Rumors said that Blair was bringing his Germans up the river to take the capitol. In near panic Governor Jackson commissioned Sterling Price a major general to organize the militia and defend the state government.

Other towns were agog with excitement. At St. Joseph, M. Jeff Thompson's long legs leaped into action. He commandeered a train of wagons to haul all the powder and lead in town back into the country, lest soldiers from Leavenworth come to confiscate it. He dispatched a half dozen Paul Reveres across the rolling hills, summoning patriots from their farms and shops to bring rifles, shotguns, and pistols. Men came on foot and on horseback, but once at the rendezvous there was no enemy to fight and no quartermaster to feed them. Jeff Thompson could get no authority from the governor to purchase supplies, and the hungry patriots trudged home disgusted. Thompson boarded a steamboat for Jefferson City.

At the capital he found panic, confusion, no leadership. He asked for an interview with the governor and was escorted into the Executive Office. Jeff Thompson was habitually a smiling man, but today he looked grimly down at the governor's deeply lined, smooth-shaven face, the silky hair curling over his ears. Jeff explained the emergency in St. Joe, stating that he could cope with it if given help. Claib Jackson replied affably but seemed undecided what to do. Thompson lost patience. "Governor," he said, "before I leave, I wish to tell you the two qualities of a soldier; one he must have, but he needs both: one of them is Common Sense and the other is Courage — and By God! You have NEITHER."

Jeff Thompson executed an about-face and marched out. He would go south and offer his services where his ability was recognized and come back triumphantly to save his Missouri.

General Harney arrived in St. Louis the day after the capture of Camp Jackson. He was much upset by his subordinate's aggressive action during his absence. The wealthy friends of his socially prominent wife suggested that the situation might be partially alleviated by ordering the German regiments out of the city. American-born citizens, he was told, resented being ruled by foreigners. Hundreds of young men from the best families were riding south to join the Confederacy or west to join Jackson and Price, hoping that one army or the other would expel "the Dutch."

Blair disapproved of any appeasement, and he feared that the advantage he and Lyon had gained for the Federal government might be lost. He hurried a delegation to Washington to explain his side of the situation to Lincoln. Harney's conservative friends sent another delegation to explain their position. The harassed President, with frantic men pounding hourly on his office door, would have to decide what to do in Missouri. He wanted peace and he wanted to hold Missouri in the Union. The Blairs knew the situation and ranked high in the administration.

Both parties returned without a decision, but on May 20, 1861, a messenger rang Blair's doorbell in St. Louis and delivered a communication from Lincoln. Blair broke the seals and read the letter. It included an order relieving Harney of the command of the Department of the West and a commission for Lyon as brigadier general. The President asked Blair to keep the papers in confidence and use them at his discretion.

Next day, May 21, 1861, General Harney announced that he had concluded a truce with Governor Jackson — the Federal government making a treaty with a sovereign state! By this agreement the governor promised not to invoke the state's military act, and Harney agreed to recognize Missouri's neutrality and use his army to enforce state laws. Blair's next action will always be open to argument. Some have maintained that the truce and due recognition of the state's neutrality would have kept Missouri in the Union and prevented the next four years of guerrilla warfare. Blair himself considered the election of Lincoln a popular repudiation of state rights. To his mind the time had come to assert the dominance of the central government — especially since his party sat in the driver's seat. On May 30, 1861, as Harney began moving the German regiments out of St. Louis, Blair sent him Lincoln's order of removal from command.

Governor Jackson saw the shadow of the Federal whip and knew that he would be eclipsed unless he could outwit the new commander. He asked for a conference at once. Brigadier General Lyon set the time and the place: June 11, 1861, at the Planters House in St. Louis. Governor Jackson came with his secretary, Thomas Snead, and his major general, Sterling Price. Frank Blair attended the council to explain his party's position. The men sat down and Blair monopolized the conversation, his tired, whining, falsetto voice repeating every plank in the Republican Party platform. Jackson and Price both presented their pleas for neutrality, promising peace and loyalty if Missouri would be allowed state sovereignty. Lyon, who had been a Democrat until Frank Pierce truckled to the slave power, fidgeted in his seat. A soldier versed in science and philosophy, he had continually made his messmates uncomfortable with his outspoken opinions. As the conference dragged on hour after hour, he became tense and nervous. Finally he could stand it no longer. Now, if ever, was the time to snap state rights across his knee. The little redhead leaned back in his chair, and his Connecticut voice struck like the gong of a grandfather's clock, calm, timeless, and cold as death.

"Rather than concede to the State of Missouri," he boomed, "for one single instant the right to dictate to my Government in any manner however unimportant, I will see you" — he rose from his chair, spurs clinking, and pointed his freckled finger at Governor Jackson's breast — "and you" — he touched the bosom of General Price — "and you" — he prodded solemn Blair — "and you" — he poked Secretary Snead, who had been watching him as an enemy and now thrilled at the man's pluck — "and every man, woman, and child in the State, dead and buried." Lyon turned formally to the governor. "This means war," he said, taking out his watch with a sunburned hand. "In an hour one of my officers will call for you and conduct you through my lines." The shaggy little commander turned on his small heels and marched down the hall. Snead listened with rapture until the clank of Lyon's saber became inaudible. What a soldier! Snead wished that the grim little man might be on the Southern side in the war ahead.

Jackson, Price and Snead returned to Jefferson City, stopping only to "wood" the locomotive, cut telegraph wires, and burn bridges behind them. There was no doubt in their minds now about Lyon's intention to attack the capital. They arrived at two o'clock on the morning of June 12, 1861, explained the emergency to House and Senate leaders and set clerks to packing state documents for a retreat. The governor locked his office door against intruders and, with Snead, toiled on a proclamation to be printed and distributed by daylight — a call for fifty thousand volunteers.

In St. Louis, Lyon worked with his usual single-track intensity. First he wired Washington for authority to enlist more men, then he commandeered railroad cars and steamboats. He purchased the finest horse he could buy — a gray stallion imported from Britain — but ordered no general's uniform for himself.

Lyon's plan of campaign was simple. One brigade of his army would move south by train to Rolla and march west to prevent Jackson from retreating to Arkansas. The main army would move up the Missouri in steamboats and take Jefferson City. It was this second part of the plan which soon involved River Pilot Samuel Langhorne Clemens in the Civil War.

Young Clemens had come to St. Louis to renew his pilot's license. Waiting in line before the clerk's desk, he noticed a pilot, named Absalom Grimes, arguing heatedly with the German in charge. The foreign official insisted on an oath of allegiance from all pilots. "I don't object to no oath," Absalom was saying, "my father and grandfather were Americans, but I'll be damned if I take the oath from a Dutchman who can hardly talk English." Grimes stormed out of the office.

Sam Clemens and another pilot followed him. The three young men boarded a steamboat for Hannibal, Missouri, and on the wharf there a few days later a lieutenant and squad of soldiers took them into custody and returned them to St. Louis. The commanding officer of the district informed them that General Lyon wanted pilots to move troopships up the river. The three men complained that they were Mississippi, not Missouri, River pilots.

"You could follow another boat up the Missouri River if she had a Missouri pilot on her, could you not?" the officer asked.

The men admitted that they could. Then, before more was said, two stylishly dressed ladies appeared at the door and requested to speak with the commander. The officer asked to be excused and stepped out to see them. The pilots looked at one another for a moment. Nodding with mutual agreement, they picked up their carpetbags and walked out the side door. Down on the levee they boarded a boat for Hannibal. Home once more, they strode promptly into the country to join a regiment of Ralls County Rangers, which they heard was organizing to defend their homes from the Dutch. At the encampment they were surprised to find only eight men in the regiment, each armed with a squirrel rifle, shotgun, or corn knife. Farmers fed them well, however, and lodged them in haylofts. The pilots allowed their beautiful locks to be snipped off with sheepshears — mustn't give the enemy any advantage at close quarters, they were told. More boys soon joined their organization, and as they waited, loafing and playing, they learned that counties all the way across the state had similar "regiments." Next to them the Salt River Tigers were assembling.

Army life agreed with these youngsters. Every man furnished his own mount. Clemens rode a little yellow mule with long ears and a roached tail which she carried straight out behind — "Paint Brush" the boys called her. Sam cut a grand military figure on her back with a carpetbag, frying pan, umbrella, and long squirrel rifle. Testy General Lyon and his two columns, one entraining for the southwest and the other going up the river to the capital, seemed far away. Distant campaigns did not disturb the rangers, but one day they learned that a third column, under Colonel U. S. Grant (assigned to active duty now), was marching into northeast Missouri to disperse them.

Watching for the enemy, Sam Clemens, Ab Grimes, and another boy were posted as sentries where the lane from their cantonment barn joined the main road. At night they took turns, one standing guard, the other two sleeping fifty yards in the rear with the horses. During Ab Grimes's tour of duty he spied, in the moonlight, a rank of Federal soldiers coming over the ridge and down across the field opposite him. Ab fled to his comrades and aroused them. The three agreed to let Sam remain and hold the horses while the other two returned to count and resist the enemy. Back on the road again, they saw the soldiers, plain enough, heads swinging in unison as they marched down the hill. Both sentries raised their guns, fired, then turned and ran. When they arrived at the spot where they had left Sam Clemens, he was gone, taking the horses. The two men raced up the lane after him. Paint Brush was slow and they soon overtook her, mounted their own horses, swore at Sam for deserting his comrades, and galloped on to camp, deaf to his imprecations not to leave him behind.

The aroused rangers mustered before the barn, guns and knives in hand to repel the invader. Soon a rattle of stones could be heard along the road and every man raised his weapon to defend his native land. Then someone shouted, "Don't shoot," and Private Clemens bobbed out of the darkness on his jigging mule. By daylight no enemy had appeared, so a squad ventured down the lane to investigate. Ab stood at the place where he had fired the opening shot and, to his amazement, noticed that mullen stalks waving in the pasture across the road must have looked like marching soldiers in the dark.

The next affray in this prelude to the war on the border was more serious. Sam Clemens suffered a wound. The "regiment" had bivouacked in a hayloft and someone's pipe set the hay aflame. Sam Clemens jumped from the loft, spraining his ankle. This was not serious, but one of his comrades at arms forked the burning hay out the window. A blazing flake fell like a blanket on Sam Clemens as he crawled away on all fours.

This hot engagement convinced Sam that he was unsuited for a military career. He dropped from the muster rolls, hiding for a few days at a plantation where a little Negro boy served as sentry down the lane on the "big road." Several times each day the little fellow raced to the house gasping breathlessly, "Miss Mary! The Yanks is comin'!" Sam would hobble into hiding and wait until he heard the reassuring treble, "Marse Sam, de Yanks is done gone!"

Such adventures failed to hold Sam Clemens. As soon as his ankle recovered, he joined his brother in Hannibal who had just been appointed territorial secretary of Nevada. The two young men set off, roughing it together on an overland stage trip to Carson City. In a lifetime of literary work as "Mark Twain," Clemens wrote little about his military service, and that little was most confusing. Absalom Grimes also dropped from the Ralls County Rangers. Craving excitement closer to the front, he determined to take an active, although subversive, part in the battles sure now to be fought on the Western border.

XII

Jefferson City, Boonville, and the
Happy Land of Canaan

Lyon sent his column into the southwest under Captain Thomas W. Sweeney, regular army man. Then, with competent young John M. Schofield as adjutant, he embarked with the main army on steamboats for Jefferson City. The latter force consisted of two regiments of St. Louis Germans recently organized as gymnastic societies and Wide-Awake political clubs. Many of them had been revolutionary soldiers abroad, and they had recently taken active part in capturing the Missouri militia and saving the arsenal. Naturalized citizens of the United States, they believed in democracy, resented the riots against them by native Americans, and intended to fight for their rights in the country of their adoption. One of these regiments was commanded by Frank Blair and the other by Henry Boernstein.

In addition to these volunteers, Lyon had his own company of the Second Infantry veterans from Fort Riley. He also had two companies of recruits for the regular army — green, incorrigible boys — and a battery from the Second Artillery commanded by Captain James Totten, a classmate at West Point with whom Lyon had little in common except military training. Totten's one recreation, after his men were dismissed, was to play poker with friends over a bottle of brandy. Lyon, when the day's work was over, sought solitude with a book or tract.

The transports steamed away from the St. Louis levee on the afternoon of June 13, 1861, entered the Missouri at dusk, and moored for the night. Two days later they arrived at Jefferson City, a town of twenty-seven hundred. The capitol stood empty on the hill. Governor, legislature, and archives had disappeared. The June weather was stifling hot and the volunteers bivouacked in the cool assembly chambers, stacking arms along the corridors. Travelers, floating downriver in a skiff, reported the "government" to be fortifying for a siege at Boonville, fifty miles upstream.

Lyon ordered Boernstein to select three companies of his regiment for police duty in the city. With the remaining forces — seventeen hundred — Lyon re-embarked on three steamboats and puffed away in the night. Four miles below Boonville the vessels anchored on June 17, 1861, near the south bank, at the foot of an island where they could not be shelled from the bluffs. The river bottom was a mile and a half wide. In the meadows the soldiers formed column and marched toward town.

Close to Boonville the river bottom narrowed, and the road wound out across a low ridge. Near the summit a lane, leading to the river, crossed the road at right angles. A brick house stood at the intersection. In it and behind the fence along the lane, Claib Jackson decided to make his stand. Major General Price was bringing up the troops when news arrived stating that the rebel militia mustering at Lexington would not be able to join in the defense as it was being threatened by a force of volunteers from Kansas. Sterling Price, prostrated by this dismaying news and a sudden attack of dysentery, turned his command to Colonel John Sappington Marmaduke, and left by boat for his home in Chariton County.

Marmaduke was a nephew of Claib Jackson's. The Marmadukes and Sappingtons formed a political dynasty. John's father had been governor of Missouri. The German immigration and the throbbing population in Kansas had upset the equilibrium of those old families. Young Marmaduke had received the appointment to West Point to which his birth entitled him. Now twenty-eight years old, he had served through the Utah Expedition with Albert Sidney Johnston in 1857 and resigned shortly thereafter. Marmaduke looked the beau ideal his name connoted. A handsome six-footer with small hands and feet, he sat his horse with consummate grace. His eyes were kindly and intelligent, his mustache and beard soft. Fine hair was brushed smoothly down on his head and flared in a glorious ruffle around the back of his coat collar. Unmarried, he was the "catch" of the river towns. A peculiar squint in his eyes was due to nearsightedness.

Marmaduke urged Claib Jackson not to pit untrained soldiers against

Lyon's regulars, but the governor insisted. With great misgivings the young commander deployed along the lane at right angles to the advancing column. Lyon spied the thin line of men waiting for his column and deployed his troops parallel to them. From the brick house at the corners, sharpshooters opened fire. Totten, methodical as though at drill, unlimbered his artillery and placed shot after shot through the brick walls. The entire Missouri line gaped at this marksmanship, sensed their own inadequacy, clambered over the fence behind them, and scampered back across the soft fields of waving wheat.

Officers swore, threatened, cried "shame." The men, soon winded by the uphill run, stopped on the crest. Feeling the confidence of green soldiers on a hilltop, they re-formed into a firing line. Marmaduke knew the danger of standing outlined against the sky and ordered the line forward twenty steps. Here the Missourians stopped and opened fire. In the fields below them Blair's St. Louis volunteers and the regulars came forward with mechanical precision, puffs of white smoke blooming in the fields like cotton bolls. The Missouri volunteers felt helpless before the indomitable advance and melted away. Within twenty minutes the action was over. Governor Jackson and his cabinet, on horseback, watched the men stream back to their tents. Here another feeble stand was made, until a howitzer on a steamboat enfiladed the encampment, scattering the defenders. Lyon's men swept in and ate the rebels' breakfasts.

Vast supplies of shoes, blankets, coats, and carpetbags were captured and with them two Confederate flags. State neutrality indeed! There was no question about the allegiance of these troops. Newspaper correspondents appropriated twenty saddle horses, laughingly saying that none of the animals was large enough to carry giant Thomas Knox of the *New York Herald*.

The Missourians made a last stand at the fairgrounds. Then the Union column entered Boonville. The district judge, with a small party of leading citizens, stood in the street with a flag of truce. Lyon and Blair assured them that noncombatants would be respected. With this guarantee the delegation retired, and the soldiers marched smartly down the main street. Many American flags waved at them from the windows.

Governor Jackson and his government had evidently fled south where the Union Army could not pursue in steamboats. With furious concentration Lyon set quartermasters to work assembling wagons for an overland campaign. He also established a patrol of police boats between Kansas City and St. Louis to prevent independent companies like the Ralls County Rangers and the Salt River Tigers from ferrying south to reinforce Jackson. Already Sweeney should have his division in southwest Missouri prepared to stop Jackson from escaping to the Confederate Army in Arkansas. Lyon had also wired Major Samuel Sturgis at Fort Leavenworth to march southeast into Missouri. Thus Jackson would be pinched from three sides and surrounded.

Sturgis started with a battalion of trained, Indian-fighting cavalry, four cannon, and two regiments of Kansas volunteers totaling twenty-two hundred men. In addition a regiment of Iowa volunteers was coming across Missouri from the Mississippi by rail to join Lyon at Boonville for the march south. Everything indicated that Jackson would be crushed quickly and the civil war terminated on the border.

Then, three days after the occupation of Boonville, Lyon was informed that Missouri had been incorporated in the Department of Ohio, with George Brinton McClellan, an ex-railroad executive, in command. This meant that the campaign against Jackson might become a side show to the big Midwestern performance, and all Lyon's constructive achievements would be wiped out. Lyon went at once to lay his troubles before the politically powerful Colonel Blair. The two men sat down together on the Missouri River bank. Lyon, careless in dress always, wore a utilitarian linen duster over his striped military trousers. Blair, in civilian frock coat, had only a military cap to show his rank. They talked for an hour. Finally Blair decided to give up his commission and the opportunity for active service, go at once to Washington where his brother was Lincoln's Postmaster General, and see what could be done to save Missouri.

As Lyon and Blair talked, the Iowa regiment was ferried across from the north shore. Quartermasters assigned it a camping place, and the volunteers eyed the regulars curiously. Regulation uniforms — blue coats over blue-gray pantaloons — appeared efficient but not so elegant as the Iowa boys' fancy costumes. These small-town volunteers found the regular soldiers uncongenial, mere mercenaries who might have marched with Caesar or Zenophon and had learned nothing since. The bustle of the great encampment, a city of tents, parks of wagons, picket lines of mules, fascinated the newcomers. As they explored the teeming levee, a steamboat swept around the upriver bend and backed to the mooring. She was loaded with buffalo hides and mountain men whose long greasy hair coiled on the shoulders of buckskin shirts. These wild fellows bounded ashore and stalked through the encampment. They had not known that the nation was at war.

Through the encampment also hobbled veterans of the War of 1812, to chuckle with toothless grins about their own battle experiences, how they had outwitted officers and evaded onerous duties. The Iowa boys laughed at their stories and matched them with better ones of their own. They, too, considered military regulations outrageous and drill a waste of time. Company E had picked up a Negro cook who tagged along without formal papers. This was against regulations but what of it. Mason Johnson was his name, and to distinguish him from the noncoms, the boys called him "Corpular Mace." Mace admitted being an escaped slave and also a veteran of the Mexican War, where he had served as body servant to Henry Clay's son, who was killed at Buena Vista. Old Mace said with a grin that "young massa's" body had been shipped home pickled in a barrel of whiskey. Thirsty sailors drank off the liquor three times, and the captain had to refill. Ol' Mace rubbed his woolly pate when he remembered how the rascals had tried to make him believe young Massa Clay drunk the whiskey his own self — yes, sah — and came outen the barrel nights hunting for mo.

The volunteers didn't sleep well at first in their new surroundings. At midnight the mules all began to bray. Corporal Churubusco — he had another name but the boys preferred this — said that in the Mexican War men kept the mules quiet by tying down their tails with sacks of rocks. Private Jacob Grimes of the First Iowa tried this experiment and found himself in the guardhouse before morning. Regular army officers didn't seem to appreciate Iowa humor, and Lyon himself was reported to be "a terror for cats." When word came down the line, "Daddy is coming," soldiers would be quiet as death. If a fellow didn't stand at attention, Lyon might dismount and kick him. Private Eugene Ware of Company E noted Lyon as an eccentric man, an educated crank, a man who knew absolutely what he knew. His reddish, scraggly beard looked unkempt and unattractive. Something about his eyes made Ware think that they did not match. Military punishments irked all the volunteers. The sight of the crumpled figure of a man bucked and gagged on the parade ground made a few of them want to fight somebody closer than the Confederates. The Iowans did not like to admit it, but they knew this was the army.

Everybody was excited on July 3, 1861, when the column started south after Claib Jackson. Would Sweeney be able to hold the refugees until the column arrived? Small boys trudged beside the soldiers with sticks and wooden swords. Their hats were marked *US* or *SC,* and they waged mimic battles as they ran. Pretty girls on sidesaddles galloped along, making their horses prance. At the van marched the First Missouri, Frank Blair's regiment, without its popular leader. Private Heustis of the Iowa volunteers called him the "bejesus colonel" and wished that the Iowans might have such a commander.

Behind the First Missouri strode the Second, which had been ordered up from Jefferson City. Colonel Henry Boernstein sat his horse like a soldier, hummed opera tunes like the impresario that he was, and read dispatches through little hexagonal spectacles. His battalion commander, Major Peter J. Osterhaus, trumpeted commands in mixed German and English through a bristling beard and mustache which protruded from his face like a megaphone.

Following the Germans came the Iowa boys, each company in a different uniform, some in military tunics, some in frock coats, Company E in outlandish hunting shirts of fuzzy, azure-gray cloth made by the girls back home. To ornament them, fair hands had stitched on the front of each bosom a broad band of venetian red, which Private Ware believed would make an excellent target. Black hats with brilliant red ribbon cockades — now faded or missing — completed the costume.

Behind the First Iowa rumbled Totten's battery, with postillions riding the six-horse limbers, one with all roan horses as alike as peas in a pod. Totten carried brandy in a wooden canteen and took a nip before drawling impersonal commands in a Virginia accent which delighted the Iowans: "Forward that caisson, God damn you, sir," or, "Swing that piece in line, God damn you, sir." Bottle-nosed Totten, they called him.

Behind the artillery marched Company B, Second United States Infantry, Lyon's hard-bitten company of plains veterans, and behind them the two hundred recruits for the regular army — tough, incorrigible youths, many foreign, selected for physical stamina regardless of mentality, already whipped into bestial automatons. Another company of regulars brought up the rear. In all, Lyon had twenty-three hundred and fifty men, of whom two hundred and fifty were trained soldiers.

The roads had become quagmires after unusual summer rains. Price and Jackson were two weeks in advance now, and if they crossed the Osage River before it flooded from the continual downpour, their lead would become greater. Sweeney's brigade might be too small to hold them. Always worrying, Lyon pushed his men through the mud with threats of the lash — suitable language for regulars, perhaps, but insulting to the Iowa boys, who gritted their teeth and decided to show the regulars, and Lyon too, how to march. When their turn came to head the column, they promptly marched away from the entire army until General Lyon sent a horseman to stop them. Next day the general put them behind the Second Infantry — his old company. Undaunted, the Iowans trod on the regulars' heels, punched into the rear at every halt, singing exultantly their favorite song, "The Happy Land of Canaan."

This melody was popular with the First Iowa, who had adopted it one night when Private Ware had been jailed in a railway warehouse for talking back to an officer. Among the stored baggage, Ware discovered kegs of Golden Grape Cognac and blackberry brandy. He sent word to his squad that a handy man with a brace and bit under the floor might find refreshments for the regiment. Before long he heard someone boring under the barrels. Then as the medium circulated through the encampment, company after company broke into song. Soon Private Ware had many companions in the guardhouse. One prisoner, French Jo, began to sing "The Happy Land of Canaan." Fellow prisoners made the guardhouse ring with the chorus. Before morning the whole regiment learned both words and music. They had sung them with relish ever since.

Lyon disliked seeing his company abused by volunteers. He had his own method of solving such disciplinary problems and decided to sweat the volunteers into submission. He halted the entire column, ordered the regulars to unsling their knapsacks, stack them by the roadside for the baggage wagons, and then march on. Let the First Iowa, carrying their packs, stifle in the dust. The Iowa boys discovered this trick when they marched past the pyramids of duffel, and they cheered derisively. The temperature registered over a hundred, but they strode along determined to prove their mettle and tread on the regulars' heels at any cost — and they did so, singing at the top of their voices about the Happy Land of Canaan.

At Grand River, a branch of the Osage, Lyon's army met the column from Leavenworth. Major S. D. Sturgis and his adjutant, rough, outspoken Gordon Granger, sat their horses watching the new men with professionals' appraising eyes. What kind of fodder were these volunteers? The volunteers, in turn, looked at Sturgis, a reputed veteran of plains Indian fighting, and saw that he was a man of medium height with black hair curled tight to his head and a bristly black beard. He had handsome features, eyes piercing but genial, and a firm mouth. Sturgis had been stationed in Arkansas when the secession cyclone struck. All his officers resigned — among them James McIntosh, who was now second in command of the Confederates in Arkansas. With resourcefulness which gained him a promotion, Sturgis extracted the enlisted men and most of the government property from a threatening cloud of secessionist militiamen. The Iowa boys respected him for this, but no officer's frailties are hidden from the thousands of eyes constantly on watch. The rank and file divined almost at once that the major leaned constantly on Granger for technical advice. The two men had known each other since West Point days and Granger — lower in rank — was the older of the two.

That night of July 7, 1861, the two columns encamped together. The Iowans evaded their guard to visit the newcomers. They found the regulars cut to the familiar pattern, but the two Kansas regiments were altogether different. Here were men from the tall-grass prairies with "issue" blue coats over civilian shirts and trousers. Unmilitary men, often in trouble for robbing henroosts, yet grim in their hatred of the slave power they had been fighting since 1854. They had seen their meetings spied upon. They had been stopped at night by patrols seeking fugitives. They had had their elections packed and their statute books defaced with laws abridging freedom of speech and the press. They were determined to crush the last vestige of a system which depended on such tactics for survival.

Colonel of the First Kansas was George Washington Deitzler, from Illinois and California, the crusading abolitionist who had negotiated under Robinson for Sharps rifles to let the Kansans defend themselves. He had served as aide-de-camp in the Wakarusa War, as senator in the Topeka government, had languished four months as a prisoner in Lecompton, and was later elected mayor of Lawrence. He had organized the First Kansas and intended to see them give a good account of themselves. One of his captains was Samuel J. Crawford, originally from Indiana, recently a member of the Kansas legislature until he resigned to accept this commission. He was a fluent speaker and writer, prone to criticize his superiors and praise his inferiors — good politics surely — yet Crawford was a man of action, too. Also in Deitzler's regiment rode Captain Samuel Walker, the Ohioan whose "hip-disease" had not kept him out of Lane's Army of the North, the fight at Fort Saunders, or the siege of Lecompton. He had been scarred for life by buckshot at Fort Titus and looked forward to settling old scores and gaining further military advancement.

The Second Kansas was commanded by Colonel Robert B. Mitchell, who had brought law books and hollyhock seeds from Ohio to a homestead in Linn County, Kansas. He had dared oppose both Lane and Montgomery in politics and had been elected to the legislature in a contest with Charles Hambleton of Marais des Cygnes notoriety. One of the captains in his regiment was Samuel N. Wood, who had been prominent in Kansas fracases since the rescue of Branson. In the ranks stood Charlie Lenhardt, onetime printer on the Lawrence *Herald of Freedom,* the same who had splashed Sheriff Jones by shooting into the water barrel. Charlie had seen his employers' printing press destroyed. He had fought with the partisans at Hickory Point, and with Sam Walker at Lecompton. Like so many of his fellow Kansans he was a veteran long before the Civil War became national. These men remembered Claib Jackson when he was an ex-legislator leading his Missouri constituents into Lawrence to vote. They wanted to "ketch" him. For them this was a grudge fight.

Twenty-five miles farther down the road from camp at Grand River the combined column halted before the swollen currents of the Osage. Jackson had crossed before the river rose, but he might be caught yet. The men set to work chopping trees, sawing planks for ferryboats. Couriers rode in from the south with a report that one of Sweeney's regiments commanded by Franz Sigel had checked the Missouri governor's army eighty miles below. Could Lyon's men get there in time to help? Lyon also learned that Blair had interceded with Lincoln in his behalf, and a new department had been created for Missouri with John Charles Frémont, the Pathfinder and presidential aspirant of 1856, in command. At last Lyon's furious energy might accomplish great things in the West. To rush aid to Sigel, he ordered all men to discard nonessentials. Let each company start as soon as it had crossed the river. Hold Claib Jackson and end the war on the border. If he escaped and joined the Confederate Mc-Culloch in Arkansas, the two might come back together, defeat Lyon's entire army, and retake the state.

The Iowans tightened their belts, discarded their tents, mess kits, and extra clothes. Private Ware said they even discarded their pocket Bibles and kept only a few decks of playing cards. Away they went, tunics, frock coats, hunting shirts flapping. "What marching legs!" "Lord God, see them go!" Lyon pulled his beard until his teeth showed and exclaimed, "[Watch] the damned Iowa greyhounds and their Happy Land of Canaan." This was as near a smile as any of the men ever saw on the general's bushy face.

And they did go, surely enough, marching forty-eight miles in twenty-four hours. Men kept on their shoes for three days. Private Bill Heustis quipped to his marching fellows: "I wish I had stayed at home and sent my big brother." Shoe soles split, uniforms wore out, hats blew away, the bottoms of trousers grew beards, and a new song verse burgeoned and spread along the marching line:

> The time of retribution am a-coming,
>   For with bayonet and shell
> We will give the rebels hell;
>   And they'll never see the Happy Land of Canaan.

XIII

Battle of Carthage

THE SECOND BRIGADE, which Lyon sent southwest to cut off Jackson's retreat, consisted of five regiments on paper. Two of them were St. Louis German gymnastic societies, uniformed in gray. Colonel Charles E. Salomon commanded one and "Professor" Franz Sigel the other. American volunteers made fun of Sigel, called him "the little red fellow in spectacles," scoffed that he "kept looking around like a weasel" to see if others were listening when he talked. The expedition was commanded by Captain Thomas W. Sweeney, newly commissioned brigadier general of volunteers. Sweeney had emigrated from Ireland to fight in the Mexican War, lost an arm at Churubusco, but remained in the service. Although Sweeney was a regular army man, West Pointers looked on him with condescension, because he had risen from the ranks. He had quarreled bitterly with Major Samuel P. Heintzelman, when the two were stationed out at Fort Yuma in Arizona. Now Heintzelman was a brigadier general of volunteers in Virginia. Sweeney lacked the West Pointers' hauteur toward enlisted men. He even joked familiarly with them in his Irish brogue. Volunteers loved him for this and because he pinned his empty sleeve on his brass-buttoned breast in the Napoleonic fashion approved for military photographs, then, with his stub, twitched the sleeve comically.

In addition to Sweeney's assignment to cut off Jackson's retreat, he was to hold the southwest Missouri lead mines, occupy the country, and discourage an incursion from Arkansas of the Confederates reported to be under colorfully dressed General Benjamin McCulloch, ex-Texas ranger famous for storming the Obispado in the Mexican War. McCulloch's second in command was James McIntosh, United States officer who had resigned to fight for the Confederacy.

Sweeney's brigade detrained at Rolla, end of the railroad, on June 14, 1861. A handsome courthouse and hillbilly shacks scattered through endless oak brush made Rolla a town of contrasts. To Northern city soldiers the natives appeared lackadaisical, long, and limber. Many were barefooted. Two Confederate flags had been left flying by a local company of home guards who had fled as the troop train steamed into town. Sweeney's men hauled down the flags and started at once to Springfield, a hundred and twenty-five miles west on the wire road. The "wire" referred to the telegraph line from St. Louis to Fort Smith, terminus of the overland stage to California.

Springfield was a hamlet of only three thousand inhabitants but important as the center of a rich farming area. In the public square loose hogs stropped their razor backs on the Doric columns of the new courthouse. The surrounding streets were lined by two-story buildings containing a bank, two newspaper offices, various stores and taverns, some with wooden awnings covering the sidewalk out to a hitch rack. Side streets led to shake-roofed cottages in garden plots separated by worm fences.

Sweeney established headquarters at Springfield and ordered Sigel and Salomon to reconnoiter to the southwest through Mount Vernon, Sarcoxie, and Neosho. Probing to the Arkansas line, Sigel learned about Lyon's battle at Boonville. He was told that the fugitive government and its volunteer army were fleeing south in his direction. Sterling Price, who had recovered miraculously from his dysentery, had already passed through, seeking aid from McCulloch, and was now encamped on Cowskin Prairie near the junction of Arkansas, Missouri, and Indian Territory. Price had left Lexington with a small guard, but hundreds of eager boys joined him on the southern march. Undoubtedly, he had communicated with the Confederates in Arkansas.

Sigel learned that other columns were coming under direct command of State Senator James E. Rains, Governor Jackson, Lieutenant Governor Reynolds, and Ex-United States Senator David Rice Atchison, who in spite of many resolutions to quit politics, had decided to take an active part on the side of the Confederacy. Rains, like Price, was a veteran Missouri politician. Long a Democrat, he had recently become a Know-Nothing to oppose the influx of hated Germans. Recently he had sat as senator at Jefferson City.

This impending multitude failed to intimidate Sigel. He wheeled his eleven hundred St. Louis Germans north to meet them. He would surely be outnumbered but hoped to hold the enemy host until Lyon could strike it in the rear. Obviously, the tables might be turned, and Sigel would be trapped between Claib Jackson and Price's men at Cowskin Prairie. Sigel decided to take this chance. Marching through Neosho — a pro-Union town — he was greeted by hilarious citizens waving from front porches and garden gates. Children, flourishing wooden swords, ran beside the soldiers, precisely as the children had done at Boonville. Flags fluttered from second-story windows. A delegation of citizens stopped Sigel for a conference, told him that they feared raids from the bushwackers or from the governor's column, and hoped that the German might leave a guard to protect them. Sigel detached ninety men for the job and sent a courier to Salomon at Mount Vernon to come, double-quick, with his four hundred. Another rider pounded up the dirt road to Springfield to appraise Sweeney of the situation.

The July days were hot and very sultry, sweating beer from every pore of the German brigade. Water in the uncovered tin canteens became nauseatingly hot. The men's cartridge boxes lacked the usual tin racks for holding the paper tubes apart. Under the steady pounding of a forced march, the cartridge covers unwound and spilled the powder, but Sigel and his men kept going. On July Fourth, after a twenty-one mile march, they encamped a mile southeast of Carthage. The town was believed to be pro-Southern in sympathy. Commissary officers rode ahead to arrange for supplies and dashed back with exciting news. Governor Jackson's commissary officers had left the village a few hours ago. The refugee "army" was only ten miles north and might arrive in Carthage any time. Moreover, the enemy had four brigades — quadruple the number of Sweeney's whole army. Price, over on Cowskin Prairie, probably had as many more, and if McCulloch crossed from Arkansas, the enemy's superiority would be overwhelming.

A cautious commander might have retreated, but Sigel had served through a revolution and was accustomed to hazards. Moreover, his men had been carefully trained in St. Louis by the best rules of European warfare, and he scorned the undisciplined American rabble. Salomon joined him, and the united forces shouldered arms to march through Carthage.

The sudden appearance of the "damned Dutch" terrified the citizens, who deserted their houses to hide in cornfields and wood lots. Sigel placed guards at all the doors to prevent looting. His army passed at quickstep — a long gray centipede winding through the village, then out over the rolling prairie beyond, and through the timber fringing Bear Creek. On the other side they crossed the simmering flats, dropped down into the Spring Creek depression, then up and on again. The eager column marched away from its four-horse supply wagons, leaving them out of sight below the southern horizon. Finally, nine miles north of Carthage, the road dipped into a half-mile belt of trees skirting Coon Creek. On the prairie swell beyond, two miles away, the enemy army stood in a long line silhouetted against the pale summer sky. Sigel reined his horse and studied the field through his telescope, as his column swung down the gentle slope toward the woods. Horseflies made the saddle animals restless, and it was necessary to dismount in order to hold the glass steady.

On the slope north of Coon Creek, Governor Claib Jackson watched the approaching Union Army from his carriage. He had feared Lyon in his rear but was unprepared for United States soldiers ahead. Marmaduke had resigned shortly after the skirmish at Boonville and had traveled East, like M. Jeff Thompson, to offer his services elsewhere. Without him Jackson had had a hard trip — holding together and feeding a partly trained rabble of over four thousand followers, including state officers, legislators, a long and elaborate wagon train loaded with furniture, official records, feather beds, pots and pans. Moreover, the governor had been suffering recently from a malignancy. Fortunately, he had been joined on the march by dashing Jo Shelby with a troop of horse trained by several Kansas expeditions. The wealthy young rope manufacturer from Waverly instilled rude discipline in the refugee army.

Senator Rains had joined the governor's column, bringing three thousand unarmed volunteers. With him, also, came a three-gun battery under gaunt Hiram Bledsoe of the cadaverous face, listless figure, bright eyes, and engaging smile. Hi's hat was so big it rested on his ears, but he was a true-born Southern cavalier of the old school with a sweeping mustache and little goatee. He loved his guns like living things — especially the one he called "Ol' Sacramento." In outbursts of affection for the relic he would embrace and kiss the polished barrel.

Many militiamen from Camp Jackson in St. Louis had also joined the column. They made light of their parole, claiming that the surrender was unjust and the parole therefore unbinding. On the march downstate a local regiment of Germans had been surprised while asleep in a barn. The Missourians killed them like sheep and took six hundred much needed muskets.

Governor Jackson's first intimation that Sigel was in southwest Missouri had been brought to him by his commissary officers from Carthage. He immediately dispatched Shelby's troop of light-horse to locate the enemy. Then, with Senators Atchison and Rains, he selected a battlefield and formed the line where Sigel found him. Jackson knew as well as the Germans did that Price and McCulloch might come up from the south and entrap Sigel.

Jackson's army had no uniforms. Officers could be distinguished from the men only by bits of red flannel or a piece of cotton cloth stitched on the arm or shoulder of a homespun jacket or broadcloth frock coat. Jackson parked his six-pounders down the slope ahead of his line with Old Sacramento between them. In the center he raised the flag of Missouri and on each flank flags of the Confederacy — a questionable presumption, for this was as yet exclusively a state army. The cavalry — a thousand of them unarmed — were placed at both ends of the nondescript line. Unarmed recruits took position in the rear.

The assembled army watched Sigel's column marching toward them, sinuously undulating around obstacles which were invisible at this distance. "Look, look," Missourians may have exclaimed, as the sun glinted on ranks of bayonets, "them Dutch have got lightning rods on their muskets."

Jackson's artillery horses and oxen were ordered to the rear, harness chains jingling as they passed through the lines. Then solid shot was rammed down the cannons' mouths and the artillerymen waited. Already the enemy's advancing column had reached the far side of the timber and was disappearing like a gray snake slithering down a hole.

Soon the van emerged from the woods twelve hundred yards away. On the open prairie, battalion after battalion deployed in column of companies — a formation to forestall cavalry flanking. The Missouri line admired the precision of the oncoming enemy's movements but were well convinced now that, counting the unarmed men, they outnumbered the "Dutch" three or four to one.

The gray-clad Germans crunched steadily forward across the coarse, dry grass. A command to halt rippled down the ranks and the formation stopped as though at drill. Sigel rode among the companies, reminding them of their battles in the old country and urging them to prove their mettle now. Then they all moved forward again. When seven hundred yards from the enemy, Sigel opened fire with grape and canister from his center and from both flanks. Jackson's six-pounders replied instantly. Both armies stood still, watching the artillery duel.

Jackson's solid shot whizzed harmlessly over the heads of Sigel's men, while the Federal grape cut holes in the Missourians' line. Here and there an unmanageable horse reared against the sky or bolted from the field. Then the infantry began to shoot. Smoke billowed from both lines. The bombardment lasted half an hour. Old Sacramento was silenced and the center line behind it broken. Could it be that the Germans were defeating four times their number? Proudly Sigel turned his telescope toward the enemy's flanks, where he saw something that chilled his military blood. Enemy cavalry were streaming away toward the south from both flanks. Sigel remembered his lumbering wagon train three miles in the rear, and he realized that it could easily be cut off. A courier raced back with orders for the teamsters to form a column of eight's and lash ahead. Meanwhile, Sigel drew back into the woods with the same precision that the Missourians had admired in his advance.

As the Germans withdrew into the trees, Jackson's men rushed down the slope in pursuit. But, at the timber, they discovered that Sigel understood the use of artillery in retreat. His shells exploded where the road entered the woods, and as soon as his army had crossed Coon Creek, projectiles churned the ford behind them. Finally, when the Missourians emerged on the south side, their advance was checked again by shells bursting along the road. In the open country beyond, Sigel placed his three batteries a thousand yards apart. Thus he could cover his retreat with two batteries protecting the removal of the hindmost. In this manner the German regiments crept back across Spring and Bear creeks, confounding frontier enthusiasts with European military science.

Late in the afternoon Sigel noted that the road ahead passed through a cut between two hills. Many of the enemy's cavalry — largely unarmed — stood above the road, evidently planning to pounce on the solid column as it trundled through with the heavy wagons. Here was a "sunken road" — a name notorious to all students of Napoleonic history. Sigel, the military tactician, decided to show the frontiersmen a new trick. He divided his column, each half marching forward obliquely. When the enemy was between his pincers, Sigel opened fire. To save themselves, the horsemen retreated down into the sunken road, out of range, and formed to charge Sigel's weakened center — a maneuver Sigel had anticipated. The ragged horsemen had hardly got in position when his German flankers gained the heights and began shooting down into the cut as Sigel swept it with well-aimed charges of grape fired along the road. Eighty-five riderless horses raced out to be captured by footsore and near exhausted Union infantrymen who had been almost ready to drop by the roadside.

At dusk Sigel's tightly knit regiments trooped through Carthage — still deserted. Behind him, Jackson's men swarmed across the meadows, firing from lanes and fences. Sigel wheeled east on the Mount Vernon road to Springfield, where Lyon should soon arrive from the north. Shortly after dark Sigel's men entered the woods east of Carthage, and the enemy abandoned the chase in the gloom of dense foliage. The tired Germans marched on for twelve and a half miles to Sarcoxie, arriving at 3 A.M. They had stopped here on the way down. Now they built fires on the old campground, cooked the first food they had eaten for twenty-four hours, and dozed against trees and in fence corners. Many lay on their backs, holding up swollen feet for the blood to run back into their bodies.

At dawn, sergeants aroused the weary men, prodding them with guttural German oaths. Sleepy soldiers lined up, answered roll call, and trudged forward into the blinding rays of the rising sun and another stifling July day. By midmorning, eighteen miles along the road, the column filed through Mount Vernon. Sigel was sure now that no enemy followed. He ordered a day's rest. Sibley tents were pitched; men washed themselves and their shirts, sitting around naked until their laundry dried. The thirty-five additional miles to Springfield were covered leisurely, and when the column marched in, Sigel reported to Lyon — recently arrived — the details of his masterly retreat: thirteen killed and thirty-one wounded. He had saved his army but lost the lead mines.

Germans across the nation lauded his successful military maneuver, and as far away as San Francisco his compatriots prepared a gorgeous flag in recognition of his military skill.

Claib Jackson's state troops, when they gave up the chase at the edge of the dark woods, returned to Carthage, stacked arms in the street, and boasted about their victory to all citizens who dared venture back to town. Next day, as Sigel rested at Mount Vernon, Governor Jackson marched triumphantly south, beside him the bluff figure of Senator Atchison talking, perhaps, about great times in Kansas. Lieutenant Governor Reynolds was unaccustomed to the hardships. Military campaigning disagreed with his plump physique and orderly mind — no facilities for filing documents with the precision that delighted him, no opportunity to display his florid literary style and elaborately schooled chirography. However, that difficulty might be corrected now by an about-face and the recapture of Jefferson City. Price's and McCulloch's army, combined, would be more than a match for all of Lyon's men.

In midmorning Jackson's column met Price's Missourians and, behind them, a regiment of neatly uniformed Louisianans — Louis Hebert's Pelican Rifles — and also a battalion of Texas boys, eighteen to twenty years old, in frontier dress. At the rear of the column came a new brigade of "butternut" volunteers from Arkansas commanded by N. Bartlett Pearce, a graduate of West Point who had served eight years in the Indian country before resigning to engage in the mercantile business. He was now back in the saddle ready to devote his military training to the Southern cause. Marching north, these soldiers had captured the entire garrison Sigel left at Neosho without firing a shot. The Federals' muskets had been distributed among the Missourians.

Governor Jackson's civilian veterans of the Carthage battle lined the road to admire the Confederates' neat gray uniforms, the resplendent Louisiana officers' gold braid, gold buttons, and stars. Real soldiers, sure enough! Military-minded Missouri boys wanted such uniforms for themselves. Huzza for the Confederacy! Most brilliant of all was General McCulloch, a man of about fifty with long hair on his shoulders. His white, planter's hat sported a wider brim than any other man's, his frock coat tails were a little fuller, his cravat flowed a little longer. He favored velvet for clothes, sat his horse magnificently, and always carried a fancy rifle in his hand. The *New Orleans Picayune* had made a hero of McCulloch in the Mexican War. He had joined the gold rush in 1849 and had been sheriff of Sacramento when Charles Robinson staged his squatters' revolt. Back once more in Texas at the outbreak of the rebellion, McCulloch led the forces which accepted the surrender of Twiggs and the Texas armaments in San Antonio, thus winning a brigadier's stars. In April, Eastern newspapers had reported McCulloch ready to dash across the Potomac and kidnap Lincoln.

Major General Sterling Price assumed command of all the Missourians. Then he conferred with McCulloch about a combined attack to defeat Lyon and retake Jefferson City. McCulloch hesitated to co-operate, at least until Price made an army with his "half-starved infantry" and "huckleberry cavalry." The great crowd of unarmed, noisy camp followers were a liability McCulloch did not care to assume.

Price, redder than usual under his long white hair, resolved to whip his mob into an army. In his straggly ranks stood many veterans who had served under him or under Doniphan in the Mexican War. Almost every man had fought at one time or another against Indians on the plains or in the semimilitary expeditions against Kansas. A little training, Price was sure, would create an army second to none.

Price marched back to Cowskin Prairie, with Atchison, Jackson, Reynolds, and the rest of the refugee government riding along. Here, where grass grew tall and beef was plentiful, Price selected experienced veterans for noncoms and set them to drilling the younger men in the school of the soldier, the school of the company, the school of the regiment. Special detachments began mining lead for bullets. Blacksmiths constructed forges to weld scrap iron into shells and canisters. The mistake made at Carthage by firing solid shot must not be repeated. On an improvised rifle range the men practiced shooting in ranks of three — standing, kneeling, and prone. This sounded simple enough, but practice was necessary to teach the prone men how to pour powder down the barrel of a muzzle-loader without rising from the ground. In this loading and firing drill, Colonel John Q. Burbridge endeared himself to the men by admonishing them to aim at the enemy's breeches' button. A wound in that region, he explained, nearly always gives the victim time to prepare to meet his Maker. Some two thousand of Price's seven thousand men still lacked guns. These recruits were drilled to follow a charge and pick up muskets from the dead and wounded.

As Price whipped his followers into an Army, Atchison, Jackson, and Reynolds left him and drove down the wire road to Fort Smith on the Arkansas River, the overland stage terminus at the edge of Indian Territory. Here they boarded the boat for Memphis. They were in a hurry, for they had learned that a convention had been called in Missouri to form a new government. Unless a Confederate Army invaded the state and brought the governor and his legislature back to Jefferson City, the people of Missouri were sure to depose them all and inaugurate a pro-Union regime. Stopping first to consult with the Confederate generals in command on the Mississippi, they traveled on to Richmond to explain the emergency to Jeff Davis.

President Davis realized the importance of getting Missouri in the Confederate fold and offered to do what he could. He ordered Brigadier General Gideon Pillow to detach six thousand men from the defenses he was building along the Mississippi, land them at New Madrid, and join the "mushrat" men M. Jeff Thompson had organized in the swampy wilderness. The ex-mayor of St. Joe was now a military man to be reckoned with. He had ridden into southeast Missouri on an old horse with a rope for a bridle and only seventy-five cents jingling in his pockets. His homespun breeches were tucked into high muddy boots and his shirt flapped outside his belt, but he fixed a gay white plume in his old wool hat and called all men to his standard who opposed being ruled by the Dutch and who considered themselves better than the "nigger." Waving a cutlass in one hand and a pistol in the other, he told barefooted recruits, "I understand you want to fight. By God! You shall have it. I am a ripsquealer and my name is fight." These "swamp rats" and Pillow's trained volunteers could now co-operate with the brigade stationed at Pocahontas, Arkansas, under General William H. Hardee. With Price and McClulloch, they could surround, cut off, and defeat Lyon in Springfield. Frémont, up in St. Louis, might try to reinforce him, but if he did, the Confederates could circle his flank and take weakened St. Louis. Thus the Confederacy planned to coerce Missouri out of the Union. (A pretty inconsistency considering that the main complaint against Lincoln was his use of the Federal Army to coerce the state into it!) Frémont saw the city's predicament and notified Lyon to save himself by coming north unless able to handle the situation alone.

X I V

Born Among the Rocks

As THE IOWA GREYHOUNDS approached Springfield, couriers reported the battle of Carthage and Sigel's escape. The Iowans, tired but exuberant over marching away from Lyon's entire division, bivouacked beside the road. They speculated about Jackson's chance of joining McCulloch and wondered if the Union men had come to take part in a fight or a foot race. Next day they bombarded the incoming regulars, Kansans, and St. Louis Germans with friendly insults: "Iowa saved the Union that time sure enough," and, "You bastards have not yet begun to die for your country."

The proud Iowans patched and scrubbed their clothes, swam in the creek, and at night played with their precious cards by the light of candles in bayonets stuck in the ground. Old Mace produced a bottle for his best friends. In the morning sutlers came out from town with a treat — a special, Springfield twist tobacco cured in molasses.

Private Guthrie of Company E, First Iowa, found a little mule that followed him around like a dog, jigging along beside him wherever he went. The First Sergeant entered into the company's fun, and when he called the roll and reached the G's, the assembled men heard: "Gregory," "Here" — "Grimes," "Heow" — "Guthrie and the mule," "Both here."

At Springfield, Lyon's army mingled with Sigel's veterans and Sweeney's volunteers, all swapping lies about their experiences. One company of St. Louisans laughed about their Fourth of July parade: "Drank so much wine we couldn't hold a line at company drill."

The entire Union command now numbered about seven thousand men. Lyon, in a terrible temper, clattered around the town on his gray stallion. Not knowing that McCulloch had crossed into Missouri, Lyon still hoped to overtake Jackson before he joined either Price or the Texan, but the quartermaster goods and supplies he had depended on for continuation of his forced march were all piled up at Rolla, a hundred and twenty-five miles away. Five days, perhaps a week, would be required to haul them to camp. After that time, it would be too late to catch the Missouri governor. Everyone blamed Frémont. The new commander up in St. Louis had sacrificed Lyon. To make the situation worse, an intercepted dispatch indicated that M. Jeff Thompson had rallied his "swamp rats" below Rolla and might cut the supply line. Moreover, the enlistment time had expired for three thousand of Lyon's seven thousand men. Some were leaving daily. The whole summer's campaign was dissolving at the moment complete victory might be attained.

Lyon decided to act at once. He knew that marching men forget their troubles, seldom report on sick call or desert. The general sent John S. Phelps, veteran congressman from the district, to plead with Frémont in St. Louis for recruits. Next he ordered reveille blown at three-thirty in the morning and the column started south. He was taking a desperate chance but, with luck, might overtake the enemy columns before they consolidated and before most of his own troops went home. Perhaps he could enlist an additional thousand local boys, but even with them his force might drop to only five thousand against the enemy's possible twenty thousand if Jackson, Price, and McCulloch had joined.

The Union cavalry trotted down the wire road in the column's van. Totten and his "God-damn-you-sir" battery rumbled after them, then into the choking dust swung the footmen swaying to the cadences of "Happy Land of Canaan." An hour's march from Springfield the wire road dipped down into the Wilson's Creek depression from the northeast and passed south of the farm home of J. O. Ray. Fording the tree-lined stream, the road skirted under a fifty- or sixty-foot bluff for half a mile. Men could climb the steep sides, but it was brush-covered and would be difficult for horse. Along the road the van could not see its own skirmishers fifty yards ahead. The bluff terminated at Skegg's Branch — a tributary from the west. The road crossed this creek and climbed out to the open prairie beyond. Farmhouses stood on the distant sky line and golden wheat stood shocked in the fields. Lyon and his adjutant, John M. Schofield, memorized the geography with soldierly attention to details. Outcroppings of limestone strata clinked under their horses' hoofs. Behind them the artillery rumbled and jolted over the rocky surface. Surely an enemy could hear a column approaching for miles.

The whole country south of Wilson's Creek looked forbidding to the soldiers. They knew that an overwhelming number of enemies waited below them somewhere. The heat was terrific. Dust billowed up from their feet in a cloud visible for miles. On the open prairie the men felt safe, but in the brushy draws they apprehended a surprise attack. Every log cabin in the hollows seemed foreign and hostile. Mud chimneys, washtubs, and spinning wheels on the stoops appeared strangely sinister. People were poorer, more shiftless than Northern farmers. The invaders considered them enemies and their property fair game. At night camps Corpular Mace milked the nearest cows and also the henroosts. His company lived well. Geese that refused to take the oath were executed without compunction. Guthrie staked his mule in the best of the secession cabbage patches. The Iowans also appropriated hats, shirts, and shoes from country stores along the road and boasted, "If our boys had been at Valley Forge there would have been no blood on the snow." A little dog was picked up by Company E. The men called her Liz and complained whimsically that she was of no practical use except to supply the men with fleas. Soldiers washed the insects from their bodies by riding naked in the rain. Veterans said that whiskey poured down a man's back, and also down his throat, discouraged the pests. One soldier quoted the Bible: "The wicked flee when no man pursueth."

After dark on August 1, 1861, the men noticed the southern sky glowing with the reflections of myriad campfires. Evidently Jackson and McCulloch had joined forces. The vastness of their fire shadows on the clouds made the Northerners' number seem insignificant. Soldiers joked — none too humorously — about being mustered out by a bullet instead of a Federal officer. Corpular Mace did not like the prospect. "They won't kill me," he drawled, rolling the whites of his eyes in the firelight. "They'll captivate me. I'se wuf two thousand dollars. I'se done sold for that mo'n wonce." The boys spit grimly in the ashes and agreed sardonically that Mace and Lyon had the most to lose. Then they piled wood on the fire for another yarn before lying down to ask the stars a few questions of their own.

Time had come to select a battlefield or to retreat. In the morning Lyon's regular cavalry probed the enemy and galloped back with the information that the two armies had joined — no question about it — and were marching around the Union forces, might even cut them off from their base at Springfield. Lyon ordered an about-face and the men swung back up the familiar road, watching over their shoulders a great cloud of yellow dust above the horizon — the enemy's flanking column. As they raced away from the enemy trap, the Union soldiers joked and played pranks. Private Bill Huestis noticed a dead man's hand protruding from a shallow grave and remarked, "That soldier is reaching for his land warrant."

The sun beat down on simmering fields and dust puffed up from the road. Marching along, Private Ware saw one of the regulars drop from the column ahead, set his rifle beside an inviting springhouse door, and step inside for a drink. Ware's musket needed repairs, so he set it beside the rifle and moved the latter. A moment later the first soldier reappeared, snatched the worn-out gun, and ran to catch his company. Ware shouldered the only gun left and joined his own outfit musing: "Them regulars will steal anything."

The rear guard fought delaying skirmishes at Dug Springs and Curran's post office on August 2 and 3. A troop of United States cavalry charged into the column of Senator Rains's advancing Missourians and stampeded Price's entire army — fifty men dispersing fifteen hundred. McCulloch's scorn for the "half-starved infantry" and "huckleberry cavalry" seemed justified. He had never been enthusiastic about the joint campaign and threatened to march back to Arkansas. His misgivings were backed by his second in command, West Pointer James McIntosh, who became known as "the man cussin' the Missourians." General Price, the ranking officer of the combined army and the oldest man, rode over to McCulloch's headquarters and offered him the supreme command if he would stay and fight the Federals. McCulloch agreed reluctantly. He was a dashing captain but not a general. The complications of a campaign annoyed and baffled him. Councils and "paper work" interfered with his daily horseback jaunts and rifle practice.

Lyon's men recrossed Wilson's Creek and marched into Springfield on August 5, 1861. News of their retreat preceded them, and townsmen were packing wagons to escape to Rolla. The rebels were known to be following close behind. Next day scouts reported the men camped on Wilson's Creek. Corn was ripening and the pastures seemed adequate for their big beef herd and two thousand horses. The encampment, over a mile wide, stretched for two or three miles along the creek. The Confederate multitude plainly outnumbered Lyon's army, and Southern sympathizers looked forward eagerly to the defeat of the "whirlwind in breeches" who had swept all obstacles before him in a summer's campaign from St. Louis to Jefferson City, Boonville, and Springfield. War correspondents had come south with Lyon's column to report his activities to papers in Chicago, St. Louis, San Francisco, and the four leading New York journals — the *Herald, Times, Tribune,* and *World.* Thomas Knox of the *Herald* was still with the troops, well acquainted now with officers and men.

Lyon found conditions worse than ever in Springfield — no supplies from Rolla and no encouragement from Frémont. Full details of a Federal defeat at Bull Run in Virginia cast an additional gloom over the encampment. An officers' council was called on August 8, 1861, at headquarters on North Jefferson Street, near the public square. Lyon outlined the situation, said that in case of a further retreat the enemy's superior force might harry them excessively. But to entrench in Springfield seemed impracticable, for the town was widely scattered and the suppy line precarious. What did the officers think of a quick attack which, if it did not conquer the enemy, would at least confound and disorganize him, thus making a retreat safer?

Colonel Sweeney, just back from a raid on the town of Forsyth, counseled attack. His old enemy, Samuel P. Heintzelman, had served as a brigadier in the recent Bull Run disaster. Now, Sweeney saw a chance to show him how army men should fight. Flushed red as a beet under his orange hair, he twitched the empty sleeve pinned to his brass-buttoned coat and shouted: "Let us eat the last bit of mule flesh and fire the last cartridge before we think of retreating." Colonels Deitzler and Mitchell of the First and Second Kansas backed the Irishman, but the majority voted for retreat. Lyon dismissed the council without a decision. Correspondent Thomas Knox reported Lyon to be a changed man. The prospect of losing southwest Missouri had sapped his former energy and decisiveness. During the afternoon Sweeney came to Lyon's headquarters, and the two regulars talked on the back porch, beyond the hearing of clerks and orderlies. After Sweeney left, Lyon went into his room and lay down on his cot. Evidently he had not made up his mind.

In the evening the supply train arrived from Rolla. Next day sergeants issued shoes and clothing, while orderly clerks distributed letters from home. Among the dispatches, Lyon received an order from Frémont stating reinforcements to be unavailable. The general must retreat, unless he felt capable of defeating the enemy with the men he had. Lyon read the order and looked out on the public square. Already two regiments had gone home, their enlistment period over. Half of the men in Sigel's and Salomon's forces had left to be mustered out. The First Iowa agreed to stay only for a battle and no longer.

Lyon replied to Frémont that the enemy was encamped five miles away. He did not say that he contemplated a battle, nor did he complain about the lack of reinforcements. The message was sealed and sent on its way. Then he ordered all companies to shift their place of encampment in order that spies might not count their number. To prevent straying, the roll was called hourly. Men were cautioned to be ready to march at sundown — but whether toward the railroad at Rolla or against the enemy was still uncertain. Old Mace disappeared, leaving no word, and Company E cooked their own supper.

Before dark Sigel came to see the general. He stamped up the steps to the brick house. The little fellow's jaw muscles gritted when he was nervous. Lyon led the way to the back porch for a talk. Sigel had fought with more rebel Missourians than any man in the army. The decision, reached by these two, came as a surprise to young Adjutant General John M. Schofield. As a West Pointer disciplined for death, Schofield also believed in a soldier's right to exert reasonable caution. An attack on at least three times their number seemed the extreme of rashness, and Lyon's battle plan seemed worse still. The general explained to Schofield that Sigel was to march that evening with a brigade — his own and Salomon's regiments, two troops of regular cavalry under Captain Eugene A. Carr, and a light battery of six guns — totaling twelve hundred men. This force was to strike McCulloch from the east at dawn, while Lyon's main army — now reduced to thirty-five hundred — would strike from the west. Thus a total of about fifty-five hundred might defeat fifteen thousand to twenty thousand men.

The adjutant general knew Sigel's reputation as a revolutionary commander in Europe. He knew also that the German had failed to hold the fleeing secessionist legislature. Schofield asked incredulously, "Is Sigel willing to undertake this?"

Lyon replied, "Yes, it is his plan." Major Schofield did not mention his own opposition. A soldier's duty was to obey without remonstrance. Neither knew that Price, Rains, and McCulloch at that moment were calling in their pickets for a night march against Springfield.

Shortly after sundown on August 9, 1861, the Federal drums beat "fall in." The Iowa men lined up before their company fires. They had no tents. In the distance they saw Lyon, on his dappled gray horse, stopping before each company to speak a few words. Finally he drew rein before Company E. Private Ware noticed that his blouse was buttoned up to his whiskers as though the hot night was cold. Red braid on the sleeves was worn and frayed. In a low voice the general said:

> Men, we are going to have a fight. We will march out in a short time. Don't shoot until you get orders. Fire low — don't aim higher than their knees; wait until they get close; don't get scared; it's no part of a soldier's duty to get scared.

Then Lyon moved on and the men stood at attention as he repeated the speech, beyond their hearing, to the next company. Finally he had gone. The men lolled over their guns, disappointed in the commander and his speech. Private Heustis said, "How is a man to help being skeered when he is skeered?" Later they compared notes with the cavalry and wished that they were commanded by Sweeney, who had twitched his empty sleeve grotesquely and told his men: "Stay together, boys, and we'll saber hell out of them." That was language the Iowa boys understood. Volunteers did not like sour-faced Lyon, although they respected his ability.

At dusk Sigel's brigade slipped out of the encampment, Captain Eugene A. Carr on lead. A born centaur, he would rather be a colonel of cavalry than President of the United States. To him the night's work was not only strictly professional but also grand adventure. Behind him strode Salomon's gray-clad German veterans of Carthage. Sigel rode along with a blue blanket tied behind his saddle. The darkened sky threatened rain from the south.

Lyon marched also at dusk, his command divided into three brigades.

At the head of the column rode one-armed Sweeney and Major Sturgis, his beard shaved off for the battle. He was marching out to fight old comrades, including James McIntosh, McCulloch's second in command, who had left him at Fort Smith to join the Confederacy. Sturgis would be accused of shaving to disguise himself from sharpshooters. At his van Captain Joseph B. Plummer led a battalion of regular infantry. Next came the Second Missouri Volunteers (two companies) with Major Peter J. Osterhaus giving German commands, then Totten's light artillery, and two companies of cavalry — one regular, one volunteer.

In the Second Brigade marched the First Missouri, commanded, in Blair's absence, by Lieutenant Colonel George L. Andrews. A dapper, likable, regular army artillery lieutenant, Johnnie DuBois, brought fifty recruits and four cannon. The splendidly mounted Fred Steele commanded a battalion of regulars. He was a small, slender soldier noted for his fastidious dress — always immaculate even after the hardest march. An epicure and also a sportsman, Steele maintained a string of race horses which invariably won money from the fastest animals his men could procure, and he always rode the best.

The Third Brigade seemed weakest by professional standards. It contained the First and Second Kansas fanatics, and some two hundred mounted home guards who had enlisted since Lyon arrived in Springfield. All were nonprofessional but with a will to fight. How would they conduct themselves? Marching at the tail of the army, the Iowa singers began to joke about the style of coffins they wanted. Private Heustis set his platoon laughing when he shouted: "I am a-going to be a great big he-angel."

Lyon heard the laughter, turned in his saddle, and spoke to the regimental commander. "They have too much levity to do good fighting," he complained. The colonel reminded him that the Iowans had outmarched the regulars and would fight well when given an opportunity. "I will give them an opportunity," Lyon mumbled in his whiskers, "but I very much fear they will disgrace themselves."

The storm clouds became more ominous. Overhead, stars twinkled through their ragged edges. Lyon, with his staff, cantered along the column, stopping to chat with each commander. He drew rein beside Fred

Steele's prancing charger, bridle chains jingling. Steele raised a velvet cuff and saluted the general. He had known Lyon at West Point and dared asked the order of the column. Where was Sigel?

Lyon replied that the German was to go by a different route and strike the enemy from behind. Steele shook his silky blond whiskers, and sputtering a fusillade of oaths in a cheerful impersonal manner, piped in his shrill voice, "Sigel is incapable of commanding an individual unit." The graceful horseman seemed almost feminine, except for his beard and blasphemy. "Moreover," he continued socially, "the entire command is much too small to be weakened by splitting."

The dappled horse galloped away with Lyon into the gloom. Thomas Knox, the *Herald* correspondent, spied the commander coming and turned his horse to ride beside him. He had talked to Lyon many times in Springfield, knew that he worried about fighting against such odds, but felt honor bound not to give up southwest Missouri without a battle. Knox had already reported the general as showing an indecision new to his usually impetuous nature. Tonight he found the commander more absentminded than usual, often unaware of questions asked him, apparently bewildered.

The entire column halted after a four- or five-mile march. Then for hours the companies and regiments moved mysteriously in the night. Private Ware remembered that his outfit sometimes marched only a hundred yards between stops, where the men napped like dogs for half an hour, and moved again. Officers rode out of the darkness occasionally and padded away, their horses' hoofs muffled in sacks. Artillery rumbled past with blankets around the wheels. No one explained to the volunteers that the entire army was being deployed in columns of companies with sufficient intervals for each regiment to be brought into battle line. Regular privates did not seem to care and slept stolidly wherever halted. In the enemy camp no sound could be heard except the incessant braying of mules.

At midnight a drizzle started, and the men sheltered themselves in fence corners, behind caissons, in brush piles and under shocks of freshly cut corn. Four or five newspaper correspondents buried themselves under new-mown hay in a field only four miles from the enemy camp. Vedettes rode out two miles farther. If McCulloch was making his surprise march to Springfield, he must have evaded both Sigel and Lyon!

Lyon and Schofield dismounted to rest between limestone slabs still warm with the day's heat. The officer of the rear guard rode up and reported no stragglers and no disposition to straggle — not a man. The volunteers all berated the cowards of Bull Run and hankered to retrieve the nation's honor. Their commanders, good politicians, were telling them that tomorrow's battle opened a war for civilization. Somewhere among the shadows, among the men resting in fence rows and crannies in the rocks, lolled long-haired Wild Bill Hickok, seasoned with the Kansas wars but still fastidious about his costume and dainty high-heeled boots. His sweeping mustache was almost long enough now to tie behind his neck. Only a month ago he had gained great notoriety at the overland stage station in Rock Creek, Nebraska, for killing three men — the McCanles gang. Since then he had been wantonly attacked by guerrillas while conducting a freight train to Sedalia and barely escaped to southwest Missouri where he was well acquainted — especially with Congressman John S. Phelps.

Across Wilson's Creek, in the enemy multitude, many Wild Bills waited for dawn. Around the campfires, enjoying a new life, lounged wealthy Shelby and his reckless riders, Cole Younger with thinning hair plastered down above a face faintly reminiscent of Charles Robinson at his age, lascivious-lipped Quantrill with his ready smile and gang of mixbloods. These slant-eyed border men from nearby Indian Territory were the rising young gunman's first command.

Out on the drizzling prairie, Schofield and Lyon crouched together. To the youthful adjutant, Lyon seemed as fanatic as Old Brown of Osawatomie. Schofield knew the barrack-room gossip about Lyon's zeal and cruelty, his almost bloodthirsty hatred of all slaveholders, the trivial anecdotes about Lyon's snatching a whip to lash the driver of a balky team instead of the horses, how the general had kicked a private he caught beating a dog and made the man kneel down and beg the animal's pardon. At Fort Riley Captain Lyon had insulted a supporter of slavery and refused his challenge to a duel. Goaded by fellow officers, Lyon had finally consented to fight and demanded pistols across a table — sure death for both contestants. No one doubted his murderous seriousness, and Major

Sibley, second for the offended party, insisted that the challenge be recalled. Yes, the general and Old Brown had much in common.

Schofield stopped his musing to brush raindrops from his jacket. He asked the silent general, crouching between the warm rocks, if he was comfortable, and heard the gruff reply: "All right. I was born among the rocks."

X V

The Battle of Wilson's Creek

On the prairie west of Wilson's Creek the rain abated at 4 a.m. on the eventful morning of September 10, 1861. Lyon roused Schofield from his meditations. Both men remounted their horses, and the Union Army moved forward toward the paling eastern sky. Marching feet swept raindrops from the grass. In low tones, sergeants cautioned men to hold intervals. Officers stood in their stirrups to scan the horizon for a glimpse of enemy campfires. Lyon, on his gray charger, looked across his advancing men. This was the first time in his lifelong service that he had commanded more than a company in battle. Strangely, no pickets challenged his approach, and his skirmishers almost reached Price's encampment before the first shot blazed against the dawn sky. Then a fusillade!

No need for silence now! Officers shouted commands. A dozen drums began to beat. Horses pranced excitedly. Columns of companies shuffled front into line. With the light of day, the men saw distant tents through a fringe of oaks. Marching into a depression, they could see nothing, but when they reached the far side, the open slope toward Wilson's Creek spread out before them. There was the wire road from Springfield. It turned under the bluff, out of sight, below them. The men knew the country well, having camped there twice in the last two weeks.

The plan of battle was plain now. Lyon's regiments were marching obliquely across the tongue of land between Wilson's Creek and Skegg's Branch. At the edge of the bluff, if they reached it, they would command the entire enemy camp. On the Federal right marched the First Missouri with a battalion of the Second Missouri under Major Peter Osterhaus in reserve to protect their flank. On the left came the First Kansas. Totten's battery rumbled along between the wings. The Second Kansas and First

Iowa brought up the rear. Captain Sam Walker was almost too ill to sit his horse, but he determined to be in this fight.

Lyon, with his staff, drew rein, sent an order to Totten, and surveyed the field. The artillery major saluted, galloped to his assigned position as methodically as though at drill, wheeled, unlimbered, and fired a twelve-pound shot at the distant tents — the signal for Sigel to attack across the creek.

General Ben McCulloch was at Price's tent when the alarm sounded. The venerable white-haired politician sat with his adjutant, Thomas Snead, who still cherished the memory of Lyon's defiance in St. Louis. McCulloch had ordered pickets drawn in last night for his proposed march to Springfield, but when the rain began at 9 P.M. (the storm reached Lyon at midnight), he canceled orders for the advance. Someone blundered by forgetting to replace sentries. Neither McCulloch nor Price suspected that Lyon was near. A cavalry detail from Rains's division had been out on the prairie all night between the roads Sigel and Lyon traveled but did not see or hear them. Eager to get back at dawn for hot coffee, they stopped only to forage a few bushels of corn which they were carrying on their saddles when they spied the enemy — long lines of men marching down upon them as far as they could see. The horsemen threw away their burdens and spurred to camp. Colonel John F. Snyder heard their breathless report and galloped down to Price's tent where the two commanders sat in conference. "Lyon," he shouted, "with twenty thousand men and a hundred pieces of artillery, is within a mile of this army."

McCulloch had had his fill of panicky Missourians stampeded at Dug Springs, and he believed this another of "Rains's scares." But soon he heard shouts, then the fusillade. Looking up Wilson's Creek, he saw a mob of men on horseback and in wagons whipping down the valley. Then Totten's cannon shell screamed across Wilson's Creek. Almost at once another cannon — Sigel's — answered from the other side of the camp. Evidently the enemy was attacking on both sides.

The surprise was complete. One of Price's regimental officers was eating breakfast when an orderly galloped up, yelling for him to form his men. "Is that official?" the officer queried, as he sipped his coffee. The next moment a shell from Totten's battery cut a sapling near the table. "Well, by —— !" he cried. "*That is official*" — and he ordered out his men.

McCulloch's army, if army it could be called, stood dumfounded — brave but confused. Louis Hebert's neatly clad Third Louisiana — the Pelican Rifles — held their formation. So did the Texans, proudly distinguished from the rabble by white muslin around their left arms. Pearce's newly mustered Arkansans were half drilled and only partly armed. Some carried their own shotguns but no cartridge boxes or other equipment. Price's men had learned to hold rough formations at Cowskin Prairie, but fully a thousand of them still had no guns or tents. At night they bivouacked in the brush and by day foraged on the prairies or loitered around the beef herd for their allotment of meat on the hoof. McCulloch still held these Missourians in low esteem and counted on his other troops to win the battle. Perhaps this was an error in judgment, for the Missouri horde in coarse cotton shirts and yellow "jean pantaloons" were veterans and, like the Kansans on the other side, they looked forward to settling old scores in this fight. Some of them had been members of the "bogus" Kansas legislature. Others had been captured and paroled from Camp Jackson in St. Louis. Men like Jo Shelby, Charles Quantrill, Frank James, Cole Younger — and they were legion — could be counted on to fight with courage and resourcefulness.

Against this grim mob, which stood scattered across two miles of brush and farm land, Lyon's long line marched steadily forward. Far beyond the creek, where the road came down past Ray's farm, Lyon saw many little figures — Hebert's Third Louisiana — climb over a fence and disappear in a broomcorn field. From that position they would be able to shoot along the entire Union line as it marched into range.

Lyon called a halt, barked an order, and Captain J. B. Plummer marched from the left flank with a battalion of Missouri home guards, ably stiffened with three hundred regulars. Let the Missourians "open the ball" in defense of their country! The army stood watching the detachment march away, drums beating, banners floating in the breeze. Lyon, as still as an equestrian statue, squinted through his telescope. Then he turned to Gordon Granger, and ordered Lieutenant Johnnie DuBois's battery with his green recruits to follow and sweep the Louisianans from the cornfield with grape and canister, before Plummer arrived. "Better go along, too," Lyon told Granger, "and see that the young gentleman has no trouble."

The halted army watched the battery gallop off, postilions leaning over the racing horses' backs. "Look at them roans," a soldier can be imagined as saying, "every one round as a dollar." A wheel hit a rock, bounded in the air spinning, but the carriage righted itself, reached the objective, un-limbered and began to puff smoke — shooting over Plummer's advancing force into the broomcorn field. DuBois's recruits acted admirably. The First Iowa volunteers and Fred Steele's battalion of regulars were ordered to protect the battery from a possible counterattack. Then the main army moved ahead at quickstep — a long, wavering line like a flight of wild geese.

An enemy battery across the creek opened on DuBois. The Iowans — hurrying to protect him — watched the shells arch through the air toward them. One hit the sod and richocheted. The company dog ran after it. A sudden and horrible neighing scream above the bombardment set all the men to craning their necks. "Down, damn you, down, sirs," officers cautioned, and the men threw themselves in the grass. The scream, they learned, came from one of DuBois's roan wheel horses. A cannon ball had torn off its shoulder. A sergeant killed the animal with his pistol.

This fight for the broomcorn field was a battle all to itself half a mile from the main forces. On the Confederate side, McIntosh — with a battalion of mounted Arkansans — calmly co-operated with Hebert. He trained batteries on DuBois and sent a detachment to charge and capture his guns. McCulloch noted McIntosh's efficiency in action, left everything to him, and rode down Wilson's Creek to see how the center was preparing to meet Lyon's oncoming line. The Louisianan's charge for DuBois's guns was countered by the First Iowa and Steele's regulars. They stepped forward in line, seeing no enemy but holding guns at ready. Officers warned them to watch the gulch ahead where treetops peeped out. In defiance, or perhaps to bolster courage, the whole line began to yell as it marched. Private Ware, of Company E, saw a man ahead writhing on the grass. The wounded youth was handsome, with blue eyes and a light mustache. As the line approached, Ware asked the stricken soldier where he was hit but heard no answer in the battle roar. He dared not stop, stepped over him, and marched on.

The Iowans saw plainly the enemy batteries across the creek half a mile ahead. Every time smoke puffed from the big guns, the men pressed themselves into the earth until the shells struck. Then they jumped up and hunted the balls or bits of shrapnel for souvenirs. Wild Bill Hickok, somewhere in the shifting columns, found himself truly frightened in the din. Frank James said later that he found the fighting slow.

Ahead of the Iowans, across the creek in the broomcorn, Plummer was outnumbered by the Louisianans almost four to one. At first he drove them back, but McIntosh, his schoolmate at West Point, rallied the Pelicans behind Ray's farmhouse, and they came crashing through the corn with fixed bayonets. DuBois fired two shells through the house, then fell wounded and was carried to the rear. Lyon saw the mishap and sent Totten galloping to the lieutenant's rescue. The veteran artilleryman rained shot and shell into the corn, wounded McIntosh, and checked his Louisianans. But it was too late. Plummer's men slunk out badly whipped. Their commander was wounded, and eighty men lay dead or in enemy hands — the price paid for protecting the main army's flank. This side action had lasted an hour.

During the fight Lyon continued his march down the tongue of land. Totten, before rejoining him, displayed his ability as an artilleryman. He pointed to a five-acre clearing across the creek, where wagons stood hub to hub. Then, with well-placed shots, he splintered the vehicles and set the loads of supplies on fire. A great black smoke, very different from cannon smoke, drifted through the oak brush. A west wind! That would help Lyon's plan of attack.

Totten watched the fire, impassive as when he won a hand at cards. With monotonous "God damn you, sirs," he ordered the guns limbered, then galloped away with them to the main field, where the army stood deployed three deep and a thousand yards long — on the right the German regiment and Osterhaus's battalion, on the left the First Kansas. In a depression at the rear stood the Second Kansas in reserve. The First Iowa soon streamed in from the defense of DuBois's battery to take a place beside the Kansans and wait, out of sight of the battle.

Across the rock-littered flat, only a few hundred yards from the front Union line, stood the enemy. The main battle was beginning here. Both sides fired continually. White smoke from the muskets drifted down the slope to the east, through the tops of hazel brush and scraggly oaks, fogging the enemy and leaving the Union line free. Confederate officers often could see nothing but smoke ahead. The sharp smell of it tingled in their noses. Union soldiers fired blindly into the cloud. Confederate deserters skulked downhill to safety without detection.

After an hour a sudden silence rang in the soldiers' ears. The Confederates had withdrawn down the bluff to Wilson's Creek. Lyon realigned his men and brought up reserves to rebuff the next charge. Officers conferred, inspected the various regiments' positions, asked one another about the enemy, speculated on the location of various batteries, and pointed to the position of Bledsoe's ox-drawn Ol' Sacramento. "Any man would recognize her bass voice — smelted from those Mexican church bells — probably shootin' trace chains and rocks at us," they may have said.

Down below the flat-topped ridge Price re-formed along the wire road beside Wilson's Creek for a second onslaught. General McCulloch decided to aid him by a flank movement. He ordered his Third Texas cavalry up Skegg's Branch where they might climb out on the ridge and slash down Lyon's thin line as Price boiled up the bluff and hit it in front. But at the place where the horsemen were to come out on the battlefield, brush and trees stood too dense for the men to ride through in formation. The horsemen straggled up to the plain and formed slowly for the charge. Totten spied them, understood the double play, wheeled his artillery and swept the cavalry back into the gulch. McCulloch watched the failure of this movement and noted Price's competence as his line clashed against Lyon's center. The Texan decided to leave the battle in Price's hands as he had left the broomcorn fight to McIntosh, and galloped to the extreme left of his army.

Lyon, cantering along the line, admonished the men to keep cool, shouting above the roar of battle, "Don't aim above their knees." He reined his gray horse over to Totten's battery and complimented the major for his marksmanship. Totten nodded. Then he noticed blood dripping from the heel of Lyon's boot and offered the general a drink of brandy from his canteen. Lyon said that the wound was not serious and galloped back into the battle fury.

Clouds of smoke obscured the movements on both sides. Soldiers coughed in the ghastly white light, stumbled over the brush. In the turmoil some companies advanced too far, others not far enough. Company E of the First Kansas inadvertently dressed on the Missouri enemy and fought with it, perplexed by seeing their supposed comrades shooting in the wrong direction. Finally, a Kansan recognized a rebel captain as the ex-postmaster at Leavenworth — a hated Border Ruffian — and shot him dead. Colonel Deitzler, of the First Kansas, was carried from the smoke — a buckshot in his thigh. In some companies almost half the men fell. Lyon whooped up the reserved Second Kansas. Colonel R. B. Mitchell, on a small dun horse, led his men proudly into the battle smoke. A company or two faltered. Mitchell and his horse both fell. Orderlies held him on another mount. In the sulfurous fog a rebel horseman appeared as by magic and was shot in a heap — the horse's legs thrashing wildly. The charger may have stampeded with his helpless rider from the enemy. Lyon, riding in the turmoil, felt his own stallion buckle beneath his knees and collapse without a struggle. A bullet creased the general's head.

Stunned, Lyon picked himself up from the ground, limped a few steps to the rear, and sat down trembling. Major Sturgis, his clean-shaven face smudged now with battle smoke, rode up inquiringly, swung from the saddle and saluted. The dazed general seemed to recognize him. Sturgis shouted for a fresh horse. "It is not necessary," Lyon said absently, but he took the proffered reins. The major noticed a trickle of blood under the general's hat and lifted it to investigate. "That's nothing, Major," Lyon said, "but a wound in the head."

The general stood up unsteadily. An orderly helped him mount a fresh horse and followed him into the smoke. Sturgis heard a distant war whoop from the enemy's right — the shrill yell McCulloch's men had learned from the Indians during their summer encampment at Fort Smith. Evidently a charge was coming. Sturgis looked at the general's bloodstained hat in his hand, threw it down, and galloped away to help hold the line.

Where was Sigel? His attacks on the Confederate rear should ease the pressure here, but no one had heard from him. Then an artilleryman from DuBois's battery noticed something familiar about the screech of incoming cannon balls. "Great God!" he exclaimed. "They're shooting Sigel's ammunition at us." A shell that failed to explode was examined and found to be Sigel's, sure enough. So the German was done for, but in spite of the discouraging news the Confederates withdrew for a second time. Surely they were not retreating. More likely they were re-forming to strike again. Now with Sigel defeated, the entire Confederate Army could concentrate on Lyon's line and the general, weakened by loss of blood from two wounds, might give way. Was Wilson's Creek to be a second Bull Run? Perhaps Lyon should save his army by retreating. But he was not that kind of soldier. Neither was redheaded Sweeney. The Kansans, although badly cut to pieces, wanted only to be led forward. Let the Confederates come again — four to one — if they dared!

The details of Sigel's misfortune were not known for several hours. He had circled east of the enemy in the dark as planned, placed four of his six guns and supporting infantry within striking distance of Colonel T. J. Churchill's Arkansas Mounted Rifles three miles from the place where Lyon was to strike. Then Sigel moved the rest of his men to attack other positions farther in the rear. When Lyon's signal gun fired, Sigel's cannon replied, and his men moved forward. Churchill was completely surprised and fled from the grapeshot whistling among the camp kettles, knocking down mules and men. The Germans rushed in, helped themselves to the rebels' breakfast and anything else they could find in the tents. Churchill's men had captured the entire company Sigel left at Neosho last month. Now the Germans wanted revenge! But Churchill's Arkansans reorganized in the brush, came back shooting, found the looting Germans completely out of control and killed or captured all of them.

Sigel, in the meantime, marching with the balance of his force south of the enemy encampment, passed the herds of cattle and the slaughter grounds near the wire road. He was now fully three quarters of the way around the enemy's army. In doing this, he crossed the open prairie. McCulloch, riding distractedly through this part of his army, spied him and estimated his number. Here was the kind of simple combat McCulloch understood. Waving the fancy rifle he always carried, the Texan whooped every man in sight against the Germans. Louis Hebert had just come in from his fight in the broomcorn. His eager men swung merrily down the road for this new assault. Sigel saw them coming — neat gray uniforms, drums bobbing against marching legs. He mistook them for the First Iowa, surmised that Lyon's victory was complete, and ordered his men to hold their fire.

Totally deceived, Sigel's men were soon shot to pieces. They lost their artillery, their battle flags, and many of their lives. Only Eugene Carr escaped with a remnant in formation. Sigel, disguised with a blue blanket around his shoulders, rode into Springfield with one orderly and went to bed exhausted.

Back on the battlefield, McCulloch assembled his men — the entire army now — for a third assault against Lyon. Churchill and Hebert brought in their victorious men to help Price. The men rallied along the wire road under the bluff — the Pelicans and Texans on the right, Churchill's Arkansas on the left. Price's Missourians lined up in the center with Pearce's Arkansas behind them. This was the largest number of men the Confederates had yet assembled for a single action. The unarmed men, thin, ragged hillbillies, some with loaded bullet bags, stood in the rear waiting for the charge that might gain them guns from the "furriners." Those with shotguns and flintlocks formed companies. "Pap" Price, in linen duster and high, black wool hat, rode before the ragged horde. "Now boys," he shouted, "here are the damned Dutch you have all been so anxious to meet: You see I am not afraid of them: Show them how you can fight."

The irregular line crossed the wire road and started up through the brush. Adjutant Thomas Snead, riding beside Price, reported his white-haired hero as shouting, "You will soon be in a pretty hot place, men! But I will be near you, and will take care of you; keep cool as the inside of a cucumber and give them thunder." (Readers may edit these words of Thomas Snead's statement as their judgments dictate.)

When the men neared the top of the bluff, Price could hear Federal officers shout commands. Brush snapped as the Union soldiers readied arms to meet the assault. The click of a thousand cocking hammers rattled along the line. Next moment, a volley crashed and a tidal wave of smoke rolled down the slope through the oaks. At the center of the line Price's Missourians stood doggedly before the blast, Old Pap riding along behind them. Several bullets ripped his clothes. One nipped him in the side. "That isn't fair," he said to Adjutant Snead. "If I were as slim as Lyon that fellow would have missed me entirely." On the Confederate left the Third Arkansas crouched low and fired at ghostly figures in the choking billows. On the right the Texans and Pelicans, elated after two victorious assaults — in the broomcorn and against Sigel — rushed through the brush with a yell. Let Louisianans show the whole Confederate Army how to fight!

For the third time the two lines met under clouds of powder smoke.

Schofield, riding beside Lyon, noticed the general's bloody wounds and dazed condition. The Kansans, fanatically furious over the loss of their two colonels, seemed eager for a desperate charge — so Schofield thought. The time seemed right to bring up the First Iowans from reserve and strike with the combined regiments.

"General," Schofield began, "let us try it."

Lyon's wan face lighted with the encouraging words, and the two officers rode back to the reserves, formed them in line. With Lyon at the right and Schofield at the left they came forward. At the firing line, Schofield's horse plunged and fell. The adjutant jumped clear, and called to his orderly for his remount, but the man had disappeared. The major used to tell later how the fellow justified himself by saying that he had retreated to save the animal. On foot, Schofield turned to his reinforcements, ordered them to fix bayonets and prepare to charge the enemy who, with flintlock muskets and shotguns, would be helpless before them. Schofield drew his sword and waving it in the air shouted, "Charge."

To his surprise the men did not follow. These volunteers had no taste for cold steel and continued to shoot into the bank of smoke ahead. Schofield found himself between the two fires. He turned quickly and hurried around the regiment's flank. As he did so, he noticed a soldier loading and firing his musket into the sky. Schofield stopped, grasped him by the arm, and shook him like a schoolboy. The man roused as from a trance and began aiming the piece rationally.

Major Schofield passed on down the rear of the firing line to rejoin Lyon and plan the next movement. The Iowa men seemed to be taking their baptism of fire stoically. One volunteer wrote a friend, after the battle, that he was knocked down and felt a sharp pain in his shoulder. He jumped to his feet and raised his gun to fire, when the man beside him said, "You are shot." This remark, and not the pain, made the field whirl before the wounded man's eyes. He turned and staggered to the rear, falling down once or twice from dizziness.

Schofield completed circling the Iowa reserves, watching for Lyon. As he walked, he saw ahead on the ground the soles of a man's boots. He recognized Ed Lehman, Lyon's orderly, sobbing over the general's body — shot through the heart, his lifeblood in a pool on the flat limestone slabs. A perplexed frown wrinkled the dead general's forehead. Schofield knelt and shouted in the orderly's ear to stop his crying and carry Lyon's body quickly to the rear, lest the fighting line become discouraged. Four men carried the limp form away, placed it in the shade of a blackjack, and covered the face with a torn blanket.

Major Schofield was unsure who should be in command now. He knew that Sweeney had been wounded and carried from the field, his stub arm twitching protest. Schofield caught a loose "secesh" horse, mounted it, and rode off to tell Major Sturgis that he was the ranking officer. Later, Schofield learned that there was a lieutenant colonel of volunteers, who might have claimed the command.

Sturgis assumed the responsibility, clattered back and inspected the fighting lines in silence. For an hour the men continued their bombardment — Missourians against Missourians in the center, Texans, Pelicans, and Arkansans against Kansans, Iowans, and Germans on the flanks. Finally the exhausted Southerners withdrew down into the brush along Wilson's Creek, and silence reigned across the field. Soldiers began to joke. They put down their hot-barreled rifles, laughed at the dirty stains on one another's faces from biting cartridges. They uncorked canteens, drank heartily, and poured water into each other's hands to wash faces and grimy necks.

A party of officers rode out into the deserted field, guiding their horses around the fallen bodies. Eight hundred and eighty-eight Confederates and eight hundred ninety-two Federals were later picked up between the Union line and the edge of the bluff. Schofield spurred to the edge of the point and looked down. Through the brush he could see the enemy reforming for half a mile along the wire road, evidently preparing a fourth charge. Sigel's captured flag was down there in the enemy's hands, being waved exultantly.

Schofield cantered back. All regimental officers were called for a conference, and as they sat on their horses talking, the rebels appeared again, Churchill's First Arkansas brandishing the flag captured from Sigel. Once again the Federals poured a cataract of lead into the oncoming line and another billow of smoke rolled over it. The Confederates faltered but did not break, and the two lines writhed back and forth in a death grapple. Finally the Southerners retired down the ridge for the fourth time, a slave belonging to Ben Griffith staggering after them, carrying his wounded master.

Sturgis watched the enemy withdraw through the dissolving smoke. He looked at his watch. The hands pointed to 11:30 A.M. His men had been fighting without food since supper the night before. Ammunition was running low. Would his tired men stand steadfast against another assault? As a veteran regular, he knew the weaknesses of human flesh. Against the advice of Gordon Granger, to whom he usually deferred, Sturgis ordered a retreat. Major Schofield stated, years hence, that the battle was won had Sturgis but known it. Perhaps it is no coincidence that Schofield, a much younger man, ended the war as a major general and so did Granger, while Sturgis was only a brigadier. Had the fortunes of battle spared Lyon, Wilson's Creek might have been the most brilliant victory of the Civil War. General Sherman blamed the next four years of strife and pillage in Missouri on Lyon's death.

Wilson's Creek battle losses on both sides were staggering. The Union killed, wounded, and missing totaled 1317. The rebels lost 1230. The First Missouri and First Kansas, which stood on the front line and almost broke before Schofield and Lyon brought reinforcements, lost 295 out of less than 800, and 284 out of 644. Company E of the First Kansas went in with 76 and came out with only 26. Of Captain Walker's 64 men in Company F of the Second Kansas, only 24 were uninjured. The singing company of the First Iowa, which had worried Lyon, did not lose a man, but the regiment suffered 150 casualties. No battle in the Civil War had a higher percentage of over-all losses. Bull Run suffered less than 10 per cent casualties. The Battle of Alma in the Crimean War, famous for its slaughter, had losses of only a fraction over 8 per cent, although the Light Brigade at Balaclava lost 36 per cent, and one regiment at Gettysburg lost 82 per cent. The casualties at Wilson's Creek amounted to over 23 per cent of all engaged.

Remarkable too, about the battle of Wilson's Creek, was the high percentage of future generals in the engagement. Of the Union officers in command seven became major generals and twenty-three would wear brigadiers' stars. The citizen soldiers' courage under fire stopped regulars from disparaging the fighting qualities of volunteers, and the Northerners marched away with the satisfying proof that a mudsill would fight as doggedly as a cavalier. Never again would an informed Southerner believe that one Confederate could whip five Yankees.

X V I

The Fall of Lexington

THE BROKEN Union Army retreated to Rolla and entrained for St. Louis. Price, occupying Springfield, prepared for a triumphal return to the capital of Missouri. His allies, McCulloch and Pearce, both withdrew with their men to Arkansas. To oppose Price, Senator James Henry Lane and General John C. Frémont each prepared to act in his own peculiar manner — both of them wrong. Grim Chieftain Lane had the vaguest authority. Although commissioned a brigadier general, he dared not accept the honor for fear of forfeiting his seat in the Senate. Yet he determined to act. Carefully signing his name to official orders as "J. H. Lane, Commanding Army of Western Border," he began a speaking tour. With all the authority of a commissioned general, he urged enlistments in a giant jayhawking expedition, apparently an independent unit of his own, to carry the old bloodstained banner of Kansas to the Gulf. He reminded prospective recruits that cavalrymen could each lead back a horse. Infantrymen could lead back one and ride another. Wild fellows flocked to his standard. Dan Anthony of the *Leavenworth Conservative,* recently acquitted of murder in the killing of the editor of the *Herald,* offered his services. Lane appointed him provost marshal of Kansas City. Thomas Ewing, Jr., chief justice of the Kansas Supreme Court, accepted a commission from Lane to enlist a regiment. Then Lane whipped away to southern Kansas where he assumed command over Jennison's and Montgomery's regiments at Fort Scott, waiting for Price's northern advance.

Frémont, in the meantime, organized the vast resources of his Department of the West, which included Illinois, Missouri, and the territory westward to the mountains. In order to work efficiently, he established headquarters in the J. B. Brant mansion on Chouteau Avenue in St. Louis.

Here, surrounded by capable civilians, West Pointers, and many foreign officers, he began shaping order out of Missouri chaos. For chief of staff he employed the stern and aloof Hungarian, Alexander S. Asboth, who had come to America with Kossuth, the revolutionist.

Efficient and systematic, Frémont suppressed disorder. He stopped open enlistments in the Confederate Army, removed pictures of Jeff Davis and Beauregard from shop windows. The city became a beehive of activity. Streets throbbed with military bands. Let traitors know the nation's might. Columns of marching men with twinkling legs and aligned muskets wheeled around street corners. Almost daily, new uniforms caused comment on the sidewalks as the wearers sauntered jauntily about. The Jessie Frémont Guard wore an exquisite cavalry cap over the right eye. It required the wearer to hold his head back, his chin in, and his chest out — all to the hussar's immense pride. The commander of this select troop was the chivalrous and athletic Hungarian, Charles Zagoni. Jessie Frémont, the general's talented and vivacious wife, was the daughter of Senator Thomas Hart Benton, rival of David Rice Atchison and leader of the antislavery Democrats in Missouri until his death in 1858. St. Louis was her home, and she drove around town in a fine barouche as to the manner born. She had married John Frémont when he was a lieutenant. Her father, with Jessie's help, had made him the popular Pathfinder. "I have tried all my life," she told a newspaper reporter, "to make Frémont assert himself. He never does. It would be better for him if he would."

Frémont had refused to send reinforcements to Lyon, because his men were needed to defend Cairo. The junction of the Mississippi and Ohio rivers seemed more important than an outpost in southwest Missouri. He had sent additional troops to the Rolla railhead, where they could threaten Jeff Thompson and be drawn in quickly, if necessary, for a sudden defense of St. Louis. He employed the potentially dangerous loafers in town to work on fortifications — expensive, yes, but cheaper to feed than fight them. He contracted with James B. Eads to build seven iron-clad gunboats, and he dispatched John Pope along the Hannibal and St. Joseph Railroad to crush out the independent ranger bands infesting northern Missouri. When Sturgis brought his shattered column in from Wilson's Creek, Frémont sent it to reinforce Pope. Major Schofield, knowing the deceased Lyon's intimacy with Frank Blair, called on the politician. Together, they went to see Frémont. Uniformed sentries stood on guard around the mansion, at the gateway, and in the halls. The basement had been converted into an armory. On the first floor sat lesser executives at their desks. Upstairs, Frémont and his staff maintained their offices. The two visitors, screened by three sets of officials, were finally ushered before the general — after a delay which annoyed politician Blair, whose brother, in Lincoln's cabinet, had helped get the Personage's commission.

This involved procedure was Frémont efficiency — self-protection to which the general was entitled in order that he might accomplish the maximum amount of work. To him, Blair and Schofield were only a colonel and a major in his command. Feverishly full of projects, he told his guests of his plan to march south, retake Missouri and Arkansas. His operation was being systematically prepared. But while talking to Lyon's best friend and the martyr commander's adjutant, fresh from Wilson's Creek, Frémont neglected to say a word about the battle. Undoubtedly it was a bitter subject.

The Blairs and the Bentons were the two most powerful antislavery families in Missouri. They had led the fight together, and for years had been intimate — visiting in one another's Washington and St. Louis homes. Now, Frémont felt his rank and seemed to be assuming full authority. The forceful Blair expected the co-operation he had received from Lyon, who also had ranked him in the army but recognized Blair's political importance. Co-operation was Frémont's weakest characteristic. He had achieved success as a pathfinder among primitive people instead of among his peers. Neither Major Schofield nor Colonel Blair remonstrated with the major general, but the latter went down the stairs, after the interview, nursing resentment.

As Frémont devoted weeks to the proper fashioning of his grandiose preparations, Senator Lane, having taken self-appointed command of the Kansas brigade in Frémont's department, pronounced the town of Fort Scott untenable in case of attack and set the men to work on a new fortification twelve miles away. He named it Fort Lincoln. The work was barely completed in late August when Price started north to retake the state with ten thousand Wilson's Creek veterans. Along the roads, farm boys joined the column bringing cherished guns, pet horses, and enthu-

siasm for high adventure. Frémont, feeling the foundations of his department quake beneath his polished military boots, sat up all night working
on a proclamation to stop the continued enlistments of Southern sympathizers in rebel forces. Early in the morning of August 30, 1861, he read
to Jessie what he had written, got her approval, and handed the document
to his adjutant. Word went out across the state and across the nation that
Frémont had put Missouri under martial law. Men bearing arms without authority were to be court-martialed and shot. Slaves belonging to
masters disloyal to the United States were to be freed.

This emancipation proclamation, designed to quiet Missouri, excited
the entire nation. The Northern abolition press praised Frémont's positive
stand, but Lincoln, who wanted to hold the loyalty of other slaveholding
border states, wrote privately to the Pathfinder, asking him to modify the
decree's severity. M. Jeff Thompson, in the swamps of southeast Missouri,
issued a counterproclamation on September 2, 1861. He outdid his opponent by announcing that for every man executed under Frémont's order,
he would "HANG, DRAW and QUARTER a minion of said Abraham Lincoln."
Then, to demonstrate his cruelty, the Swamp Fox promptly hanged a
horse thief, forded a bayou saddle-skirt deep, dashed into the town of
Charleston, took $56,000 from the bank to finance his further operations,
and disappeared into the watery wastes of Mingo and Nigger Wool
swamps.

The national excitement and the renewed disturbances in eastern Mis-
souri drew attention from Price's threatening advance in the West. On
the day before M. Jeff Thompson replied to Frémont, the left wing of
Price's army was spied by Lane's men on Dry Wood Creek east of Fort
Scott. Montgomery's regiment skirmished with them and withdrew into
Kansas. Price did not follow. He was interested only in repossessing Mis-
souri. A few captured rebels told Lane that Old Pap was heading first for
Lexington.

This wealthy little town was the headquarters of Russell, Majors and
Waddell's overland freighting business and the most important center of
population between St. Louis and Kansas City.

Lane, with only two thousand men, dared not turn and attack Price's
ten thousand. Instead Lane sent a messenger galloping north to beg reinforcements from Major W. E. Prince at Fort Leavenworth. Then, in

Price's wake, Lane started north to indulge his men in a special kind of warfare which the Grim Chieftain believed suitable for the emergency.

Meanwhile, Lane's message reached Major Prince on September 7, 1861. The major telegraphed Frémont. His wire was one of a series of annoyances which harassed the Pathfinder in rapid succession. First, Lincoln had censured him for his radical attempt to restore peace by threatening abolition. At the same time the President had taken five thousand of his much-needed troops East. Then, to cap the cumulating adversities, came Prince's wire announcing the advance of Price's ever-victorious army and the threat that the guerrilla bands north of the Missouri might join with him and perhaps take over the state. In desperation, Frémont wrote Lincoln that he would not alter the proclamation, and he sent Jessie hurrying to Washington to explain the situation to the President in person — a futile act, for Lincoln replied to Frémont by canceling the emancipation proclamation. The general, in the meantime, ordered Pope and Sturgis to concentrate on Lexington and prevent its capture. He also ordered Lane to fall back on Fort Leavenworth.

Colonel James A. Mulligan, at Jefferson City, a hundred and twenty-five miles downriver from Lexington, learned about Price's incursion at the time of the Dry Wood skirmish. As yet he did not know Price's destination. Perhaps he was headed for Jefferson City. The tall, dark-eyed Irishman had recently married and might be expected to wait in his comfortable surroundings at the capital, but Mulligan was an excessively ambitious Chicago politician. His sensitive and delicate features belied his brave and combative heart.

The roads had been churned by rain into troughs of mush, but Mulligan ordered out his men and plodded away, hunting the enemy. Constantly his scouts sloshed in with nothing to report. Finally Price was located, sweeping north toward either Lexington or Kansas City. Mulligan headed for the former town and on the ninth day of his march saw the brick buildings of Lexington peeping over the green trees on the highlands above the Missouri River. Mulligan ordered his regiment halted. Men broke ranks to wash their faces, brush mud from their clothes, polish guns, and joke about the pretty girls who would admire their uniforms as they marched briskly through town.

The glittering column swung down the main street, the Stars and

Stripes beside a green banner embroidered with a golden harp. The marching men watched for girls, noted the substantial buildings, some with grillwork shipped upriver from New Orleans. A colonnaded courthouse stood on a green knoll, and yonder was the strongest bank in western Missouri with gold enough to whet the appetite of any invader. It was hard to believe that the fabulously wealthy firm of Russell, Majors and Waddell with their 6000 teamsters and 45,000 oxen was now bankrupt. The extravagance of the Pony Express had finished it. That rich partnership and this rich town were notorious for working together in 1856, searching steamboats, confiscating free-state settlers' guns. Let them suffer!

North of Lexington, on a verdant campus overlooking the Missouri, stood the white-pillared Masonic College. The Irish brigade wheeled north to the academic gates. Here Mulligan found Colonel Thomas A. Marshall with a regiment of Illinois cavalry and three hundred and fifty home guards. The collegiate oaks had already been chopped down preparatory to fortifying the location. The two colonels compared commissions. Mulligan held seniority, thus giving the native-born countrymen another reason to complain about Lincoln's rule by foreigners — "Yer dam Dutchmen, yer Poles, Eyetalians, yer Swiss, Danes and French." As a matter of fact, only about a third of the garrison was Irish, but the force was soon joined by a German regiment from Kansas City under Colonel Everett Peabody, thus giving a strong foreign flavor to the whole.

Mulligan selected the college buildings as his headquarters, requisitioned $900,000 from the bank, buried it under his tent, set his men pointing the felled oaks into abatis, and sent a courier downriver to Frémont for reinforcements. The Pathfinder was as yet unprepared to take the offensive, having barely enough men to suppress the rebels in St. Louis. Moreover, his administration was being thwarted at every turn by Frank Blair, and it might be necessary to arrest his old friend for the good of the service. To do so would be a bold act which Frémont hesitated to take, but Blair's destructive criticism must be stopped. With his own headquarters and the whole department in jeopardy, Frémont could send no more men.

To Mulligan the situation looked bad. He had, all told, twenty-eight hundred soldiers to meet Price's ten thousand. The Irishman determined to fortify the seventeen acres around the college with heavy breastworks. The town, its fine courthouse, business block, and many mansions would be abandoned to the enemy.

The elaborate work was hardly commenced on September 11, 1861, when Price's van appeared south of town, halted, deployed a guard, and bivouacked. All night Mulligan's men worked feverishly with their spades. At dawn on September 12, before the day shift took over the shovels, Colonel Peabody rode out with three companies, burned the bridge over which the Southerners must come, and fired at their encampment. The invaders withdrew, circled to the Independence road from the west, and in the afternoon felt out the defenses on that side. To meet them, Mulligan sent out six companies, which opened fire from lanes and hedgerows. A Union battalion in the cemetery used the mounds and monuments as fortifications.

Again the enemy withdrew, but the Federal soldiers noticed new regiments coming in hourly from the south. During the afternoon Henry Guibor — paroled at Camp Jackson — arrived with his battery which had made a name for itself at Wilson's Creek. Taking position, he blazed away with grape and homemade canister at the hedgerows. One shell exploded near a group of Federal officers and sent them racing pell-mell into Lexington, where they drew rein, shamefacedly explaining that the noise had made their mounts unmanageable.

Mulligan ordered a battery to reply to Guibor. A lucky shot hit one of his guns and exploded a caisson. Workmen threw down their shovels to cheer as the smoke mushroomed into the sky.

Price had little ammunition in his van. He retired a third time to establish camp at the fairgrounds and wait for his entire army before renewing the fight. Hundreds of country people came to town on horseback, in wagons, and on foot to watch the impending battle — see the "furriners get licked." They crowded the streets as at fair time, packed the taverns, slept in livery stables and on the lawn before the ornate courthouse.

On the morning of September 13, 1861, General Monroe M. Parsons sent a flag of truce to Mulligan. Parsons had started an active military career as a militia officer on the Missouri border in 1860. At Carthage and at Wilson's Creek he had gained deserved recognition. Now, as commander of Price's van, he asked for a cessation of hostilities to permit removing the wounded. Parsons reminded Mulligan that a similar courtesy had been allowed the Federals at Wilson's Creek. The Irishman acquiesced.

Evidently Price felt no need to hurry, no fear of Frémont's converging troops. He placed each new regiment, as it arrived, in a circle around the college grounds. His men camped in the town streets, on residents' lawns, and in the churches. Federals, behind their fortifications, heard all the enemy bugle calls. They feared a surprise attack at night and moved from their tents to dugouts in the trenches. On Sunday, September 15, Father Thaddeus Butler said mass on the hillside beyond the college buildings. Then the men returned to their duties — rolling cartridges, shoveling dirt to strengthen breastworks. Supplies were running low and Mulligan cut rations in half. Especially unfortunate was the scarcity of horse feed for the large number of animals in the besieged ramparts.

On September 17, 1861, Price's ammunition wagons arrived. The town was cleared for action. Houses in line of artillery fire were knocked down and all civilians were ordered to leave. Among them went Mrs. Mulligan, the nineteen-year-old bride of the commander out at the fortified college.

The Federals watched Price's preparations and knew that the day of reckoning had come. Mulligan's long, waving hair and sweeping mustache appeared constantly above the fortifications. He watched the enemy's advancing banners and gleaming guns, listened to the threatening tattoo of drums. General Rains posted his men east and southeast of the college. General Parsons deployed on Main Street and moved north within striking distance of the fortifications. Colonels B. A. Rives and John T. Hughes, the latter a kinsman of Price's and ex-clerk of the Kansas legislature, deployed a thin line of men through the tall weeds along the Missouri River below the bluff. Thus the college grounds were completely surrounded and the Federals cut off from water. A steamboat, moored below the fortifications, was captured without resistance. In the ominous silence, Father Butler walked along the Federal embankments blessing the men.

At 10 A.M. on September 18, with the sun beating down mercilessly, Price opened with sixteen guns. The concussion broke windows in town.

Hiram Bledsoe had been wounded at Dry Wood and was not present, but the dull boom of Ol' Sacramento was recognized by people who had heard it thunder here in Lexington on many a Fourth of July. Under the bombardment General Rains moved his men forward, and as he passed the batteries, he offered a gold medal to the artilleryman who could shoot down the flag on the battlement ahead. Then, turning to an aide, he sent out word that the descending banner would be the cue for a general assault which would put his men ahead of any other division — optimistic braggadocio, for the flag was still flying at midmorning.

Over on the river, the thin line of skirmishers complained about shots coming from brick building two hundred and fifty yards outside the Federal battlements. A hospital flag flew from the structure, so it had been spared. Now a few rebel companies organized under the riverbank to rush and capture the hospital. At a given signal they scrambled up the slope, through weeds tall as a man. Here and there hidden mines exploded, wounding some. The rebels skipped over or around the smoking craters, and stormed in the hospital's main entrance, up a circular stair, and down the halls. The building was a hospital, truly enough, with many sick and wounded in cots on the second floor, and in the basement a pack of huddled slaves. But the snipers had hidden or escaped. From the balcony and from roof gutters the invaders looked down into the college fortifications. What a place for sharpshooters to pick off Union officers!

Mulligan, watching from the college, saw that the hospital must be retaken if possible. He called for volunteers. The men looked at the two hundred and fifty yards of open ground between them and the well-defended building, with no cover but wild flowers. None volunteered. Mulligan strode down before his Montgomery Guards. He owed his success in politics and in war to fluent oratory, and now he delivered the speech of his life. Frankly, he said that the building must be taken and that he was asking his guards to do what others had refused to consider. Would they go? The Irishmen cheered, eager for the chance. A company of Peabody's Germans asked to go with them.

The assault party rallied behind the sally port. Officers, about to die perhaps, drew their swords, and the companies marched out at quickstep, formed in line, and started at double time. Finally, as the distance shortened, they broke into a mad rush. Shots from the hospital sprawled some of the men among the weeds, but the survivors stormed in the door and up the stairs shooting over the cots at fleeing figures in the wings. Three trapped Southerners surrendered and were bayoneted while under guard. Another climbed in bed with a wounded Illinois soldier and thus saved himself until the furor subsided.

Almost exhausted from the charge and from the stifling heat in the hospital, the victors, finding no drinking water, fought among themselves for swigs from the bloody buckets used by surgeons to wash wounds. Thus disorganized and desperate, they were unprepared for the counterattack which drove them back to their fortifications at dark.

During the night, Mulligan strode around his lines. His men had been driven from several other outposts besides the hospital. The seven hundred horses within his fortifications were suffering for food, and worst of all, his two cisterns of drinking water were almost empty. Horsemen had stolen most of it for their animals regardless of the men's need. Mulligan detailed men to dig wells. The river was only two hundred feet below, and two springs on the bluff outside his lines indicated a high water table. As the well diggers set to work, soldiers at a hundred fires molded bullets for tomorrow's fight.

The next day, September 19, 1861, dawned hotter than ever. The water shortage behind the Union fortifications became acute, and the prospect of relief from Frémont seemed hopeless. Dead horses polluted the air with a sickening stench. Some men suffered from swollen tongues and cracked lips. The saltpeter in the powder tortured them every time they bit a cartridge. Blood trickled down their chins. Then a sudden downpour brought temporary relief. Men wrung their saturated blankets over basins and sucked the healing water. Mulligan rode around the wet and shining earthworks, encouraging the men to hold out one more day. Surely reinforcements would come from Frémont in St. Louis or from Lane in Kansas. The regiments under Pope and Sturgis north of the Missouri might arrive hourly. Mulligan did not know that, as he talked, Sturgis was across the river within fifteen miles of Lexington. He had detrained his men at Utica on the Hannibal and St. Joe Railroad, and while quartermasters were impressing supply wagons for the march to Lexington, his boys raided neighboring apiaries for honey. Irate owners stormed into camp, claiming damages. Sturgis lined up his men, picked out those with honey on their beards — and then marched them away without punishment. He could hear cannonading ahead and needed every man for the fight. At the Missouri River bottom, where the road emerged from the uplands and dipped into lush corn lands, a Negro stepped out in the dirt road, hat in hand.

"Ginral, don't go down dar. . . . Dey's captured de ferry, and dey knows you is comin', an' five thousand on 'em's hid in de woods by de river to kill ye."

Sturgis, the regular, with the same caution he displayed at Wilson's Creek, wheeled to the right and marched to Kansas City. His decision seems justifiable, for General Parsons was waiting for him with an adequate force to ambush his six companies. However, two other Union regiments and a battalion totaling in all thirty-three hundred men were within a day's march. Lacking communications, each unit feared to come in alone, and Lexington was abandoned to the enemy.

Mulligan knew nothing about the failure of the relief columns. Big guns pounded endlessly at his fortifications, geysers of sticks and dirt spraying along the line. Several incendiary hot shot thumped into the college rooms. Men with shovels saved the building by throwing the hot balls out the windows.

Meanwhile, the Federals' bombardment set several houses in town on fire. One cannon ball chipped away part of a column on the courthouse. Price's men laughed at a farmer volunteer who joined their lines with gun and dinner pail. Taking a position in sight of the parapet, he shot every head he could see above the embankment until noon, then retired, ate lunch, smoked his pipe, and returned to the grisly job. Another citizen volunteered a novel idea to end the siege. Why not advance to the enemy position behind a movable breastworks of hemp bales? Price thought the device worth trying, and wagons lined up before warehouses. All afternoon bales were hauled down to the river to be drenched, then up the hill to the hospital. During the night of September 19, 1861, the bales were arranged like a wall extending in two wings from the brick building.

Next morning the Federals saw a dark barrier lying like a snake across the ridges and hollows. As they watched, the line twitched and moved forward, crushing down weeds and sunflowers. It parted for trees and joined together after passing them. Men with levers were obviously prying the line forward. Sputtering rifles warned the Federals to beware.

Mulligan called up his artillery and ordered hot shot fired at the twitching line, but the wet bales did not burn. Occasionally a direct hit sent a bundle bouncing, but the gap was quickly filled. Absalom Grimes of the Ralls County Rangers, in action now, reported seeing a captain knocked flat by the impact of a cannon ball against the hemp bale he was hiding behind, but most hits rocked the compressed bundles harmlessly. Mulligan sent out a few daredevils to charge the line, but they failed to take it. Nothing he could do stopped the slow and relentless advance.

Sudden shouting at another part of the line attracted Mulligan's attention. At several places white flags appeared, contrary to his orders. Price sent over a courier to arrange the truce. Mulligan sent him back saying that he knew of no white flag unless Price had raised it. Then, on inquiry, Mulligan learned that one of his majors, who had twice been threatened with death if he dared surrender, had waved a handkerchief on a ramrod. Other discouraged men had done likewise. There was no doubt about the offer to surrender.

Mulligan called his top officers together and asked their decision. They voted to quit the fight — four against two. The Irishman dispatched the verdict to Price and all firing ceased. Price acknowledged the surrender and asked why the United States flag was not hauled down. Mulligan replied that his Irishmen had nailed it to the pole. This satisfied the serene and white-haired Price. He ordered troops formed for the capitulation. All enemy muskets were to be stacked. Officers and men were to keep side arms, personal property and horses — magnanimous provisions typical of Price.

Dutifully the defeated men emerged from the battlements and gave up their guns. A captain of the Thirteenth Missouri offered his sword to his brother on Price's staff. Meanwhile, inside the fortifications, the Irish regimental band began to play defiantly. General Rains looked inquiringly at Price, but the commander smiled indulgently. The irate Irish were marching and countermarching around their green and gold standard. In due time they, too, came out the gate, stacked their arms, and the siege was over.

The rebels had captured Marshall, Mulligan, and Peabody (the two latter wounded), the entire army, a thousand horses (suffering for feed and water), a hundred wagons, five pieces of artillery, three thousand muskets, and all that was left of the commissary. Their losses amounted to only twenty-five killed and seventy-two wounded. Price invited the vanquished officers to a champagne dinner, and immediately opened negotiations to exchange the prisoners for Missourians taken by Lyon at Camp Jackson. As yet, Price held no commission from the Confederate government, so his negotiations were an anomaly, but a cancellation of paroles was arranged. Then, after dallying two weeks in Lexington, Price ordered his army to march south. The crops were already harvested, so there was no necessity for a supply line. Field corn — sustaining if not appetizing — could be grated into meal by rubbing the hard kernels on sheets of tin roughened with nail holes. General Price endeared himself to the men by living on the same harsh rations. They also admired his chivalrous treatment of wounded Colonel Mulligan and his bride, who had come back after the surrender. The couple accompanied the column in Price's private carriage and had their tent pitched near the commander's at night. Undoubtedly the two politicians had much in common. A few complained that Price was much too benevolent for a military man.

The North wailed over the defeat louder than it had after Wilson's Creek. Frémont was accused of sacrificing Mulligan as he did Lyon the previous month. Critics complained that he had twenty-five thousand men available and ten days to get them to Lexington — a statement ignoring the necessity of troops in other theaters. The fact remains, however, that Frémont failed to force available troops, under Sturgis, Pope, and Prince, to strike Price in the rear and divert him from the siege. Perhaps the Pathfinder's mind was overly harassed by the quarrel with Blair, for during the height of battle at Lexington, he arrested his old family friend. Critics also asked what had become of Senator Jim Lane and his new kind of warfare which had promised so much in this emergency?

XVII

Osceola, Zagoni, and Frémont's Recall

LANE had obeyed Frémont's order to march north, but instead of trying to overtake Price's big army, he decided to destroy all towns along his wake which had welcomed the rebels. Lane told his eager followers, "Everything disloyal, from a Shanghai rooster to a Durham cow, must be cleaned out." His chaplains even plundered furnishings for the churches in Lawrence. Regardless of Lincoln's modification of Frémont's emancipation order, Lane distributed copies of the original as he marched.

His progress northward was interrupted by the report of a raid on the town of Humboldt, forty miles west of Fort Scott, on September 8, 1861. The Grim Chieftain detached two hundred men in charge of James G. Blunt, a Kansas doctor who had been associated with John Brown's underground railroad. Riding west to chastise the raiders, Blunt met young Preston Plumb, a candidate for the legislature now, with nineteen men from Emporia, also seeking the marauders. The companies combined and overtook the raiders at the Quapaw Agency. In a short skirmish they killed several men, including the leader, who was identified as John Mathews, Indian trader and Osage squawman. In Mathew's pocket, Lane's men found an order from Ben McCulloch to enroll the Quapaw Indians under the Confederate banner. So the South had stooped to winning the war with the scalping knife! The North screamed resentment — all but Jim Lane. He had been considering doing the same thing, himself.

Marching leisurely northward, distributing the barred Frémont proclamation, Lane's army came to Osceola, ninety miles south of the Missouri River, on September 22, 1861 — just two days after Price had occupied Lexington. Osceola, with a population of two or three thousand, was an important wholesale distributing point at the head of navigation on the

Osage River. Lane's advance cavalry complained that townsmen had shot at them. To retaliate, the horsemen thundered down the main street firing indiscriminately. Montgomery's regiment marched in behind them. Soon Lane himself arrived. Inspecting warehouses while his men reveled, Lane found tons of lead, kegs of powder, and a large supply of cartridge paper. Could this be Price's depot? His foraging men rolled out barrels of brandy, 3000 sacks of flour, 500 pounds of sugar and molasses, 50 sacks of coffee, a quantity of bacon, and camp equipment — all suitable for Lane's army.

Lane impressed teams and wagons from the livery barns and neighboring farms. One set of men loaded the supplies, while a drumhead court-martial sentenced and shot nine citizens. Then Lane announced that Osceola must be "knocked into Herculaneum." The courthouse, with its records, and all but three of the houses were burned to the ground. Lane drove out of town with three hundred of his men in wagons — too drunk to march. In addition to the supplies, Lane's plunder included 350 horses and mules, 400 cattle, 200 Negroes, and a fine carriage which the Grim Chieftain sent to his family in Lawrence. The rear guard nailed an American flag to a tree in front of the charred wreckage of Senator Waldo P. Johnson's house. He had been a colleague of Lane's in Washington, but a member of the opposition party. The property destroyed or appropriated was reckoned to be worth a million dollars — ample compensation for the Southerners' capture of Lexington, according to Lane's calculations.

Lane's reputation galloped ahead of his column. Negroes by the dozen joined him at every crossroad, shouting "Bress de Lord." Some brought fine horses and good wagons, evidently taken from their masters' plantations.

Major W. E. Prince, in Leavenworth, learned about Lane's depredations, and wrote him that he hoped the looting might be stopped. Governor Robinson appealed directly to General Frémont. Lane feared trouble and whipped away from his column to harangue the people in his favor. Rallying audiences at Leavenworth and other Kansas towns, he defended his actions as the quickest way to stamp out treason. He urged the enlistment of more jayhawkers and also Indians to sweep across the South with fire and tomahawk.

Lane's oratory pleased the radicals in both East and West. Righteous adventurers flocked to his banner. John Brown, Jr., with sixty "sharp-shooters" eager to join Lane, passed through Chicago singing, "John Brown's Body." The idea of an Indian expedition kindled Eastern imaginations. *Harper's Weekly* printed a picture of Lane and his red men. The Grim Chieftain wrote Lincoln that ample troops were available but that Governor Robinson was working "in season and out of season" to ruin his plans for victory. He urged the President to sidetrack both Robinson and Frémont by creating a new Department of Kansas, and he offered to resign his seat in the Senate if given command.

Lane's army of twenty-five or thirty hundred men encamped outside Kansas City. Their reputation attracted the curious. Soldiers from Pope's army — the troops who had concentrated to save Mulligan but failed to do so — visited the notorious riffraff. Lieutenant Seymour D. Thompson of the Third Iowa, reported Lane to be "the last man we would have taken for a general. He had on citizens' pants, a soldier's blouse, and a dilapidated white hat. He rolled under his dark brows a pair of piercing eyes, and between his jaws a huge quid of tobacco. . . ." A *New York Times* reporter described the Grim Chieftain as being full of rollicking humor, a "Joe Bagstock Nero fiddling and laughing over the burning of some Missouri Rome."

Visitors described Lane's army as "a ragged, half-armed, diseased, mutinous rabble, taking votes whether any troublesome or distasteful order should be obeyed or defied." The men boasted about plundering. All seemed to be hard up for cash and eagerly offered to sell rebel caps for souvenirs at ten cents each. Negroes and Indians mingled with the white rowdies. Fall Leaf, the Delaware from the reservation above Lawrence, had joined with fifty-four red men dressed in a mixture of savage and civilized attire. Still speaking broken English, this Hercules of an Indian, who had brought back the nuggets which started the Pikes Peak gold rush, stalked proudly through the throng. Thirty Wyandottes also enlisted as a company in Lane's army.

Lane issued an order prohibiting his men from appropriating private property for personal use, but few obeyed him. One party of travelers on good horses was robbed at the edge of his camp, and the leader of the thieves, according to a newspaper account, was Montgomery himself.

As these jayhawkers roistered around Kansas City, Sterling Price marched his army leisurely southward, living off the country. The roads became excessively muddy, and the horses contracted "grease heel," compelling their riders to dismount and lead them. Proslavery farmers along the road greeted the column hospitably, treated them to pitchers of cold buttermilk from their springhouses, invited them to join games and dances. Charles Quantrill, who had followed the command with his slant-eyed crew, deserted with his gang somewhere on this southern march. A man of liquor and women, reckless when in command, he fretted under the disciplined routine of a large army. The distant border offered more excitement than he could find in his homey farm-boy cavalcade. Most of the other volunteers followed Old Pap with childlike devotion. They wrote home about their patriotic emotions, whistled at the girls in country towns, and shouted at those who waved from farm porches. Private Grimes described a jolly "church social" down near the famous battle-field of Carthage. In a game called King's Chair, one of Absalom's comrades volunteered to be "it." He was ushered into a room full of people who could hardly keep their faces straight. The gallant volunteer was asked to sit down on what appeared to be a sheet-covered bench between two very pretty girls. As a matter of fact there was no bench. The girls were sitting on opposite ends of a sheet stretched over a washtub between two stools. As the soldier sat down, the girls stood up amid shouts of merriment as the victim jackknifed into the water. Ab Grimes laughed until his sides ached. Then another game was suggested. A charming brunette offered to wager Ab a kiss against a dime that he could not balance her ring on his forehead and toss it into a funnel in his belt. Ab felt confident that he could win the bet — but let him tell what happened:

> While my head was pushed back one of those sweet, gentle girls whom I had admired so highly, poured a half-gallon dipper of cold water into that funnel. . . . There was but one place for the water to go and it went there without delay.

Next day the boys marched away, their heads dizzy with memories of laughing feminine faces. In the evening Ab and his friends met more Confederates marching south by another road. Both columns exchanged funny experiences and trudged on together.

Price's leisurely retreat gave Frank Blair renewed opportunity to blame

Frémont's administration. The Pathfinder had released him from arrest and Frank determined to get a full measure of revenge. It was said of the Blairs that when they went in for a fight, they came out with a funeral. Jessie Frémont had been unsuccessful in her interview with Lincoln, and Frémont saw that he was losing favor. Maliciously, Blair and his associates publicized the Pathfinder's shortcomings. They exaggerated his guilt in the Wilson's Creek and Lexington defeats, even blamed him for Pope's failure to quell Mart Green, the guerrilla, in north Missouri. Frémont was censured for coming tardily to St. Louis after his appointment. Blair described his extravagances in constructing useless fortifications and scoffed at his military panoply. Frémont was also accused of employing men of questionable reputation, of building up a political machine — a rival to Blair's! Many of the Pathfinder's California friends had come to St. Louis seeking cushioned chairs and had found them. Most notorious were Colonel I. C. Wood, who had screened visitors from the Presence, and Captain L. Haskell, chief of the St. Louis police. Several of the big Eastern newspapers which had supported the Pathfinder turned against him, especially the powerful *New York Times* and the *Herald*.

Only one thing could save Frémont. He must win a smashing military victory. His army, after three months' training, was in the pink of condition — so Frémont thought. He wrote Winfield Scott, the commanding general in Washington: "I am taking the field myself, and hope to destroy the enemy either before or after the junction of forces under McCulloch. Please notify the President immediately." But Lincoln had already made up his mind that Frémont was unsuited for his job. Scott replied tersely that Lincoln "expects you to repair the disaster at Lexington without loss of time." The President also sent Adjutant General Lorenzo Thomas and Secretary of War Simon Cameron to St. Louis with a signed order for Frémont's removal. Frémont knew that they were coming, and when they arrived in St. Louis, he had left to join his army. Just before boarding the train for Jefferson City, he had rearrested Frank Blair.

Frémont's army of forty thousand men was distributed in five divisions with planned supply lines at strategic points across Missouri. General David Hunter's division headquartererd at Versailles; John Pope went to Boonville, Franz Sigel to Sedalia, Asboth to the terminus of the Pacific Railroad at Tipton, John McKinstry to Syracuse. The five divisions were all in communication and could work together. In addition, Senator Lane and Brigadier General of Volunteers Sturgis had approximately five thousand men on the Kansas border.

Such an army should be able to defeat anything Price could muster, but the campaign had flaws. Elderly General Hunter, Lincoln's aide on his inaugural trip to Washington, had personal ambitions which might be helped by Frémont's failure. John Pope had been quietly thwarting the Pathfinder all summer, and his failure to relieve Lexington still rankled in the general's heart. McKinstry had been accused of diverting the few available reinforcements from Lyon at Wilson's Creek — an oversight at the root of Frémont's unfortunate situation. Lane, on the border, was always undependable to the verge of insubordination. He might appeal orders directly to the people. Only the foreigners, Sigel and Asboth, seemed completely loyal, and it was at Asboth's headquarters in Tipton that General Thomas and Secretary Cameron overtook Frémont. Fall rains had made the roads almost impassable, but the inspectors found Frémont's engineers prepared to bridge or corduroy as required. The efficient Pathfinder had anticipated every emergency, and the soldiers' morale was high. They merrily promised themselves Thanksgiving dinner in Memphis and Christmas in New Orleans. Subordinate officers praised their commander and pronounced his emancipation the quickest way to restore loyalty in Missouri.

Secretary of War Cameron showed Frémont the order for his removal. The Pathfinder begged for time to demonstrate the power of his army after months of training. Cameron agreed to give them a chance, put the order back in his pocket, and returned to Washington, but Thomas published a scathing report which delighted the Blairs. Fifteen of Frémont's ranking officers sent a round-robin letter to Lincoln commending their commander.

Left to himself again, Frémont ordered a general advance. His five columns were close enough to consolidate within twenty-four hours in case resistance was encountered. On the Osage, below the charred remains of Osceola, the bridge was gone. Frémont's expert technicians constructed a new eight-hundred-foot span in thirty-six hours, and the column continued. "New Orleans and home again by summer," soldiers shouted with glee, but Frémont, in spite of his men's military confidence, knew that personal enemies were plotting constantly against him. Worrying about these conspiracies but outwardly calm, he rode beside his ten-year-old son, who dressed gaily in the full uhlan uniform of the guard. Bayonets and sabers radiated from the Presence. The air behind him was fragrant with the smell of shoe polish and saddle soap. This pageantry appealed to his military followers, but farmers along the road and volunteers in his army who had enlisted to uphold democracy began to feel that Price's simplicity was more American.

On October 24, 1861, the elaborate column came within sixty miles of Springfield. Rumor said that the rebel legislature was in session down there and that Price guarded the place with only four hundred men. October 25 was the anniversary of the charge of the Light Brigade at Balaclava. Major Zagoni asked permission for the guard to celebrate the great day by a surprise attack on the rebel capital. His men were eager to belie their reputation as "parlor pets" in fancy uniforms and kid gloves. Even their glossy horses had been pointed out as toys.

The country ahead was being spied upon by Major F. J. White with a squadron of some two hundred United States Prairie Scouts scattered in small parties across the countryside. Frémont agreed to let the guardsmen go, if they would take White and his scouts along.

At 8:30 P.M. on October 24, Zagoni and his men rode south. Frémont's son stayed behind to nurse a bruise from his horse's kick. Halfway to Springfield they came to the scouts' camp. The combined force now numbered three hundred and fifty. Zagoni waited two hours to rest his horses and muster the scouts. Then they all set off in the night. Major White, being ill, said that he would follow in a carriage when well enough. Shortly after dawn the column surprised an enemy foraging party and captured all but one man — who galloped furiously away toward Springfield. Zagoni knew now that all hope of a surprise attack was gone. Moreover, the prisoners told him that Springfield contained at least two thousand soldiers. To attack them openly was folly, but to return without fighting on the anniversary of the charge at Balaclava and be taunted by the men who had called him a parlor pet was more than the proud Hungarian could stand. Price would expect him on the north road. An attack from the west might catch the Missourian unprepared. Zagoni sent a courier back to Frémont requesting ample reinforcements for him to fall back on if repulsed. Then the Hungarian wheeled his column to the right and galloped away seeking the road to Springfield from the west. He had completely forgotten Major White, who convalesced and drove along the north road until he entered the enemy lines and was imprisoned.

Zagoni's guard reached the new road without being stopped. His guide said that Springfield was very close now. The highway ahead skirted a quarter of a mile of dense woods, then came to open fields on both sides. At the left the meadows sloped down to a brook — the headwaters of Wilson's Creek. On the hill beyond stood Springfield. Zagoni ordered his resplendent column into line. Riding before them, he explained that the hour had come. The odds were at least five to one. Let all cowards withdraw now. "We have been called holiday soldiers for the pavements of St. Louis," he shouted in his quaint accent. "Today we will show that we are soldiers for the battle. Your watchword shall be 'Frémont and the Union.' Draw saber! By the right flank — quick trot — march!"

The men swept past the woods, their uniforms gay as the autumn foliage. Vines and underbrush screened the view toward town. As they entered the fenced lane between the open fields, a volley from the left tumbled seven horses in a space of twenty feet. The entire column halted in confusion, mounts bumping together, ranks of four intermingling. The enemy stood at the edge of the timber beyond the fence at the left, safe from the horsemen. Zagoni waved his saber in the air and spurred down the lane through a flank fire from the woods. With him raced the survivors of the first company. Those behind them returned to the protection of the woods. As Zagoni spurred along the lane, he noticed a gap in the fence on the left, bounded through it and down the slope to the brook. In the hollow, out of sight of the enemy, the first troop drew rein. A riderless horse, which had followed, whinnied frantically, turned, and raced back, bridle reins flying in the wind.

At the edge of the woods the second and third troops had ventured out on foot to tear down the fence for a proper cavalry charge. Seeing their commander aligning his troop out of rifle range along the brook below them, they ran the gauntlet down to him, the loose horse following again with flapping stirrups. White's scouts, at the rear, could see little of what was happening in the confusion. Some of them joined the race to the brook; others stayed in the protection of the woods. Along the brook, the three troops of the guard and part of the scouts, re-formed. The enemy waited out of sight on the hill above. All firing stopped. "They have discharged their pieces — don't give them time to load again," Zagoni shouted, and led a charge up the hill. The solid rank of Confederates scattered before the oncoming horsemen. Some backed away as they loaded their guns. Others made the fatal mistake of turning to run, thus enabling the enemy to ride them down and saber their skulls. With little opposition the guard galloped into Springfield. A Southern lieutenant, cut off from his men, refused to surrender. "He was a brave man," Zagoni reported. "For that reason I felt some pity to kill him."

On the new courthouse flagpole the guard raised their banner. Unhorsed guardsmen rallied to it. Prisoners were brought in. Zagoni mustered his men and inspected the wounded. He censured a bugler who had failed to blow a call when ordered. The musician, a Frenchman, displayed his instrument with the mouthpiece shot away. Major Zagoni's own tunic had been ripped across the breast by a bullet. One of his privates had received a ball through the "blacking box" in his kit but was unhurt. Another had been stung by a bullet that penetrated coat, vest, and shirt but did not break the skin. A third lad was shot through the nose. "My boy," Zagoni said to him, "I would give anything for that wound."

A hundred and seven Confederates were reported killed — an exaggeration, perhaps, but their loss seems to have been greater than Zagoni's. Of the hundred and fifty guardsmen in the charge, fifteen were killed, twenty-seven wounded, and ten missing.

At dark the major decided it best to leave town before the enemy came back in force. Taking $4,040 in gold from the bank, he abandoned his wounded and dismounted men, then rode north. At Three Mounds Prairie he met Colonel Eugene Carr with eight troops of cavalry, coming from Frémont to relieve him. Zagoni's guard had ridden eighty-five miles, having stopped only to rest and feed the horses.

Frémont, with his vast army, came on at a slower pace, entering Springfield two days later without opposition. The general sent heroic dispatches announcing a great victory — atonement at last for Bull Run, Wilson's

Creek, Lexington, and Ball's Bluff (a recent Northern defeat back in Virginia). Surely this would offset the criticism being poured constantly into Lincoln's ears.

Establishing headquarters in the brick building formerly occupied by Lyon, Frémont watched his army divisions march in, day and night. Lane and Sturgis both arrived from Kansas. The Grim Chieftain's men were loaded with plunder, and hundreds of freed Negroes loafed around his camp. General Frémont recognized Fall Leaf, who had guided him on exploring expeditions.

A great city of tents sheltering over thirty thousand men rose around Springfield. Smoke from thousands of campfires floated in Indian summer haze above the treetops. Members of the guard prowled up and down the slope where they had made their charge, telling and retelling personal experiences.

Frémont renewed his magnificent parades. Frank Blair and his threats seemed far away. With the guard, resplendent as imperial uhlans, the Pathfinder rode out to Wilson's Creek battlefield. He had at last retrieved the territory won by the ragged little "captain." The key to Missouri now lay once more in Federal hands. Price, down at Neosho, eighty miles away, tried feebly to maintain his government by firing a hundred-gun salute to announce the convening of the rebel legislature. Both houses lacked quorums, but with alleged proxies an ordinance of secession was passed, and General Rains was elected to the Confederate Senate. Price, still quarreling with McCulloch, urged him to come to Missouri and help fight Frémont. The Texan insisted that the Pathfinder be lured into Arkansas. In the open country north and east of Pea Ridge the Federals might be trapped and annihilated.

Frémont, in Springfield, understood the game being played against him. He knew that Price had insufficient men to strike alone and that many of them would refuse to leave the state and fight in Arkansas. Thus the two armies could be fought separately. Everything seemed to be turning to his advantage.

On the evening of November 2, 1861, Frémont's plans were suddenly changed. All his divisions but Hunter's had come in. Frémont sat writing at a long table in his tent when a messenger presented himself, and delivered a letter. The general frowned as he read it. Then the messenger ripped an order that had been sewed in his coat and handed it to Frémont. The general glanced at the paper, slammed it on the table, glared at the courier, and demanded, "Sir, how did you get admission into my lines?"

Frémont called in his division commanders and showed them the order relieving him of command and appointing General Hunter — who had not yet arrived — in his place. Lincoln, with characteristic caution, had sent the order with instructions that it be withheld in case Frémont had fought a winning battle, was in personal command in battle, or was in the immediate presence of an enemy. General Asboth offered to resign at once. Sigel did, too, then changed his mind — another retreat. Osterhaus ground the point of his scabbard into the gravel. Soon the news spread through the camp. Soldiers raged with resentment. As schoolboys they had been taught to revere the great explorer and refused to see him deposed. Indignation meetings were called around open fires. Officers who had been quarreling over military preferment forgot their differences. Whole companies threatened to throw down their arms. A dozen bands began to serenade Frémont, all at the same time.

General Frémont ordered the bands hushed. The men must submit. During the evening a hundred and ten officers, including every brigadier, came to Frémont's tent. They begged to be led against the enemy at once, and thus invalidate the order. Frémont agreed to wait one more day for Hunter. Then, if he had not appeared, they would march. All next day plans were drawn up for a battle. Lyon's tactics at Wilson's Creek were to be repeated. Sigel and Lane were to circle and attack from the rear, Asboth would march in from the east, McKinstry and Pope from the north. Soldiers rehearsed for this movement, actually believed that the enemy had come and a battle was imminent. But the Pathfinder knew better.

After dark, Hunter arrived and the elderly brown-wigged general rode to Frémont's tent to assume command. The Pathfinder explained the plan for attack in the morning, gave Hunter the file of orders which had been issued, and withdrew. At Sturgis's tent he stopped to clip the stitches on his shoulder straps saying, "When I take these off I will be equal to any of them" — "God knows I never prized them much." To Jessie in St. Louis he wrote that the order reached him when in face of the enemy.

Hunter, he said, had arrived in the night after the order to march had been given.

In the morning Frémont rode away toward Rolla with his guard and a few others. The months of worry had ended in the worst possible way. Yet the final decision came as a relief. His companions noted that the deposed commander seemed almost gay as he cantered along. Rumor whispered that he had challenged Hunter to a duel, but no sign of unhappiness showed on his face this morning. In St. Louis snow was falling and sleighs jingled along the streets. He was met by Jessie and a throng of admirers. Called on for a speech, he was reported to have maligned Lincoln "as weak and imbecile." With his wife and two staff members he entrained for New York, evoking much interest from passengers.

General Hunter was a very different man from Frémont — a plain, dark-complexioned soldier with the calm, Oriental air of a mandarin, and a dyed mustache that curled down around the corners of his solemn mouth. He had served at Fort Dearborn soon after graduating from West Point and while there married the sister of John H. Kinzie, pioneer Chicagoan. Hunter's personal habits were frugal. He dressed in the regulation double-breasted military coat buttoned neatly to the old-fashioned linen stock around his neck, and rode about the encampment with one orderly. Ascertaining that no enemy was concentrated nearby, he ordered a council of war on November 7, 1861. The assembled generals agreed that Price's army was at least seventy-five miles away, but in case the Federals withdrew, the Southerners would retake the country. Some officers suggested that the situation might be remedied by adopting the "Lane policy." At every village an American flag should be erected with the warning to residents: "Let that flag come down and your town will go up in smoke like Osceola."

Such severe medicine was not acceptable to regular army men or to many of the Eastern volunteers. Hunter would not countenance it and ordered the retreat north in three columns — one under Sigel to Rolla, one under Pope to Sedalia. The third under Sturgis and Lane marched north along the Missouri border. Sigel pronounced the retreat "an outrage without parallel in history."

Union people along the way knew that the Southerners would take revenge on their farms. For self-protection they joined the columns by hundreds. Other refugees flocked to St. Louis ahead of the army. Men, barefooted and in smocks, women shivering with children under dirty shawls, claimed to have been driven from their cabins by the rebels. With this pitiful horde came news of Hunter's retreat, and some St. Louisans prophesied a collapse of Federal authority. Wealthy women even dared drive downtown displaying Confederate flags in their carriage windows.

A different story followed in the wake of Lane's column. When planters laughed at him for retreating, their plantations crackled up in flames. At every crossroads Negroes waited to join his procession. Sturgis sternly kept slaves out of his lines and restored them to their masters. Lane welcomed them and soon had all his foragers could feed. He organized the Negroes into a brigade under his three chaplains. A wagon train a mile long carried their children and furniture. Old muskets that would not shoot added a martial appearance to the colored cavalcade.

Lane ordered his "Black Brigade" to leave the column, march west to Kansas and help harvest the fall crops. Singing under a "moon with her half filled horn," they marched seventeen miles the first night. Glory, glory, hallelujah! At Dry Wood Creek, six miles from the Kansas line, they camped to forage for corn and kill a "traitor's" beef. Feasting until almost daylight, they were interrupted by a Negro woman exclaiming, "There are streaks of light." Freedom for all men was dawning in the east, and the Negroes crowded the road to be on their way. The rising sun illuminated the distant hills of Kansas. A free state! The slaves surged forward with another song. One of the chaplains thought that the demonstration "must have equalled the shouts of Israel after the passage of the Red Sea." The Reverend Hugh Fisher halted his section and rode before the ragged Negro multitude. Standing up in his stirrups, he raised his hand for silence. "In the name of the Constitution of the United States," he boomed, "the Declaration of Independence and the authority of General James H. Lane, I proclaim you forever free."

Sturgis was outraged at this violation of military orders to protect private property. He censured Lane for disobeying regulations. The Grim Chieftain promised repeatedly to stop plundering and freeing slaves but only chuckled when it continued. His one great interest seemed to be a giant jayhawking expedition to the gulf.

Lincoln replaced Hunter on November 19, 1861, with a younger man.

General Henry M. Halleck was a West Point graduate, an owl-eyed scholar with bulging forehead and receding chin. Like Frémont, he was a furious worker, though very different from him in other ways. Then Lincoln carved from the old command a new Department of Kansas — a division which Lane had wanted. However, instead of assigning it to the Grim Chieftain, the President appointed Hunter to the new post. In high dudgeon Lane returned to his seat in the Senate.

General Halleck moved into Frémont's St. Louis headquarters. He prided himself on issuing more orders and devising more plans than anyone else. He taxed wealthy Confederate sympathizers to support the refugees who continued to come in from the South. He housed the homeless in mansions owned by disloyal citizens. At the same time he scoffed at the possibility of Price's invading north Missouri again. General William Tecumseh Sherman, on an inspection trip to Halleck's department, warned the commander that Price was coming, sure as death and taxes. Halleck wrote his wife that the general must be touched with insanity.

Then Halleck was rudely jarred from his academic complacency by a report that Price had reoccupied Missouri as far north at Osceola. A thousand of his men had even dared march to Lexington and help ferry recruits for the Confederacy who had enlisted north of the Missouri River.

To get Price out of the state, Halleck gave the command of southwest Missouri to Brigadier General Samuel S. Curtis, an Iowa congressman with military experience and a record for engineering competence. The assignment was becoming more difficult daily, for the Confederacy realized the importance of Missouri. On December 27, 1861, Jeff Davis's newly appointed Secretary of War, Judah P. Benjamin, wrote General Braxton Bragg that the state had become of "supreme importance to us." Then, without warning, hundreds of ragged and destitute Indians appeared along the Kansas border. The starving red men claimed that the slaveholding members of their tribes had driven them from Indian Territory. What did this mean? Could Price and McCulloch be going ahead with the plan to enlist Indians to invade the North?

X V I I I

The Five Nations Secede

JOHN ROSS, principal chief of the Cherokee, paced back and forth in the handsomely furnished withdrawing room of Rose Cottage, his beautiful home near Park Hill, Indian Territory. He was a small, dignified man with the suave, shrewd expression of New York's political wirepuller Thurlow Weed — and with a career behind him fully as brilliant as Weed's. John Ross's seventy-two years of life had known much violence, many great negotiations, and also great material success — attested by the chief's fine house and well-fed waistline. Only a trace of Indian blood flowed in his veins, but he was a legitimate tribesman by the quarter-blood mother who had married his Scotch father. Chief Ross's first childhood memories were of Lookout Mountain in Tennessee near where he had been born in 1790. Both the English and Cherokee languages came as naturally to him as did the responsibility of chieftainship. His first wife was Cherokee, but in 1845 he had married Mary B. Stapler, a Quaker from Wilmington, Delaware.

The decision that perplexed John Ross as he paced his Park Hill mansion concerned the future of his own position as chief, as well as the entire well-being of his people in case they became involved in the Civil War. He had received a letter from the newly appointed Confederate Indian commissioner, calling his attention to the Federal withdrawal from southwest Missouri and asking if it might be to the best interests of the Cherokee to join the Confederacy. The letter must be answered.

If the proposal was accepted, Chief Ross would violate his people's treaty with the United States and forfeit payments of some five million dollars to the tribe for land vacated in North Carolina, Georgia, and Tennessee. If the proposal was rejected, the Confederate commissioner might appeal to Ross's rivals in the tribe and throw him out of office. The opportunity to oust him would be welcomed by several wealthy slaveholding mixbloods who had become more akin to Southern planters than to their Indian ancestors. John Ross himself owned a hundred Negro house servants and field hands. From the pillared portico of Rose Cottage he could look across his well-tilled fields and orchards — a peaceful scene where life and property were apparently as much respected as in adjoining white settlements. But Ross knew that the specter of assassination peered nightly in all the tall windows of his house. He lived luxuriously with his wife and her sister, amid imported furniture brought from the East at a cost of $10,000. Their mansion could accommodate forty guests. A half-mile driveway, bordered with roses, led to its imposing colonnade. When the family went driving, a black boy in livery sat on top of the coach in a special seat at the back. But beyond the whitewashed fence surrounding the estate, the Rosses had only a few friends of their own class. All others were jealous enemies.

Out in the wooded hills, beyond the mansions of the wealthy Cherokee, stood hundreds of log cabins occupied by full bloods who had adopted the backwoods culture of the Carolinas and Tennessee before being shipped to Indian Territory some twenty years ago. These red-skinned settlers raised a little corn and tobacco, cured their own pork, made hominy and soap, kindled fires with flint and steel, baked dodgers and fried meat in the fireplace. On holidays a full-blooded Cherokee delighted in a gay calico shirt and a plume in his turban or broad-brimmed hat, but his costume was no more picturesque than that worn by white frontiersmen. Like frontier whites, most Cherokee owned flintlock shotguns, but they also used bows and arrows for killing small game and fish. A Cherokee husbandman, with all the outward appearance of a peaceful farmer, was still an Indian at heart who would flush with rage when an enemy gave the ancient "turkey-gobble challenge" — a fighting gesture that stirred primeval passions.

In recent years a nostalgia had appeared among the full bloods for the ancient long-house culture. A new and popular secret society dedicated members to the preservation of tribal customs. Keetoowah, as it was called, claimed some two thousand devoted members. John Ross knew that his opponents accused him of using Keetoowah to hold the full bloods' loyalty to himself, to retard their progress toward a Southern-planter way of life. He knew, too, that Northern missionaries had sponsored the secret order and were said to be preaching abolition to its converts. Thus allegiance to the North, abolition, and tribal gods had become a trinity in the fullblood Indian mind, just as abolition, self-government, and freedom of the press had become a trinity in the Kansas free-state mind.

Liberal mixbloods scoffed at the Indians who looked backward instead of ahead, called them "pin" Indians in derision — a name said to have originated from the clandestine meetings of Keetoowah in the hills, like Washington Irving's mythical little men who bowled above thunder clouds in the Catskills. More likely the name referred not to ninepins, but to the order's insignia — a poor man's pins fixed in a cross on coat lapel or hunting shirt.

John Ross, pacing to and fro with the important letter in his hand, understood the curious problems before him and his people. In addition to the conflicting tugs of the planter civilization and the ancient Indian way of life, a third force had invaded the red men's cabins since the Cherokee had come West. The great plains, with limitless grass and wild bison, lay only two or three days' ride toward the setting sun. Young Indians of the civilized tribes rode out there on excursions and came back with some of the "horse Indians'" adventurousness — a new sense of values, all Indian, but very different from the Keetoowah concept of tribal customs in the Blue Ridge Mountains of Tennessee.

These conflicting pressures were baffling enough, and now civil war had come to cut the red men off from council with their traditional White Father. Bewildered and excited, security gone, the confused Indians might stampede down any of the new paths that promised safety. Chief Ross knew that his reply to the Confederate commissioner's letter might precipitate some rash and unforeseeable action.

The elderly chief had known other crises and he had invariably surmounted them. The greatest had been the removal of the tribe from Tennessee. At that time the mixblood families had betrayed the full bloods by signing away the tribal lands, excusing the act by saying that removal was inevitable and their treaty a better one than Ross could make.

Chief Ross had promptly turned this defeat into victory by contracting with the government to carry out the removal terms of the treaty, thus adding thousands to his already ample fortune and at the same time holding the friendship of the dispossessed tribesmen, who retaliated against the treaty signers by calling them from their houses at midnight and stabbing them all to death — all but one. Stand Watie alone had escaped the knives, and John Ross had good reason to believe that Watie blamed him for the deaths of his friends and hoped constantly for revenge. The Civil War might furnish the opportunity Stand Watie wanted. Suppose Ross turned down the commissioner's request to join the Confederacy and Watie accepted it in the name of the mixbloods? Backed by the Southern Army, Watie might become chief. Old John Ross had outwitted such clever schemers before. He must do so again.

Stand Watie was three-quarter Cherokee — much more Indian blood than John Ross could boast. He had been born in Georgia, spoke English perfectly, and his brother, Elias Boudinet — murdered by the "pins" — had edited the *Cherokee Phoenix:* a widely circulated Indian newspaper printed partly in English and partly in the peculiar written language originated by the scholar Sequoyah.

Ross, in his mansion, surrounded with loyal retainers, had little to fear personally from Stand Watie, but he could not think unemotionally about that swart little man and what he might do in this crisis. Watie had the advantage of being sixteen years younger than Ross. He looked like an Indian, wore his hair proudly in pompadour, spoke abruptly or not at all. Moreover, his legs were bowed from years in the saddle. Confederates might find use for him as a guerrilla, but they would be mistaken to believe him a savage, for Stand Watie possessed great natural ability. As sole survivor of the treaty-party leaders he had assumed large and complex business responsibilities. He had settled claims of the heirs of the assassinated chiefs. He had managed the affairs of their widows, leasing their slaves to supply income, mortgaging some to obtain ready cash. He had straightened out titles to their land and had found employment for their children, or arranged for their schooling back East. But with all his competence in the white man's business world, Stand Watie prided himself on being an Indian. He had named his daughter Minnehaha — though she now wore Eastern clothes, could quote the Bible and read Latin.

With the specter of Stand Watie's vengeance always before him and a lifetime of amicable relations with the Federal government behind him, John Ross had discouraged all sympathy for the Confederacy among his people. He had quashed a proposed plan of the Five Nations to act in concert against the North. The gaudy Texan, Ben McCulloch, had called in person at Rose Cottage seeking an alliance, but Ross stood firm. Next had come Albert Pike, newly appointed Confederate Indian commissioner with $100,000 to be used in getting control of Indian Territory. Jeff Davis realized the importance of the Indians' half million cattle.

John Ross met Pike as he had McCulloch. The small, punctilious chieftain extended his hand to the majestic mountain of flesh capped with flowing locks. Pike's face was notably marble calm, statuesque, profusely bearded — round as a pansy. His dress was untidy, but John Ross knew him to be an accomplished scholar versed in Indian languages and also in French, Spanish, Greek, Latin, and Sanskrit. Ross also knew Pike's reputation as a gentleman on the dueling field, how he had stood serenely before an admiring crowd while his antagonist's bullet twitched those pansy whiskers.

Strangely enough, this man Pike understood Indians and Indians' ways as well as, probably better than, the Indian chief. In addition to being a successful attorney for the red man, Pike, as a youth, had ventured out on the plains among wild Indians and had survived. But he, like General McCulloch, failed to convert John Ross.

Disappointed, Pike had left Park Hill and driven south to negotiate successful treaties with the Choctaw and Chickasaw and to encourage the enlistment of Indian regiments to be commanded by their agent, Douglas H. Cooper, hard-drinking Mississippian appointed by President Pierce. The *Little Rock Times and Herald* lauded the new allies as "these noble sons of the west, [who] armed with the long rifles, Tomma-hawks and scalping knives, swear that nothing but the scalp of the Yankee will satisfy their vengeance."

With the Choctaw and Chickasaw treaties in his portfolio, Commissioner Pike drove north again to visit the Creek and Seminole — both weak tribes surrounded by the powerful Cherokee. If these nations dealt with Albert Pike, the Cherokee would be the only civilized Indians to remain neutral. Most ominous of all, Stand Watie had begun to raise an independent battalion of Cherokee with himself as colonel. Other officers included his nephew Elias C. Boudinet, Arkansas newspaperman who had recently been chairman of the Arkansas state Democratic convention. Ostensibly the battalion was to police the border, but the implications were clearly political.

Really worried by Stand Watie's military preparations, Ross had watched Pike negotiate treaties with the mixblood factions of both the Creek and Seminole, regardless of the protests of many purebloods who appealed to Chief Opothleyoholo to resist or revolt. Then, with an escort, the commissioner drove westward nonchalantly, cigar smoke curling serenely around his long hair and beard. He was bound for the frontier posts where he hoped to make treaties with the half-wild Indians on the edge of the plains. Suppose he succeeded and came back to the Cherokee Nation offering one of his treaties to Stand Watie and his mixbloods! Such a trick must be stopped if possible. Ross sent a messenger to the western plains' chiefs to beware, to remain united and neutral like the Cherokee. He also published an open letter for the press assuring all Southerners that the Cherokee wanted only peace and neutrality. No white settlement need fear the tomahawk.

Waiting anxiously, Ross learned from bits of news printed in Texas and Arkansas newspapers and from a constant dribble of riders coming across the western horizon what was happening out on the frontier during the hot July days of 1861. Pike, with his elaborate escort, tents, tables and chairs, drove to Forts Washita, Arbuckle, and Cobb — all deserted by the Federal garrisons. Sturgis and Totten had moved north by this route, abandoning the posts in haste. Doors stood ajar and dust blew through broken windows. Indians and renegade whites had prowled through the buildings, pawing over the canvas cots, old blankets, and castoff shoes. Irregular troops of Texans, Choctaw, and Chickasaw — the latter commanded by English-speaking mixbloods — now camped in some of the rooms. The half-wild Comanches, Osages, and Wichita in the area were baffled by the soldiers' retreat. Frightened and confused, some of them had packed their savage accouterments and trailed away over the horizon to live independently like wild Indians or to go to the fabulous land of freedom called "Kansas." Others remained sullenly in their rude shelters along the brushy creek beds.

Pike had called the remaining chieftains to grand councils and explained his proposed treaty. The headmen asked to be given time for deliberation, then stalked away to talk all night among themselves. As the old men debated, young savages stripped naked and smeared their bronze bodies with paint for a dance. The civilized irregulars watched them and some days later staged a dance of their own under a Confederate flag, stamping out two generations of missionary teaching to the rhythm of a plains Indian war dance. By morning the civilized Indians were half savage and the half savages were still reluctant to sign a new treaty.

Pike turned his attention to the possibility of an alliance with the wild Indians. He inquired about Jesse Chisholm, the famous trader with the half-wild Wichita. Chisholm operated a "factory" on a tributary of the Canadian where the bottoms supplied ample grass, wood, and water for Indian encampments. The Wichita, having learned white men's ways, acted as middlemen for the wild tribes beyond, and they might be important in Pike's plan to enlist plains savages against the Federal government. Jesse Chisholm traded extensively with them, and his buildings could not store the bountiful accumulation of pelfries and buffalo hides. Deerskins, beaver, otters, and wolf furs were ricked like hay outside the cabins awaiting transportation to Milt McGee's warehouse in Kansas City. From the wild Indians Chisholm also purchased occasional Negro slaves captured in Texas, and he resold them, together with his pelts, in Missouri. Some wild villages of Kiowa and Comanche occasionally offered white prisoners for sale but feared to come near trading posts with them.

Jesse Chisholm spoke the Wichita and Comanche dialects fluently. English and Cherokee were his native tongues. He had come with the Cherokee from east Tennessee to the territory. His mother's sister had married Sam Houston when that Tennesseean resigned the governorship to go West and native. Jesse's wide knowledge and experience promised to be of great help to Pike in his effort to amalgamate the badly split Indian factions and get a treaty that represented entire tribes.

To entice the red men to councils, Pike purchased great quantities of goods. He gave presents and feasts, all costing many thousands of dollars. He distributed bolts of gingham and calico to Indian women, playing cards and "store pants" to favored chiefs. His grocery purchases included such camping luxuries as canned corn, green peas, peaches, oysters, salmon, asparagus, lobster, sardines, pineapple, six bottles of Schnapps, two of Worcestershire sauce, and two of castor oil.

To consume such inducements, wild Indians jogged in under a flag of truce, wanted to "talk" as long as the grub lasted. Then they rode off across the ocean of grass, leaving Pike wondering if they might be spies from the abolitionists in Kansas. Obviously it was food, not constitutional principles, that interested them. Some Indians became outright insolent in their demands. Buffalo Hump, George Washington, and Pock Mark displayed contempt for Pike and the Confederacy, too, unless properly paid to change their ideas.

Pike boasted that he negotiated a favorable treaty with the Comanches, but it was really with some members only — the old trick used against the Indians so many times, the subterfuge John Ross feared Pike might use next against him by treating with Stand Watie.

Chief Ross was pondering this dilemma when Sterling Price rode to McCulloch's encampment on the Missouri-Arkansas border and induced the Texan to come north and fight at Wilson's Creek. The newly enlisted Indian regiments had not gone with McCulloch to fight the "cold weather people" but remained to guard their own homes. However, a few red men enlisted in Arkansas regiments and at least one, John Benge, was killed. The survivors came back with horrendous tales of the slaughter and of Lyon's death. The spectacle of dead and dying horses impressed some of them more than the sight of mangled men.

Commissioner Pike learned about the Federal defeat and wrote again to Chief Ross, summarizing the hopelessness of the Federal cause and asking the chief to reconsider his decision to remain neutral. This was the letter which now caused Chief Ross so much perplexity as he walked up and down in his handsomely furnished home. He had withstood all the pressures, the blandishments, had watched the powerful Choctaw and Chickasaw join the Confederacy, saw the lesser Creeks and Seminole quarreling on the verge of civil war. Always John Ross had hoped that the United States Army would assert its authority and give the Cherokee the protection specified in their ancient treaty. However, the Washington government had failed. Ross had seen Sturgis and Totten evacuate Little Rock and the frontier posts, give up Fort Smith without firing a shot. Rumors that Jim Lane and James Montgomery would come down and discipline proslavery mixbloods, as they had Missourians, did not materialize. Then Lyon, the only Federal general in the West, had been killed and his army retreated. Certainly the time had come for John Ross to make the best treaty he could before Stand Watie betrayed him. Chief Ross decided to answer the commissioner's letter affirmatively. He called in his head men, and sent out riders summoning all the people to meet on August 21, 1861, at Tahlequah, the Cherokee capital, and consider joining the Confederacy.

Over four thousand Cherokee flocked to the capital, unhitching their teams and pitching tents in the wind-sheltered valleys tributary to the Illinois River. Little parties marched up the hill in single file, the women behind, to the council house and outdoor rostrum in the square of taverns, trading houses, and restaurants. John Ross's brother Lewis, the Cherokee treasurer, met the newcomers and mingled with the growing crowd. Today he must persuade the full bloods to join the Confederacy — and they were reputed to be a stubborn people. He shook the hands of turbaned chieftains, patting shoulders clothed with gay calico shirts. Quietly and persistently he urged them to vote for the new alliance. Mixblood Cherokee, fair as Anglo-Saxons, were sure to acquiesce. Dressed in frock coats and tall hats, with their women in ballooning crinoline, these men felt themselves a part of the Southern civilization.

At midmorning John Ross mounted the speakers' stand in the square and explained that the permanent disruption of the United States seemed probable. He asked consent to take preliminary steps for an alliance with the Confederacy. The assembled Cherokee granted his request and voted to authorize John Drew, of the Ross party, to raise a regiment and tender its services to General McCulloch — a shrewd request, as this organization should neutralize the power of Stand Watie's battalion.

With the Southern alliance assured, a jubilant mob whipped out to Park Hill and prepared to erect a Confederate flag on the lawn at Rose Cottage. John Ross stopped them. Mrs. Ross and his sister-in-law, the chief said, being Pennsylvania Quakers, objected to the emblem of slavery. Suspicious observers might have seen duplicity in Ross's action, but on the surface he appeared loyal to the Confederacy.

A treaty was duly drawn up with Albert Pike, and during the first week in October the commissioner came to Tahlequah to celebrate the alliance. Around the speakers' stand Colonel Drew assembled his green regiment of Ross supporters. Beside them Stand Watie's horsemen stood in military array. The swart leader held a commission now from Jeff Davis. He had come to give lip service to John Ross's chieftainship, but he also intended to see his own party get rightful recognition.

On the platform, the mixblood leaders mingled with Ross's followers under the Confederate flag — first time in a generation these traditional enemies had met on friendly terms. Bewhiskered Pike, a Mont Blanc towering above the rugged black heads of both factions and beaming cordiality, shook hands with everyone. Then, tossing his majestic pate in characteristic manner, his long hair hanging down his back, Pike welcomed the Cherokee Nation into the Confederacy. Chief Ross removed his stovepipe hat and responded, outlining the generous features of the newly adopted alliance. He concluded by presenting a Cherokee flag to the commissioner. Pike then gave a Confederate flag to Colonel Drew's regiment. Next Chief Ross walked across the platform and extended his hand to the squat figure of Stand Watie. The short man looked into the chief's ingratiating face and blurted out that the two parties should have acted like this long ago, but even now there would be no peace between the factions so long as the "pins" remained a political organization. Ross replied suavely that he knew nothing about them — a questionable statement. Was he still planning an underground movement to hold the Cherokee with the Union?

In any event, John Ross wrote, with apparent good faith, to the recalcitrant chief of the Creeks, Opothleyoholo, to come "where we may all smoke the pipe of peace and friendship around our great council fire," let all the civilized nations acquiesce in allegiance to the Confederacy. With Ross's letter Commissioner Pike sent another, offering a colonel's commission to the Creek chief and complete amnesty for most of his followers. Surely the little Creek and Seminole nations could not stand alone, now that the powerful Cherokee had joined the Confederacy. The victory seemed complete and an exultant Southern press urged the newly formed red regiments — the Choctaw, Chickasaw, and Cherokee — to strike at southern Kansas while the abolitionists, defeated at Wilson's Creek, were running north as fast as their legs would take them.

X I X

Slaveholding Indians Declare War

Opothleyoholo replied to Chief Ross by messenger. A large group of his people, he said, were determined to remain loyal to the Union, to repudiate the Pike treaty. He must comply with their wishes. The eighty-year-old chief was a blanket Indian. He painted his face and could neither read nor write, but his brain was powerful. He owned many slaves and cultivated two thousand acres of land, keeping all the details of his business — various mortgages and payments — and the income and expenses of the Creek Nation in his mind.

Like the Cherokee schism, the split among the Creeks was an ancient one. At the time of removal from Georgia it had almost flared into open warfare. The Creek chief in those days had been William McIntosh, wealthy mixblood planter and brigadier general under Andy Jackson. His first cousin — all white — had been governor of Georgia. The full bloods had murdered William McIntosh for selling their tribal lands and agreeing to move the nation West. The chief's oldest son, Chilly McIntosh, had escaped on that horrendous night. Chilly's brother, Daniel N. McIntosh, twenty-two years his junior, had been reared in the traditional fear and hatred of those distant days. He seemed more like a white man than an Indian, wore his long hair curled at the ends in cavalier fashion. His beard grew vigorously and he shaved it with care, leaving a handsome mustache and goatee. An ordained minister in the Baptist Church, he scoffed at Opothleyoholo's pagan Indian beliefs and hoped to educate all the Creeks to a Southern-planter way of life.

Chilly and Daniel had persuaded the Creek Council to treat with Albert Pike, and Chilly had joined the escort which went west with the commissioner to help convert the wild Indians. Daniel, at home, had enlisted a

Creek regiment and, proclaiming the hatchet "dug up," hoisted a Confederate flag over the Creek agency. Opothleyoholo fled to his plantation, fearing the McIntoshes' revenge as much as Chief Ross feared Stand Watie's. All Creeks loyal to the Union joined his encampment.

The Seminole were also split into treaty and nontreaty parties, dating back to the removal. The treaty party was led by John Jumper, rich pure-blood, unable to read or write but a would-be Southern gentleman. A magnificent figure of a man and a fluent speaker, benevolent but strong, he was followed with religious devotion by Baptist converts. His influence had induced some Seminole to agree to the Pike treaty. The opposing faction, led by Billy Bowlegs and Alligator, flocked to Opothleyoholo's standard.

Many Creeks and Seminole, however, refused to join either group. Instead, they packed their wagons and drove north behind the retreating United States Army. Some traveled on to Washington to lay their predicament before Great White Father Abraham.

Lincoln listened to the grievances of the picturesque delegations. He had already discussed the problem with Jim Lane, who wanted to enlist the red men for his great expedition into the South. Lincoln had objected to fighting Southerners with Indians, but he approved a series of councils with them in the Kansas towns of Humboldt, LeRoy, and Fort Scott. To these meetings the Union factions of the Creek, Seminole, and minor nations sent representatives. All expressed their loyalty and asked for United States soldiers to protect them from the Confederates. John Ross, they repeated over and over, was for the Union but dared not express himself.

Opothleyoholo knew about these councils and, no doubt, expected the government to save the refugees who came constantly to his home. Their total number will never be known. Contemporaries estimated them as high as four thousand, including a thousand to seventeen hundred warriors. They came on foot, horseback, and in wagons piled high with duffel. Squaws perched on top of the loads. Children drove milk cows. Many runaway slaves from other tribes joined the throng. These civilized Indians, camping together on the plains, soon reverted to the primitive. Woman stitched savage embroidery on the edges of their men's homemade breeches. At night the men danced to the rhythms of plains Indian chants. Rumor said Lane's jayhawkers were coming down to help them.

The refugee's livestock soon ate all the grass around the chief's plantation. Opothleyoholo decided that he and his followers must move. He
stowed the Creek Nation's money in a barrel and with a slave drove back
into the hills to bury it. After returning, tradition says he ordered the
slave killed to insure secrecy. Perhaps so, perhaps not. In any event fortune hunters ruined much of the chief's land, digging for the money.

Opothleyoholo's subsequent movements are also controversial. He said
that he led his people toward the open Western country to establish a
"cow-pen" — an idiom common in the Eastern mountains during the
Revolution. Confederate sympathizers tried to stop him, and he fought
them on November 19, December 9, and December 26, 1861, in battles
known by various names. His exact route and purpose can only be surmised. Certainly Opothleyoholo started from home in a westerly direction
as though planning his "cow-pen." Confederate Indians accused him of
driving off their cattle, taking their women and children, and three or
four hundred of their slaves. They complained that the Kansas jayhawkers
had joined him and were raiding Confederate Indians' homesteads.

Opothleyoholo replied that the cattle belonged to his own people, that
no Kansans were in his party, and that the women and children followed
of their own free will. Some cabins owned by the McIntosh faction were
robbed, and the trading house of John W. Taylor, a Confederate sympathizer, was burned to the ground. Taylor and his son barely escaped with
their lives.

To stop the exodus, the McIntoshes and John Jumper called for help
from the brigade of Choctaw, Chickasaw, and Texans which liquor-loving
Douglas Cooper had raised at his agency. Long-haired and goateed Daniel N. McIntosh hastened enlistments in his all-Creek regiment by promising that captured cattle and Negroes — free or slave — belonging to
Opothleyoholo's supporters would be sold and the money used to start a
new Creek treasury.

The entire Confederate force, red and white, numbered at least fourteen
hundred. With high confidence they jogged away to catch Opothleyoholo,
then march "on to Kansas." At the column's head rode Cooper's Fourth
Texas Cavalry, next came the Creek regiment commanded by Colonel
D. N. McIntosh. Behind his regiment straggled the Creek and Seminole
battalion under John Jumper and Chilly McIntosh — the latter, in his

buggy, whetting toothless gums in anticipation of revenge for the assassination of his father. The giant Major Jumper, astride a suitable charger, appeared as dignified and benign as though leading his congregation to church. In the rear came Colonel Cooper himself, with his Choctaw-Chickasaw regiment.

The column marched four days hunting Opothleyoholo. An abandoned campground was discovered — matted grass, dead fires, boot tracks and the print of children's bare feet; battered kettles, discarded rags littered over an area fifty yards square. Wagon tracks showed the route ahead, so the column followed them.

From day to day, scouts studied the horse droppings between the wheel ruts. One morning they pronounced them fresh and Colonel McIntosh ordered a slave to gallop ahead, overtake the fugitives' train and order it to halt or suffer awful vengeance. The Texans followed as an advance guard for the army.

In midafternoon the slave returned. He reported overtaking the fugitives, said that he had ridden along the creeping column warning everybody from the gray and wrinkled Opothleyoholo in his buggy in front to women in the slowest, swaying oxcart in the rear, but not a team stopped.

The Texans yelped with gleeful anticipation and spurred away. At four o'clock they spied a skein of smoke on the horizon, halted for a moment to examine it, then broke into a gallop, hoofs thrumming across the level plain in an ever-lengthening line — a spectacular horse race. The smoke proved to be a delusion. The riders found only a deserted outpost, the fire still burning merrily.

The sun was sinking now, shining in the riders' eyes as their heaving horses formed company front again. The Creek regiment was close behind, and the Texans, intent on being first, dashed off again, determined to whip the enemy before the main army arrived. As they spurred along, the leaders noticed that the wagon tracks dipped down a gentle slope toward a line of leafless timber skirting a stream. Beyond, against the darkening sky, they could see the outline of two flat-topped mounds. Below, twinkling through the bare tree branches, they saw a constellation of campfires — Opothleyoholo's main party at last.

An exultant yell rippled along the charging line as the Texans rushed down the slope. It was too dark now to see one another clearly. At the edge of the black woods a sheet of red fire roared out from under the trees. Horses rolled over like rabbits. Others stumbled, reared, pawed the air, bumped together in confusion. Men rocketed through the darkness, pitched to the ground, staggered to their feet in the tall grass. Those unhurt tried to re-form, back on the prairie, but found themselves vulnerable marks against the stars. Arrows whistled past their ears. Shots in the distance flickered like fireflies. Others spit with sudden viciousness from nearby bushes. Texans and attacking Indians were undistinguishable in the blackness. No hope except retreat to the main army! In desperate straits the Texans started back, with enemies hooting signals to each other like wood owls in the gloom, and stealthily picking off stragglers.

A roll call of the survivors who reached Cooper's camp disclosed twenty missing with their flag. Next morning scouts ventured toward the timber and found that Opothleyoholo had moved away during the night, leaving a few old ponies, the chief's buggy, twelve broken-down wagons, thirty yoke of oxen, and some sheep. Partly consumed sacks of sugar and coffee indicated a hasty retreat. Mangled bodies of prisoners were found with skulls bashed in by squaws' hominy pestles. Among the dead on the prairie lay the sprawled body of John W. Taylor, merchant to the Creek Nation, who had ridden with the Texans.

Colonel Cooper policed the battleground, collected the booty, and jogged off toward Fort Gibson, an old army post on the Neosho sixty miles west of Fort Smith. He excused himself for not following up the left-handed victory by saying that McCulloch needed him in case Lincoln's newly appointed General Hunter continued Frémont's demonstration against Arkansas.

So ended the battle of Round Mounds on November 19, 1861 — first engagement of the Civil War in Indian Territory. Opothleyoholo fought only on the defensive. He made his stand at the edge of the Creek country as though hesitating to go farther. Shortly before the fight a friendly Cherokee rode into the Creek camp offering hospitality in his village at the Big Bend of the Arkansas. Opothleyoholo accepted the invitation, and after the battle fled northeast toward it during the night. Obviously he had no fixed purpose now, except escape, and always in the minds of his people Kansas stood for freedom under the government.

As Colonel Cooper jogged south toward Fort Gibson with his Indians and Texans, after the battle of Round Mounds, he intercepted many fugitive red men in bands much smaller than Opothleyoholo's, all headed for the promised land in Kansas. He captured them, usually without resistance, and marched them back to their homes in the territory. Many other parties evaded him. Some were miles away to the east or to the west. Among these was Jesse Chisholm — certainly no abolitionist — with the Wichita who depended on him and his trading post, now on wheels, as their only source of civilized supplies.

Before Colonel Cooper reached the fort, he learned from a messenger that General Hunter had retreated from Springfield, Missouri. The danger of invasion had passed, and Cooper's Indian brigade would not be needed to reinforce McCulloch and Price. The colonel halted, where grass stood tall and well-cured on the stem, to rest his men and horses for another attack on Opothleyoholo. Soon his brigade was joined by the full-blooded Cherokee regiment recently recruited by Colonel John Drew. Stand Watie had not yet increased his battalion to regiment size but sent word that he would come later.

Cooper, now having near two thousand men, decided to strike Opothleyoholo front and rear. A mixblood scout named Clem V. Rogers (father of Will Rogers) pointed out the trail taken by the fugitives. Clem's father, a member of the treaty party, had been killed by the Ross faction, and the son felt no sympathy for full bloods, be they Creek or Cherokee. But when the attacking army surrounded Opothleyoholo, Drew's regiment of full bloods refused to fight full-blooded Creek and Seminole whose sole offense was loyalty to the United States. This defection cut Cooper's army down to Opothleyoholo's size, but the colonel's men still smarted from their defeat at Round Mounds and determined to attack. The battle was fought along the south bank of Bird Creek and in the cane and brush thickets bordering the stream. At dark Opothleyoholo still held his ground.

During the night Cooper reassembled his men on the plain and received reports from his commanders. He listed his casualties as fifteen killed and thirty-seven wounded, Opothleyoholo's as "probably five hundred." Without doubt the latter's loss was "probably" less than Cooper's. Moreover, Indian Agent Cooper had tired of fighting. Perhaps his stock of liquor was running out. In any event he ordered his men back to Fort Gibson.

On the march, Cooper's Indians joked about their encounters and escapes. Their second failure became a victory as the distance from Bird Creek increased. Before long the Chickasaw boasted that they had taken fifty scalps while the Choctaw claimed a hundred and fifty. McIntosh's Creeks excused themselves from the grisly game by saying they could not scalp their own people. Lieutenant A. E. Folsom, of Company E, Second Choctaw Regiment, wrote home happily: "I shot the first man killed, got his horse and saddle, two scalps, and almost lost my own."

This bravado did not conceal the Confederate Indians' defeat. Southern newspapers foresaw disaster: Would "the Yankee abolitionist" Opothleyoholo, with his four thousand warriors (he had less than a quarter of that number) crush Cooper's little force and thus take the entire Indian Territory from the Confederacy? Colonel Cooper spurred ahead of his men to confer with Chief Ross and General McCulloch. He wanted an explanation for the desertion of the five hundred Cherokee, and he also wanted some white soldiers to stiffen his Indian brigade. To his disappointment Chief Ross equivocated and McCulloch was absent in Richmond, Virginia, conferring with President Jeff Davis about his conflicting authority with Sterling Price. The command had devolved on James McIntosh — no relation to the Creek — and this proved good for Cooper. McIntosh was always less cautious than his chief. He agreed to come to Cooper's aid with thirteen hundred and eighty Wilson's Creek veterans, catch Opothleyoholo or "pull a wheel off." Again the plan was to strike the Union Indians front and rear, the Indian brigade to march up the Arkansas, the Americans up the Verdigris.

McIntosh led the way. The weather turned cold with snow hissing through the gloomy blue hills. At noon on December 26, 1861, a company of his Texans probed the thin ice for a ford across Shoal Creek — a tributary of the Verdigris. Distant rifle shots peppered the slope behind them. The lead squads splashed across and hid behind the creek bank on the enemy's side. McIntosh halted his main army out of range and studied the country ahead. Beyond his crouching men a prairie stretched four hundred yards to a ridge dotted with boulders and blackjacks which undoubtedly sheltered the enemy. The Wilson's Creek veterans prided themselves on being able cavalrymen, but a successful charge could hardly start along a frozen creek and end at an impassable hillside.

McIntosh turned to his shivering men. He ordered them to dismount and warm themselves by deploying rapidly in line. Then he shouted to the company behind the creek bank to open fire by squads, spatter the hillside with lead until no Indian dared raise his head. Next, he turned to his bugler: "Blow the charge!"

Down the bank and into the half-frozen creek the Americans splashed, then up the other side and out across the open prairie, running hard now in their wet clothes, straight for the rocks and trees that sheltered the Indians. Here from rock to tree, the Americans worked their way up the hill. By 5 P.M. the action was over, except for a few squads still firing at fugitives in distant valleys.

Bugles sounded assembly and the men trudged in to cook supper, dry their clothes, and prowl through Opothleyoholo's deserted camp where a hundred and sixty women and children and twenty Negro prisoners quaked in a huddle. Guards were assigned to care for seventy yoke of captured oxen, thirty-nine wagons, five hundred ponies. All warriors not dead among the blackjacks had escaped into the wintry dusk, with only the scanty supplies they could carry in their hands, on saddle horses, and in a few wagons. Perhaps some courageous women had escaped too.

As dark settled over the bivouac fires, Stand Watie clattered in from the south at the head of three hundred Cherokee horsemen — the first Indians to arrive at the scene. McIntosh was ready to march back to Fort Smith and call the war finished, but Stand Watie and his nephew, Elias C. Boudinet, warmed their brown hands before the open fire and promised themselves a chase after the fugitives next day. Following behind them, Cooper's big brigade of Choctaw and Chickasaw whooped for vengeance after their double defeat at Round Mounds and at Bird Creek.

In the morning McIntosh returned to Fort Smith, as he planned, but the red regiments galloped ahead tracking the refugees. The few who had escaped with wagons were easily overtaken. Those on foot or pony-back were harder to find. Heading blindly north across a hundred miles of bleak plains, their only thought was to reach the mythical "Kansas." By day, little parties of them cowered along the brushy creeks sheltered from the biting wind. After dark they ventured across the open plains, guided by the stars and hoping to reach the next timber before dawn when Stand Watie's keen-eyed horsemen were sure to spy them. The fugitives killed and ate their horses, used the hides for shelter and cut them into rude moccasins for frosted feet. Women crept from hiding places in gullies, after the pursuing horsemen had passed, and picked kernels of corn from the horses' droppings to chew for food. Mothers, terrified and discouraged, threw their babies into freezing mudholes and trampled the life out of them.

A few families decided to give themselves up, others determined to fight boldly to the death. Major Boudinet's battalion captured seventy-five prisoners and twenty-five pack horses. Alligator, a Seminole from the swamps of Florida, died rather than surrender. Cooper's brigade, riding more leisurely, apprehended stragglers missed by Watie and Boudinet. Persistent as bloodhounds, they followed all fresh tracks in the drifting snow, scoured brushy watercourses, and unearthed little parties in miserable shelters, killing or capturing them. Not all were followers of Opothleyoholo. Many were independent groups fleeing in terror toward Kansas. One party of Delawares was stopped, interrogated, and released when found to be relatives of Confederate sympathizers.

The rout was complete, with seven hundred Indians perishing in the flight. Confederate newspapers crowed exultantly, reported Stand Watie as sweeping victoriously north across the "Boston abolition strongholds, leaving Fort Scott, Topeka and Lawrence in ashes." Delegates from the civilized nations were received in the Confederate Congress in Richmond. Albert Pike was commissioned a brigadier general to command the entire Indian Territory. He forthwith prepared a long "talk" for the recalcitrant Comanches and Kiowas who had refused to accept his treaty. Jesse Chisholm — having come back down what would soon be called the Chisholm Trail after delivering the Wichita in Kansas — was employed to carry the "talk" to the wild Indians. Runners took copies of it to the nomadic Apaches, Cheyenne, and Arapaho. On the Comanche reservation a battalion enlisted. Old Buffalo Hump, George Washington, and Jim Pock Mark sent word that they loved Pike like a brother. When would he deliver the presents?

In Fort Leavenworth, Agent George A. Cutler wired Washington: "Heopothleyohola . . . needs help badly. . . . Hurry up Lane."

X X

I Must Have St. Louis — Then Huzza!

As THE REFUGEE Indians dribbled into Kansas, Curtis marched his column south to redo the work of Lyon and Frémont, to retake Springfield, and defeat Price. At the Rolla railhead, Curtis left his wife and daughter to act as nurses at the army hospital established there. Although solicitous for his wife's welfare, letters to her were pompously signed "yours Saml R. Curtis." Only to his brother, back in Nebraska, could the general become confidential — even sentimental, when recalling boyhood days together.

The cold winter of 1861–1862 that wreaked such hardships on the Indians also caused suffering in Curtis's army. Roads were almost impassable. Mudholes froze over every night strong enough to hold a man, but wagons broke the ice and sometimes sank to the hubs. At Lebanon, halfway between Rolla and Springfield, Curtis halted for his men to thaw out and reorganize. They were equipped with round Sibley tents, each with a conical Sibley stove in the center. Around this the men slept packed snug as wedges of pie, their feet to the fire and heads out. Lieutenant Nathan Harwood of the Forty-sixth Iowa Infantry remembered how, when a man wanted to roll over, he shouted the command: "Spoon right," or, "Spoon left," as the case required.

Beyond Lebanon, where the hill country came to an end, prairie roads were quagmires. In addition, people on the rich level land did not welcome "abolitionists." Curtis noticed, too, that long cold rides tired him more than they had a quarter of a century ago when he studied soldiering at West Point. Fifty-seven now, he was putting on weight. Civilian life and two and a half terms in Congress had softened his muscles. The fine wavy hair on his head was thinning. Curtis's natural slowness of thought and action, his prominent forehead above a dish-face, had seemed pompous in boyhood, and companions made fun of him, but in maturity his calm bearing and massive figure would ornament any army column. Bad roads failed to disconcert him. As an engineer on the old National Road in Ohio he understood the technical problem ahead. As former city engineer of St. Louis, under Mayor Luther M. Kennett, he had been an efficient administrator. Exact in small details, Curtis also possessed constructive ideas — a rare combination that should serve him well against Old Pap Price. During the Mexican War Curtis had created a highly successful espionage system. Now, in southwest Missouri, he employed adventurous young men to disguise themselves as hillbillies and collect information. Twenty-five-year-old Wild Bill Hickok joined this service. To slip away in the night, hide in the woods by day, loaf around mountain cabins, attend "secesh balls" and even enlist in the enemy forces suited his daring disposition. Only two drawbacks marred Hickok's usefulness. His ego demanded gaudy clothes, and his fantastic mustache made him a trifle too conspicuous for successful spying.

Curtis believed that he understood the causes for Frémont's failure, and determined to strike quickly — a difficult task for one of his deliberateness. But he inherited competent officers. Sigel, Carr, and Osterhaus were all veterans of Wilson's Creek, now commanding divisions. All of them were familiar with the enemy and the country ahead.

Spies reported that Price and McCulloch were still at odds. The Texan had gone to Richmond to clarify his position. Price's men were said to be suffering from much sickness. Discipline was reported to be lax with Old Pap "drinking too much" — good news for Curtis.

The Federal Army moved cautiously forward, through the mud, toward Springfield, with Price's men retreating before them. The Union soldiers entered the town on February 13, 1862, as the rebels marched out. Curtis arrived with his staff shortly after the occupation, found his men gulping beer and gingerbread looted from the stores and promptly established martial law. He set up his headquarters in the deserted residence of Mrs. Grane. Price had lived here and he left the place immaculate. All the owner's bric-a-brac were carefully put away in a closet where they would not be disturbed. Truly Price set an example hard for commanding generals to follow. Curtis's aides opened their general's baggage, spread out the papers. Quartermasters began to inventory the town's supply of forage, flour, and army stores. Curtis ordered Grenville M. Dodge to ride south with the Fourth Iowa Cavalry and keep in touch with the retreating enemy — a job Dodge understood, for he knew the prairies, having surveyed west from Council Bluffs what he hoped would be a transcontinental railroad. "Level Eye" the Indians called this solemn, hundred-and-thirty-pound, stoop-shouldered engineer.

Hour after hour the troops streamed into Springfield to be assigned proper camping places. Veterans who had been here before noticed the ravages of war on the little town. The shade trees along the streets of 1861 were now lifeless stumps. Broken fences, muddy wagon tracks across meadows, and patches of dirty snow added to the unsightliness. Every day vedettes brought in parties of rebel recruits who believed Old Pap still held the town. Among these was Brigadier General Edwin M. Price, the commander's son, returning from northern Missouri. This distinguished prisoner was sent to Rolla and thence to St. Louis where Department Commander Halleck agreed to parole him with the understanding that he reside in a Northern city.

Private Absalom Grimes and a companion were also caught away from their company when Price retreated. Coming back from a foraging expedition, they noticed blue-clad soldiers in the roads and knew something was wrong. They turned and spurred away, riding south all night. Next morning, tired, sleepy and very hungry, they spied some cavalry horses hitched around a farmhouse — evidently Price's rear guard. Eager for a warm breakfast the foragers dismounted, opened the door, and stepped into a crowd of men in blue who promptly took their arms and sent them back to Springfield under guard, to be imprisoned temporarily on the second floor of a double house which Curtis had converted into barracks. Before long some Federal prisoners were pushed in the room. Drunk, they soon fell asleep. Grimes took a cap and overcoat from one of the snoring culprits. Then, when the guard downstairs changed, Grimes donned the cap and coat and marched his fellow Confederate past the new sentry and along the street to the Logan sisters' house at the edge of town. Here Grimes and his companion were renewing old friendships with the girls when a party of Federal cavalrymen knocked at the door, asking to share the house's hospitality. Grimes and his friend hid in a back room, and as darkness settled over the prairie, they stole outside, unhitched the reveling cavalrymen's chargers, and trotted south in the night, happy to feel loaded dragoon pistols on the pommels of both saddles! Price's army might be far off, but by keeping away from main traveled roads, Ab and his companion hoped to reach it.

Ahead of the fugitives, had they known it, Dodge scoured the country with his Fourth Iowa "Black Coats" and the Thirty-sixth Illinois. Prodding Price's retreating column, Dodge fought three skirmishes in February. In every fight Price offered only slight resistance. He abandoned many horses, supply wagons, and an occasional cannon. One captured gun was equipped with prolonges, and a discarded cap indicated that it belonged to Hebert's Louisianans. Obviously Price was making a general retreat with no thought of standing for a battle, at least until he could join and co-operate with McCulloch — the old situation which had divided the command before Wilson's Creek. Curtis determined, as Lyon had, to strike before they resolved their differences and combined.

Dodge's two regiments led the van enthusiastically. The weather was fine and the men reveled in Southland sunshine, razorbacks, and an occasional wild turkey. Along the road they saw piles of rebel equipment, dead and broken-down horses and mules. The enemy must be flying in distress. At country stores and crossroads, farmers in homespun stared at the marching column. The Yankees stared back. They told one another that the Ozark girls were something to look at — all kept their hair nicely combed "by crawling through the brush-fence after the pigs." In front of some cabins, whole families stood begging mercy. They had been told by Price's men that the Yankees would kill all men and ravish the women. Dodge's men laughed and forged ahead with long, swinging route steps. They outmarched their supply train and went on short rations, but still they failed to overtake Pap Price. Hungry now, they began to loot farmhouses. Abashed at first, they soon learned to storm in closed doors, rummage deserted premises. In some houses they found washtubs filled with clothes, the soapy water still hot. Clocks ticked ominously on the mantels of silent rooms. Foragers from the Fifty-ninth Illinois were startled by the meow of a hungry cat that rubbed against their legs and begged for food.

Suddenly the weather turned bitter cold. Sigel froze his feet. On the rolling farm land between Sugar Creek and Pea Ridge the van fought a skirmish, but Price got away once more. Curtis noticed that the area seemed ideal for maneuvering troops in battle. Twelve miles below, the Union soldiers marched into McCulloch's winter cantonment at Cross Hollows. It, too, was abandoned. Blackened timbers still smoked among red brick chimneys — barracks enough to house ten or twelve thousand men. So McCulloch and Price were both retreating now! Could this be a trap? Sick and wounded lay unattended in hospital buildings. Fires still burned in cookhouse ovens. Food bubbled in kettles on the ranges. Plates and tin cups stood on mess-hall tables. Wire pens contained two hundred game fowl kept by the Louisiana boys for sporting purposes. The Yankees devoured them with glee, became ill, and complained that they had been poisoned. The discovery of some brass knuckles set the Northerners to speculating about "chivalry's" brutality.

Eighteen miles below the abandoned cantonment stood Fayetteville — an intellectual oasis largely Union in sentiment — on a tree-tasseled knoll at the edge of the Boston Mountains. Fayetteville supported two female seminaries and Arkansas College — institutions attended by the well-to-do whites and by Creek, Cherokee, and Choctaw "ladies of refinement." Asboth, with his St. Louis Germans, reached the town as McCulloch evacuated it, leaving the stores looted and many houses on fire. Asboth's men were fighting the flames when a courier from Curtis ordered them to retreat. The general feared his line had extended too far for safety.

Seated in his tent back near Cross Hollows, on February 25, 1862, General Curtis wrote a happy letter to his brother. He liked to camp in the open, to sit in full uniform and spurs, live close to nature and the good ground even when a house was available. Solemn and sentimental always, his big hazel eyes looked across the farm land his men occupied. The sun shone warmly after the cold snap, and he wrote about the singing birds. The farm belonged to an avowed secessionist who now sat in the guard tent while the Union soldiers pitched their Sibleys in his grain fields, butchered his cattle, and tore down his fences for firewood. Curtis could hear the man's wife and four little girls on the porch of the farmhouse lamenting the destruction of their property. Curtis told his brother about the successful march and expressed pride in the campaign so far. Driving Price from Missouri might seem a small accomplishment beside Grant's recent victories at Forts Henry and Donelson, but it was nonetheless a real military achievement.

His correspondence completed, Curtis settled down to the routine of organizing his position, of establishing his communications along the wire road to Springfield, Rolla, and St. Louis. He was aroused from his concentration over these details on March 3, 1862, by the distant booming of cannon. He counted forty precisely timed discharges — the salute for a major general. So a top-ranking officer had come to take command over Price and McCulloch! Here was a challenge to Curtis from the unknown.

Jeff Davis had solved the quarrel between McCulloch and Price by the oldest of devices. To appoint either as supreme commander would alienate a large number of the other's loyal supporters. To discharge either would lose the services of a valued military leader. Therefore, Davis kept both generals in their respective commands and created over their heads a new military department — the Trans-Mississippi Department No. 2 — including the commands of Price and McCulloch as well as Pike's four regiments of Indians and M. Jeff Thompson's "swamp rats," a total of forty-five thousand men under the command of Major General Earl VanDorn with specific instructions to defeat Curtis.

VanDorn was a soldier by profession, a Mississippian by birth, and a grand nephew of Andy Jackson's. He loved weapons and women — including other men's wives. A dashing captain of horse he had been twice brevetted for gallantry in the Mexican War. As he assumed command of the new department, he was convalescing from a bad fall while attempting a dangerous ditch jump. His aide, duty-bound to follow, had been seriously injured.

On the day of his appointment VanDorn wrote his wife, "I must have St. Louis — then huzza!" Crushing Curtis and his ten thousand five hundred men seemed only incidental. Up in the Missouri metropolis, society matrons sympathetic to the Confederacy planned for VanDorn's reception. One wealthy widow who had become notorious for selling "secesh aprons" and "secesh fans" boasted that her house was open to the Southern champions when they arrived.

Hot-blooded VanDorn was the ideal soldier to restore Missouri chivalry. Surely he could outmarch and outfight slow, methodical engineer Curtis.

With characteristic éclat he halted the retreating Confederates in the Boston Mountains south of Fayetteville, and ordered an about-face. With Napoleonic language, in the wintry woods of Arkansas, he addressed the army:

> Soldiers! Behold your leader! He comes to show you the way to glory and immortal renown. . . . Awake, young men of Arkansas, and arm! Beautiful maidens of Louisiana, smile not on the craven youth who may linger by your hearth when the rude blast of war is sounding in your ears! Texas chivalry, to arms!

This ornate eloquence was followed by an order for the men to prepare three days' cooked rations for a forced march north. On March 4, 1862, they set off with a gale blowing wet snow in their faces. "In like a lion, out like a lamb," gave them little immediate comfort. Cavalrymen tried to warm numbed fingers between saddle blankets and their horses' backs. The hot sweat felt good at first but finally left their hands colder than ever. Infantrymen fared better by swinging their arms and legs naturally. In addition to horse and foot, VanDorn brought sixty pieces of artillery, including ox-drawn Ol' Sacramento, under command of bright-eyed but cadaverous Hi Bledsoe.

On another road, west of the Boston Mountains, Pike's Indian column was coming to join the Confederate army with from one to six thousand men — estimates vary as much as that. In all, VanDorn was using from sixteen to twenty thousand of the men in his department in an effort to defeat Curtis's ten thousand five hundred.

The Indians marched in a long straggling line, many mounted, some trudging on foot. At the head, in a carriage, rode poetical and bewhiskered Pike, decked out like a Sioux in feathers, leggins, and beaded moccasins. His Negro body servant Brutus accompanied him with the tribal papers and pay rolls in carpetbags. With Pike rode conservative John Ross in frock coat and stovepipe hat like President Lincoln's. General Cooper brought his Choctaw and Chickasaw. One unit of the former called themselves the "Blue Eyed Company," but it would be a mistake to consider any of them not Indians. Both factions of the Cherokee Nation were represented. The mixbloods, under Stand Watie and Elias C. Boudinet, rode with the Texas battalion — all veterans of the fights against Opothleyoholo. Twelve hundred full-blooded "pins," who distrusted Stand Watie's "slick skins" more than they did the enemy, rode with John Drew. Pompous John Jumper, dignified as an archbishop, came with six hundred Seminole. The Creeks were led by long-haired Daniel McIntosh with eight members of his family holding commissions in the regiment, among them the tooth-less Chilly with a battalion of two hundred. Surely as bizarre an army as ever rode into an American battle! A VanBuren, Arkansas, newspaper re-porter described McIntosh's Creek regiment as being a mixture of all ages and colors, including many Negroes with no uniforms and few arms. They had practiced a unique drill unknown to the pages of Hardee's manual. For the newsman the tatterdemalion gang lined up and at a given command all emitted a savage yell, broke ranks, ran a hundred yards to timber, fired by squads, cleaned their guns, and stood waiting further orders. Just how this kind of warfare would work on a battlefield was anybody's guess. None of Drew's Cherokee showed much enthusiasm for military glory. Some wanted to desert. Others still sympathized with Opothleyoholo and, as they marched along, plotted to kill their Con-federate allies in the first battle. The pay promised them by General Pike was long overdue. He had received it from Richmond but, in his leisurely way, had failed to make the payments. Now his negligence proved a bene-fit to the service, for he promised to pay the companies at stations ahead. Thus few men deserted his column on the march.

Back at Curtis's encampment near Cross Hollows, a tough little jockey of a man drove north along the wire road. Bandy-legged Captain Phil Sheridan did not know that his team of prancing black chargers was car-rying him away from an impending battle. A short time after he left, Wild Bill Hickok and a party of scouts brought word that the enemy was coming in force. Curtis decided to concentrate and fight in the area be-tween Sugar Creek and Pea Ridge, some twelve miles to the north. Eu-gene Carr and Jefferson C. Davis were stationed there already. As veteran regulars they could be counted on to prepare adequate fortifications. Carr, the bearded Cossack, had distinguished himself at Wilson's Creek. Davis had been in Jefferson City when Mulligan made his march to Lexington. He was a silent, lonesome-looking man with cold eyes that habitually peered down a long sharp nose. Fellow officers considered him a recluse on account of his abstract devotion to duty. Certainly he would work inde-fatigably under Curtis's instructions. Davis had been a lieutenant of artillery in Fort Sumter at the time of its surrender eleven months ago. Now a brigadier general of volunteers, he commanded a division.

Curtis sent couriers racing out through the night to call in Sigel's division from northwest Arkansas. He warned the German to come at once lest VanDorn cut him off. Then Curtis mounted his saddle horse and rode toward Pea Ridge. He arrived at 2 A.M. on March 6, 1862, aroused Carr and Davis, and outlined plans for the defense.

The couriers found Sigel's men widely scattered. Riders galloped off to all the units with orders for them to pack up in the night and start north. By late morning on March 6, 1862, all but two regiments were within ten miles of Pea Ridge and these, as Curtis had feared, were pinched off by VanDorn. Sigel halted his entire line to help them out. Curtis on Sugar Creek, riding around to inspect the progress on his earthworks, heard the distant bombardment and guessed the cause. He ordered Asboth, the austere Hungarian, and the voluble Osterhaus to check the Confederates and help Sigel come through. They found the little German executing another of his spectacular retreats, with his artillery in the center of infantry columns. A wall of bayonets prevented Shelby's Confederate cavalry from sweeping in from the flanks to kill the artillery horses.

Throughout the day, as Asboth, Osterhaus, and Sigel fought their way to Pea Ridge, Curtis put the finishing touches on his defenses. He planned to meet the enemy where the wire road from Fayetteville to Springfield dipped into the Sugar Creek hollow. Here Davis and Carr had constructed elaborate fortifications of dirt and logs, behind which cannon could be fired — an engineer's innovation. Grant and Sherman, back East, were still unlimbering artillery in open fields. Curtis fully expected Van-Dorn, with his superior numbers, to deploy before the breastworks and then extend his line around the Yankee's left wing. The Federal right and rear seemed safe under Pea Ridge, but his left was exposed at the north end of the ridge, where the Elk Horn Tavern stood on the wire road, and Curtis sent strong forces to occupy that area of the field.

The Elk Horn Tavern was a frame house with a two-story porch on the south, and copious chimneys at both ends. This building was the first telegraph station south of Springfield. The operator, a Mr. Cox, lived here with his mother and young wife. Immediately behind the tavern a side road dropped down into a defile much too steep and narrow for maneuvering troops. The east end of Pea Ridge began at the west side of this gulch and extended south for two miles. The precipitous granite escarpment, feathered on top with trees, sloped gradually north to a road through the woods. At the west end of Pea Ridge, and back from the wire road, stood the hamlet of Leetown — since disappeared — a dozen houses with blacksmith shop and grocery.

At dusk on March 6, 1862, Sigel came tearing in with Asboth and Osterhaus. Shelby's cavalry followed them to within sight of the fortifications. Curtis moved his men north between Pea Ridge and Sugar Creek to make room for the Germans. At his extreme left he placed Carr, near the Elk Horn Tavern. In the center he stationed the gloomy Jefferson C. Davis. Next to him he placed Asboth, whose division had arrived first, then Osterhaus. The extreme right, where the fortifications were strongest, he assigned to Sigel. The little German directed his men to the position, rode to Curtis's tent, dismounted, threw back the flap, walked in and said that he was hungry. Curtis would have preferred some remark about the adequacy of the fortifications or the selection of the battlefield. What kind of man was this fellow Sigel?

The four Federal divisions, waiting in line for tomorrow's battle, made merry during the night, cheering defiantly around their roaring campfires. The snow, which had been pelting VanDorn in the south, began to fall at Pea Ridge, whitening the ground. In plain sight, across Sugar Creek, the Confederates' bivouac fires appeared like yellow stars twinkling along the blue-white wire road as far as the Yanks could see. Closest to them were Shelby's horsemen. Next Price's Missourians squatted around their fires. Behind them stood McCulloch's and McIntosh's Arkansans and Texans. Colonel Louis Hebert followed with his Third Louisiana. These veterans of Wilson's Creek were eager to give Curtis some of Lyon's medicine. At the rear, Indians streamed in until midnight, lighting new fires as they turned out of the road to bivouac.

VanDorn's army had marched fifty-five miles in three days against wet, driving snow. Their rations were gone and in the morning they would fight for the enemy's supplies. Out in the dark wintry fields, two figures stumbled into the light of a bivouac fire. Humped with cold, hands in pockets for warmth, they held their horses by looping the reins under their arms. Private Grimes and his companion asked where, in these thousands of men, they might find their outfit — the First Missouri Cavalry, Company K.

March 7, 1862, dawned cold and clear, with not a man in sight south of Sugar Creek. Where had VanDorn's army gone? Curtis's men lined up around their cook fires for a good hot breakfast as they asked this perplexing question.

X X I

The Battle of Pea Ridge

The battle of Pea Ridge began at about 10:30 A.M. on March 7, 1862. General Curtis was a precise engineer, so his recollection of the minute must be correct. VanDorn had slipped quietly away from the bivouac during the night, leaving fires burning deceptively along Curtis's front. In the darkness he had marched around the north side of Pea Ridge to strike Curtis in his left rear at the Elk Horn Tavern. He expected Curtis to concentrate and fend off this blow. Then VanDorn planned a second surprise attack around the south end of Pea Ridge at Leetown. The maneuver was much the same as Lyon's strategy at Wilson's Creek, but VanDorn had more, instead of fewer, men than his antagonist. The night march was longest for Sterling Price's Missourians, who traversed the full length of Pea Ridge to the defile behind the Elk Horn Tavern. McCulloch and McIntosh, with their Texans, Arkansans, Louisianans, and Pike's Indians, were assigned the shorter march to the southern end of the ridge.

Daylight came long before VanDorn's men reached their stations. The delay gave Curtis ample time to discover the enemy's new plan of attack and, instead of being struck in the rear, Curtis ordered an about-face and stood ready to meet the foe on a reversed front. Moreover, his men — with the exception of Sigel's — were fresh and eager to fight the tired Confederates. Although outnumbered, Curtis had shorter communication lines and could shuttle reserves as needed. On the Confederate side, VanDorn felt ill. He had rashly swum on horseback across an icy river to join the command, although he had not recovered from the earlier fall from his horse. However, VanDorn was not one to postpone a battle for personal indisposition. He determined to direct the battle from an ambulance with his blooded trotting mare hitched to the side for emergencies. The benign and bell-voiced Pap Price followed the vehicle on his charger, answering questions, identifying passing military units, watching respectfully his commander's Airedale mustache, aggressive, imperial, and jaunty kepi at the ambulance's uprolled curtain.

A mile from the Elk Horn Tavern the Union pickets fired at the advancing Confederates and retreated up the gulch through the brush. Price's butternuts deployed slowly in the scrub oak, pushing their lines out on the steep hillsides until they reached the summits.

Waiting for them in the open country at the head of the hollow by the tavern, General Carr placed his twenty-five hundred men and twelve cannon to hold the sixty-five hundred, then galloped along the line — a perfect horseman, his Cossack beard covering the upper four brass buttons on his blue coat. With the critical eyes of a professional soldier, Carr appraised his position. At the extreme right he ordered frock-coated Colonel Grenville Dodge, pale from a recent illness, to dislodge the enemy in the brushy slopes east of the hollow and open a flank fire on the enemy in the gulch. Level-eyed Dodge moved a battalion of his Black Coats into the russet underbrush. Then Carr ordered skirmishers down the road into the hollow to meet the enemy column. He watched them pull hatbrims over their eyes as they entered the danger zone, as though to protect themselves from rain instead of bullets. Behind the foremost battery, beside the tavern, Carr placed a blue wall of reserves. His guns were unlimbered along the wire road at proper intervals to protect each other. From the east end of the tavern's second story, Carr could direct the fire into the hollow. Puffs of smoke down there and whistling shells overhead disclosed the enemy's guns in the woods. Carr recognized a familiar boom — ox-drawn Sacramento firing as she had at Wilson's Creek. "Always count on splay-footed cattle to outhaul spike-footed mules in the mud!"

Along the Union line, bursting shells kicked up dirt around the advance battery. A well-placed shot disabled three of the four guns. Two caissons exploded, killing all the men. A moment of silence followed the bombardment, then a horde in homespun charged up the hollow, boiling into Carr's divisions, threatening to roll up Curtis's whole right wing. This was the first blow VanDorn had planned.

Carr, desperate for reinforcements, sent a messenger to headquarters.

The courier delivered his note to the twenty resplendent horsemen who surrounded General Curtis with a gleam of gold and blue, and shining saddle leather. Another courier from the west end of the line dashed in with a request from Osterhaus for help at the south end of Pea Ridge. VanDorn's second blow had struck there. The aides, on their pawing chargers, waited respectfully for their commander to decide which way the reserves would be sent.

Over at the left, Osterhaus had got into a hornets' nest. Shortly after breakfast he probed around the west end of Pea Ridge, hunting for the enemy. Beyond Leetown his scouts sighted a multitude of men across a field, all dressed in outlandish costumes. The Germans had no time to retreat, so Osterhaus unlimbered his flying batteries behind a rail fence around a cabin dooryard. Then, before he could deploy his cavalry, the horde rushed on him, a great disorderly mass — black, white, and red — with guns, cutlasses, bows and arrows.

Osterhaus and his men had never seen anything like this before and were not trained to meet it. The Indians swept forward brandishing rifles, knives, and tomahawks, while barking shrill, unearthly signals. Osterhaus's trained infantry battalion broke and fled, some scampering this way, some that. Soon Choctaw, German, and Texan were milling in a confused and bewildering rabble, shouting, shooting, and running.

Osterhaus's cavalry, armed with revolvers and sabers, wheeled their horses and spurred back through Leetown, back through the fluttering yellow flags which marked the hospital area, back through the waiting lines of the Fifty-ninth Illinois Infantry beyond, shouting as they passed: "Turn back! Turn back!"

Texans led the Confederate charge, and behind them came Stand Watie's dismounted cavalry and next, on horseback, Drew's regiment — the "pins" watching for an opportunity to change to the Union side, or go home as they had in the fight with Opothleyoholo, but the excitement of sudden victory confused them. With shouts of laughter they danced around the abandoned "shooting wagons," roaring delightedly as they held horse collars around their necks and pranced about with harness chains jingling. "Me big In'gen, big as horse."

McCulloch took instant advantage of this break in the Union left and launched a third attack on Curtis's center, where Jefferson C. Davis's precious reserves waited under the protection of Pea Ridge. Osterhaus, in the meantime, tried to take back his batteries with a charge by the Twenty-second Indiana and the Thirty-sixth Illinois, sending at the same time to Curtis for reserves. This courier had arrived at headquarters just as Carr's appeal for help reached the commanding general. With the Union right being pushed back and shot to pieces, with the Indian horde crumpling the left, and a wedge being driven in the center, Curtis must act quickly. Which way should his reserves be sent?

On the Confederate side, Pike gloated over his Indians' achievements until he tried to reorganize them for another charge. Then he discovered that the red men were uncontrollable under artillery fire. They refused to lie down and let the shells pass harmlessly overhead. Most of the Indians wanted to fight individually — to climb trees or shoot from behind rocks at the distant enemy, perhaps at their fellow Confederates, for Drew's confused regiment still wanted to fight for the Union. With the Indians almost useless, McCulloch determined to hold the new line. He brought up the Sixteenth Arkansas behind a tree-lined fence and sent it forward against Osterhaus's infantry, which had stood fire when the cavalry skedaddled. General McCulloch, conspicuous in dove-colored coat, sky-blue pantaloons, and Duke of Wellington boots, rode immediately behind his skirmishers and ahead of the Sixteenth Arkansas's advancing battle lines. The Thirty-sixth Illinois, crouching behind a fence, opened fire and drove them back, retaking much of the field. The routed Arkansans re-formed and charged again in the tall grass. Sixty yards from the fence they stumbled over the limp body of an officer stripped of arms and gold watch but still wearing Wellington boots.

General McIntosh, hearing of his chief's death, rallied the men for vengeance and went forward — to fall dead himself within an hour. Thus the top command of the Confederates' right wing devolved on Albert Pike, who did not learn about his new rank until 3 P.M., when his Indians were too disorganized to even hold the line.

The Federals, swarming back over the field where the Indians had captured the battery, found thirty or forty scalped corpses. Some of the dead men's skulls had been cleft with bowie knives "mangling brains, and blood and hair." A private of the Ninth Missouri, finding his brother scalped, determined to retaliate tomorrow.

VanDorn's entire right-wing action had been a feint to draw reinforcements from the Federal center while Price pushed the Confederates' left column up the wooded hollow against Carr at the Elk Horn Tavern. Curtis responded to the feint as the Southern commanders expected. He reinforced his left and trusted Carr, the regular, to hold the right without help. Carr, watching the road for reinforcements as he rallied his men, pushed the Confederates back into the hollow, then galloped over to see Dodge on his extreme right. He found the chunky little black-coated colonel wounded. A surgeon was binding his arm as he sat in the saddle — no time to dismount. His artillery was raking the brushy hillside ahead of his skirmishers to hold back the enemy from turning his flank. While Carr talked with Dodge, there was a lull in the enemy's artillery fire back at the tavern. Then butternuts charged up the hollow again and plunged into the Federal lines within three hundred yards of the tavern. The Union commander in charge there during Carr's absence, Colonel John S. Phelps, the Springfield congressman, rode courageously behind the Union Missourians. Three horses were shot from under him and a hundred and seventy-five of his soldiers fell, before Price's men slunk into the hollow a second time.

Carr, galloping back to the scene, expected Price to re-form and attack again. He feared that his men could not stand a third onslaught and sent another desperate message to Curtis. The general, surrounded by his epauletted staff, calculated constantly the shifting battle risks, and the number of daylight hours left for the fight. To keep him posted on every area of the field, a corps of couriers dashed back and forth along the dirt roads and scudded across the fields, bounding fences, jerking their mounts to a halt for the receipt or delivery of messages. One of these riders was Wild Bill Hickok, the spy, and during the day he used up four horses — one killed, three exhausted. Curtis fumed to himself because Sigel, tired from yesterday's retreat, took little part today. Both wings seemed to be crumbling, and efficient Jefferson C. Davis's reserves were now fighting to save themselves from the Confederate regiments which had slipped in from the south, under Pea Ridge, and threatened to pierce the Union center. Curtis could spare no men from that line.

Carr's men, waiting at sundown behind the Elk Horn Tavern, listened hopefully for reinforcements. They knew the meaning of the silence down in the gulch where the enemy had withdrawn. The Ninth Iowa formed in solid ranks around the mouth of the hollow to make the best defense they could against another charge. Artillerymen regrouped batteries where they could rake the enemy as it came over the crest. The men were hardly in position around their guns when Price's artillery began tossing shells along the wire road again — wrecking battery after battery. Another silence followed this carnage, then, in the twilight, hundreds of butternuts fanned out of the hollow once more, swirled around the tavern, thumped across the wooden porch — the owner and family cowering in the basement — and roared down the road.

The Iowa artillerymen fled from their disabled pieces, but one of them, before he ran, tossed a blazing quilt on an abandoned caisson. Seconds later, as the rebels swarmed around the captured guns, he heard an explosion and looked back to see gory tatters of men tossed into the paling sky, some to hang dripping from the trees, others to plummet down through the branches and thud among the mangled bodies on the ground. Soldiers at Leetown, two miles away, saw the column of smoke, and Curtis sent two divisions under Asboth to relieve Carr. They arrived at dusk and Carr's and Dodge's bleeding regiments retired through their ranks.

In the dark Curtis rode around his battered lines. The scene was grim. His men had been pushed in at every front. Enemy campfires illuminated the tavern up to the elk horns on the rooftree. On the lower porch corpses were corded like wood. The Union soldiers lay on their arms a quarter of a mile down the wire road. The enemy, under Pea Ridge, bivouacked in places so close to the Federal line that their low grumbling voices and an occasional nervous laugh could be heard in the dark. One Union caisson drove, by mistake, into an enemy's camp. Back at safer distances, boyish voices on both sides sang the same sentimental songs. Southern boys enjoyed shouting:

> Jeff Davis is a President;
> Abe Lincoln is a fool;
> Jeff Davis rides a big bay horse;
> Abe Lincoln rides a mule.

After finishing his inspection in the dark, General Curtis returned to headquarters and learned that Sigel was marching his men back to their encampment for supper. Curtis had been irritated all day by the German's relative inactivity. Now, contrary to his deliberate nature, he snapped a peremptory command: "Let Sigel's men hold their lines. Send supper out, not the men in."

In Curtis's tent, orderlies had spread blankets on a pile of straw. The general lay down, fully dressed, and summoned all division commanders to a council. At midnight the tired officers dismounted stiffly in the chill night air and limped in for the conference. Carr, Dodge, and Asboth — all of them wounded — were gloomy about success. Lieutenant Colonel Frank J. Herron, the Captain Herron of Wilson's Creek — youthful head of a Dubuque bank established by wealthy Pennsylvania parents — had been left wounded in the field for the enemy to capture. Not a single commander could report an advance. Supply lines and all communications were completely stopped. Sigel maintained that the army's only hope was to cut its way out in the morning — a movement in which he excelled. The advantage seemed to be with the Confederacy, truly enough, but Curtis moved too slowly to give in at once. He knew that McCulloch and McIntosh had both been killed, that the Louisianan, Louis Hebert, was a prisoner, that the Indians were probably disorganized permanently, and that by drawing the Federal wings together, his forces could be reknit to strike with double strength.

Curtis's commanders trooped back to their lines with orders to consolidate and renew the fight at dawn. Colonels passed the word to captains who whispered orders along the fence rows. In hollows, out of sight of the enemy, soldiers built fires, cooked flapjacks, and boiled coffee in muddy snow water — their first food in almost twenty-four hours. Cramming victuals into ravenous mouths, they exchanged experiences, and vowed to beat the enemy in the morning. One man displayed three bullet holes in his hat, another told how a buckshot had snapped the ramrod from his fingers. Private Peter Pelican of Company B, Thirty-sixth Illinois, displayed a gold watch he had taken from an officer in top boots and "sky blue britches" after shooting him from his horse. Pelican's squadmates cherished McCulloch's belt and pistols. A German in the Thirty-fifth Illinois claimed that one of the earrings he wore to preserve his teeth (a superstition of the time) had been shot away, and while he was telling a comrade about the freak incident, a second bullet snipped off the other one. Privates in the Fifty-ninth Illinois joked about the recruit in their outfit who had dirt kicked in his eyes by a musket volley. "Damn the thing," he said, then turning his other end, exclaimed, "Now . . . shoot and be d---ed."

In the Confederate camp VanDorn studied the cost he had paid for victory — if a victory. He had learned about the deaths of McCulloch and McIntosh in midafternoon but had kept the information from Price's men, until Pike stumbled in with the remnant of his Indians during the night. Only Stand Watie's Cherokee and Chilly McIntosh's two hundred Creeks remained loyal to the Confederacy. Drew's disorganized regiment was already on the way back to Indian Territory. VanDorn ordered the Indians who stayed to take positions on top of Pea Ridge at the extreme right and await the opening of tomorrow's battle.

Saturday, March 8, 1862, dawned without a breeze in the blue sky. Smoke from the battle hung like drapery over the fields, woodlands, and mountains. The sun shown wanly, through a copper haze, on the waiting men. VanDorn opened the ball with a cannon blast into the smoke, arousing the Union boys from naps after breakfast. They were better fed and better rested than the enemy, in spite of the ground they had lost.

Curtis rechecked his constricted position. Confederates held Pea Ridge, the fields below it, and the Elk Horn Tavern. Their lines stretched east of the wire road for a mile — the area which Carr and Dodge had occupied yesterday. Curtis decided to strike the nearest enemy first. He ordered Sigel, who had taken little part in yesterday's battle, to assume the initiative at once. The stubby little German deployed his forty guns against the enemy under Pea Ridge. Two hundred and fifty yards behind his batteries he placed the infantry, with orders to lie down in the muddy fields. Then Sigel rode calmly among the guns, as dignified as though being watched on parade. Often he dismounted, personally sighted a cannon, and gave orders for the fire. He was a genius with artillery this morning. Young Churchill Clark, Confederate from St. Louis, a son of Meriwether Lewis Clark and grandson of the explorer, felt a shell brush his mustache and quipped, "God! That was a close shave!" The next cannon ball took off his head. Hot shot kindled dry leaves in the woods. Fire crackled through the tall grass, burning the helplessly wounded, setting able-bodied men along the worm fences to dancing desperately, as though fighting bees. Clark's cousin, Captain William Clark Kennerly, remembered the horror of that day. Passing a field hospital under the ridge, he saw amputated arms in shirt sleeves, and legs with boots on feet, tossed out on the ground from operating tables. Hurrying across a cornfield under fire, he wondered why the farmer had not cleared off the fodder last fall, then wondered why he wondered why. The human mind acts strangely when afraid.

In the inferno Curtis galloped around the field. Shells exploded over his flying head and under his horse's twinkling hoofs. Two orderlies were killed near him, but the engineer-commander remained absorbed in military calculations. Noting a weak line, he ordered the requisite number of men forward to strengthen it and dashed away consulting the second hand on his watch to see if the men appeared at designated locations on time.

Under Sigel's persistent bombardment and Curtis's consolidation of troops, the Confederate regiments evacuated their positions below the ridge — Old Sacramento booming defiance to the last. Sigel ordered his guns forward, and soon his shells puffed along the ridge, scattering Stand Watie's Indians, blowing up Confederate batteries silhouetted in the trees. Within half an hour none remined. VanDorn sent replacements, but Sigel had learned the range so accurately that he blasted the new gun carriages as soon as the horses appeared against the sky. Meanwhile the Federal infantry advanced and opened fire. Their rifles crumpled butternut soldiers whose short-range shotguns left them almost helpless. Curtis noticed that the enemy was withdrawing before his fire superiority. Surely the time had come to turn a retreat into a rout. He ordered forward the Third and Seventeenth Missouri, the Thirty-sixth and part of the Forty-fourth Illinois. In solid formation, drums beating, flags waving, the ranks writhed across the fields like a great python. One undulating end coiled up the ridge. The center followed like a serpent moving sideways. Reserve regiments on the fields below cheered, hats and handkerchiefs sparkling like popcorn from the mass of men. "O, dot was lofely," Sigel exclaimed. Curtis pronounced the charge the finest ever "made on the American continent."

Beyond the tavern, Carr's and Davis's soldiers looked back over their shoulders and saw the great snake coiling up the side of Pea Ridge. They pleaded for a charge on their own front and with a cheer the officers let them go. In no time they swarmed through the woods, capturing three cannon and the Dallas Battery's silk flag. Confederate reserves heard their yell and thought their own men were charging. They rushed forward to participate but met the routed Texans coming helter-skelter to the rear. False rumors that Price and VanDorn had both been captured added to the confusion. As a matter of fact, Price's arm had been severely wounded, but he carried it in a sling and refused to leave the field. By eleven o'clock butternuts streamed down from the mountaintops — some going east, some north, some down the deep hollow behind the tavern — a disorganized rabble of exhausted men. All firing ceased and dignified Curtis shouted like a boy. Spurring along his lines, brown eyes dancing, he yelled, "Victory, victory."

The men broke from their ranks, scattered out over the fields hunting souvenirs. They found many dead soldiers robbed of shoes and stockings — things needed most by the rebels. At one spot corpses lay so thick a man could walk on them for a hundred yards. The private of the Ninth Missouri who had found his brother scalped took nine in payment.

A sudden alarm ended the gruesome revelry — a call to arms! Merrymakers had spied an oncoming column of butternuts marching down the road. Drums beat the long roll, men ran for their encampments and "fell in." Nose bags were snatched from tired horses and the protesting animals were kicked around in their places before gun carriages. Then, with the army organized for action again, the invading column hove in sight with a white flag. The leader wanted permission to bury his dead.

Curtis granted the request and handed the officer a letter rebuking Van-Dorn for permitting his Indians to scalp their victims — the beginning of a provocative correspondence which terminated in the next few days in a way Curtis did not expect. In the meantime, Curtis repaired the battle damages and tallied his seven or eight hundred prisoners — among them the notorious Louis Hebert of the Third Louisiana and the insignificant Private Absalom Grimes. The former would be exchanged for Lieutenant Colonel Herron. Private Grimes would renew the anxiety he had previously caused his captors and gain notoriety by novel efforts to escape, once by tunneling through a wall under his bed, and again by impersonating a mechanic, oil can in hand, whom the guard left when all prisoners marched off a steamboat. Curtis's captives also included Bill Price, a nephew of Ol' Pap's and a member of the "so-called Confederate Congress." Eleven "civilized Indians" had been taken. The prisoners were marched north to Springfield with a suitable guard. Grim little Grenville Dodge, short neck bent and shoulders stooped from years behind a surveyor's transit, went along for hospitalization in St. Louis. His black frock coat was riddled with wagon nuts, bits of chain, and pebbles shot from cannon in the last hours of the fight. The Indians were to be exhibited as proof of Confederate barbarity, but none of them reached Rolla. Fearing torture, they tried to escape, one by one, and were all shot down by the guard.

VanDorn entered the conflict with an army estimated as numbering from 16,000 to 25,800 men, and on March 11, 1862, he was reported to have only 2894 answer roll call — a misleading statement, for many more reported later. VanDorn declared his losses to be 1000 with an additional 300 made prisoner. Curtis, with 10,500 men before the battle, admitted losing 1384 in killed, wounded, and missing.

The day after the battle was warm, with a gentle rain sopping the blood-stained field, washing away the scars of war. Mrs. John S. Phelps drove down from Springfield with wagonloads of lint and medical supplies. The humid air soon became tainted with decaying flesh, and Curtis ordered the encampment moved to a more healthful atmosphere. At the new site his tent was pitched beside a clear stream babbling from under blossoming branches of sugar maples, pawpaws, cherries, and budding grapevines. He wrote his brother — always more sentimentally than to his wife — that upland Arkansas resembled the Ohio woodlands they had known as boys. At dawn, he said, he awoke to music from striped woodpeckers, cooing doves, and bluebirds. Every evening he dropped to sleep with the carols of spring frogs in his ears. He described the scene of the recent battle as "silent and sad." "The vulture and the wolf have now communion, and the dead, friends and foes, sleep in the same lonely grave." The rocky ridge above the battleground, he hoped, would perpetuate the memory of the men who fell "for Civil and religious liberty" — surely a new motive for the Civil War.

The routed rebel army fled in three directions, and Captain Shelby covered the retreat so skillfully that Sigel, following one column, sent back word to Curtis that VanDorn might readily re-form, and surround the

Federal Army. Sigel always wanted to cut his way out in a masterly retreat.

VanDorn himself wrote his sister on March 16 that he had withdrawn from the field "with tears in my eyes," the first time in his life to fall back from an enemy. "My eleventh battle." . . . "Hungry for two days."

Many of Pike's Indians who started home on the first day of the battle looted the Confederate wagon train as they retreated. Pike, with his staff, a day later, skulked through the fields for forty miles until he overtook them. Stand Watie withdrew his mixbloods in good order.

VanDorn, retreating in an opposite direction, replied to Curtis's complaint about Indian atrocities by saying that his red men were considered as civilized as the Germans who had killed Confederate prisoners in cold blood. VanDorn hoped that in the future all perpetrators "be brought to justice, whether German or Choctaw." Years later a Choctaw woman remembered that her people mailed scalps back to friends and relatives in Mississippi. At the time, the duly assembled Cherokee Council passed a resolution against atrocities "incompatible with usages of civilized nations."

The main Confederate column withdrew down the Fayetteville road. Citizens of that charred and gutted village heard many rumors before it arrived. During the battle they were told that the South was winning and that Sigel had been killed. Then, to everyone's surprise, a carriage rolled into town containing McCulloch's body. The team stopped to display the corpse, then plodded on to Fort Smith where undertakers prepared it for burial — the fatal bullet falling from the general's clothes.

In an hour, another carriage drove into Fayetteville with the body of General James McIntosh. He was carried into a residence and citizens filed past looking at his bearded face, his thinning hair, and the dead leaves still clinging to his overcoat.

Next day the defeated army streamed into town, not the neat column of four men abreast that had marched north but a rabble filling the fifty-foot road. Few had guns, knapsacks, or blankets. Many were bareheaded. The mob seemed endless, but at sundown came two cavalry regiments in formation — obviously the rear guard. For a week longer, gangs of miserable men straggled through town. Others were found camping in the woods. Many scattered to their homes, never reporting again for muster. Others organized as bushwhackers to live by plunder. During the summer one gang of a thousand freebooters encamped on the edge of Fayetteville, their presence terrifying everybody.

Price retreated with his Missourians toward the east, earning for himself the nickname of "Old Skedad." The St. Joe *Herald* poked fun at the two-hundred-and-ninety-pound giant running away and reported, "As a racer he has seen few equals for his weight." Evidently enjoying the joke, the editor continued: "General Price is said to be careless in some of his military arrangements but he always keeps his rear open."

Curtis followed Price cautiously, but the Confederate legislature at Little Rock packed to flee. Other armies were concentrating for a decisive battle east of the Mississippi near Shiloh, and VanDorn hurried the remnant of his army across to take part and re-establish his military reputation. Price urged his Missourians to follow. Some did so, but many turned back to Missouri to lurk in the woods near their homes, to live by stealing, and eventually join Quantrill or other freebooters.

To stop Curtis, a new commander named Thomas C. Hindman appeared in eastern Arkansas. He was a dapper little man, five feet one inch tall, who dressed in tight-fitting clothes, ruffled shirts, and patent-leather boots. Lamed in an accident, he wore one boot heel higher than the other but considered himself the mirror of fashion. He had killed his man according to the gentleman's code, had written a sentimental novel, and been elected to Congress. In 1860 he resigned to preach secession, joined the Confederate Army. As a member of a family of politicians — his father had participated in the Plaquamine Parish voting fraud — Hindman understood every angle of practical politics. He determined to prevent General Curtis from crossing Arkansas to aid the Federals east of the Mississippi and in the emergency ordered all available forces to bushwhack Union pickets, to burn bridges, destroy all food including growing crops, to pollute water "by killing cattle, ripping the carcasses open and throwing them in." Let men without arms forge their own pikes and lances, kill stragglers, break up wagon trains, scorch the earth so that no Union soldier could reach the Mississippi.

XXII

The Bloodstained Kansas Banner

Up the soft dirt highway into southwest Missouri rode Stand Watie with his Cherokee battalion. The soggy spring woods stood empty in April 1862 — deserted by the Federal defenders who had gone to fight at Shiloh. Here and there old men, cripples, and boys assembled in local farming communities to defend their homes from the Cherokee. Neosho and Cowskin Prairie were far away from Lincoln and his military advisers. Nearer theaters of war demanded their attention. In Virginia, McClellan seemed exasperatingly inept. Grant's success at Donelson had been eclipsed by confusion and butchery at Shiloh. Casualty lists were still coming in. Only Jim Lane kept nagging incessantly for attention, for adequate protection on the border. Constantly he urged the enlistment of refugee Indians in Kansas. Let these embittered people drive back Stand Watie's raiders and reassert Federal authority in the territory.

Lincoln finally consented, specifying that the red men must not be employed in the giant jayhawking expedition Lane had advocated, but only as a punitive force — Indian against Indian. Lincoln had sidetracked Lane from the command of the larger proposed expedition to the gulf. Now he authorized a Lane man, William Weer, to command a smaller project. Weer was a lawyer from Wyandotte, Kansas, with military ambitions and a fondness for drink. In the territorial days he had captained a gang of jayhawkers, and stolen Missouri horses in accordance with the Kansas code.

William Weer was authorized to enlist two Indian regiments — one Creek, the other Cherokee — making fifteen hundred in all. To stiffen these units, two regiments of white infantry, three of cavalry, and two batteries were added. The column started south in June when the grass became tall enough to sustain the horses. A missionary, Evan Jones, accompanied the force with a confidential message for Chief John Ross. The North showed little interest in the expedition. New Orleans had just fallen to "Beast" Butler, and dispatches from the Crescent City monopolized the news.

All uniforms issued to the Indians seemed to be too large or too small, with sleeves overhanging hands or reaching only below elbows. High-crowned hats perched precariously on heads with braids dangling below shoulders. The warriors' faces were carefully painted like plains Indians'. As they jogged along, in column of four's, a war song started in the front ranks and surged to the rear. Over the prairie ahead, a thunderstorm blackened the sky like "a lid on a pot." Private Albert Greene, in the white cavalry — the Ninth Kansas — thought he could hear Stand Watie's laughter in the thunder.

Colonel Weer marched rapidly in his search for Watie, but the chief galloped back into the territory, refusing to fight. Without firing a shot, the Federal Indians captured Tahlequah, the Cherokee capital. Seventy-two-year-old John Ross surrendered readily. His young Quaker wife and her sister, as well as household treasures and the Cherokee Nation's archives, were loaded in several carriages to be sent to Washington. Cherokee flocked to Weer's encampment by dozens asking to enlist. Many claimed to have been in Drew's brigade at the battle of Pea Ridge, said they had wanted to change sides there but were unable to make themselves understood. Weer organized them into a third Indian regiment under the command of Colonel William A. Phillips, the Scotsman who had made a name for himself in Kansas as an antislavery reporter for the *New York Tribune*. Horace Greeley had offered him $10,000 a year to be his correspondent with the Army of the Potomac, but Phillips preferred active service with a colonel's pay in the West. Of the three Indian regiments his became the best.

Inactivity and torrid summer heat soon broke the brigade's morale. All the Indians resented restraint. They hunted, rode, and frolicked independently. The white soldiers fretted under the simmering sun. Colonel Weer, drunk in his tent, lost control of his army. Finally the officers went in a body, arrested their commander and marched back to Missouri under Frederick Salomon, ranking colonel.

The border, during the brigade's absence, had lapsed into near chaos. Deserters from Price's column at Pea Ridge had returned home to pillage the countryside. Charles Quantrill was making a name for himself and a new guerrilla, Bloody Bill Anderson, had joined his band. Then in July 1862, after the distressing Seven Days' Battle in Virginia, Lincoln called for three hundred thousand additional men. The freebooters cheered. Let the border send its quota and Confederate guerrillas would take over Missouri.

Across the state line in Kansas, buoyant, irrepressible Senator Lane offered to raise five regiments for Lincoln's call. He pointed to the success of enlisting Indians — questionable certainly — and asked now to recruit Negroes from the thousands who had escaped into Kansas.

Lincoln needed those five regiments, but he still opposed giving the Grim Chieftain a commission to march freed slaves into the South under "the blood-stained Kansas banner" which Lane advocated. The President sidetracked Lane again by appointing him Commissioner for Recruiting in the Department of Kansas with verbal authorization to organize Negro regiments — probably the first in the Civil War. The plan was to feed, clothe, and drill these fugitives until Negro troops were officially authorized.

Lane opened a recruiting office in Leavenworth. He appointed his son-in-law colonel of one regiment and Thomas Ewing, Jr., whose brother-in-law, William Tecumseh Sherman, was now major general of volunteers, to head another. With the histrionic oratory which Kansas relished, Lane stumped the state talking down to the rabble, purposely mispronouncing "Topeka" as "Topeko" and "Leavenworth" as "Leavingsworth." His enemies censured him for his methods, said that it would split the Republican Party, even urged citizens to protest the enlistment of Negro soldiers. "Great God!" Lane replied in an answering speech. "They say Jim Lane can't enlist colored troops at Junction City! That is what I'm here for. And" — taking a blank sheet of paper from his pocket — "I hold in my hands a list of the copperhead, disloyal and rebel element in this community; and when I get through organizing colored troops, I am going to draft these men as cooks for the Negro regiments."

By mid-August the newspapers reported Negroes in red pantaloons, drilling with great precision. Jokers called them Zouaves d'Afrique. Others quipped that scarlatina had broken out in the Kansas army. Lincoln, as agreed, was sending them new uniforms purchased, in the emergency, from France, but as yet no money was available for the Negro soldiers' pay.

The recruiting had hardly commenced when Quantrill, on August 11, 1862, captured Independence, Missouri. Several women were suspected of conspiring with him to betray the town. Already, the fair sex was beginning to romanticize the slim bandit with the broad mustache and voluptuous smile. In the raid, he captured an exceptionally fine brown horse which he named Charley, his own given name. Almost immediately, Quantrill was commissioned a captain in the Confederate Army. He appointed George Todd and William Gregg lieutenants. Todd had been an itinerant stonemason and ditchdigger in Kansas City. Though worthless and sulky as a workman, he had made a name for himself as a dogged fighter. Gregg, a more intelligent man, had served as deputy sheriff of Jackson County.

Five days later, on August 16, a band of guerrillas under Upton Hays attacked and fought a comparable number of Union guards at Lone Jack, twenty-five miles below Independence. The embattled farmers on both sides fought desperately. A hundred and twenty-five men were killed before Hays called in his men and rode south with Quantrill to plan more mischief.

With the worst of the bushwhackers gone and most of the soldiers in Tennessee preparing for the battle shaping itself at Corinth, trouble bubbled from a new source. The "farmer" Sioux in Minnesota had joined the "blanket" Sioux in the massacre of two or three hundred white settlers. A delegation of the Sioux' tribal enemies came to Leavenworth offering their people's services to Senator Lane. The Grim Chieftain knew that General Pope — after his defeat at Second Bull Run — was being sent to quell the disturbances in the Northwest, so he merely promised to help the Indians protect themselves by furnishing them with what guns he could spare — which was none — and leave the question of their service to the great White Father.

On August 24, 1862, Confederate Hindman became the official commander of the District of Arkansas, which included Missouri and Indian Territory. The jaunty little fellow with the curls, rose-colored kid gloves, and rattan cane had made a name for himself by impeding Curtis's march to the Mississippi after the Confederate defeat at Pea Ridge. He had been especially successful in organizing guerrilla bands. Although unpopular, he was a dynamo of ideas that succeeded miraculously even if they gained him many personal enemies. All his life Hindman had been a man who got whatever he sought. In 1856 he had married the girl of his choice despite the fact that her disapproving father had incarcerated her in a convent school. Hindman, disguising himself, entered the sanctuary and they eloped. Craving a fine brick house, he built one, despite a lack of money to pay the bills. This audacious wonder man had raised an army of twenty thousand in his district after all available men had, presumably, been shipped east of the Mississippi for the Corinth campaign. With supplies cut off from the East, he had commandeered muskets, medicine, and money. He started to manufacture percussion caps and small arms, operated the lead mines and tan yards, discovered and began digging saltpeter for powder. He established chemical laboratories, making calomel, castor oil, and spirits of niter. Under him, women organized sewing circles to knit socks for soldiers. Even some Negroes became enthusiastic about his program. In VanBuren they were reported to have given a ball, charging fifty cents admission for the benefit of the "Suddern Fed'cy." Most important of all was his successful propaganda to exaggerate the number of his forces and then keep Little Rock in Confederate hands after Memphis had fallen and White River was open for gunboats to within sixty miles of the capital.

Hindman learned of the guerrilla victories at Independence and Lone Jack. The successful bushwhackers were reported to be riding south, and Hindman proposed to join them for a new conquest. He organized three regiments of exiled Missourians under Shelby and called on Albert Pike to bring his Indian brigade. Pike responded slowly. He had quarreled with McCulloch for persistently taking the Indians' uniforms and supplies. Hindman, never one to be denied, repeated the order, and Pike resigned. Douglas Cooper immediately applied for Pike's post — Indian commissioner and brigadier general. As Indian agent he had great influence with the Choctaw and Chickasaw, and he had commanded them in battles against the "pins," but his reputation for sobriety had not improved since his retreat from Bird Creek in December 1861. However, he was appointed acting commander and moved the brigade north along with the battalion under Stand Watie, new chief of the Cherokee since the "capture" of John Ross.

The combined column was now reported to number forty thousand — another Hindman exaggeration perhaps — so Schofield, commander of the district, appealed for reinforcements from Department Commander Samuel Curtis, who had succeeded Halleck at St. Louis. (Successful officers were rising like rockets to the top echelons of command!) Curtis sent down a brigade from Kansas under command of James G. Blunt, the soggy-built terrier of a man, with dark, deep-set eyes, bristling black mustache, and little aggressive goatee. A born scrapper with a mathematical brain and flair for artillery, this rip-roaring abolitionist hurried south, met Salomon and learned that Upton Hays, Shelby, and Cooper — only part of Hindman's army — held an impregnable position behind the stone walls of Newtonia, a town between Springfield and Neosho, Missouri. Hindman had reorganized Shelby's riders into an organization its leader delighted to call the Iron Brigade. Schofield himself came to direct the attack against this Confederate concentration. On October 4, 1862, he sent the rebels flying. Upton Hays was killed. Cooper retreated to Indian Territory. Shelby led his wild horsemen into the brushy Boston Mountains southwest of Fayetteville.

Blunt led a pursuit and overtook Cooper's Indians at Old Fort Wayne, Indian Territory, on October 22, capturing all their artillery and scattering them like chaff in a fan mill. With no tangible army left to fight, the Union column came back to Arkansas. Schofield being ill, and believing the campaign finished until spring, returned to St. Louis.

The Union Army settled down for a winter of border-patrol duty against guerrillas. Headquarter encampments were located for over a hundred miles along the wire road. Blunt remained at the southern extremity on Lindsay's Prairie. Other divisions camped at the Pea Ridge battlefield and at Wilson's Creek, where "Bottle-nosed" Totten, a division commander now, was in charge but temporarily absent on court-martial duty. His command devolved on wealthy, handsome, and vain Frank Herron, recovered from his wound at Pea Ridge, and already — at the age of twenty-five — a brigadier general commanding two divisions. The popular young general's men fretted at the old campground. They had satiated their appetites for souvenirs from the Wilson's Creek battlefield. Many of them had dropped rocks on the ever-increasing pile which marked the site where Lyon fell. Now they were eager for action. To hell with a winter camp here, when glory waited on other battlegrounds.

Late in November, Blunt's scouts set the Lindsay's Prairie cantonment agog with a startling report. A division of Hindman's horse was coming through the Boston Mountains under the leadership of Marmaduke. This young Missouri officer had redeemed his performance at Boonville in 1861 by gallantry at Shiloh and now commanded all of Hindman's cavalry — Missouri volunteers, Shelby's Iron Brigade, and the bushwhackers routed from Newtonia in October — as reckless and picturesque riders as ever cinched a saddle. Quantrill's men joined them too, but the guerrilla chief had gone back to Richmond seeking a higher commission. Quantrill's lieutenants, Todd and Gregg, were in charge. Dangerous men for Quantrill to be with or be away from!

Blunt started south with five thousand men and thirty cannon to meet Marmaduke. After a thirty-five-mile march he found the enemy, on November 28, 1862, encamped at Cane Hill, a hamlet on the Fayetteville-VanBuren road just north of the Boston Mountains. The Confederates had looked forward to wintering in the rich and hospitable farming country west of Fayetteville, famous for its peach and apple brandy. Many of them remembered luscious feasts and gay dances here. Poetic Shelby likened his riders to Scottish Highlanders come to make merry on Lowland marches.

Blunt deployed quickly for battle. He ordered Colonel Salomon to hold one division in reserve, and with the other two Blunt opened the attack. The Eleventh Kansas under Colonel Thomas Ewing, Jr., deployed with newly issued long-barreled muskets, each loaded with a .72 caliber ball and three buckshot. Beside the Eleventh advanced the Tenth Kansas under Colonel William Weer, sober when stimulated by the prospect of battle. Next came Colonel William Phillips, the real Scotsman — not the Sir Walter variety — with the Third Cherokee, best of the Northern Indian organizations. Lieutenant Colonel L. R. Jewell led the Sixth Kansas Cavalry.

Shelby's "Scottish Highlanders" and Marmaduke's more prosaic Missouri farmers fell back before the "Lowland" resistance. The two commanders discussed the situation as they sat with chivalric staffs on neighing stallions, banners snapping in a northwest wind, russet leaves fluttering before an approaching storm. Marmaduke decided to entrap Blunt in the Boston Mountains — or at least get away before being defeated. He would dismount his horsemen and retreat, fighting through a defile so narrow that the restricted firing line would offset the disparity in his and his enemy's numbers.

For this maneuver, Marmaduke selected a road hemmed by brushy hills and gulches where Blunt could not flank him. He backed away toward it. As he did so, the sun pierced a rift in the clouds, illuminating a patch of scrub oak. Diminutive Shelby, always watchful for the spectacular, spurred to the spotlight and striking an attitude before his Missouri farm boys, pointed a gauntleted hand and shouted: "It is the sun of Austerlitz" — brave words from a guerrilla preparing to run for his life.

Blunt saw under the lowering storm clouds Marmaduke's broad line funneling into the defile. He realized that his enemy might escape under cover of the approaching rain and called for volunteers to charge, stop the vortex, and prevent an orderly retreat. Lieutenant Colonel Jewell of the Sixth Kansas offered to accept the risk. He raced down the road with half his regiment, lost his own life, and failed to seal the entrance.

The last rebel horseman passed out of sight. Blunt followed, knowing that his superior numbers availed little in the restricted defile. The Confederates arranged their companies so they could fire by volleys against the advancing Federals, then retreat through their own lines. Thus Blunt was always faced by a solid rank with loaded muskets — the trick Sigel had played with artillery at Carthage. Shelby, conducting the retreat, rode always behind the firing line to hold it firm. One of his captains fell beside him, red blood spurting in Shelby's face as the victim slid from his horse. Was there a couplet in Sir Walter Scott for such an experience? The black plume on Shelby's own hat was clipped off by a bullet and horse after horse — all sorrels — collapsed between his legs. Shelby boasted that he was bulletproof when riding a horse of that color.

Once Shelby made a countercharge, hoping to turn the tide of battle, but he found Blunt's line as impenetrable as his own. Fifteen miles down the road, having fought every foot of the way, Marmaduke sent back a flag of truce asking to gather the dead and wounded. Blunt granted the request and inquired the name of the commander he had been fighting.

He was told that it was Shelby — Shelby of Waverly, Missouri, who had crossed with his horsemen so many times to vote in Kansas before the war.

During the night both sides withdrew. Shelby and Marmaduke sank deeper into the gloom of the Boston Mountains. Blunt decided to avoid a possible ambush in the winter woods. He turned around and marched back, fanning out on the rolling Cane Hill country. Half of the Union men had seen no action in the narrow defile, but his Eleventh Kansas had had its battle baptism. Colonel Tom Ewing's experience ranked far below brother-in-law Sherman's, which now included Bull Run, Shiloh, and an unsuccessful attack on Vicksburg. In the fighting, Major Plumb had lost his horse and he trudged along on foot. Captain Crawford — also with political ambitions — mused to himself that the battle had begun awkwardly and was won gallantly — typical Crawford phraseology, thus lauding men in the ranks. The generalization seemed worth remembering. He might use it to advantage when these enlisted men voted in the next political campaign.

Blunt settled down at Cane Hill. Major Plumb found an old printing press with fonts of English and Cherokee type which had been left behind by Evan Jones, the missionary. Plumb, a printer by trade and a politician by preference, started a regimental newspaper, the *Buck and Ball*. He had printed fifteen hundred copies when the startling news reached camp that Marmaduke was coming back again, this time with an army of twenty-five thousand men under Hindman — fifteen thousand by the most conservative estimate. The Confederate was bringing the Arkansas conscripts he had mustered so miraculously in his district. With them came the Indians Blunt had dispersed at Old Fort Wayne and Stand Watie's chivalrous mixbloods. Obviously Blunt's best maneuver to save his five thousand men was to retreat up the wire road and consolidate forces with Schofield in the District of Southwest Missouri, but black-eyed terrier Blunt did not know the meaning of the word "retreat." He telegraphed directly to Department Commander Samuel Curtis for reinforcements and prepared to meet Hindman at Cane Hill.

X X I I I

The Battle of Prairie Grove

At his camp on Wilson's Creek, Brigadier General Herron received a wire from Department Commander Curtis at eight o'clock in the morning of December 3, 1862. It described Blunt's predicament at Cane Hill and requested that reinforcements go to his aid. Herron did not wait for confirming orders from his immediate superiors Totten or Schofield. Self-reliant and brave to rashness, he grasped this opportunity of a lifetime to command two divisions in battle. His men were ordered to pack knapsacks and be ready to march at noon. Sensitive about his society background, Herron realized that the ordeal ahead would be a test of his own and his men's mettle. He warned the soldiers that he expected them to make a record march without tents or equipment. Knapsacks would be hauled in wagons. They must traverse a hundred and twenty-five miles of country roads before Hindman marched less than half that distance and overwhelmed Blunt.

Herron's men started south, swinging at route step, night and day — thirty-five miles in each twenty-four hours. They often ate their pork ration raw, as they walked, and at every stop fell asleep in their tracks with half-chewed hardtack in their mouths. At day rests, without knapsacks, they drank coffee from tin cans picked up along the road. Officers prodded laggards and stragglers with the menace of death from guerrillas or imprisonment by Confederate regulars: "Andersonville or hell!" Crossing the Pea Ridge battlefield on December 5, 1862, the men were too tired to hunt souvenirs, but noticed the scars of cannon balls on the Elk Horn Tavern.

At midnight on December 6, the first companies of Herron's infantry reached Fayetteville. A provost guard stood before each house with drawn sword to prevent looting. The men bivouacked in the streets, hugging fires piled high with pickets from dooryard fences. Hoarfrost, white as snow, covered the ground. Residents in sympathy with the Union passed among the soldiers with buckets and pitchers of hot tea. One more day's march — twenty-five miles — should put them at Cane Hill. Surely they would beat Hindman to Blunt's encampment.

In the Boston Mountains, Hindman was confident that he would defeat Blunt before reinforcements arrived. Shelby led his van — an unpleasant job, for the weather turned suddenly cold in the hills. Icicles tinkled on the horses' beards and on the men's mustaches, too. Shelby had no tents or wagons. At night his sleepy men suffered around their campfires — always too hot on one side, too cold on the other. December 2, 1862 (the day before Herron started his relief march) dawned with a change of weather. Rain poured from the leaden skies, pattering on the dry leaves, hissing in the fires. The troopers climbed, blinking and shivering, into wet saddles and slopped along through dreary scrub oaks. Shelby's new black plume became limp with water. At four in the afternoon snow began to fall, and he ordered a halt for the night. The men warmed their stiff muscles by chopping brush for shelters and building fires to dry their drenched clothes. Before morning the rain stopped and the weather turned cold again, with stars twinkling above bare twigs overhead. After breakfast they started another day's march. At three o'clock the van stopped when shot at by a scouting party from Blunt's Sixth Kansas. Shelby's men captured twenty-two of them. The rest retreated toward Cane Hill.

Shelby interviewed the prisoners, slyly trying to deceive them about the size of the Confederate Army. Then he paroled them on their word to fight no more and sent them back to the Union lines. He hoped that they would report being captured by a battalion of raiders instead of by the advance of a big army.

Blunt was not deceived by the paroled prisoners' story. His spies had already informed him of the advance and he prepared to meet everything Hindman could send. On December 5, 1862, the Confederates appeared within eight miles of Cane Hill. Herron's infantry was still streaming past the Elk Horn Tavern, fifty miles away, but advance detachments of his cavalry were arriving at Cane Hill every few hours. One more day or day and a half should be sufficient for Herron to come in. Then, let Shelby, Marmaduke, and Hindman attack at their own peril! Blunt sent Frederick Salomon with his reserve brigade to guard the wagon train at Rhae's Mills and prepared his other two brigades for battle.

After dark, Hindman emerged from the rough country below Cane Hill. Regiment after regiment coiled, snakelike, from the woodlands — horse, foot, and artillery, including grinning, ladder-backed Bledsoe with a new battery. Old Sacramento had been confiscated at Pea Ridge. Hindman knew that Herron might reach Fayetteville before morning and that the Confederates' only chance was to strike one army or the other before they joined — divide and conquer. Always full of ideas and a good manager as well, he called his top officers to a midnight conference at his headquarters in a farmhouse on December 6, 1862.

Stumping back and forth on his good leg and high-heeled boot, Hindman explained that he must "chaw up Herron for breakfast, and then turn and gobble up Blunt at dinner." To do this, campfires should be left burning for miles opposite Blunt's front to give the impression that the whole Confederate Army was waiting to attack at dawn. Hindman explained that the moon would set early in the morning and when it did, all but a skeleton force was to slip off around Blunt's flank to the Fayetteville road, march east, and meet and defeat Herron, wherever he might be. General Marmaduke's horsemen were to lead the flank movement. He could use Shelby, Quantrill, and Stand Watie as seemed best. Colonel James Monroe, with the skeleton force, must hold Blunt's attention by continual feint attacks and skirmishes. Always efficient to the last detail, Hindman distributed leaflets to be given to the men. Better to have them read, or puzzle over a printed page, than sit nervously idle in the calm before a battle! Hindman believed in putting into his army the careful thought which had made him successful in organizing the civilian economy of the state. Besides, he knew that many of his conscripts might be Unionists at heart. Let them read and ponder the principles for which Confederates fought. His leaflets warned them not to fire until ordered to do so, to shoot only after singling out a victim, and then to aim as low as his knees. When possible, pick off officers and kill all artillery horses. The instructions also included a list of "don'ts:"

Don't stop with your wounded comrade. The surgeons and infantry corps will take care of him. Do you go forward and avenge him.

Don't break ranks to plunder. If we whip the enemy all he has will be ours. If not, the spoils will be of no benefit to us. Plunderers and stragglers will be put to death upon the spot. File-closers are especially charged with this duty. The cavalry in the rear will likewise attend to it.

Remember that the enemy you engage have no feelings of mercy or kindness towards you. His ranks are composed of Pin Indians, free-Negroes, Southern Tories, Kansas jayhawkers, and hired Dutch cutthroats.

Tomorrow's orders completed, Hindman bade his officers a peremptory good night. They mounted their horses and rode off into the darkness, admiring their general's efficiency though disliking his egotism.

At four in the morning of the seventh, with no sign yet of the winter dawn, Hindman's sergeants aroused the soldiers from their fires for the stealthy flank escape. The moon had set and the night was black as pitch. Coughing, spitting, rubbing sleep from swollen eyes, the men grumbled in low tones about auguries and presentiments of good and bad luck for the day's fighting. Some felt a hidden meaning in the distant howl of a dog, the nearby shying of a horse, the memory of a trivial incident before the last battle, and its happy conclusion. While they stood in line before their fires, Shelby rode by. He reined his horse in front of Major David Shanks and told him to start with detachments from two regiments, one containing Quantrill's bushwhackers. (Quantrill himself was still in the East.) Shelby said that he would follow with a second force after a suitable interval.

Shanks listened to the instructions, smoothing, as he did so, a stray lock on his horse's mane. Then he lifted his plumed hat with a "Shelby salute" and galloped away. "Come on, brave boys!" In the van rode Quantrill's men in stolen blue uniforms — true bushwhacker disguise. Dave Pool, grimacing little comedian, commanded the outfit. The James boys, Frank and fifteen-year-old Jesse, rode in the ranks. Up hill and down, out of sight beyond the flank of Blunt's army, they galloped toward the Fayetteville road. Shelby waited. Then as dawn, like milky water, diffused the sky, he followed the van's horse tracks along the byroad through the winter woods.

The blue-clad bushwhackers swept down on the Fayetteville road, capturing twenty-one commissary wagons headed for Blunt's lines under guard of a newly enlisted Arkansas troop of "Mountain Feds." The Confederates did not know that a detachment of Hubbard's Third Missouri from Herron's column had just passed. The Mountain Feds, baffled by an attack from men in blue, turned tail and fled toward Fayetteville with Shanks and a half regiment yipping after them like a pack of hounds. Behind Shanks, Shelby slashed down through the trees as planned, gave quick orders for confiscating the wagons. Almost immediately he was attacked by the detachment of Hubbard's Third Missouri which heard the shooting behind them and came back. Completely surrounded and overwhelmed, the Iron Knight and all his staff surrendered. However, before side arms were handed over, Shanks and Poole loped back and captured Hubbard's three hundred seventy-three Union soldiers. Shelby, a free man once more, sent the prisoners with a detail to Marmaduke. Then Shelby aligned his forces and clattered down the Fayetteville road to find Herron and hold him until Hindman's infantry came to "chaw up Herron for breakfast, and then turn and gobble up Blunt at dinner."

Meanwhile, back at Fayetteville, where Herron's troops had rested, shrill bugle calls roused them before dawn. The soldiers staggered off along the dark road. At seven o'clock their tired eyes saw horsemen pounding toward them — the "Mountain Feds" returning in panic, hatless, hair streaming, newly issued uniforms discarded and rumpled, eyes wild with fear. "It was with the greatest difficulty," Herron reported, "that we got them checked, and prevented a general stampede . . . but with some hard talking, and my finally shooting one cowardly whelp off his horse, they halted."

At this point in the battle maneuver, Hindman had the advantage but instead of following the Fayetteville road and aggressively attacking Herron's exhausted troops as they straggled toward him on the morning of December 7, 1862, Hindman lost his nerve, and stopped when he reached Prairie Grove church, on a ridge overlooking Illinois Creek between Fayetteville and Cane Hill. Below him, to the east, lay a patchwork of withered cornfields crosshatched with worm fences. Methodically, Hindman placed Frost's and Parsons's Missourians, the conscripted Arkansans, Stand Watie's Indians, and Marmaduke's cavalry — eight thousand of his fabled horde — in a two-mile line to wait for an attack from Herron's six thousand footsore regiments, while Blunt, with at least eight thousand more Federals, stood on the alert eight miles away.

To this battlefield Herron's tired column marched in solid formation with a battery on lead and the general riding close by. As his big guns splashed across Illinois Creek, Hindman's first shell burst over them. Other shells churned the ford and Herron knew that he dared not cross more guns or men. He ordered the first regiment in the column to lie down under the protection of the creek bank — and they did so, promptly dropping to sleep with Hindman's shells whistling overhead. Then Herron, with his characteristic rashness, galloped around the selected battlefield, alone except for one aide. He examined the terrain, floundered back across the ford, and ordered his engineers to cut a road through the woods to another crossing half a mile above. His batteries forded here and opened fire on Hindman, who was still concentrating his shots on the first battery that had crossed. Hindman immediately turned his artillery on the new guns. Thus, with the shelling diffused, the Union soldiers poured over Illinois Creek, extending their line opposite the enemy's, while their eighteen guns pounded the Confederates on the ridge. After two hours' bombardment Herron ordered his infantry to advance, under cover of worm fences, wood lots, and farmhouses. However, Shelby, at the extreme right, saw the Federals coming and prepared a decoy to entrap the lead companies. He abandoned four guns, with their horses tied in plain sight. Behind them, at point-blank range, he masked Collins's flying artillery, cautioning the commander, "When you see their hands upon the wheels, Dick, FIRE — not before."

In a peach orchard an Irish regiment, the Twenty-fifth Illinois, spied the battery and ran toward it. "Be jabers but Rabb plays hell today with the rebs," one man shouted, as they swarmed around the guns, cheering, raising their canteens. The horses stood impassive. One master was as good as another to them. An officer ordered the animals killed, but no man obeyed. In a sharper tone he repeated the order, and the brutes were shot down, quivering in their chain harnesses. Then the hidden Confederate battery belched over the Irish soldiers, scattering twisted bodies through the orchard. One man hobbled away using his musket for a crutch. The commanding officer's horse — its saddle empty — staggered drunkenly through the trees, then collapsed. Behind it, the colonel limped to the rear using his sword for a cane. From their hiding place the "rebs" scampered out to loot. An Illinoisan with a shattered leg looked at a rebel: "For the love of God, friend," he begged, "kill me and put me beyond such intolerable misery."

"Are you in yearnest," Shelby's rough Missourian asked, "and may I have your overcoat and canteen?"

"Yes, yes — everything," gasped the dying man.

"Well, here goes — shut yer eyes and hold yer breath — 't will be over in a minnit." The Confederate placed his musket at the wounded man's head, blew out his life in a puff of smoke, and coolly took his coat. Uncorking his canteen, he smelled excellent Fayetteville brandy. "Huzza! Have one on me." Soon all corpses were being rifled for their canteens. "Three cheers for the Confederacy!"

Hindman decided that the critical hour of the battle had come. A smashing blow now might bring victory. He resolved to counterattack with his entire line, but, to his dismay, he learned that one Arkansas regiment had deserted, leaving only its colonel and a few officers. These conscripts could not be trusted. Hindman had forged an efficient dictator's chain around Arkansas, but it might be only a chain of sand. He decided to cancel his order for attack and hold the line only.

Herron charged twice more but failed to budge the Confederates. Where was Blunt, who had summoned him for this battle? Herron knew himself to be outnumbered, but he did not know about the deserting Arkansans. He expected Hindman to charge successfully any moment. Union officers, versed in the Napoleonic wars, told one another, "We must have night or Blücher."

Eight miles away at Cane Hill, stubby, black-haired Blunt, still unconscious of the departure of Hindman's main army, waited for an attack. His two divisions stood in battle line. South of them Blunt could see Colonel Monroe's skeleton force deployed in what appeared to be a far-flung battle line. Once a Confederate officer on a white horse rode across a distant wheat field, obviously — perhaps too obviously — inspecting the ground for an advance. A few random shots were exchanged between pickets but nothing more. Blunt's nervousness cumulated with the rising sun. Officers remembered that he had lacked consideration last night, seemed nervous and upset. In the dark the Tenth Illinois Cavalry, from

Herron's column, had ridden into his lines after a ninety-mile forced march. The horses' hair was mud-caked and dead-looking from the long ordeal, their hocks bumped when they walked — evidently near exhaustion — yet Blunt had ordered the cavalry into line for a night patrol. The colonel remonstrated and Blunt admitted his error, assigning the regiment to a place for rest. At reveille they had turned out with all the men and stood in line, although still tired. The monotonous wait with no attack was irritating everybody. Some men lay down to sleep. Others burrowed into nearby strawstacks for warmth. By contrast, Blunt's Kansans, fully rested and eager for battle, danced hornpipes and scuffled on the stubble. A distant band played "Annie Laurie." An orderly rode up to General Blunt, saluted and presented him with a bottle of liquor, "with the compliments of General Salomon" — who had taken the first brigade to protect the wagon train at Rhae's Mills. Blunt put the bottle in his saddle pocket and dismounted to tighten his saddle girth. A colonel rode up. Blunt offered him a drink. The colonel declined.

"Yes," Blunt drawled, "I think we've more important business on hand just now." Obviously he was hiding nervousness behind casual manners.

Line officers busied themselves driving restless soldiers back into ranks, keeping them from straying. By eleven o'clock in the morning, Blunt's nervousness became more apparent. No dispatch riders had come through from Herron, so the Fayetteville road must be blocked. Blunt leaned forward on his pawing charger, stroking its mane absent-mindedly. Then he heard the distant boom of Hindman's guns opening on Herron at Illinois Creek.

"What was that?" Blunt sat erect in his saddle. Another, and another explosion throbbed in the distance. "My God, they're in our rear." Blunt snapped out quick orders to his aides. Drums began to roll, bugles screamed commands. Regiment after regiment shouldered arms and wheeled across the fields toward the Fayetteville road. Major Plumb thought first of his unpublished regimental paper. He staggered to an ambulance with all the copies he could carry, tossed them in, admonished the driver to follow, and then joined his battalion. Infantry, cavalry, and artillery arrived on the road at the same time, jostling and pushing. "What are we doing?" "Which way?"

Above the tumult, Blunt's voice was heard. "Tell the —— —— fool to turn to the right and come on." The little general galloped away, his charger's hoofs throwing rocks and clods over the rabble. The men cheered and followed, treading on laggards' heels. At every field and prairie, cavalry regiments spurred around the infantry. Artillery postilions lashed their horses every jump, gunners lying flat on the carriages shouting "faster, faster" as the spinning wheels bounded from rock to hummock. In the contest Blunt outran his staff, arriving on the battlefield alone. With a practiced eye he selected battery and troop positions. Then his army rumbled in, artillery horses tired but excited, ears laid back, eyes wild from lashing, nostrils dilated and red as blood. Wheeling into battery under Blunt's orders, gunners jumped from the carriages like sailors in a gale, and stood at their positions. Two shots from the lead batteries announced to Herron that Blunt had arrived — two shots that unhappily landed among Union skirmishers, for Blunt was, as yet, unfamiliar with the entire field. At first Herron mistook the shots for those of the Confederates and feared that he had been flanked.

Across the battlefield Hindman recognized the newcomer as Blunt and hoped to demoralize him with a charge before the new Union lines were formed, but another regiment of Arkansans on his left wing sulked. These Ozark conscripts were ruining his army. He feared another defection like the one on his right and ordered Marmaduke's cavalry to drive them into action. Goaded from behind, the Arkansans marched forward reluctantly and the charge failed. Blunt formed his line and, with Herron, had forty-two guns to spray grape and canister on the Confederates.

After an hour's bombardment, Blunt ordered an advance. The way lay across farms, through bare orchards and shriveling stalks of corn. Soldiers moved from rail fence to hedge, and on to dwellings, stamping through barnyards amid squawking fowl and grunting hogs. Women and children cowered in cellars. Hindman's left wing retreated back into the woods, but Shelby galloped reserves along the line and the lost ground was retaken. Confederates on the edge of the timber dared the "Feds" down in the fields to rout them out. Colonel A. W. Slayback of Marmaduke's staff, dreaming of days gone by "when knights wore greaves and vizors, and when that war-cry rang over the iron of Bannockburn — 'St. James for

Argentine,'" challenged any man to meet him in single combat. The Arkansas hill men, Missouri Union farmers, Illinois and Iowa small-town boys gaped in wonder, but they admired his courage too.

From the Union lines rode Lieutenant Thomas Willhite, a Southerner to the manner born but commissioned in the Union Army. He was willing to pit his courage against the flower of Hindman's chivalry. Twenty paces from his adversary he fired his pistol. Slayback shot back at him. Neither man was hurt. Both fired again. Willhite lurched in his saddle, wheeled his horse and cantered back, slipping down in his own lines, a bullet in his thigh. Other champions on both sides galloped out to exchange shots, "chivalrous as Bayard" — or irresponsible as Sioux warriors, according to the point of view.

Darkness crept over the armies' sputtering lines, a few last shells blazing fiery arches across the night sky. Several strawstacks caught on fire. Wounded men were known to have crept into them for warmth, but nothing could be done about that now. While the moon was still high, Blunt ordered his wagons from Rhae's Mills to Fayetteville, so Salomon's fresh division could join tomorrow's battle. In addition, stragglers from Herron's forced march continued to arrive all night, swelling the Union numbers.

Although obviously defeated, Hindman claimed the victory because his men held their original lines on Prairie Grove ridge when firing ceased, but he retreated secretly, after dark, with blankets wrapped around his cannon wheels. In the morning he sent back a white flag asking for a twelve-hour truce to tend the wounded and bury the dead. Blunt, deceived again about the withdrawal, granted the truce. Men from both sides trudged out with stretchers and many women came on horseback and in carriages to care for the wounded. They found some of Herron's men dead without a wound. Exposure in the December cold while exhausted from the march had killed them. The worst scene of horror was around the charred strawstacks. Here the smell of burning flesh had attracted hogs during the night. They had rooted through the black ashes, dragging out, fighting over, and devouring morsels of human bodies — intestines, heads, arms, and even hearts.

Opposite Blunt's batteries, where Hindman had herded the Arkansas conscripts into an unwilling charge, the bodies lay close together and the ground was muddy with blood. The salvage crews picked up unshot bullets by the hatful. The conscripts had bitten them from the cartridges and fired only blank loads against their nation's flag. In their pockets searchers found the propaganda leaflets Hindman had distributed.

Blunt's burial details reported that the Confederates were picking up arms from the field instead of wounded men. Blunt ordered this stopped. Some Confederate parties clattered away in high dudgeon to join the retreating army. Others persisted in salvaging guns, until Blunt arrested them and sent them north with other prisoners. The total battle casualties were between twelve and thirteen hundred men on each side. Fayetteville churches and college buildings became hospitals, with suffering men laid out on the floors. Emergency operations were performed without anesthetics, and eighty per cent of the patients who suffered amputations died.

In St. Louis, District Commander Schofield had learned that Herron was marching to Blunt's relief. He believed a battle imminent and, ill though he was, Schofield raced to the front but failed to arrive before the battle of Prairie Grove was ended and all chance of gaining personal credit had passed. A pouting man when well, this educated upstart who had risen from lieutenant to brigadier general in three months whined that both Blunt and Herron had been outmaneuvered, and escaped annihilation only by chance. Why, he asked pointedly, had not Blunt gone part way to meet Herron, and why had Herron attacked with exhausted troops? Regardless of these technical errors, the victory was badly needed for Federal morale. Without it, 1862 would have closed with the disasters at Fredericksburg, Holly Springs, and Stone's River. In spite of Schofield's censure, both Blunt and Herron received major general's stars for the action. Herron became the youngest man with that rank in the Northern Army. Thus both outranked Schofield.

After the victory, Blunt and Herron rested while Major Plumb published his newspaper from the ambulance. Then the Union forces marched southwest. Colonel Phillips retook Fort Gibson with his Indians, and Blunt surprised Hindman at VanBuren, chasing his Texas cavalry, bareback, bareheaded, and half dressed, down the main street. Four steamboat loads of Confederate supplies were burned and many wagons captured. Downriver, at Little Rock, the Confederate legislature packed up a second time to retreat. But Blunt was now far from his base, and Schofield, unhappy about the battle of Prairie Grove, called him back. Phillips, too, was ordered in from Indian Territory, and Fayetteville became the North's southwestern outpost.

Shelby and Marmaduke could both teach Schofield the futility of staying close to a base. They planned cutting loose and raiding with a brigade across Missouri in midwinter. Shelby, like many a young man who has been reading poetry, felt the creative urge himself and wrote:

> Still Collins plies his lurid torch
> Where balls will rend or powder scorch;
> Still Shanks and Gordon, side by side,
> Like veteran heroes stem the tide.

The Marmaduke-Shelby expedition was joined by Quantrill's guerillas — commanded in the continued absence of their chief by Gregg and Todd. This column struck first at Springfield, Missouri — a hundred and thirty-five miles north of Blunt's headquarters — on January 8, 1863. The Union commander resisted them with two thousand men in four partly finished blockhouses. Shelby dismounted three regiments and advanced in infantry formation. A female academy was taken and one Federal gun was captured, but the blockhouses proved impregnable. Quantrill's men refused to fight on foot, and spent their time dragging Federal militiamen out of warm beds in the neighborhood. They also raided the much-abused farm of General John S. Phelps, who had been appointed, "on paper," the military governor of Arkansas. Blunt started up the wire road after them, but the raiders did not wait for him. Instead, they galloped eastward along the frozen road, reaping bountiful harvests of horses, Negroes, wagons, and overcoats on the way to Hartsville and Batesville. Shelby wanted to turn north and raid all the way to his home country, around Boonville and Lexington, but the weather turned cold in mid-January, and Marmaduke ordered a return to Arkansas. Shelby closed his report of the campaign with his usual poetic description:

> On the last day of December, 1862, when the old year was dying in the lap of the new, and January had sent its moaning winds to wail the requiem of the past, my brigade . . . [was] on the march for forays on the border's side [through] the grand old mountains standing bare

against the dull and somber sky, their heads heavy with the storms of centuries.

Finally, with further veiled inference, he reminded all interested friends that Missouri was one of the Confederate States — even if a quorum had failed to assemble for the secession vote. Shelby also added that he looked forward to renewing old acquaintances when bushwhacking became more pleasant as the leaves unrolled next spring.

X X I V

Quantrill Redresses Gettysburg

CHARLES QUANTRILL returned from Richmond disappointed over receiving only a colonel's commission. President Davis was insufficiently impressed by the freebooter's lascivious grin. The winter of 1862–1863 had been more severe than usual in the southwest. Natives complained that the "dam-yankis" brought their climate with them. On the border Quantrill was greeted sullenly by his lieutenants. George Todd, William Gregg, and Bloody Bill Anderson had carried on without him at Cane Hill, Prairie Grove, and Shelby's raid on Springfield. They resented Quantrill's renewal of authority. Quantrill dared not push the issue of rank to a conclusion with such quick-trigger men. Instead of permitting them to challenge his authority, he stayed away, loitering in the brush with a *gamine* he called Kate Clarke.

The whole Confederate department had been reorganized. Hindman, after his defeat at Prairie Grove, was replaced by Theophilus Holmes, a stooped, sixty-year-old crony of Jeff Davis's, whom he commissioned lieutenant general. Pike's place was filled by William Steele, an ex-captain from the United States Army. Bushwhacking had become a recognized offensive. Out West the popular Confederate song, "Maryland, My Maryland," was sung with new words:

> Jo Shelby's at your stable door;
> Where's your mule,
> Oh, where's your mule.

The guerrillas were given further encouragement in April 1863. As new leaves began to protect woodland prowlers, Grant called on Curtis for all available men to help with a proposed siege of Vicksburg. Curtis knew the danger of abandoning Fayetteville and other southwestern posts, but he obeyed, holding only Helena and a few garrisons along the Mississippi. To fill the vacuum created by the withdrawal, he called in the Second Colorado from distant Denver for border patrol. Phillips's brigade of "pin" Indians and Kansas Negroes was ordered to march into Indian Territory and take the posts vacated by Union soldiers. Thus red men and black would be pitted against mixbloods in the southwest, and the Colorado boys could test their courage against Missouri bushwhackers — a savory assignment for Pikes Peak prospectors who had survived among wild Utes and Arapaho.

Bushwhackers greeted the newcomers derisively. In the first skirmish with them, Dave Pool, the freebooting comedian, dared any of the Colorado "cowards" to single combat. His challenge was accepted instantly. A Colorado rowdy stepped out between the lines and promptly pinked Dave with a bullet. The bushwhacker was happy to return alive to his own men. He could grimace and laugh, but his companions knew that they were confronted with formidable fighters. Quantrill, always a man of moods — long periods of languor interspersed with burning activity — continued to dally with Kate in the brush, but he watched the new turn of affairs and waited for an opportunity to assert himself.

The red and black replacements sent into the southwest proved equal to the job. Phillips's column of twenty-five hundred "pin" Indians and Negroes re-established Federal authority in the territory, protected the loyal Cherokee who met in formal council, repudiated the treaty with the Confederacy, outlawed Stand Watie and his fifty-five hundred followers. The rebel Indians' property was confiscated and all debts due them declared void. Henceforth, Watie's faction could be counted on to fight with the desperation of the condemned.

To counter the continued Federal success, William Steele worked constantly to revitalize the Confederate Indian brigades. He also sent runners out among the wild Indians to gain their co-operation. This was not a new plan. Pike had tried it unsuccessfully in the summer of 1861, but no one was prepared for the concrete proposals of 1863 and the recoil which shocked the Western border in May. That month two Osages rode into Humbolt, Kansas, to report the massacre of some white men by their warriors. Being half civilized, the head men feared the white man's might, and led Federal investigators to their village where snake-eyed warriors with roached hair, pates daubed with vermilion, and ears slit to ribbons and dangling with trinkets watched them sullenly.

A few scalps were displayed: one coarse and curly — a man's beard, not head hair. The victim had been bald, the guide explained, so the disappointed warrior took the best substitute available. Other relics of the massacre were extracted from the savages' duffel — some papers! These indicated that the dead men had been commissioned by the Confederate government to organize the "wild" Indians of the plains, the miners, Mexicans, and others beyond the border.

The party seems to have numbered twenty-one, most of them officers of the Confederate Army. They had ridden stealthily for eighty miles across the Osage lands in what would later be Montgomery County, Kansas, and on the fatal day nooned in the shade of some oaks. A small band of Osage horsemen spied them and rode into camp as the whites were saddling. The Indians, disliking trespassers in their country, asked the white men's business, and insisted on taking them to the nearest Union garrison for identification. In the argument someone shot an Osage and the whites, now mounted, galloped away through a flurry of arrows. Unknowingly, they ran toward an Osage village. Over the prairie swell ahead, they saw hundreds of feathered warriors sweeping down upon them. The Confederates wheeled, raced to the nearby Verdegris, slid down the bank, and sprinted out on a sand bar where, with their guns, they hoped to hold back bow-and-arrow pursuers. However, the situation seemed hopeless, and they raised a white flag in surrender. The Indians rode out, took their weapons, and scalped or beheaded them all. The only survivors were two men who had dropped out in the race — one of them Warner Lewis, kinsman of Meriwether Lewis, the explorer. These men hid under the riverbank until dark, then — guided by the stars — trudged across the prairie toward Missouri, night after night, hiding in daytime, until they reached the settlements.

Thus Confederate plans for military diversion in the southwest misfired again! Grant, engrossed with his campaign against Vicksburg, called for more trans-Mississippi soldiers. Halleck in Washington levied a second draft on Curtis's department. Curtis replied that he could spare no more. Without further warning, Lincoln removed him and gave Schofield his department. Curtis was nonplussed and chagrined. His great victory at Pea Ridge had made him invulnerable, he believed. Yet Lincoln let him go. The reason seems plain enough. Lincoln's first consideration was to get every man he could for Grant. Governor Gamble had sufficient militia to replace Curtis's troops in Missouri but refused to co-operate because he disagreed with the general's "charcoal" radicalism. Not being able to remove Gamble, Lincoln explained later, he therefore removed Curtis. The solution, however, proved no solution, and it served only as another of the circumstances shaping themselves for Quantrill's great day.

Schofield, aged thirty-two, took command on May 24, 1863. He found forty-three thousand men in his department and immediately sent almost half of them to Grant, then mustered Gamble's militia to police Missouri. Like Curtis, he retained his hold on Helena, Arkansas, and with Phillips at Fort Gibson, Indian Territory, raiding successfully toward Fort Smith on the Arkansas line, Schofield noticed that Little Rock lay between the pincers of his military machine. If he could capture the capital of Arkansas, and hold Missouri at the same time with half the number of men Curtis had used, he would make a great name for himself.

But Schofield did not reckon with his host. The split in the Republican ranks, started by Blair and Frémont, was wider now than ever. The radical abolitionists who had supported Curtis against Governor Gamble now accused Schofield of being too lenient to traitors. They said that his militia was in collusion with the bushwhackers, that freebooters joined only to get guns. The disconcerted radicals appealed for help to Jim Lane, the rabble rouser who considered anybody who voted against him a traitor.

Lincoln saw at once that Schofield's administration would be hopelessly hampered by these contending forces, so he reorganized the West, creating the District of the Border between Missouri and Kansas. To command this buffer between Lane and the Missouri moderates, Lincoln promoted Colonel Thomas Ewing, Jr., to a brigadier's rank, jumping him over radical abolitionist General Blunt. Ewing had been a moderate Lane man who should blend adequately between the Grim Chieftain and conservative Schofield. Moreover, Ewing's father was influential in the United States Senate. Young Ewing was no colorless stopgap, however. His slightly protruding lower lip indicated stubborn determination. Already he was wearing his beard clipped close to his cheeks like his brother-in-law

Sherman, who with Grant was still floundering around Vicksburg in what seemed to be an endless effort to capture that stronghold.

Quantrill, rousing from his dalliance, sneered at the new appointment. "Ewing commands the district," he scoffed, "but I run the machine" — braggadocio of a commander who dared not exact discipline from his own lieutenants. But Quantrill saw in the lawlessness around him an opportunity to regain prestige. His bushwhackers — acting on their own initiative — raided under Ewing's nose. George Todd even dared take a captive Union man along on a foray and then send him to Ewing as a witness. In Arkansas elderly General Holmes realized that the border development opened a rosy opportunity to demolish both prongs of the pincers threatening Little Rock. He must take Helena and drive Blunt out of Fort Gibson, tidy victories which might divert some of the Union troops hammering at Vicksburg. Holmes proposed to strike at Helena with an Arkansas brigade, Price's Missourians, and Marmaduke's cavalry, which included Shelby's Iron Brigade. To take Fort Gibson, Stand Watie was to capture a big wagon train rumbling down from Kansas with supplies for Blunt and Phillips and thus starve them out. It seemed as easy as that.

This double maneuver west of the Mississippi began as Robert E. Lee crossed into Pennsylvania, sweeping along the roads toward Gettysburg. Consequently, the curtain was rising on four military theaters — Gettysburg, Vicksburg, Helena, Fort Gibson — and the first week in July promised to be decisive in the war.

All four engagements went against the Confederacy. Lee marched back to Virginia, very lucky to escape. Pemberton surrendered Vicksburg to Grant. Holmes failed to capture Helena. He almost lost Collins's flying battery, and Shelby received a bad wound. Stand Watie's attack on the Fort Gibson supply train was equally fruitless. He ambushed the three hundred wagons at a flooded crossing of Cabin Creek on July 1, 1863, but failed to capture it after fighting three days against the guard of "pin" Indians and Lane's Negro soldiers. With the full length of the Mississippi in Federal hands after these battles, the Trans-Mississippi Department was completely cut off from Richmond — an island of rebeldom that must be self-supporting or perish. General Holmes asked friend Jeff Davis to relieve him from such a hazardous responsibility and assign the post to his assistant, E. Kirby-Smith.

The new commander of Kirby-Smithdom, as the department was soon called, tried to retrieve victory from the recent defeats by a quick counterstroke. He would combine his Arkansas troops with Stand Watie's horsemen, surround Fort Gibson, and destroy at least part of one prong of the pincers threatening Little Rock. Hard-drinking Cooper — who still held a line command — was ordered to join the assault with his Choctaw Chickasaw regiments, Texas cavalry and batteries.

Blunt learned that these troops were concentrating at Honey Springs, a village where the Texas road crossed Elk Creek eighteen miles below Fort Gibson. With his Negroes, "pin" Indians, and a battalion of Colorado boys, he marched all night and at dawn on July 16, 1863, struck Cooper's Indians. Stand Watie was absent and without him the Cherokee gave way. Chilly McIntosh's Creeks retreated "to consolidate their position" and failed to stop. The Choctaw and Chickasaw regiments became confused and marched away seeking reinforcements. The Arkansas conscripts coming up the mail road dragged their feet in the red dust. They objected to fighting outside their state boundaries, and whole companies of them deserted, making it all but impossible for the few loyal men in the column to close intervals. The remnant arrived at Honey Springs in time to take care of a hundred and forty-seven dead and wounded which had been left by Blunt as he marched north with fifty-seven prisoners, all of the Indians' supplies of bacon, flour, dried beef, and three or four hundred handcuffs brought to shackle his Negro soldiers and lead them back into slavery.

Confederate sympathizers along the border were incredulous of this series of defeats. But Quantrill saw in them the opportunity of his lifetime. He called his captains for a conference and outlined plans for the greatest raid of the war. Lawrence, Kansas, epitomized everything the South despised in the North. Its New England reformers, its widely circulating newspapers had roweled the nation with abolition propaganda for seven years. The hated Jim Lane was out there now on vacation from the Senate. Why not destroy him and the vile nest of nigger thieves all at once! Such an achievement would immortalize the participants — and regain for Quantrill his old prestige over the phantom regiment of Confederate guerrillas.

Quantrill's captains listened sullenly. They rode away without agreeing on any plans. Then an accident happened and the situation changed. In

the campaign to stamp out bushwhacking, many women had been arrested on their homesteads for sheltering guerrillas. The prisoners included
three sisters of Bloody Bill Anderson's, the Munday girls, Martha and Sue,
whose brother was with Price in Arkansas, and a female cousin of Cole
Younger's. Jesse James's mother and sister had also been taken from their
home by Union soldiers. Most of the disloyal women were incarcerated at
Kansas City in an old brick building on Grand Avenue between Four-
teenth and Fifteenth streets. The first floor contained stores. The second
floor, where the girls were imprisoned, was reached by an outside stairway
at the rear. The country girls noticed that some of their fellow prisoners
were women of bad character — Quantrill spies, too — and refused to
speak to them. When Ewing assumed command, he made it a point to treat
his charges with consideration. The prostitutes roomed by themselves. All
were allowed playing cards and musical instruments. The Munday and
Anderson girls sent home for their own bedding. Those who would pledge
their word not to escape were permitted to go downstairs, under guard,
and visit the stores. Major Plumb, the Good Bishop, was put in immediate
command over them.

Gossips in the grog shops whispered that a tunnel was being dug to
free the prisoners. Others said loose hogs had rooted dangerously under
the foundation. The old brick walls bulged noticeably. Then one day after
dinner a guard felt the floors quiver. "Get out of here," he shouted, running down the wooden steps. "This building is going to fall."

Some of the girls, but not all, raced down the steps behind him, long
skirts ballooning above white stockings. Behind them the walls teetered,
swayed, then collapsed under a cloud of reddish-yellow dust. Major Plumb
ordered a company to the scene and surrounded the ruins with fixed bayonets, while rescuers pried under the debris. The bodies of an Anderson
girl, Cole Younger's cousin, and several others were carried out. Female
survivors wrung their hands and screamed imprecations against Ewing,
and Lincoln's tyranny.

Back in the bushy hills of Johnson County, Quantrill called another
meeting of his captains. This time they all voted to join in a raid and
wreak vengeance. Captain Pardee's farm in Jackson County, only a short
day's ride from Ewing's headquarters, was selected for the rendezvous. On
August 18, 1863, each captain jogged in with his followers to camp in the

woods and meadows along the Blackwater. Sturdy Todd, his oval, smooth-shaven face hard and stubborn as granite, brought a troop of immigrant Irishmen as illiterate as himself. With Bloody Bill came Frank James and the Youngers. William Gregg, commanding the cream of the Border Ruffians, served also as adjutant and aide to Quantrill. He reported a hundred and ninety-four men "present and accounted for." An equal number was to be picked up as the column advanced.

On the morning of August 19, 1863, scouts disguised as farmers ambled along the roads watching for Federal troops. They reported the way clear, and Quantrill, in hunting shirt — the bushwhacker uniform — embroidered by the fair hand of unclean Kate, mounted his fine sorrel horse, called his men from their leafy bowers, formed them on the dirt road, and rode leisurely forward. Quantrill's longhorn mustache paralleled the brim of a low-crowned black hat garnished with gold band and tassels. Four pistol butts raised their ugly heads above his belt. His short-cropped hair emphasized the smallness of his head on a giraffe neck — a pervert among unkempt and bearded followers.

After riding ten miles along the hot summer road, the column halted to feed horses and eat a snack. Quantrill addressed the wild assembly, his big loose mouth telling the men for the first time their destination, the rich booty in prospect, and the opportunity for revenge: "Kill every male and burn every house in Lawrence!"

The guerrillas resaddled in the cool of the evening and rode southwest, apparently toward Fort Scott and Indian Territory instead of toward Lawrence. This might deceive spying Federals. During the night the column was joined by Colonel D. Holt with over a hundred additional riders. Next morning, August 20, 1863, at seven o'clock, as a sultry sun began to heat the air, the bushwackers watered their horses on upper Grand River four miles from the Kansas border. Here another contingent of bepistoled horsemen rode in, making four or five hundred men in all. Time had come now to slip through Ewing's patrol into Kansas — then dash fifty miles to Lawrence.

All morning long, scouts examined the roads ahead while the guerrillas rested in dense woods. At three o'clock in the afternoon the way was pronounced clear. The bushwackers mounted and, in solid formation, crossed the state line near Aubry where a hundred Federal soldiers were garrisoned. United States Captain J. A. Pike saw the invaders and mustered his men but, being outnumbered, dared not attack. Instead, he sent a courier up to Little Santa Fe spreading the alarm. In two or three hours Ewing should receive the message in Kansas City, and Quantrill could not reach Lawrence — if that were his destination — in less than ten or twelve.

Every man in Quantrill's force was a seasoned rider, skilled in getting the most out of his mount. The race ahead would test Quantrill's leadership of light horse. At first he ordered a swinging trot. Twelve miles across the border, when darkness had fallen, Quantrill called a halt to graze the horses. Grass-fed animals must eat often. After an hour, the men were ordered to tighten saddle girths and mount. Riding through the sleeping village of Spring Hill, the column turned northwest, heading now for the first time straight toward Lawrence. At eleven o'clock they clattered into Gardner and, shortly beyond, left the road for a northerly route across the prairie. Lawrence slept less than twenty-five miles away.

Quantrill counted the miles against the midnight hours and watched the stars. The crisis of his lifetime had come. Many of his men strapped themselves in their saddles, hobbling their stirrups, in order to sleep on the march and be ready for tomorrow's butchery. These outdoorsmen knew their way across open country, but new fences and brushy creek crossing might delay the march. Quantrill took no chance. At homesteads he impressed sleepy farmers to guide the column. When the country ahead became strange to a guide, a bullet ended his usefulness. Ten were thus shot in eight miles.

The column forded the Wakarusa by Blue-Jacket Crossing and drew rein on a prairie swell half a mile from Lawrence. West of them at the foot of Mount Oread lay the village asleep in the dawn twilight. Or was it? Perhaps the townsmen had been alarmed and were waiting to ambush the guerrillas!

Quantrill ordered two scouts to ride ahead. They were to signal if the inhabitants were on guard. While they were gone, Quantrill ordered roll call. His veterans eyed the village critically. It was larger than they expected. Some men protested. To rush a town the size of Lawrence seemed folly. Besides, Federal soldiers must be coming from many directions. Best to gallop away now while they could. Quantrill's broad, voluptuous lips sneered. He would take the town if he rode in alone! Remember:

"Kill every man and burn every house." Quantrill touched his good-luck horse with the spur and moved forward under his black silk flag. The column followed at a fast trot to the edge of town, then roared in with a yell.

Mayor George Collamore had been warned that Quantrill might come some time. He had collected guns for defense, but the citizens scoffed at his precaution. To them the war seemed far away. They had fought it out with the Missourians seven years ago and now felt safe inside Federal lines.

In one of the outlying homes, the Reverend Hugh Fisher, chaplain for Lane's expedition to Springfield, had risen early this morning of August 21, 1863. He felt ill and stood at the window looking up the street. His neighbor, the Reverend S. S. Snyder, pastor of the United Brethren Church, came out of his house with a milk pail and sat beside his cow. Fisher watched him absent-mindedly until aroused by the rabble of racing horsemen — a motley, bearded crew in broad hats and dirty shirts. He saw puffs of white smoke from their pistols. The Reverend Mr. Snyder slumped from his stool, bucket upset, cow limping away. Next moment the yipping riders were gone. It was like a dream — hard to believe anyone had been in the road. But before Mr. Fisher had time to arouse his wife and draw on his trousers, squads of riders were patrolling every street, shooting at anyone who appeared. The whole town lay helpless in the bushwhackers' hands.

Quantrill had proved his competence. He led the way first toward the rebuilt Eldridge House, detaching patrols on all side streets. His vedettes galloped to Mount Oread to watch for approaching soldiers. Guests in the hotel heard pistols popping like firecrackers below their windows and peered down at the surging riders, at Quantrill — his hunting shirt, open now at the breast, disclosing his white body. Someone, with a dinner gong, marched up and down the halls admonishing the guests to be calm. The manager waved a sheet from a window.

Quantrill agreed to spare the guests if they would dress quickly and come out. One of them was a spy who might be useful in identifying victims. He had recently associated with Lane — the man wanted above all others by the guerrillas. Quantrill ordered the guests searched for weapons, then sent them under guard to the City Hotel, or Whitney House, where he established his own headquarters and demanded luncheon. Quantrill said that he had boarded at this hostelry when he lived in Lawrence and would protect it from destruction.

The street patrols robbed all houses systematically. At the gate to each residence two or three men waited on their horses. Others dismounted, strode up the walk, spurs jingling, and knocked. If the door was opened by a man, he was shot down, if by a woman, she was ordered to deliver all money, watches, and jewelry in the house. Then the dwelling was set on fire. Any man who appeared from the smoke was killed. Some women grappled with their husbands' murderers. Most of them stood with their children, helpless and horror-struck. An occasional heroine ran recklessly to her spouse only to feel him killed in her arms. Through it all, no woman was harmed — for the bushwhackers adhered to a code. As the houses burned, women were allowed to salvage rugs, curtains, prized furniture, and keepsakes. Occasionally a man escaped from his house by hiding under a carpet as it was carried out. Others saved themselves by crouching under their wives' hoop skirts. Still others died rather than "hide behind petticoats."

The Reverend Hugh Fisher's wife saved her husband by crafty procrastination. He had run to the cellar and when the raiders demanded candles to light them on a search for him, Mrs. Fisher replied that she had only kerosene lamps — mechanical inventions more elaborate than Missouri bushwhackers had yet seen. Ordered, at pistol point, to light one, she artfully turned the wick down into the coal oil. The delay, while the curious countrymen gaped at the novel machinery, permitted her husband to crawl under the house and hide between a dirt bank and the foundations. The thwarted raiders set the house on fire and galloped away for more loot than could be found in a minister's home. Mrs. Fisher called from the cellar stairs. When her husband came up, she covered him with draperies and smuggled him from the blazing building.

A more harrowing experience awaited G. W. E. Griffith, owner of a store on Massachusetts Street. He heard the shooting while still in bed. Looking from a window, he saw a Negro with a baby in his arms run across the street. A moment later the man pitched forward, shot dead. Griffith knew at once what must be happening. In a few moments he heard a knock, unlatched the door, and — instead of being killed — was told to deliver all money and valuables in the house, then come down to his store and open the safe. Griffith hurried his wife to a neighbor's and as he was led away heard a woman scream. Turning, he saw through the neighbor's open door the man of the house tumbling lifeless down the stairs. The murdered victim's wife tried to run to him but was held back. The house burned down with the stricken man crumpled in the hallway.

On Massachusetts Street, Mr. Griffith looked at all the business buildings, doors shattered, looted goods scattered under the hitch racks in the street, smoke curling from broken windows. Other merchants, like himself, had been aroused from bed to open their safes before being killed. Boys, as well as men, lay sprawled along the street — among them two sons of John Speer, the newspaper editor. Griffith recognized a few citizens who had saved themselves by mingling with the mob and pretending to be bushwhackers. As his captors looted his store, he too dodged into the crowd. Joining the Eldridge House guests, he walked safely to the Whitney House under guard. Here all felt safe, but after Quantrill dined, he rode away, leaving the house unguarded. Two men on routine burning duty spied the unharmed building and dismounted. Why was this house spared? Orders were orders: "Kill every man and burn every house."

The proprietor, Quantrill's friend, stepped out the door to identify himself and explain the commander's order. The raiders were in a hurry and nervous. A pistol slug downed the hotel man. Terrified guests watching from the hall, turned and ran out the back door, jumped from windows. Better take a chance and be shot running than wait and be murdered! Besides, two men with pistols could not kill a dozen before some reached safety. In backyards and along alley fences, sunflowers stood tall as a horse's back. Griffith plunged into the weeds and scurried out of harm's way along the Kansas River.

By nine o'clock in the morning, Quantrill decided to leave Lawrence. The prairie air was already heating under the August sun, and sentries on Mount Oread reported a cloud of dust — soldiers no doubt — visible in the east. He assigned William Gregg the job of forming a rear guard, of gathering drunken and unruly raiders. Others assembled for the retreat, with stolen horses. Toy flags from the book store had been plaited in some animals' tails. Piano covers and damask curtains served as new saddle blankets. A hundred loose animals were to be led back or driven.

Most men had acquired at least one horse and a watch or two. Almost everyone had a pack horse loaded with bolts of cloth, shoes, or other dry goods. Morose George Todd, the stonemason now high in command, strutted in a new and splendid uniform looted God knows where! A few surviving prisoners at the livery stable were ordered out. Quantrill watched them from under his level-brimmed black hat. "Select one to drive an ambulance with two of my wounded men," he said to the guard. "Shoot the rest!"

Quantrill turned his sorrel horse and ambled away, listening to the fusillade in obedience to his orders. His men waited in a long line, bundles on their saddles, pack horses bulging with goods. "By God, Atchison never whipped Lawrence like this," it would have been like him to have said, "nor did Robert E. Lee march out of Pennsylvania with such a victory."

"Four's right: MARCH."

One man may have been left behind, too drunk to ride. A stranger in that condition was found by the citizens as they assembled from hiding places along the riverbank, from patches of tall sunflowers, from the graveyard. Men crept out from under the board sidewalks, too shocked to grin at one another's escapes. Mayor Collamore was found dead in his well. He had let himself down, with a rope, to hide and had smothered. A man who went down to rescue him also suffocated. On the streets, in gutters, on porches, in yards, a hundred and eighty-three men and boys were found dead or dying. A million to a million and a half dollars' worth of property had been destroyed. The new house built by Senator Lane lay in ashes. The Grim Chieftain himself had escaped by crouching behind a log as the raiders passed. Knowing that Quantrill wanted him particularly, Lane, in his hiding place, decided to kill himself rather than be tortured to death by the guerrillas. His only weapon was a small penknife, but he planned to thrust this little blade above his eyeball into his brain where the skull was thin. His brother John, an officer in the Seminole war, had killed himself in this manner with his saber.

Charles Robinson and George Deitzler had also escaped and hidden in a gulch on the side of Mount Oread. Ex-Governor Shannon, a resident of Lawrence now, was not in town and his house was spared.

Lane was the first man in town to rally a pursuit party. Calling on every able-bodied citizen to follow, he bounded, spiderlike, into a buggy and whipped up the road after Quantrill's men — Lane in a buggy chasing the deadliest killers on the border! A few farmers joined his party, making in all some thirty-five men on mules, draft horses, and in wagons, with long rifles, shotguns, and pistols. Those who stayed behind hanged the drunken stranger and dragged his stripped body by a rope along Massachusetts Street.

At noon Lane overtook the guerrillas. They were going back to Missouri by a route south of the road on which they had come. Near Baldwin City, the raiders fanned out for a mile along the creek in order to let all the horses drink at the same time and not delay the escape. Senator Lane knew this country, had been baptized — twice at least — in this creek. He also knew it to be unwise to charge with his little force. Moreover, a courier on the road reported the entire country aroused, soldiers converging from north and east, Major Preston Plumb coming with two hundred and fifty cavalrymen.

The neighborhood here was partly settled. Plumb's column stumbled into Lane's line, horses exhausted and almost useless from a forced march. His tired men and Lane's disorganized farmers advanced and fired a few shots at the fleeing raiders, but Quantrill ordered Gregg to hold them back with his rear guard while the bushwhackers' main column moved ahead at a spanking pace. Late in the afternoon Quantrill noted something familiar about the tree-rimmed horizon ahead. Surely his column was riding straight toward Paola, where he knew a strong Union force was garrisoned. Quantrill spurred along the rocking line of riders to the guide — a trusted follower — and called a halt.

"Where are you taking us?" Quantrill probably asked.

"Through Morristown, yender."

"That's not Morristown. It's Paola. You can't fool me. I'd know its hide in a tanyard."

As they argued, distant shots announced the approach of soldiers — the Paola garrison. Quantrill wheeled his men out of column and, counter-charging, drove the soldiers back to town where they laid an ambush should he come in after dark. But Quantrill's one idea was to escape, and the friendly Missouri woodlands were only twenty miles away. He re-formed his column and, swinging south of town, his horsemen leaned forward in their saddles for the last lap of the race to safety.

Major Plumb, in the meantime, stumbled along in Quantrill's rear until stopped by darkness. Then he turned toward the glimmering lights of Paola to rest his men and feed his horses. Straight into the ambush he led his squadron of cavalry. The Paola guards raised their guns, sighted along the barrels in the darkness. The commander waited until all the line was in range. Major Plumb, near the head of the column, turned stiffly in his saddle with that characteristic toss of his head, shouted encouragement to his exhausted men. The Good Bishop's voice was well known on Kansas hustings. The Union commander recognized it.

"By God, a minnit mor'n we'd a-fired," soldiers must have murmured as they lowered their pieces.

Safely in town, the exhausted and still tubercular Plumb was helped from his horse to bed. During the night, scouts rode in to report that Quantrill had camped for an hour to graze his horses on the rich bottom lands along Bull Creek. Plumb, tired as he was, dreamed always of his political future and determined to be on the spot at dawn to follow Quantrill's trail when light enough to see. Bugles called his soldiers from their blankets, and the column padded off in the dark, leather squeaking, sparks flying as horseshoes clinked on loose rocks. With the first paling light, Plumb saw the trail and trotted forward. At intervals he walked the horses to keep them fit. He knew that the enemy must be only ten or fifteen miles ahead. Telltale "scourings" from the retreating horses revealed them to be weakening faster than his own. Soon Plumb's horses began to shy at discarded booty along the road — bolts of silk and calico, a stack of new hats nested one in the other.

Finally Plumb sighted the enemy column worming over the undulating prairie ahead. The Missouri state line lay somewhere out there only five miles away.

"Come on, men!"

But Plumb was too late. Quantrill reached the Missouri woodlands before his pursuers, and grinning triumphantly under his long mustache ordered: "Each man for himself." His raiders knew all the cowpaths through the thick brush in this country and every cabin where sympathetic women would feed them grits and cracklings. By a hundred trails his little army vanished.

Senator Jim Lane raved up and down the border, tearing off his shirt with the eloquence he had used in territorial days, shouting for volunteers to march into Missouri, kill, confiscate, and collect. Eager men flocked to his noisy standard until General Schofield dared order him to quit — a risky liberty to take with a United States senator. Outwardly, the Grim Chieftain obeyed the order with meekness. He told his recruits that their righteous expedition had been prevented by "Skowfield." The sneering mispronunciation indicated that the senator might fight the general in the Senate and even appeal to President Lincoln, if necessary. Perhaps Lane's ruthless methods conformed more with the people's wishes than did Schofield's moderation. As the war dragged on endlessly, many people cried out for cruel and crushing blows. A mob in Chicago shouted: "Give us Jennison the Jayhawker: Give us our man of blood."

In Leavenworth, the radical Dan Anthony blamed the sack of Lawrence on Ewing and sent dispatches across the nation censuring him for negligence. Ewing replied with an extreme measure: Order Number Eleven expelled all people, loyal or disloyal, from Jackson, Cass, Bates, and Vernon counties, Missouri, excepting only certain areas near the large towns. Thus the bushwhackers' haven, to which Quantrill's men had fled, was to be depopulated — not a cabin left to hand out corn pone, a chunk of hog meat, and information about the "Feds."

Dispossessed homesteaders packed their wagons, drove into Kansas City and Independence to live miserably on government bounty as the Creeks and Seminole had been doing since the winter of 1861. Across America the copperhead press, striving for peace between North and South, conjured up harrowing stories of loyal Unionists torn from their hearths and homesteads by rude soldiers. Ewing had hoped to follow a neutral course between the Missouri moderates and the Kansas radicals, but he had to admit that Order Number Eleven put him in the camp of radical Jim Lane — a personality he had hoped to avoid. Only General Schofield still believed moderation to be the best policy, and the Grim Chieftain reached now for "Skowfield's" scalp. Like Curtis, before him, the department commander depended on Lincoln.

X X V

Baxter Springs

Lincoln was troubled about the demands for Schofield's removal. The war had turned definitely for the better since Gettysburg and Vicksburg, but was far from won. In Virginia, the Confederates were as unconquered as ever. In Chattanooga, Rosecrans seemed helpless before the Confederate, Braxton Bragg, and news from the Western border reported four thousand Texans marching north to join the Indians whom Steele was mustering since the Honey Springs defeat. Once reorganized, the small Federal garrisons holding the territory would be no match for them. Scrappy little Blunt, convalescing from smallpox, marched out of Fort Gibson to investigate the rumors and break up all concentrations, as he had done so successfully in July. Here was a soldier after Lincoln's own heart. Unlike Meade in Virginia, who wanted to take Richmond instead of defeating Lee, this Westerner realized that the enemy armies, not the enemy towns, were the important objectives. On August 24, 1863, Blunt knocked McIntosh's battalion of Creeks to pieces, then marched through the Choctaw country hunting for defenders and destroying Confederate supplies. He detached Captain Samuel Crawford to scour the country, hunting all organized bands of civilized Indians, while he marched into Fort Smith without firing a shot. War Department maps in Washington could now show western Arkansas and all of Indian Territory under the Stars and Stripes. Moreover, the pincers on Little Rock had been established once more.

Blunt's triumph in Indian Territory inspired Jo Shelby to retaliate with a fifteen-hundred-mile raid into Missouri with six hundred raiders. Starting September 22, 1863, his poetic eyes scanned the heavens and he wrote:

> The weather was propitious and the glorious skies of a Southern autumn flashed cheerily down upon the waving banners and glittering steel as we marched by the white-haired chieftain, General Price, and his healthy benediction was solemnly prophetic of my entire success.

Riding triumphantly toward the center of the state, Shelby was joined by bushwhacking bands until his column numbered fifteen hundred. He might well capture Jefferson City and expiate the loss of Little Rock, which had recently fallen into the hands of the now notorious General Fred Steele in this boundaryless war. Could not Schofield stop these annual raids across Missouri? Lincoln read the report along with an account of the Union defeat at Chickamauga which trapped Rosecrans in Chattanooga. At the depth of the President's despondency over these military reverses Senator Lane requested an audience. He had come with a delegation from Missouri and Kansas. Lincoln walked down the White House stairway to meet them in the East Room. Lane had lined up his delegation along three sides of the chamber. After introducing them to the President, he asked the chairman of the delegation to read their request for "Skowfield's" removal. Lane never forgot an old enemy.

Lincoln, the politician, listened to this canvass thoughtfully. He believed in the people's right to rule. But this high-pressure demand from a selected group presented a challenge to the administration. Lane explained that the delegation before him represented the will of the Republican Party in Kansas and Missouri — one thing on which the two rival states agreed at last. Peace between them might be restored by dismissing Schofield.

Lincoln's personal secretary, John Hay, watched his chief under the pressure of this temptation. Lane had built a strong case, and these men had great political influence, but their motive was obviously personal power rather than the nation's good. Lincoln asked for specific errors committed by Schofield and heard none of importance. Yet the delegates were united in wanting the general ousted. A smear campaign in newspapers controlled by these men might damage the administration. A weak executive would have submitted, but John Hay noticed that Lincoln stood firm. He would abet no injustice to a competent officer. Schofield had his faults, to be sure, but he was resourceful, knew his department, had done a good job, and Lincoln had no intention of ordering him to walk the plank because a deputation said that his elimination would make better relations between Kansas and Missouri. Lincoln suggested that the committee give him time to consider their complaints.

Lane was too shrewd to be forestalled in this manner. His delegates demanded an answer *at once.* Lincoln evaded this trap, too. He said that he would answer them *at once,* not orally but in writing — an artful way to scotch the possibility of a smear campaign, for the first letter the press could publish now would be Lincoln's case, and the committee would be caught defending themselves.

Senator Lane led the way out of the White House. His scheme had been defeated, but with his usual resiliency he stopped for speeches on his way back to Kansas — not against Lincoln and Schofield, as might have been expected, but against the horrors of slavery and for abolition and the continuance of the war. Always aiming his remarks at the level of his audience's intelligence, he sniffed at the popular Copperhead slogan: "Would you have your daughter marry a Negro?" Amalgamation, Lane said, had been more common under slavery than it ever would be in freedom. Then, bending over the audience in his confident and ingratiating manner, he continued:

> When I was a child, I was not of much consequence. My mother was not very well and she put me out to nurse with a nigger wench in Kentucky. [Lane was always born in Kentucky when talking to slave-state people.] This nigger wench had another baby, not near as white as I was; we slept in the same cradle — we wrestled together — we went swimming together — it was a boy, I remember. Nothing of the kind transpires among Northern people. . . .
>
> Amalgamation? I tell you that . . . slavery . . . is but a system of prostitution.
>
> And I say another thing, that a young person of pretention is not considered fit to move in good society till he has fallen in love with a nigger wench. I say, abolish slavery and it would take a thousand years of freedom to so systematize the crime of amalgamation as it is in slavery. Why, sirs, in your own State, while Lane's brigade was lying in Springfield, as beautiful and as white slaves came into my camp as refugees from slavery as I ever looked upon — hair as straight. The bleaching process has been going on in the slave states ever since slavery was there.

Lincoln never could be very angry with such an irrepressible fellow. He told his secretary, John Hay, that radicals made lots of trouble, but he liked them. "They are utterly lawless — the unhandiest devils in the world to deal with — but after all their faces are set Zionwards."

Lincoln had been perplexed by another Kansas radical. General James Blunt clashed continually with the conservative Schofield, but he did win battles. To ease frictions, Lincoln had transferred Blunt from the Department of Kansas to command the Army of the Frontier in Indian Territory. The little black-headed scrapper had cleaned out rebel Indians and bushwhackers wherever he went. Now in October 1863, Blunt decided to establish headquarters in Fort Smith, which he had captured twice, over Schofield's remonstrances. He marched south triumphantly, with reinforcements and a military band suitable to his new position — and as he marched south, Shelby marched north only a hundred miles farther east, in Schofield's department. Let "Skowfield" stop him if he could, Blunt would fight his own battles!

With Blunt rode General Curtis's son, Major H. S. Curtis, serving his country as his sister had at Rolla until she died in the nursing service the year before. Also in the jubilant column, the twenty-two year old wife of Captain Chester Thomas, brigade quartermaster, sat in an ambulance anticipating a reunion with her husband at Fort Smith. Nobody expected an attack, at least not until Stand Watie's Cherokee country was reached.

On October 6, 1863, Blunt's column approached Baxter Springs, located in a great prairie where army livestock was sent regularly to recuperate on the lush grasses. To protect the animals, a post had been established. The buildings stood in a hollow near the water and out of sight of the vast plain. A hundred men were garrisoned here, two thirds of them colored. They were eating dinner when a gang of broad-hatted riders swept down with wild yells and began shooting from hiding places between the mess tent and the soldiers' sleeping quarters. Dave Pool was in command. The gang were an advance detachment of Quantrill's bushwhackers, riding south to winter again on the good grass in Indian Territory.

Quantrill himself was riding a short distance behind the van, with his "regiment" divided in three troops. He had rendezvoused at his Johnson County headquarters on the Pardee farm southeast of Independence — just outside the boundaries vacated by Order Number Eleven — and had ridden south for a hundred and thirty miles without being stopped or detected. The blue Federal uniforms worn by his raiders may have deceived many people along the way, but surely Schofield was unduly lax in letting him pass. If he was keeping no better control over central Missouri, Shelby had a good chance to capture the capital.

When Quantrill rode in toward Baxter Springs from the northeast behind Dave Pool's company, he saw Blunt coming down the road from Fort Scott with about a hundred men, an elaborate band wagon, commissary, and ambulance train. Quantrill saw at once that he outnumbered the Federals. He formed company front a short way back from the road and waited. General Blunt watched the blue-clad soldiers forming. He had not heard the shooting below the plain at the springs, so he believed these horsemen had come from the garrison to welcome him formally. Flattered by the recognition, Blunt turned off the road and marched in file parallel to it. He planned a left face for a grand salute with both his companies extended in rank, but when his file came within point-blank range, the guerrillas opened fire. The surprised Federals fled in panic, Blunt and Curtis shouting desperately for them to stop and fight. In no time the two officers stood alone among the wagons with twenty-five or thirty dead under foot. They could do nothing now but flee for their lives. They led a spare horse to the ambulance for Mrs. Thomas, lifted her hurriedly aboard, legs shockingly astraddle, and too short for the stirrups. Her feet were thrust into the straps and she was told to hold to the saddle pommel for dear life — all useless gallantry, for no woman had been harmed by Quantrill's men, even in Lawrence.

Away the three fugitives raced over the prairie. Ahead of them a ten-foot gully gapped across the plain. The three horses gathered themselves for the leap. Two soared over. Curtis's mount flinched at the brink. A bullet had struck its hip. Horse and rider slapped into the far bank. A second bullet pierced Major Curtis's skull, killing him instantly. The jump had thrown Blunt from his saddle to his horse's neck where he clung like a monkey on a stick until out of range. Only Mrs. Thomas, the novice, sailed gracefully across to safety.

The wagon carrying the band of fourteen unarmed musicians and a drummer boy whipped for the post. A front wheel hit a hole and came off, spilling all the occupants among their brass. Guerrillas surrounded the wreck, killed the musicians, and set the wagon on fire. Other bushwhackers hunted down retreating soldiers on the plains, shooting sixty or seventy of the hundred in Blunt's command. Then Quantrill called back Dave Pool from the fort. Why fight all day down there and maybe lose some men? The victory was good enough already. Looting the wagons, each one took what food and liquor he could carry. Quantrill, himself drank until he became noisy — a rare excess for him. "By G-d," he boasted, "Shelby could not whip Blunt; neither could Marmaduke, but I whipped him."

Reeling happily in their saddles, the guerrillas circled around the fort and galloped south along the road to Fort Gibson, killing a few Negro and Indian soldiers who happened to be on detached duty along the way. Eighteen miles above the fort the bushwhackers crossed the Arkansas, swerved out over the plains around the garrison and on October 12, 1863, joined Cooper's Indians in the Indian Territory — safe again for another winter's rest where horse's feed was good.

Blunt had never suffered such a defeat. He limped, chagrined, into Fort Smith and was soon removed from command of the Army of the Frontier. But Lincoln did not dismiss him from the service. Instead, Blunt and that other fighting firebrand, Jennison, were assigned the duty of recruiting Negro regiments on the border. Both men had proved so popular that their names would draw crowds of admirers wherever they went.

In mid-October Lincoln decided to cut the knot in some of his Western problems of command by appointing Grant over all the departments. As President, however, he did not relieve himself of responsibility. The radicals continued to complain about Schofield. They pointed out that his dependence on Governor Gamble's "Copperhead Claybank militia" had proved to be a terrible mistake. Guns issued to them were going straight to the bushwhackers. Lincoln inquired about this. Schofield replied that, in order to send every available man to Grant, he had enlisted ex-rebels, but he defended the policy, maintaining that all officers were of unquestioned loyalty.

Lincoln accepted the explanation but at the same time read reports of Shelby's march to central Missouri. At Boonville the mayor offered the raiders peaceful admission, and Shelby began enlisting soldiers from north of the river. Then he returned to Arkansas without serious interruption from Schofield's troops. This was as bad as Frémont at his worst. Exultantly Shelby reported that he had destroyed a million dollars' worth of Federal supplies, and railroad property worth eight hundred thousand dollars, and that he had brought back six thousand horses and mules and eight hundred recruits from northern Missouri. He claimed, in addition, that he had diverted ten thousand Federal troops who might otherwise have reinforced Rosecrans after his defeat at Chickamauga.

Lincoln was busy at this time urging General Meade to attack Lee in Virginia and destroy his army, instead of shadowboxing for Richmond. Meade made excuses. With them came Schofield's report of Shelby's raid — so different from the newspaper accounts. Schofield wrote that the raider had been expelled after losing half his men and gaining *no recruits* except the robbers under Quantrill. The dispatch ended: "This is gratifying as showing that the rebel power in Missouri is completely ended."

Lincoln had received too many communications like this from frustrated generals to be much deceived. How was Grant, the new top commander in the West, going to handle this?

Lincoln turned to the myriad papers on his desk — especially the forecasts of local elections which would indicate the strength of his administration. Grant ignored the Missouri problem and concentrated on the relief of Chattanooga. Let the border suffer. Stand Watie, noticing the ease with which raids could be made behind Federal lines, bypassed Colonel Phillips at Fort Gibson, destroyed the Cherokee capitol at Tahlequah, and burned beautiful Rose Cottage.

Kirby-Smith, ruler of an isolated domain, reorganized his army, militarized his industry, began running the Texas blockade to sell cotton abroad. On December 11, 1863, he replaced General Steele, commander of Indian Territory, with Samuel B. Maxey, able, fire-eating orator from the Lone Star State, now a major general in the Confederate Army.

Under the new command Stand Watie started to invade Kansas, but on December 18, 1863, he was overtaken and turned back by Phillips's brigade of Indians and Negroes. The Confederate Cherokee swerved away from this defeat, rode straight for the Department of Missouri to take advantage of Schofield's shortage of man power, and raided into southwest Missouri.

The continued inability of Schofield to police his department against the bushwhackers, against Shelby, against the Cherokee gave credence to the radicals' complaints. Here was just cause for removal, not just the fabrication of politicians seeking power. Lincoln replaced him on January

22, 1864, with William S. Rosecrans, a skillful commander, yet one who had failed in Tennessee. To decide the next Confederate offensive, the rebel Indians met in council at Amstrong Academy on February 1, 1864. General Maxey attended the meeting. The two most important plans discussed were the practicality of another raid into Kansas and of an alliance with the plains Indians to fight Western settlers — Pike's perennial objective.

X X V I

Lincoln's Re-election Campaign
on the Border

GENERAL MAXEY'S PLAN to repossess the Indian Territory and strike north
and west was changed in the early spring of 1864 by the grand strategy
of the top Union command. This was election year. The victories of 1863
had been stalemated, and something must be done, or Lincoln would not
be nominated for another term. Two plans to split the South and hasten
a Northern victory were considered. Lincoln favored cutting Louisiana
in half, then marching across Texas to the gulf. Grant and Sherman preferred to capture Atlanta and then jayhawk across Georgia to the sea.
In case Lincoln approved this plan, Sherman promised to give the command of a division to his brother-in-law, Tom Ewing, who was now in
charge of the District of St. Louis, which included southeast Missouri.
Both Ewing's wife Ellen and his adjutant, Harrison Hannahs, believed
that Ewing made the mistake of his life when he declined this offer and
remained west of the Mississippi. Whether a mistake or not, the decision
may have caused his physical shake-up, for he soon suffered from neu-
ralgia and a boil on his neck. He became irritable with his wife, complained about her spending — too little, not too much — and admonished
her for talking about the possibility of dying when her expected baby was
born.

The plan to split Louisiana was tried first, under command of Nathaniel
Banks, the political general who — as speaker of the House — had appointed the committee to investigate the Kansas troubles in 1856. He
floated seventeen thousand men up Red River while it was still navigable
with the spring freshets. Generals A. J. Smith and Joseph A. Mower were
to join him with ten thousand soldiers, and Fred Steele, the high-voiced

dandy, was to come down from Little Rock with an additional fifteen thousand. Thus, with forty-two thousand men, Banks could easily clean up Kirby-Smith's twenty to twenty-five thousand soldiers, no matter how reckless and dashing his horsemen under Marmaduke and Shelby proved to be.

Threatened by this invasion, Kirby-Smith ordered General Maxey to bring all the guerrillas and Indians he could muster in the territory. Thus the new general relinquished his designs on Kansas and started his men — red and white — to Louisana. Now, the Creek and Cherokee country was safe again for Northern Indians. The United States Indian Superintendent, W. G. Coffin, estimated that he had nine thousand of these dispossessed red men on relief in Kansas and hoped to return them to their homes. He assembled five thousand refugees. The Seminole were left behind on account of smallpox which had laid many of them low. Chief Billy Bowlegs had succumbed to the disease. Coffin was in a hurry to get his charges back to their own lands in time to put in a crop. In case the long trip was made too late for the growing season, the problem of feeding so many Indians during the winter in distant Indian Territory would be staggering. Annoying details kept him from starting as soon as planned. He had trouble hiring sufficient wagons and teams necessary to haul the emigrants' gear. Then on May 7, 1864, he received a message from Washington to postpone the expedition indefinitely. The Red River expedition had failed. Receding flood waters stranded the army in central Louisiana, and the supporting columns had not come as planned. Now the Union armies were returning to their bases. General Steele had started back to Little Rock, fighting engagements on the way and losing his wagon train with a guard of twelve hundred men — mostly enlisted Negroes — when surprised by Marmaduke's horsemen at Poison Springs. The black men who surrendered had been killed mercilessly. With the danger ended in Louisiana and Arkansas, the rebel Indians and guerrillas were spurring home to the territory, and the refugees, if they attempted the hegira, would be preyed upon by their enemies. Indian Commissioner W. P. Dole, in Washington, feared especially that Quantrill might sweep across the plains and massacre the Union Indians as Marmaduke's men had massacred the Negroes at Poison Springs. Such inhumanities would be blamed on Lincoln, and this was election year!

Superintendent Coffin reassured the commissioner that he had ample military protection. His supplies had been purchased and his wagons hired. To delay longer would be inexcusable extravagance, so the commissioner allowed him to proceed. The expedition left the Sauk and Fox Indian Reservation in Kansas on May 16, 1864. Three thousand men, women, and children walked ahead and behind the wagons in a procession six miles long. Two thousand old people, mothers, and babies rode in the wagons with bedding, coops of chickens and ducks, and at least five hundred puppies. Around the wagons and running along with the footmen trotted some three thousand grown dogs. Superintendent Coffin wrote Dole: "If we had a Bayard Taylor with us he would furnish articles for the *Tribune* for a season." Behind the procession came a private ox-drawn train of three hundred more wagons with supplies for McDonald and Fuller, sutlers at Fort Gibson. From their perches on duffel in the wagons the travelers watched the sky line for guerrillas.

The weather was sultry, with frequent cloudbursts muddying the roads. Wet clothing steamed on hot human bodies. At the Osage Catholic Mission the refugees halted. From here on they must cross the dreaded enemy country. The prospect of danger upset the travelers' nerves. Stand Watie and Quantrill were said to be waiting for them just below the horizon. The frightened people refused to leave the cluster of buildings, yet the planting season and their own chance of raising a crop became shorter with each day's delay.

Finally the refugees were persuaded to venture out on the last leg of their journey. But instead of being attacked by warlike Indians, a band of thieving Osage crept into their camp at night and drove away thirty oxen from the train. Another accident marred the passage. In one of the daily rainstorms a Negro interpreter was struck by lightning. The bolt fired every load in his revolver, blowing his feet and ankles to ribbons.

The thirty-one-day march ended June 15, 1864, with the red Israelites splashing across the flooded flats into Fort Gibson. Coffin reported that he had brought the wayfarers through with only six deaths — and sixteen births. Three children had broken legs by falling from wagons and being run over. One man in the military escort drowned on the night of arrival. He had been thrown from his horse crossing Grand River, and the weight of his weapons sank him.

The refugees had reached home at last, but Superintendent Coffin's troubles were not ended. His wards had arrived too late to put in a crop, even if they dared venture from the fort to their deserted homesteads. Moreover, the expected supply boat *Williams* had not arrived from Fort Smith, and instead of feeding the five thousand emigrants he had brought, Coffin estimated that sixteen thousand refugees had congregated on these far-off flats. Many of them had come south with the Indian regiments in 1863. Others had ventured home independently. Fort Gibson was three hundred tortuous miles upriver from Little Rock, a hundred miles above Fort Smith, and a hundred and seventy-five overland miles from Fort Scott. Supplies here fetched fabulous prices. Flour in the store owned by the Ross family of Cherokee cost twenty-five dollars for a ninety-eight-pound sack — a prohibitive price for Coffin's dwindling funds. He was writing a report of his predicament when he received word that the boatload of supplies he expected would not arrive at all. Stand Watie had attacked and destroyed the vessel twenty miles above Fort Smith.

The stern-wheeler *Williams* had started with a full load and a guard detailed from the Twelfth Kansas. Stand Watie realized the vessel's importance to the refugees and laid an ambush for it. A nineteen-year-old Creek lieutenant, G. W. Grayson, recently back from school in the East, joined him with a company of Indians eager for military service. Watie assigned Grayson the task of preparing a screened battery on a riverbank where the vessel might be captured. Grayson, proud of his first important commission, selected the heavily-wooded shores seven miles below Webber's Falls, planted his three cannon on the south bank, and waited. Colonel Stand Watie's scouts rode inconspicuously along the shore beside the doomed vessel. On June 15 — the day the refugees arrived at Gibson — Lieutenant Grayson watched through the sheltering leaves as the *Williams* splashed up the middle channel toward his guns. When the steamboat was broadside, he ordered a shot fired across its bow. An answering volley from the boat ripped the branches above his head where the telltale smoke cloud from his cannon drifted through the trees. Lieutenant Grayson ordered his other two guns and all his men to fire. Watie's regiment also galloped in to join the fun. Through the smoke they saw the Federal guards splashing off through waist-deep water to the north bank. The pilot waved a white flag from the texas, and whooping Indians waded out to climb over the gunwales. They found the boiler pierced and useless. One man lay dead. The cargo consisted of barrels of hominy, and salt pork — grand rations for guerrillas. Hour after hour they unloaded. Then the stripped vessel was set on fire and allowed to drift downstream.

Stand Watie sent a courier to General Cooper, inebriate commander of Choctaw and Chickasaw, requesting transportation to haul away the rich booty, but before wagons arrived, Stand Watie learned that Union soldiers were coming in force from Fort Smith. He ordered young Grayson to stand guard with a platoon of his Creeks and hold the Federals, should they arrive before dawn. In the meantime, Watie's Cherokee loaded their horses with all the supplies they could carry and scattered away in the night, each man for himself — true Quantrill tactics.

Lieutenant Grayson exulted in this second responsible assignment. Proud of his Creek blood, he gloried in the prospect of showing his courage in the unequal fight ahead. Let the world know that Creeks could whip Federals twenty-five to one! Carefully he placed each of his men on guard for the night. Then he rode back along his picket line to be sure all knew their duties. To his dismay every picket had deserted. Grayson alone remained to fight the Federals. He neck-reined his horse from the line of duty and cantered away. In any event, the Union refugees, with their supplies destroyed, were in a predicament.

War was becoming a long holiday for the civilized Confederate Indians, and so long as Sherman drew away most of the Union soldiers for his investment of Atlanta, the license promised to continue. A lack of soldiers on the plains emboldened the wild Indians. Stage lines to Denver and Salt Lake City had been completely stopped by Sioux, Cheyenne, and Arapaho warriors. No one could be sure that they were allied to the Confederacy, but their bullets and arrows killed just as effectively. Southern prisoners of war were offered their freedom if they would enlist to fight these savages, but only a few volunteered. Some of the sparse troops on police duty against guerrillas in Missouri, Arkansas, and the territory were ordered to the plains.

Frustrations, battle reverses, and campaign stalemates extended to the Eastern seaboard in the spring of 1864. In May, when the Red River expedition was acknowledged a failure, General Phil Sheridan had made a dash for Richmond, Virginia — chronic objective, seasonal as Price's raids to Jefferson City, Missouri. At Yellow Tavern the chivalric Jeb Stuart thrust his horsemen in front of Little Phil and saved the Confederate capital, but paid with a wound from which he died next day. Among Stuart's many casualties was Henry Clay Pate, Fifth Virginia Cavalry — "the so and so you've heard so much about." The man who hoped to take Old Brown, until Old Brown took him, had had a checkered military career since leaving Westport. In the Confederate Army he had once been court-martialed for mutiny, but in the end he died honorably as a lieutenant colonel.

The military deadlocks and reversals weighed heavily on President Lincoln. Many members of his party turned against him, blaming military defeats on his inefficiency. Joe Medill, editor of the *Chicago Tribune,* wrote Congressman Elihu B. Washburne to have Lincoln restore Frémont to command of the Department of the West if he wanted to be renominated for the Presidency. He said that the *Tribune* subscribed to twenty-five German newspapers, and their translator reported the Germans to be incensed about the treatment accorded Frémont, Sigel, Osterhaus, and Carl Schurz. The Germans also resented Lincoln's disregard of the Missouri radicals.

A convention of Lincoln's party opponents met in Pittsburgh on May 31, 1864, and nominated Frémont as Republican candidate. A week later — June 7 — the regular convention assembled in Baltimore. Senator Lane was in temporary disgrace for being cowhided by a woman in Washington. Lane explained the mishap by various stories. He said the woman had attacked him because he had kept her from annoying the President. He also said that Governor Carney, Robinson's successor as governor in Kansas, had employed her in order to discredit him and get the patronage Lincoln had given him. Talking to rallies of the "bhoys," Lane winked, shifted his quid to the other cheek, and admitted that he might be quite a man with the ladies.

Thus restored to favor with the masses if not with the classes, Senator Lane traveled to Baltimore where the delegates were congregating to nominate a President to quash Frémont. On the incoming trains groups of delegates protested the renomination of Abraham Lincoln. Anybody would be better, they complained. The Grand Council of the Union League met to select their candidate the night before the convention. Needless to say, their recommendation would weigh heavily on the morrow. Powerful and practical politicians stood up, made suggestions, pounded their fists. All seemed to agree that Lincoln's failure to end the war was sure to drag down the party in November. Finally Senator Lane, a trage-dian's thoughtful frown on his high forehead, paced down the middle aisle. Time and again he had stood before hostile border men who mali-ciously patted the pistols in their pockets. Yet always his magic voice had turned hatred to hosannas. But now he faced a different audience. These politicians believed themselves to be educated and intelligent, sophisti-cated, cynical, and capable of resisting the emotional appeals of hustings oratory. This was not Baldwin City and Lane did not purposely mispro-nounce "Leavingsworth" and "Topeko." Instead, he began with broad-cloth language and gracious style:

> Mr. President, Gentlemen of the Grand Council: For a man to produce pain in another man by pressing upon a wounded spot requires no great degree of strength, and he who presses is not entitled to any emotion of triumph at the agony expressed by the sufferer. Neither skill nor wisdom has been exercised in the barbaric process. For a man, an orator, to pro-duce an effect upon sore and weary hearts, gangrened with bitter disap-pointments, so stirring them up, even to passion and to folly, demands no high degree of oratorical ability. It is an easy thing to do, as we have seen this evening. Almost anybody could do it.
>
> For a man to take such a crowd as this now is, so sore and sick at heart, and now so stung and aroused to passionate folly, now so infused with a delusive hope for the future, as well as address himself to such an assem-bly, and turn the tide of its passion and excitement in the opposite direc-tion — that were a task worthy of the highest, greatest effort of human oratory. I am no orator at all; but to precisely that task I now set myself, with absolute certainty of success. All that is needful is that the truth should be set forth plainly, now that the false has done its worst.

Lane's speech was short, but it hit the mark. He concluded: "If we nominate any other than Abraham Lincoln, we nominate ruin." The converted council resolved to endorse the Rail Splitter, and next day, in the Republican Party's formal convention, Senator Lane nominated him. Lane has also been credited wth the selection of Andrew Johnson as Lin-coln's running mate, and with securing the right to vote in the convention for delegates from reconstructed Arkansas, Louisiana, and Tennessee.

After his slate was approved unanimously, Lane returned to Kansas to stump for Lincoln and also for a legislature that would re-elect him, Lane, to the United States Senate. He would need all the funds he could raise for this campaign, and when he arrived in Kansas, he learned that a new mania, exciting as the Pikes Peak gold rush, had swept the state. Thousands of cattle were being driven in across the Indian Territory to be sold at absurd prices by shady characters. Some cattle were coming all the way from Texas, but most of them were animals that had been abandoned by the warring factions of civilized Indians. Enterprising individuals among the refugees stranded in the midst of this multitude of beef began driving cattle north by the Chisholm and a dozen other trails. In Kansas the animals were sold for a pittance.

Soon, white border toughs saw the opportunity for easy wealth. They outfitted roundup camps, drove south, and gathered all the loose cattle they could find. At Humboldt, the commanding officer of the garrison patroling the Kansas state line reported herds of from a hundred to a thousand cattle passing through his lines daily. The men who brought the cattle had little or no title to them, but they made money selling out for a nominal figure to brokers who resold the animals to butchers, ranchmen, and army contractors. Lane's own supporters were becoming rich in this trade, as were many others — all voters. Among the prominent free-state men implicated were Samuel N. Wood, the Quaker abolitionist who had rescued Branson from Sheriff Jones in 1855, thus bringing on the Wakarusa War. He had become a brigadier general in the militia and a state senator. Shalor Eldridge and Dan Anthony were both accused of participating in this illegal trade. So was Lane's partner in the *Conservative,* Daniel Webster Wilder. Even Governor Carney was not free from suspicion.

Lieutenant Colonel Plumb, Colonel William Phillips, and others tried to stop the stealing at the border and were relieved from duty. Evidently someone with great power in the army was profiting by the wholesale robbery. Senator Lane was implicated, by inference, but the cloud of accusations against him did not appear to jar his confidence. At the Republican state convention at Topeka on September 8, 1864, the Lane-Lincoln ticket triumphed with Samuel J. Crawford the nominee for governor. Crawford's military record from the early days with Montgomery around

Fort Scott to his service at Wilson's Creek and with Blunt at Fort Wayne all added prestige to his political stature. Republican Robinson seemed to be pushed permanently aside by the Lane machine. The New Englander consoled himself by endorsing Frémont's merits and maligning Lincoln.

Senator Lane set off in high good humor with his menagerie, as it was called, to tour the state for his ticket: Lincoln, Crawford, and a legislature that would elect him again. Everywhere he went, audiences were promised grand entertainment, always something new. General Ewing, who had decided to run against Lane for the Senate, gave up the idea, and wrote his wife that the humbug was almost sure to carry the state. Two months before election, Sherman captured Atlanta and asked final permission to undertake his march to the sea. At the same time, his brother-in-law Ewing prepared to leave on furlough for Lancaster, Ohio, where his wife expected to be confined at about election time or sooner. But before he left St. Louis, he learned that Shelby's horsemen were probing his outposts in the southern part of the state. He had heard rumors since last April that Price planned another invasion, but nothing had come of it. The route ahead of Old Pap, if he attempted it, was twice as long as Sherman's proposed march to the sea. However, the white-haired patriarch had become an expert at living off the country on long marches — in fact, had taught generals like Sherman that it could be done successfully. Now if Sherman dared cross Georgia to Savannah, Price might disconcert him by marching north to take St. Louis. The South's strategy to foil Sherman was plain enough. Did Sherman dare take such a chance, at least before election?

The problem of stopping Price in southeast Missouri devolved on Rosecrans's district commander, Tom Ewing. The political-minded officer gave up his furlough, wrote his wife that he could not come, duty called: Kiss the children and give "ten cents for Will, ten for Mary and five for Tom with Papa's warmest love to his darlings."

XXVII

Cabin Creek and Pilot Knob

GRAY-HAIRED Pap Price rode exultantly north on his gray-haired horse Bucephalus, hoping to counteract Sherman's victories in the southeast. At the same time, Stand Watie planned another march northward into Kansas. He had been raiding the Fort Scott-Fort Gibson road for weeks, killing Negro workmen, burning mowing machines and hay, carrying off what little booty his men could find. This had diverted only a minor number of Federal troops. For the really important raid Watie planned, he urged General Richard M. Gano, new commander of the district, to join him with the Choctaw, Chickasaw, two regiments of Texans, and John Jumper's Creeks and Seminole. Watie had learned that a wagon train was lumbering down the Fort Scott road toward Fort Gibson, carrying supplies worth over a million dollars to the garrison and refugees restricted to a beef diet since the destruction of their stores on the *Williams*. The train had a strong guard of Federal Indians, but Watie and Gano, combined, could muster two thousand men and four cannon — surely enough to overpower the wagon guard. General Gano agreed to join Watie and capture the train.

Like Price's raiders, these Indians were dressed in rags of Confederate uniforms — and some in shoes and blue coats taken from dead Federals. The equipment issued Westerners, red or white, had usually been picked over by Southern quartermasters before it crossed the Mississippi. At best the clothing made in Confederate factories was inferior. Indian soldiers complained that their issue hats of unscoured wool smelled like a sheeppen. When wet, the brims hung around the men's ears like squaws' dresses. The eager column under Gano and Stand Watie looked forward to new clothes and good food when they captured the great supply train coming south.

Circling carefully west across the plains, out of sight of Fort Gibson, the column crossed the Canadian, then the Arkansas and the Verdigris. On the second day's march, September 16, 1864, they came to the military road ten or twelve miles above the fort (near where Wagner, Oklahoma, would later be). A crew of Negroes was cutting hay here for the Federal cavalry. Guards with rifles stood on the hills to ward off raiding Indians, but no preparation had been made to check the sizable army which swept unexpectedly across the horizon.

Gano and Watie galloped their line to within rifle range, then unlimbered their cannon. A few shots of grape scattered the Federal guard, and the exultant victors rode unopposed into the hay-cutters' camp. With guns across their saddles, the ragged Confederate Indians jogged up and down through the uncut hay and the tall weed patches, shooting hidden Negroes like rabbits. Some black men rose from the weeds calling, "O! Good master, save and spare me," but all were shot down. Some were found submerged in the water under the creek banks, only their noses above the surface. These were killed like the others and their bodies dragged out on the pebble bars.

When all were dead, the column burned three thousand tons of hay stacked for Fort Gibson. Then the raiders remounted and jogged north, weather-beaten hats flapping, braids of hair bouncing with the ponies' trot. On September 17, 1864, the column encamped on Wolf Creek (near present-day Salina). Next morning General Gano scouted ahead with four hundred Texans. He spied the train — three hundred wagons — encamped in the little cluster of houses on the bluffs above what was known as the Military Crossing of Cabin Creek. Gano watched stealthily from a distance. Obviously the Federal commander expected to be attacked, for his guard of a thousand Creeks and Seminole were working on fortifications — building a stockade and piling hay bales into a breastworks.

Gano dispatched a runner for Stand Watie to bring up his Indians during the night. The red men had waited all day on Wolf Creek. Eager yet nervous, they made "medicine" and tried to recall old battle omens of their vanished long-house culture. Too bad the hated "pins" and their abolitionist Keetowah medicine men were on the other side! The country hereabouts had been unlucky for Confederate Indians. Stand Watie's attack at Cabin Creek on July 1, 1863, had failed. Was his "medicine" wrong? Indians in the ranks were discussing this seriously when Greenbrier Joe saw a vision — a white deer near the encampment. He believed this a "sign" of victory, and the column was confident as it rode away to join Gano.

The moon shone brightly and at midnight the Indians saw, across the silvered landscape, yellow flames from many enemy campfires. Soon Watie's and John Jumper's brigades joined with Gano's. They surrounded the Federal encampment and closed in until near enough to hear shouting and laughter within the palisades. The teamsters and Federal Indian guard were drinking and making merry. In the darkness the raiders shouted taunts at them, and Indians in the barricade replied. The turkey-gobble challenge shuddered back and forth. No Cherokee of spirit could ignore that call of his blood. One wagoner, bolder than the rest, emerged from the stockade and stumbled defiantly toward the raiders' hidden lines. Told to halt, he sneered from the darkness at the cowardly attackers, went on, and was shot down.

Major Henry Hopkins, commanding the Federal guard, ordered a volley fired into the darkness. Gano replied with small arms and with artillery blasting the campfires, upsetting wagons. A herd of mules stampeded in confusion. The terrified animals dashed in panic over the one-hundred-fifty-foot bluff, braying shrill screams of pain and terror. With daylight the attacking Indians saw, through the tall grass, the cabin roofs, canvas wagon covers, baled hay barricades. Without orders they began to shoot — white smoke balls blossoming in the tall grass. Gano ordered the firing stopped, but individual Indians advanced alone before admiring tribesmen, snapping pistols at the enemy barricade, and urging comrades to follow in a general charge. Captain Grayson's Creeks handed around "medicine," rubbed it on their bodies or clothing. His first lieutenant, Tsupofe Fixico ("Thomas Benton" in English), offered some to his chief. The educated young captain scorned the fellow's superstition and walked boldly up and down the line under fire, to demonstrate that "medicine" was superfluous.

Billows of smoke from the Federal guns fogged the fortifications. Major Hopkins decided to abandon his train and save his men under cover of the murky clouds. He retreated, fighting up the road toward Fort Scott. The ragged Confederate Indians, intent on loot, swarmed in among the deserted wagons. They poured captured brandy into their empty stomachs. Crazy drunk, they killed and mutilated wounded prisoners, and tossed property over the bluff into the creek for the sheer joy of watching its destruction. The commanders realized that they must get away or be crushed by a counterattack from Fort Gibson. Half the supply wagons stood fully loaded, but the mules that had survived shied and kicked at the staggering strangers who did not know their harness or understand which animals worked best at wheel, swing, or lead. Finally, a train of a hundred and thirty wagons was hooked up and started south by a new route west of the military road. Within an hour the sobering Confederates sighted Federal soldiers riding up the road from Fort Gibson. Scouts exchanged a few long-range shots with them, but the Confederate column was laden with too much loot to stop and risk a battle.

Federal losses in property amounted to hundreds of thousands of dollars. The sutler firm of McDonald and Fuller, who were handsomely supporting Jim Lane's campaign — as well as Abraham Lincoln's — valued their lost goods at sixty thousand dollars. The Confederates boasted that they had acquired sufficient clothing for two thousand men, besides bountiful foodstuffs. In addition, they had cut off communication between Forts Gibson and Scott. The isolated refugees, in spite of their bounteous supply of cattle, might flee again to Kansas. Worst of all: Where would these Confederate Indians strike next? People wondered while they watched for reports of Price's advance across Arkansas.

Old Pap started his march north triumphantly. Would Lincoln dare let Sherman march to the sea while this horde menaced the West? As Price rode north, Marmaduke joined him with two brigades. General James S. Fagan marched to his standard with three. Fagan was a popular and extremely handsome Arkansas politician who had rendered distinguished service at Shiloh, and was always sure to give a good account of himself. Early in September, Price's column crossed the Arkansas River, between Little Rock and Fort Smith. The Federal garrisons at both posts let him go without attacking. Thus Price severed his communications and marched ahead, precisely as Sherman expected to do in Georgia if Lincoln would give him permission.

The Confederate invaders told each other that Fred Steele, in Little Rock, feared to come out and, like an Oriental prince, reveled with a harem of romantic women surrounded by dogs, race horses, and the luxury necessary to his velvet-collared, shrill-voiced existence.

At Pocahontas, Arkansas, Shelby joined Price's column with three more brigades — perhaps they should be called regiments. Already Price had marched as far as from Atlanta to the sea and was now more than half the distance to St. Louis. On September 19, 1864, he crossed into Missouri with twelve thousand men — only eight thousand of them armed — marching in three columns. Marmaduke commanded the right, his raiders skirting the swamps and bayous along the Mississippi. On the left, spritely little Shelby's horsemen galloped along the Ozark Mountain roads. In the center, Fagan's brigades escorted the wagon train and a thousand beef cattle. Thomas Reynolds, swarthy-skinned and urbane, rode along in a carriage, planning an eloquent inaugural when Price restored the government in Jefferson City. Cancer had killed Claib Jackson.

Up in St. Louis, General Rosecrans, the department commander, feared that the Knights of the Golden Circle might rise, join the heroes, and take over the state. He impressed every available man into service. Provost marshals stopped soldiers on furloughs and hurried them into ranks. The district commander, Thomas Ewing — giving up his trip home to be with his wife during childbirth — boarded the train for Pilot Knob, the railroad terminal in the iron-smelting and coal-mining region halfway to the Arkansas border. At all bridges he posted guards and sent scouts south, hunting for Price. At Pilot Knob a Union fort contained less than a thousand men. This was the main garrison in the area. The fort was a heptagonal earthwork with walls nine feet high and ten thick, surrounded by a deep moat with perpendicular sides. Behind the walls stood seven guns. The magazine in the center of the fort was protected by four-foot walls.

Ewing's scouts came in here with prisoners captured from Price's column. They reported the advancing Confederates to have from twelve to fifteen thousand men, ragged, poorly armed, but excellently mounted. Moreover, many of them were Missourians coming back to repossess their homeland and expel the "damned Dutch." Certainly they would fight desperately. Rosecrans sent word to Ewing not to risk a battle against overwhelming numbers and, unless sure of victory, to fall back on St. Louis.

Ewing — his wife fast approaching her time of confinement — discussed the situation with his officers, and they agreed that the fort was impregnable. They wanted to test its walls against horsemen and were not afraid of ten times their number. Ewing decided to fight. His men, noting his protruding lower lip, judged themselves due for a real battle. Ewing believed it good strategy to delay Price as long as possible at Pilot Knob, in order that troops might be transported from Tennessee and Alabama by boat and thus save St. Louis. Let Missouri's Thermopylae be here! He sent all the railroad rolling stock back to St. Louis and set the men to work digging additional trenches outside the fort.

Pilot Knob was named for a volcanic cone of iron, sixty per cent pure, rising six hundred feet above one side of the fort. Across from it, on the other side of the fort, rose Shepherd's Mountain. Lookouts reported the enemy coming up the valley between them. For two days Price's army streamed in, pitching tents, moving from place to place. At night the Federals heard their picks and shovels preparing gun emplacements. General Price, however, was somewhere in the rear, for he did not expect a major battle here. Shelby's horsemen scouted the roads to the west, watching for reinforcements who might be coming to aid Ewing.

On September 27, 1864, Marmaduke, who was concentrating in the east, sent a rider with a message under a flag of truce to the Pilot Knob fort. Ewing opened the dispatch and read a demand for surrender. He sent the horseman back to his own lines with a defiant challenge.

The Confederate Army moved closer, standing by thousands in the fields and along the roads to display their preponderant numbers. Then another flag of truce advanced to the fort. This time Ewing sent back word that he would fire on a white flag if another was sent. Confederates had taken Fort Pillow under a flag of truce and then massacred the Negro garrison. "They shall play no such game on me," he said.

Rebuffed twice, the Confederates opened fire from a distance with their big guns. Puffs of white smoke disclosed battery locations on Shepherd's Mountain. In the fort Ewing's cannon fired back, spraying dirt among the white clouds. To the south, in the broad valley, Ewing saw four solid walls of men moving forward on foot. His men in the outer trenches waited until the enemy was within rifle range, then mowed down the first rank like wheat straw before a scythe. The ranks behind charged, shouting vengeance and death for the author of Order Number Eleven — the order which had vacated whole counties in Missouri. A regiment of gallant ragamuffins under General Cabell drove the Federals from the outer trenches and reached the moat. The Union artillery commander, Lieutenant David Murphy, leaped on the parapet in full view and strode along, stepping over leveled rifles, swearing abusively at the enemy, and urging the Federals to double their fire. Those bushwhackers fought with a recklessness that chilled the blood in the bravest defender of the fort. Again and again the rebels formed and re-formed, charging desperately. Soldiers peeped over the fort walls to see dead bodies sprawled face down, arms flung out; face up, arms clutching their shirts; bodies arched back over a rock or brush, eyes and mouths open. The Federals counted sixty-seven of them in a space no larger than an acre. In six hours the Union soldiers killed or wounded one and a half times their own number — a record for battle, Ewing's adjutant reported. The Federals told themselves, and may have believed, that the enemy had been crazed by a ration of whiskey mixed with gunpowder. Finally, the Confederates retired, still undefeated, to build scaling ladders for tomorrow's assault.

At night a curtain of darkness dropped around the earthworks. Distant bivouac fires sparkled like sequins on Shepherd's Mountain and like city lights down in the valley. The heptagonal fort remained brilliantly illuminated. Enemy shells had ignited a smelter's charcoal pile which burned like an incandescent lamp. Brigadier General Ewing called his officers to a sheltered bastion. A quarter of his forces were casualties. Price's expedition had been delayed three days and as many more would be consumed before they could continue the march. This interruption would undoubtedly give Union soldiers sufficient time to come up from the south and defend St. Louis. To fight Price's vast army another day at Pilot Knob seemed futile. The garrison's only alternatives were retreat or surrender. In the dazzling light of the burning charcoal pile, retreat might be impossible. Would the officers take the risk? Yes, by God.

In order to keep out of sight, the soldiers mustered in the shadow of the moat. A drawbridge was constructed on the dark side of the fort and covered with canvas to muffle the sound of artillery wheels on the boards. Then a long fuse was laid to the powder magazine and the men marched into the night in column of two's, heading west toward Rolla, terminal of the South West Branch Pacific Railroad from St. Louis. When the last knapsacks on the last retreating backs had dissolved in the outer darkness, a rear guard lighted the fuse.

The column was a mile on its way when the explosion pulsed beside the flaring charcoal pile. Confederate vedettes edged forward to investigate, and at dawn Price's men thronged over the wrecked earthworks. The fort, the town, the mines, and the Iron Mountain Railroad were theirs with direct connection to St. Louis, but they had not a car or locomotive to take them there, and before they could march the hundred miles to the city, Union reinforcements were sure to have arrived.

Marmaduke begged for permission to gallop ahead of Ewing and, with Shelby on the south, surround and rub him out. Price demurred. Delays had possibly cost him St. Louis, but he might still capture the Missouri River towns and the capital. His supporters lived in western rural areas. With them and an uprising of the Knights of the Golden Circle, Missouri might yet be won for the Confederacy and Reynolds inaugurated governor. To do this, Price must keep his army together. A few of his vedettes scouted within thirty miles of St. Louis, but the three big columns wheeled west, marching straight for Jefferson City. As they crossed and recrossed the Pacific Railroad tracks, they destroyed bridges, water tanks, and stations.

General Ewing fought delaying skirmishes with the advancing army and read, in dispatches, that General Alfred Pleasanton was coming from St. Louis to strike Price in the rear with seven thousand horse and eight cannon. Pleasanton was a regular army man trained at West Point and also in the hard schools of active service in Mexico and in the West. A veteran, fifty years old, he had participated in the big battles of the Civil War — South Mountain, Antietam, and Fredericksburg. At Chancellorsville, he had been credited with saving Hooker from complete rout. At Gettysburg, he commanded all the Union cavalry. Although Price had a larger army, Pleasanton was a dangerous man to have at Old Pap's rear. Ewing determined to delay the invaders as much as he dared.

Among the official military communications coming to Ewing as he fell back before Price's advance was a personal letter from Lancaster, Ohio. Wife Ellen wrote him, praising God that his life had been spared in the battle — and hers, too, for on that day she had borne a baby daughter. "Our dear little ones [were] perhaps never, never in such danger of being left both Fatherless and Motherless in the same day," she wrote. Then sensing the importance of the victory to her husband's political future, she added, "Your career is now onward and upward."

The general was not so sure. Order Number Eleven would hurt him with the Democrats, and Lane was still a great man among the Republicans in Kansas. There was no telling what trick the Grim Chieftain might pull next from his political bag.

XXVIII

Centralia

SHELBY was disappointed when Price wheeled west from St. Louis in October 1864. He wanted to strike the city, cross the Mississippi, and sweep through Illinois, Indiana, and Kentucky. The Knights of the Golden Circle would rise everywhere, he said, to join the liberation. Price, however, was a Missouri politician. He had brought "Governor" Reynolds to inaugurate him in Jefferson City. Knights in his own bailiwick awaited him. Hopefully the three Confederate columns — Marmaduke's, Fagan's, and Shelby's, all under Price — moved westward. Every twelve or fifteen miles they camped to interview and recruit young blades who craved a chivalrous life.

Price had planned with all the bushwhackers who wintered in the South to prepare Confederate sympathizers in Missouri to rise and join his invasion. He knew that many of Schofield's militiamen enrolled solely to get arms and might now fight the Union. During the winter Quantrill and Anderson had quarreled openly and separated. Bloody Bill received a commission from Price and rode North with his own gang. Only George Todd had remained with Quantrill and his men. They started back to Missouri together. After a hard ride, they were irritable when stopped by a Federal patrol, and during the skirmish which followed, Todd refused to obey Quantrill's orders. The two parted on the field. Quantrill sought the company of Kate Clarke. Todd, who had a commission like Anderson's, trotted away with fifty trusted gunmen for a summer's freebooting until Price arrived.

Price had urged all guerrillas to attract attention from his advance by fomenting disturbances north of the Missouri River and thus draw troops away from his columns. He urged them to cut all transportation lines and

destroy bridges. The rich landowners up there had been proslavery sympathizers since Kansas days. Many of them had ridden as Border Ruffians.
With the coming of the Civil War, local employees of the Northern Missouri Railroad quit work rather than take the oath. Many had joined
ranger bands as Sam Clemens and Absalom Grimes had done, and eventually went south to enlist or become bushwhackers. Paroled after various
defeats, those who came home could surely be counted on to fight again
for revenge.

On September 27, 1864, as Price fought Ewing at Pilot Knob, and Stand
Watie distributed his Cabin Creek loot, Bill Anderson rode into Centralia,
fifty miles north of Jefferson City, with a hard-faced following of bushwhackers — many of them reckless and insolent boys in their teens and
twenties. He had recently captured a wagon train near Rockport in the
extreme northwest corner of Missouri, getting thirty thousand rounds of
ammunition and bounteous rations. Federal soldiers were congregating
to catch him up there when, to everybody's surprise, he appeared at Centralia, considerably over two hundred miles away. With him rode assorted
gangs of gunmen under solemn George Todd, John Thrailkill with the
curled and perfumed hair, and Dave Pool, the little, bearded joker. From
Linn County, one Holtzclaw brought his gang. With Anderson's men
rode Frank James and his brother Jesse, a narrow-faced, blue-eyed veteran,
now in his seventeenth year. At 11 A.M. the four-horse stage from Columbia rolled unsuspectingly into town. The bushwhackers met it with leveled
pistols. Eight or nine occupants stepped down from the vehicle and handed
over their money and watches.

At 11:30 a train from the East chuffed into the station. Passengers
heard a volley of bullets rip the car sides. Then Anderson, in a blue military coat, black trousers, and jaunty military hat pinned up at one side,
ordered the travelers out of the train. Twenty-four unarmed soldiers with
discharges or furloughs were on board. Some of them hesitated on the
platform when they saw the assembled bushwhackers. Anderson fired his
revolver twice. Two soldiers tumbled dead between the cars, and all other
passengers, military and civilian, crowded down the steps in confused submission. Anderson ordered the soldiers to line up at one side, civilians on
the other. Ruffians with drawn pistols stood guard over all. Then Anderson, a slim handsome figure of five feet, ten inches, with black beard and

long hair inclined to curl at the ends, strode in front of the uniformed men. "You Federal soldiers have just killed six of my soldiers, scalped them and left them on the prairie," he said. "From this time forward I ask no quarter and give none. Every Federal soldier on whom I put my finger shall die like a dog. If I get into your clutches I expect death. You are all to be killed and sent to hell. That is the way every damn soldier shall be served who falls into my hands."

The Federals shouted protests, said that they had nothing to do with killing his men. They were just from Sherman's army on the other side of the Mississippi. One waved a crutch. Anderson ordered them to take off their uniforms. His men could disguise themselves in blue coats. Then Anderson turned his head, long curls waving. He ordered: "Fire."

All the soldiers fell but one who ran desperately toward the executioners, plunged through their line, darted under the cars, then under the station platform. Excited guerrillas set the station on fire and waited, with drawn pistols, until the frantic man emerged from the smoke, club in hand. He knocked down two bushwhackers before he fell, riddled with twenty balls.

Next, the raiders turned to the terrified passengers. All were ordered to deliver their watches, jewelry, and money. One young man traveling with his mother slipped a hundred dollars in greenbacks into his boot leg and handed over a few bills and change. The amount seemed small and the robber asked if he had hidden any. The young man said "No." Told that he would be searched and if funds were found, he would be shot, the chap confessed. The guerrilla slipped the money from his victim's boot and killed him. A gold watch was found in the boot of a German and he, too, was killed. The raiders found $3000 in the express car, set the train on fire, and galloped away.

Two hours later Major A. E. V. Johnson pounded breathlessly into town with three companies of soldiers. They dismounted and were tending the dead and wounded when Anderson swept back, scattering them before his pistol balls. Then the guerrillas dashed off once more. Major Johnson rallied his soldiers and followed. He found the bushwhackers bivouacked on a hillside in Fullenwider's pasture, three miles from town. The guerrillas had watched him coming along the road, knew that they outnumbered him, and decided to fight.

Johnson ordered his men to dismount. Every fourth man held horses. The other three loaded their muskets, fixed bayonets, and advanced. The guerrillas, all finely mounted, waited in line, one foot in the stirrup, one on the ground. Each was armed with three or four Colts. At the end of the line George Todd lifted his hat to Bill Anderson — the Shelby salute. Anderson lifted his to Pool. Then with a yell all swung aboard and rushed up the hill, lying low on their horses' necks. Johnson's men fired one volley overshooting the target and hitting only three men — a common mistake when shooting downhill. Next moment the horsemen were upon them, killing every soldier where he stood.

The men holding horses behind the line fled toward Centralia, some on foot, some mounted. Most of them were overtaken and killed along the road or in outhouses in town. Of a hundred and forty-seven soldiers only twenty-three survived. Major Johnson lay among the dead, said to have been shot by Jesse James. Dave Pool, capering as usual, bragged that he could walk the length of the enemy's rank on the bodies of dead soldiers without stepping on the ground. To prove his statement, he staggered along on the yielding corpses, seldom having to jump. Serious-minded Todd protested, "That's inhuman."

"Aren't they dead?" Pool grimaced. "And if they're dead I can't hurt them."

The Centralia victory was as complete and devastating as the Lawrence raid. It had been won without Quantrill. Todd and Anderson exulted over their achievement and sent their erstwhile chieftain an insulting message.

The Eve of Austerlitz

THE CENTRALIA MASSACRE augured well for the success of Price's expedition, but when ten miles from Jefferson City, Shelby reported a tragic victory. As his van came to the ford on the Osage River, the local militia fired on it. According to Shelby's report, "The swift and beautiful water was torn into foam-flakes that hurried and danced away to the sea. . . . [Shanks, the Confederate commander,] pressing on far ahead of his best and bravest . . . fell in the arms of victory — a bullet through and through his dauntless breast."

Shanks's command was given to grinning M. Jeff Thompson, sharp-faced Swamp Fox who gloried in ivory-handled pistols, brass buttons, canary vests and coffee-colored frock coats. The victory Shelby reported was complete, for the enemy militia, after their initial fire, turned their arms over to the invaders, either through fear or treachery — first fruits, perhaps, of the Golden Circle plot to deliver Missouri to the Confederacy. Could there be more to this conspiracy than was generally known?

As Price approached Jefferson City, he tried vainly to learn the number of its defenders. The failure of an uprising in town made him apprehensive. He knew that transports could steam up the Mississippi and the Missouri faster than he could march. Pleasanton must be somewhere close. Grant, now supreme commander, had sent A. J. Smith and Joseph Mower with reinforcements from the Tennessee theater. Among the incoming regiments was the notorious jayhawking Seventh Kansas. In its ranks stood a young Apollo named Bill Cody, the boy whose father had homesteaded on Salt Creek in 1854. Bill, on a drunken lark in February, had enlisted at Leavenworth.

Price's legions assembled before Jefferson City on October 7, 1864. The scant troops at Columbia, thirty-five miles north of the river, hurried to the capital's defense. Citizens up there, left to the mercy of bushwhackers, organized under self-imposed martial law. Male residents were ordered to report, with the family musket, at a newly constructed blockhouse, or be listed as rebels. Some ignored the order, loaded their movable property in wagons, and followed the soldiers. With them traipsed two or three hundred Negroes, white-eyed with terror of what Price's men might do to them. Women packed their best clothes in trunks, hoping to save them in case their houses were burned. The women themselves had little to fear from the bushwhacker code. Left in their houses alone, they congregated in little groups to sew, drink tea, and gossip.

Price's men looked eagerly at the capitol on the hill above the autumn-tinted trees. There stood the legislative hall from which Jackson and Reynolds had been expelled by Lyon in 1861. Confederate raiders had sighted that classic building every year since. Now, at last, they might occupy the city and hear the erudite "lieutenant governor" deliver his first gubernatorial inaugural with all the poetic allusions lacking in the rougher Claib Jackson's speech when he took the oath in December 1860.

Jefferson City's defenders — the number was still meager — watched the host forming in the fields south of town. Dark clouds in the west threatened rain. Against the lowering sky, majestic Price — a shining knight — rode to and fro on Bucephalus. Time and again curious citizens saw the flash of a thousand blades drawn for a charge, but no horsemen came. Throughout the night sentries watched and waited in the rain. At dawn the russet hills, the shining roads and lanes were empty. Price had gone. Pudgy "Governor" Reynolds, wet and miserable in his carriage following Price, cursed the general's timidity, and henceforth noted the commander's ineptness.

Old Pap had moved in the nick of time, for early next morning General Alfred Pleasanton rode in with his cavalry. He was a handsome middle-aged man with finely chiseled features. Sinewy and athletic, his slim figure delighted military tailors, and his trim uniform was reflected in the tidiness of his whole command. A confirmed bachelor, Pleasanton had married the service and looked for no other charmers. In place of swords, he and his staff wore whips on their wrists — a badge of the drive he demanded of himself and his men. Although outnumbered by Price, he would pound mercilessly at the rebel's rear.

On October 9, 1864, Price appeared at Boonville, forty miles above Jefferson City. The town, always pro-Southern, welcomed the invaders and delivered to them the small Federal guard whose leader was executed without trial. The Confederate liberators stacked arms, like Indian teepees, in the streets. Farmers and townsmen swarmed among the soldiers, inquiring for friends who had gone south. Brothers met and embraced, beard in beard. The ragged invaders reveled in the stores, swaggered along the sidewalks in gay and fantastic costumes. Many of them had not been in a town, slept in a bed, or eaten at a table for months. Bloody Bill Anderson jogged in from north of the river with human hair fluttering from his horse's bridle and three hundred bushwhackers in his train. Even Shelby's Iron Brigade watched these wild fellows with admiration. Supplies were plentiful and Price spent his Confederate money with lavish hands. His officers purchased the best in horseflesh and pranced along the streets displaying their mounts.

Boonville differed from much of Missouri. Elsewhere the citizens failed to greet the liberators as some Knights of the Golden Circle had predicted. A majority of the people still favored the Union, and Price could save himself only by moving. His chivalric standard attracted romantic-minded youths, however, and when his roistering horsemen left Boonville, many of the fifteen- to eighteen-year-old boys in town left with them. A few mothers complained that their sons had been "pressed" into his service, but most admitted that they went willingly, eyes aflame with enthusiasm. In a deserted street, after the last raider had gone, a soiled notebook was picked up. People turned the pages curiously and read: "wee hav plenty of corn bred and pore beefe to eat and sasafras tee to drink."

Price followed the road toward Lexington. Bill Anderson returned to the north side of the river. Panic and consternation fanned ahead of both columns. Mary Gordon, Columbia "schoolma'am," recorded her excitement in a diary. On October 15, 1864, when the courthouse bell tolled alarm — falsely — that Bloody Bill was coming, she scribbled: "It was but the work of a moment to get a bonnet and go flying" after the children. Merchants for miles around closed their stores, buried their goods, or hid them in the woods. Doctors hesitated to visit the ill. Pallbearers at one funeral were disturbed by the sound of approaching horsemen, but it was a false alarm, for Bloody Bill had ridden north by a different road. He was killed within the month. In his pockets were found $300 in gold, $150 in treasury notes, and several written orders from Price — a blot on the general's benevolent character, always.

As Price moved westward toward Lexington, traversing ninety miles of twisting hilly roads, the telegraph wires east of Independence were cut. Kansas City, Leavenworth, Atchison, Lawrence, Topeka, and all farming areas of eastern Kansas speculated blindly on their fate. Visions of many more Lawrence massacres haunted every hamlet. The Department of Kansas was commanded by Samuel Curtis, placed there by Lincoln to atone for his removal from Missouri. Curtis met the looming emergency by establishing martial law and urging Governor Carney to mobilize as militia all able-bodied men, black and white, from sixteen to sixty.

Governor Carney was busy with the last days of his campaign for re-election against Lane's candidate, the veteran Samuel Crawford, but he stopped long enough to issue a mobilization order. The call was answered by more than ten thousand farmers and mechanics — as unsoldierly an army as had risen to defend their homes since the days of the American Revolution, according to one volunteer. These militiamen were commanded by George Deitzler. Sam Walker and "Colonel" Harvey both led regiments. A battalion of conscripted Negroes marched under Richard J. Hinton, the Scotsman. Blunt had arrived with the Second Colorado and Sixteenth Kansas from the plains. He was eager to lead the way into Missouri and fight the enemy in their own country.

The military excitement came at a time when the Grim Chieftain's political campaign had turned sour. Lane himself broke under the mounting disapproval, becoming ill in bed at the Mansion House in Leavenworth. Voters still wanted to "elect old abe," but Lane had become a stumbling block. He could still provoke laughter with stories about his Platonic affinity for the ladies. The "bhoys" cheered the crass manner in which he claimed to have stimulated Lawrence intellectuals with his knowledge of Latin by glibly repeating, *"e pluribus unum," "ne plus ultra,"* and *"multum in parvo."* But political savants shook their heads, said Lane's sands were running out. They were sure that the majority of voters backed the Carney and Robinson faction. Lincoln might be defeated in Kansas next fortnight.

The political campaign was interrupted by a flood of news about Price's triumphal advance toward Kansas. All Missouri was said to be flocking to his standard for a Border Ruffian invasion of a magnitude never known before. Politician Lane saw an opportunity to retrieve his fortunes. Exchanging his sickbed for a buggy, he whipped away to Wyandotte, crossed the Kaw to Kansas City, drove to Independence and down to Hickman's Mills. There was no question about the impending danger: What an opportunity for him to regain his popularity by becoming the minuteman who saved Kansas!

Lane mounted the stump with fiery energy. Why did Governor Carney keep the militia idly waiting in Kansas? Let the battle be fought on enemy territory! Carney newspapers branded the alarm as political demagoguery, a trick to get anti-Lane voters out of Kansas on election day. Carney politicians visited the militia camps, burned Lane in effigy, paraded a donkey labeled "Blunt," and urged the men to disobey orders to cross into Missouri.

In the political confusion some Kansas militia regiments remained on the border, others crossed. Senator Lane rode with Blunt, at the head of the Second Colorado and Sixteenth Kansas, all the way to Lexington, marching into this once wealthy Missouri town ahead of Price. They expelled a company of local bushwhackers who were preparing to welcome the Confederates. Blunt and Lane marched another twenty miles along the road toward Waverly, Shelby's home town. Here they met M. Jeff Thompson, leading Price's van, and opened fire — the first shots in a week-long running battle through a hundred and fifty miles of western Missouri.

In the opening days of the battle, Price's column marched parallel to the Missouri, his right wing protected by the river. Behind him Pleasanton followed with a smaller number of cavalry. On Price's left flank came A. J. Smith's veterans and a rough regiment from the District of Southwest Missouri under Colonel John E. Phelps — son of Congressman John S. Phelps, whose farm near Springfield had been ravaged periodically by invading Confederates. One of Phelps's men, Wild Bill Hickok, was riding as a spy in Price's column. In front of Price, Blunt's brigade harried his advance skirmishers but constantly fell back.

Thus Price was surrounded, with inferior numbers of enemies on three sides and the Missouri River on his right. Directly ahead of him stood Independence, Kansas City, and Westport, practically undefended except for Blunt's two regiments, unless Curtis had mustered enough soldiers in his Department of Kansas to come over in Rosecrans's bailiwick. Price was confident that he could outride Pleasanton, sideswipe Smith and Phelps, and overpower Blunt. His main uncertainty was Curtis, whose natural slowness seemed to be increasing with his age. Moreover, Curtis had never regained full confidence in himself since Lincoln had removed him for his inability to get along with Governor Gamble. Now Curtis was caught again in a similar situation. Would Governor Carney be as jealous with his militia as Gamble had been?

Price marched rapidly toward Independence, kicking Blunt's little force ahead of him. Ten miles from town Old Pap rested in a roadside meadow as his men streamed past. (He always lay on a carpet sipping a toddy, according to "Governor" Reynolds's jaundiced recollections.) A squad of horsemen came up the road counter to the marching column, and turned into the field where he rested. The sullen-faced leader spoke a few words to Price's orderly and strode toward the general, reporting that his prisoners were from Lawrence, Kansas. Price noticed something familiar about the captain's dull features and asked, "Who are you, young man?"

"I am George Todd," the captain replied. His prisoners winced. They knew Todd to be a man who never brought in prisoners alive.

"Are you Captain Todd?" Price asked, for he had commissioned a bushwhacker by that name.

"Yes, sir," Todd said, then turned to his prisoners, told them to dismount and go before the general. Todd and his companions rode off with their horses — the last ever seen of these animals and of Todd, too, except his dead body.

Price queried the prisoners, asked how many men were ahead of him and their plan of battle. The prisoners said that the opposing army was led by Generals Blunt, Jennison, and Tom Moonlight — a Kansan who had distinguished himself as a captain with one cannon at Dry Wood in September 1861. These men intended to make a stand on the Little Blue, a stream east of Independence, flowing north into the Missouri. Behind them, between the Big Blue and the Kansas line, Curtis had his department volunteers and the newly mustered Kansas militia under George Deitzler, totaling twenty-eight thousand men — almost three times Price's own force. Price did not believe it and asked a breakdown of the number. When told that seventeen thousand — an exaggeration — were Kansas militia, he said so young a state could not raise so many. The prisoners assured him that they knew the number and that the first fight would be at the Little Blue, the second on Big Blue just outside Kansas City.

Price dismissed the prisoners and ordered his army to strike at the Little Blue. The weather turned cold and misty. Through the fog his sentries found the Union forces concentrated as he had been told. Shelby drove them from the Little Blue crossings, and Price's superior numbers pushed them back into Independence. Fighting block by block for four hours, the Confederates cleared the town. This was Price's first severe battle since Pilot Knob. His kinsman John T. Hughes, ex-clerk in the Kansas "bogus" legislature, who had been with him since Wilson's Creek and Lexington, was killed. The bushwhacker George Todd also fell here. Farm boys, who had enlisted for glamor a few days before, died in the muddy streets, but the survivors could joke about the antics of excited commanders. Colonel Casper Bell was one such officer. He was known to his men as a rural parson who strengthened his faith in the Lord with bourbon whiskey, and chewed tobacco while he preached. Before delivering a prayer, he was wont to spit copiously, then lift his head, close his eyes, and begin. In the clang of battle he delighted his men with a vocabulary of unchurchly profanity.

Blunt's men, fighting as they backed through Independence, and Curtis, waiting at the Big Blue, and Deitzler, with the militia at the state line, all knew that Pleasanton was coming to help them, but they had no direct communication with him. Curtis, with his engineering skill, had constructed breastworks along the ridge west of the Big Blue from Byram's Ford to the Missouri River. West of the ford, where the road traversed a hollow leading to the rolling country south of Kansas City, he had felled trees so that their branches pointed downhill. The limbs had been sharpened to impale soldiers advancing against them. Thus, Curtis hoped to halt Price at the Big Blue. Then if Pleasanton would strike quickly from the rear, the Confederates could be trapped between the Big and Little Blues. Deitzler's raw militia might even consent to cross the state line and fight behind the breastworks.

To explain this plan to Pleasanton, a message must be sent across Price's army to him. One of Deitzler's men, Daniel W. Boutwell, volunteered to float down the Missouri at night, pass Price's right wing and climb out in Pleasanton's lines. The project seemed feasible and he set off after dark in a boat, drifted onto a sandbar, climbed out on the south bank — not into Pleasanton's lines as he hoped, but into a party of Blunt's soldiers who had been pinched off from their regiment by Price's advance. These men were hiding in the woods and hoped eventually to be picked up by Pleasanton. In order to increase the chance of escape, Boutwell separated from them before dawn, slunk over the hills and fields, eluded Price's rear guard, was challenged by and admitted to the advancing Federal lines. He asked to be taken before Pleasanton. The army had halted for a morning rest, and the bedraggled soldier was taken to the immaculate West Pointer. Pleasanton listened to the man's story. Convinced of its truthfulness, he snapped a crisp order. Bugles piped "Boots and Saddles." The call rang down the road. Other bugles picked it up far out in the fields. The distant figures of horsemen in formation, each troop with a fluttering guidon, trotted to assigned positions on the march. If Price was being held at Independence, he might be trapped and crushed to death this afternoon.

Price, however, had not been stopped as planned. Elderly General Curtis lacked the necessary tenacity. He distrusted the Kansas militia, feared that Governor Carney — jealous of Lane — might recall them at any time. This Curtis was a different man from the victor of Pea Ridge. As Blunt and Jennison were pushed out of Independence, they retreated slowly through Curtis's defenses west of the Big Blue. Jennison's Fourth Kansas Cavalry was assigned to hold the abatis at Byram's Ford against the enemy.

Shelby's cavalry were the first of Price's van to reach Curtis's line. The Iron Knight surveyed the defenses along the ridge as far as he could see toward the Missouri River. Probing south up the Big Blue, he encountered the abatis at Byram's Ford and pronounced it impregnable. Galloping farther upstream, he came to the end of the Federal line, splashed across the creek, and rode down the ridge on Jennison's flank.

The Kansan was caught with his elaborate defenses in the wrong place. He withdrew, and with him went all the troops along the ridge. Shelby took possession of the abatis. Marmaduke, Fagan, and the Confederate wagon train forded unmolested and rumbled up the hollow among the felled trees — a good defense now to stop Pleasanton when he came. Far to the north, in the bare trees along Brush Creek just south of Westport and Kansas City, Curtis formed another line. His new position extended around Westport and stopped at the Kansas border where the companies of Deitzler's militia who had not crossed into Missouri were massed to defend their state.

Price could have swung his column to the south now and started for Arkansas in good order, but Shelby urged a quick thrust at Curtis, then an about-face to knock out Pleasanton when he reached Byram's Ford. Napoleon might have done this successfully. Why not Shelby and Price?

Old Pap ordered his wagon train to turn south on the road, be safe in case of a general retreat and accessible in case of victory. Marmaduke remained to defend the ford. Shelby and Fagan marched north across the rolling plateau. The short October afternoon allowed only a few more hours of daylight. Curtis retreated before the advancing Confederates and made a new stand north of Brush Creek at dusk. Shelby's division bivouacked on the wooded crest south of the creek, with M. Jeff Thompson's brigade at the extreme west in sight of the lights in Westport. General Price established headquarters at Old Boston Adams's farmhouse. His generals rode in during the night to caution him about the danger of an attack and the advantage of retreating in the morning — all but Shelby, who fired the white-haired patriot's spirits, convinced him that a fight would be successful. With Price's promise for a general offensive at dawn, Shelby galloped happily through the dark to his men's bivouac on the wooded ridge south of Brush Creek. The night was frosty and the soldiers huddled close around fires. Those on sentry duty warmed their hands against their horses' bodies. Shelby dismounted and lay down, his back to a tree, for a wink of sleep, his goateed chin sunk deep in upturned coat collar. Napoleon had rested so on the eve of Austerlitz. Or had he?

X X X

The Battle of Westport

DURING THE NIGHT of October 22, 1864, Brigadier General Jennison, Colonel Moonlight, and Lieutenant Colonel Plumb moved detachments of Kansans along the state line from Westport south to below the Shawnee Mission — the red brick buildings already sacred in the struggle for a free Kansas. The veterans of Lexington and Independence mingled contemptuously with the militia who had remained timidly near the state line. In the darkness they could hear Shelby's troops moving into new positions for tomorrow's offensive. Sporadic rifle fire flashed red in the night where venturesome pickets clashed.

Many of the Kansas militiamen were strangers to war. Others had seen service in the political skirmishes of territorial days. Among these was J. S. Reader, a Kansas dirt farmer who had marched with Harvey and his "forty thieves," fought with them at Hickory Point in 1856, but since that time had taken little part in politics or war. That summer campaign had been a picnic compared to this one with its cold rain almost every day and no tents to shelter the men on their march from Topeka to the Shawnee Mission. Now they were more comfortable in pup tents, but they did not feel like soldiers. All of them had reported for duty in their work clothes, and on the march each man wore a sprig of sumac in his hat. This made them feel more like an army in uniform. At night strolling Negroes entertained some of the men with capers, jokes, and tricks around the campfires, but hardships kept most of the soldiers growling. Tonight, on the eve of battle, they were all hungry. Wagons with rations were promised before dawn. In the distance, over Independence way, the unhappy militiamen could hear Pleasanton bombarding Price's rear. The dull booms lasted until midnight. "I'd rather hear the baby cry," Private J. S. Reader heard one man say. The fellow admitted being scared and said he expected to be killed in the morning. Reader tried to reassure him that the future state was probably better than this one.

"Well, I don't know about that," the man replied.

Reader wondered why he himself was out here in the cold. He had responded to the draft because everybody else did. Personally, he was uninterested in Lane's political maneuvers and would rather be back on his farm than dead on a Missouri battlefield. To build his own morale for tomorrow's fight, he unrolled a clean shirt from his clothes sack and put it on.

During the night all Federal officers of brigadier rank or higher congregated in the Gillis House in Kansas City to plan tomorrow's action. Practically all the Kansas militia had moved now from two to four miles across the state line, and Governor Carney had become ridiculous for claiming the invasion to be a political scheme of Lane's, but his continued outcry had permanently shaken General Curtis's confidence. In the afternoon and evening, as Price's men swarmed up from Byram's Ford, Curtis had ordered his wagon train to retreat to Fort Leavenworth, and even some units of his line south of Kansas City and Westport were withdrawing, while the Kansas militia watched them go. Militia officers had overtaken General Curtis, driving north. At their insistence he came back for a council of war in order that all might co-operate. In a private parlor of the hotel Senator Lane, General Blunt, Captain Crawford (the candidate for governor), and a half dozen more were waiting for him. They persisted in fighting to save Kansas City and Westport. Curtis complained, said he had but four thousand trained men. The sixteen thousand militia under Deitzler — being state troops — might refuse to obey his orders. (This was eight thousand less than Price had been told was ahead of him, but with Pleasanton's force the number was close.) How could a general be expected to fight with such an assortment? Rugged old Curtis looked tired and unkempt.

The Lane men were furious. Kansas would be overrun, with ample defenders marching away from the fight. They urged and pleaded, but Curtis displayed the stubbornness of old age. At two in the morning some of the officers took Blunt to the other end of the room and whispered that there was but one thing to do: Disregard Curtis's superior rank, put him under arrest, and assume command.

"Gentlemen, that is a serious thing to do." Blunt had been in trouble twice for precipitous acts, and he was not seeking any office in next month's election.

"Yes," candidate Crawford replied, "but not so serious as for this army to run away like cowards and let Price sack Kansas City and devastate southern Kansas," ("and keep me from being elected governor," he might have added).

"Will the army stand by me?" Blunt asked.

"Yes, and we will stand by you while making the arrest."

Blunt turned and walked toward massive General Curtis, who was still arguing with Senator Lane. "General Curtis," — Blunt spoke with the positive tone of a man used to command — "what do you propose to do?"

Curtis turned his large dish-face down to Blunt's upturned terrier profile. From under his shaggy eyebrows Curtis saw the determined countenances of the officers around him. For a moment he seemed uncertain. The loss of a son and a daughter and the reprimand from Lincoln had shaken his usual determination. "General Blunt," he said, "I will leave the whole matter to you. If you say fight, then fight it is."

The officers all turned happily on their heels and soon the patter of horses' hoofs could be heard as the commanders galloped through the night to their respective positions.

Over at Independence, on this same night, General Pleasanton established his headquarters and rested after a hard day's fight through the town, having given Price the first reverse on his expedition. Pleasanton's Third Brigade under General John B. Sanborn had endured the brunt of the day's battle. Before retiring, Pleasanton ordered Colonel E. F. Winslow of the Fourth Brigade to take over and pound Price until midnight, forcing him across the Big Blue. At dawn General Egbert B. Brown with the First Brigade was to relieve Winslow, cross Byram's Ford and push the enemy to the top of the hollow. Brown had lost one arm in action. His men believed that he had never thoroughly regained his nerve, but he saluted dutifully and rode off with his men. Pleasanton's next problem was to flank Byram's Ford and isolate Price's wagon train beyond. For this he selected General John McNeil, a man who knew the country well. The assignment was distasteful to him, but he could say nothing. The enemy blamed him for killing some prisoners and had sent word that if captured, he would be shot without trial. McNeil saluted as Brown had done and rode away.

On the morning of Sunday, October 23, 1864, Pleasanton mounted his horse and with his staff and resplendent general's flag rode from Independence toward Byram's Ford to see how well General Brown had obeyed his orders. Sitting on the ground near Brown, Colonel John F. Phillips of the Seventh Missouri State Cavalry was changing from boots to shoes for the charge across the ford when Pleasanton thundered down the road.

Phillips had never seen Pleasanton before and turned his head to watch curiously. The slim, handsome veteran commander halted his horse in front of General Brown, shook his cowhide whip in Brown's face, and with a volley of oaths demanded to know the reason why his division had not moved forward at dawn as ordered.

General Brown saluted with his one good arm and replied that Colonel Winslow's men had blocked the road ahead.

"You are an ambulance soldier and you belong in the rear," Pleasanton retorted. The general and his ranking colonel, James McFerran, were ordered under arrest. Then Pleasanton shouted: "Who is next in command here?"

Nearby officers indicated Colonel Phillips.

"Where is he?" Pleasanton barked.

"Here I am," the sock-footed colonel replied.

"What are you doing down there on the ground?"

"I am getting ready to lead my men into that fight down there."

"If you want a fight you shall have it," Pleasanton called. "You take charge of this entire brigade and go down there and put those people out."

Pleasanton neck-reined his horse to one side and, raising his whip, cantered away hunting General McNeil, who, like Brown, had not pushed forward on schedule. He, too, was arrested on the field and sent to the rear.

Colonel John F. Phillips remounted his horse, put two lieutenant colonels in charge of each regiment in his brigade, placed a battery to shell the abatis across the river, and by eight o'clock started down toward Big Blue and the ford. Balls from Marmaduke's men chipped the leafless trees around his advancing men. Phillips's horse had never been under fire, and the colonel felt the animal's heart beat between his knees. At the ford the stream ran breast high. The men crossed holding their rifles and cartridge boxes above their heads. Phillips splashed through on horseback. A shell exploded in the water behind him, blowing a horse and rider to shreds of flesh and putrescence. The colonel felt sick and had to steady himself in the saddle.

Ahead, the road up the hollow seemed impassable through the abatis. Marmaduke's sharpshooters fired at every man who exposed himself. Phillips ordered his men to lie flat under the bristling stakes, while details went back for axes. Then he checked the range with his artillerymen and ordered a barrage. Behind this wall of fire his men chopped paths through the impediments. The honor of charging up the road to the top was given to Lieutenant Colonel Thomas Crittenden. Marmaduke's sharpshooters, in a cabin on the rim, picked off the advancing officers. Crittenden ordered his men to advance on hands and knees, stop for breath behind stumps and hillocks while rear companies fired volleys at the cabin and surrounding works.

In the tumult a private ran back with the information that Crittenden had been killed. Colonel Phillips strode up the hill to investigate and take command. Among the stumps and roadside gullies sprawled the dead and wounded. Phillips recognized a captain with the back of his head blown off. The colonel took some letters from his pocket, one addressed to his fiancée. Farther up the road Phillips came to a lieutenant with his breast torn open to the lungs. The young man tried to salute as he slumped into a heap. Beyond him Crittenden lay on the ground, face white as death, hand clutching his side. The colonel ripped open the blouse and shirt. He saw a black spot on the man's stomach, but the skin was unbroken. Phillips held up Crittenden's head, poured some peach brandy into his sagging lips, saw his eyes open. A cough racked the prostrate man, color flushed his cheeks, and consciousness returned. A richocheting bullet had punctured his vest pocket, striking a leather wallet filled an inch thick with shinplaster money. The paper stopped the ball, but the impact had knocked the lieutenant colonel senseless. He soon stood up and stumbled after his men to the head of the hollow where they had stopped, having gained their objective.

The victorious Union Missourians looked west across the rolling table-land between the Big Blue and the Kansas state line. Toward the south, stone fences crosshatched the farmsteads, and a brick mansion with white pillars — the "Wornall house" — stood by a road running north to Kansas City. In the fields to the west and south as far as the Federals could see stood Price's army — twenty thousand men, they estimated. As the Union soldiers gazed with wonder, Pleasanton rode up under his general's flag and watched. Pointing at the distant figures, he shouted, "Rebels, rebels, rebels, fire, fire, you damned asses."

At the northwest end of the battlefield, during the forenoon of this tumultuous Sunday, as Pleasanton's men had fought their way up the gulch from Byram's Ford against Marmaduke, Curtis had been maneuvering against Shelby and Fagan along Brush Creek. Early in the morning the general had ridden from Kansas City to Westport where he stationed himself with a telescope on the roof of the Harris House — the old pro-slavery headquarters in territorial days. Curtis's aide, Major Preston Plumb, fresh from a midnight tour of the lines, could explain the terrain of each sector. Curtis ordered a general advance across Brush Creek. The men crunched through ice, window-glass thick, and trudged into the frosted woods. Within half a mile all of them were stopped by Shelby's and Fagan's lines. Some regiments were driven back across the creek.

Curtis, scanning the tree-lined crest ahead of him and receiving reports of reverses along the line, heard — far to the southeast — Pleasanton's cannon begin their morning bombardment at Byram's Ford. Over there General Brown had just been arrested on the field, and the advance was beginning. Day before yesterday, Curtis had planned a double attack on Price, front and rear. Perhaps he could execute one today. He lowered his telescope and called for his horse. The general would lead a charge up the brushy ridge in person. This might be the decisive moment of the battle.

General Curtis rode along his own and Deitzler's lines to prepare the soldiers for a charge. An old man tottered up to his horse, said he lived in these parts and that a gulch "yender" penetrated the enemy's line. Curtis looked where the aged man pointed and ordered Blunt, with a strong force of his fighting regiments, up the hollow to flank the enemy, then notified Deitzler to prepare his entire line for an advance when Blunt's men opened fire. Curtis also invited the aged man to ride with him during the day and watch, but the patriarch declined — too old, he said.

The maneuver succeeded. Blunt emerged from the gulch with Shelby on his left and M. Jeff Thompson on his right. Having flanked both their positions, he began firing down their lines, and thus forced them to move south to the next low ridge. As they retreated, Deitzler's long line advanced through woods south of Brush Creek and occupied the vacated Confederate positions. General Curtis consulted his watch — a habit with him in battle. The time was 11 A.M.

Price saw now that these Kansas militiamen who outnumbered him two to one would fight like veterans. He learned, too, that Marmaduke was being forced back by Pleasanton in the hollow across from Byram's Ford. Price realized that Shelby's plan was failing. Instead of defeating Curtis and then turning on Pleasanton, the Confederates were losing ground on both fronts. The two Union commanders might soon join forces and, with a solid line, hit the Southerners on three sides — perhaps cut Fagan and Shelby off from Marmaduke and the wagon train. Price ordered all his divisions to concentrate for a general retreat toward the wagons on the road leading down the state line. But he had not reckoned with Jo Shelby. The goateed and poetic cavalryman did not want to retreat unless whipped and, like John Paul Jones, believed that he had not yet begun to fight. He moved his brigade south to another ridge on the rolling farm land, unlimbered his cannon, and bombarded the Federals who followed him.

Between the lines lay a sloping valley of brown, frost-killed grass. A Federal battery galloped up the north ridge, unlimbered, and opened fire on the Confederates' position. Colonel J. H. McGhee, with a regiment of Arkansas cavalry, decided to stop the Federals' impudence. In battalion front he raced across the swale to capture the guns. Colonel Jennison saw him coming. He turned to Captain Curtis Johnson and ordered him, with Company E of the Fifteenth Kansas Cavalry and a squadron of the Second Colorado under Captain Green, to countercharge. Let horse meet horse on the open sloping prairie — one of those chivalric displays seldom seen in real battle. As the two lines charged, Johnson and McGhee singled out each other. With poised revolvers both fired. Johnson was hit in the arm,

McGhee through the heart. The two lines of riders clashed, shooting and slashing. Then the Arkansans spurred back to the protection of Shelby's lines — all except the dead and badly wounded.

Vastly outnumbered now, with Fagan, Marmaduke, and Price all hurrying south with the wagon train on the Little Santa Fe road, Shelby and M. Jeff Thompson retreated once more to stand on the ridge beyond. It was their men and Marmaduke's whom Pleasanton saw when he swore at his men: "Rebels, rebels, rebels, fire, fire, you damned asses."

Shelby discovered Pleasanton on his right flank when it was almost too late. Marmaduke was out of sight now, and from the west, Colonel Moonlight galloped in to completely surround him. Stone fences two miles away promised cover. Shelby ordered his men to mount and fly. His wounded — who had been placed in the brick Wornall mansion, while the womenfolk cowered in the cellar — were abandoned. Shelby himself barely got away, hatless, six-shooter in hand, long sandy hair waving in the wind. At the stone walls he dismounted again and stood the enemy off until dark, then slipped away. Eight hundred of his best men lay behind him on those brown fields.

Thus ended the battle of Westport, biggest Civil War engagement west of the Missouri with over 29,000 men in the field — 20,000 Federals, 9000 Confederates. Both commanding generals — Curtis and Price — lacked their usual spirit and resolution. At no time did Price have more than a third of his men in action. Subordinate Generals Marmaduke, Shelby, Pleasanton, Blunt, and Jennison fought desperately. The only western battles comparable in point of numbers engaged were Pea Ridge with 26,700, Prairie Grove, with 24,000, Lexington with 21,000, and Wilson's Creek with 15,575. In every one of these engagements, except Pea Ridge, the army with the greatest number won the victory — a commentary on Curtis's generalship when at his best. Thomas Ewing, Jr., in St. Louis, now out of the political race and hurt because he had not received the recognition he felt due for Pilot Knob, wrote his wife Ellen:

> You see Price is making for Kansas. Look out for outrageous lying dispatches from Lane, Blunt, Carney and co. They have each a pack of most [*undecipherable*] and scoundrelly liers that ever filtered filth through a goose quill: who tag after them to make cowardice appear courage, disasters victories, and skirmishes decisive battles.

X X X I

Retreat from Moscow

ON THE NIGHT of October 23, 1864, after the battle of Westport, Generals Curtis and Pleasanton met for the first time. The conference was held in a farmhouse behind Price's retreating column. Pleasanton was ill. Outside, in the dark, both Union armies bivouacked in the rain — some had forged ahead for miles on Price's trail. Pleasanton's men complained with pride that they had eaten nothing since Saturday noon, October 21, that the water dripping from their hat brims and running into their beards provided poor refreshment.

October 24 dawned wet and blustery. A dozen regiments streamed down the road in a column fifteen miles long. Curtis and Pleasanton rode in the same ambulance, but their armies jostled jealously for position on the march. Colonel Moonlight, with the Second Kansas Brigade, struck off independently down the state line, intent on reaching and defending Fort Scott in case Price headed for that depot. Blunt, with his veteran First Brigade, followed Price. Beside him, to the east, rode the hero of Byram's Ford, Colonel John Phillips, at the head of Pleasanton's column.

Price's army marched in four parallel columns — compact, hard to cut, easy to defend, and disciplined with despair. Crossing the state line into Kansas, Phillips's brigade harried Price's rear for half the night. At dawn, October 25, Old Pap ordered Marmaduke to deploy on a prairie below the Marais des Cygnes — the "Mary Dasun," one of the soldiers called it in his journal.

Phillips's men, tired, sleepy and munching raw field corn, blundered into Marmaduke's lines and opened fire. The Confederates fell back fighting. As they retreated, Blunt rode in with two regiments — both tired after two nights' bivouac in a cold rain, but eager to knock out the enemy.

Seeing Phillips's troops on the vacated field, Blunt was furious. Why had the Missourians crossed into the Department of Kansas to steal a battle from the soldiers who belonged there?

As the Union commanders glared at each other, Price moved, in good order, down the road. Phillips and Blunt both rested their exhausted men. A few miles south of them Price decided to stop and form again for battle. He selected a site on Mine Creek where the tree-bordered stream crossed an open prairie — ideal for a cavalry engagement. North of the stream Marmaduke deployed his division in line. South of him, in the open country beyond the creek, Fagan's division formed a second line of defense. ·

Samuel Crawford, with a small party of men, had shadowed Price and now watched the Confederates form for battle — the first to be waged between regular troops on Kansas soil. As candidate for governor in the impending election, Crawford determined to take an active part, and waited on the open prairie for Union soldiers to arrive. The first to come was Colonel Phillips, with his two tired regiments from Pleasanton's column. They deployed slowly in battle line. Crawford waited, looking for Blunt. Some of Deitzler's militia arrived, but still no Blunt. Crawford suspected that the black-headed scrapper was sulking because Pleasanton's men had struck ahead of him on the Marais des Cygnes.

Finally, Crawford became convinced that Blunt was not coming. He rode over to talk to Colonel Phillips. "I never like to be fired upon," he said; "let's charge them." The leading regiment was ready, and away they went. Accounts differ about the details of the ensuing events. Crawford described the action on many a hustings in the years to come as a spectacular cavalry charge with the two lines riding as though on parade. Marmaduke's line, he said, was not parallel to the oncoming Federals. The two struck first at one end. Then, like closing shears, the clash of steel rang down the ranks — a rip tide of wielded sabers.

Other participants saw the melee with more confused eyes — the Federals charging in column of regiments, bugles blowing, guidons crackling, the whole brigade a swirling chaos, men fighting on horse and on foot, slashing and shooting, all semblance of military lines lost in the turmoil. Many of Marmaduke's men retreated through the Mine Creek tree belt, falling over one another on the trails in a panic to reach Fagan's deployed line. In the confusion Marmaduke's saddle horse became unmanageable, threw its rider, and galloped away, head held on one side, reins flying. Deitzler's advancing militia became as confused as the cavalry. Private J. S. Reader, of Topeka, found himself alone. He heard distant shooting and saw men running all about him. Not knowing which way to go, he wrote his name on a piece of paper, pinned it in his drawers, and walked in the direction he believed toward home. Private James Dunlavy, Company D, Third Iowa, noticed a big, farmerish Confederate in rain-streaked blue jeans and leveled his gun at him. The portly man held up his pistol by the barrel with one arm. The other arm hung limp and wounded. Dunlavy disarmed and marched the big captive back up the road, inquiring the way to General Curtis's headquarters. He found the commander in his ambulance, reported that his prisoner claimed to be Major General Marmaduke.

General Curtis looked from under his shaggy eyebrows at the captive. "How much longer have you to serve?" he asked Private Dunlavy.

"Eight months, sir."

The general turned to his adjutant. "Give Private Dunlavy a furlough for eight months," he ordered. The proud Iowa boy saluted and strode off with Marmaduke's belt and sword for souvenirs. Brigadier General Cabell, four colonels, a thousand men, and ten pieces of artillery had also been captured.

When Crawford — according to his account — saw Marmaduke's line disintegrate, he rallied as many of his Kansans as he could find and with Phillips's two disciplined regiments, crossed Mine Creek to where Fagan stood on the prairie a thousand yards beyond. Candidate Crawford felt sure that Fagan's line would crumple as Marmaduke's had done. Colonel Phillips was willing to risk another assault. But he noticed the haggard condition of his men and their mounts, so he ordered them to deploy slowly and rest along the tree border of Mine Creek. Let the horses eat grass for a few minutes. While the men waited, a courier from Pleasanton arrived with an order for Phillips to recall his troopers.

Crawford, with his handful of Kansans who had remained in formation, watched Phillips's brigade retreat north as Marmaduke's retreated south. Unwilling to admit defeat, Crawford followed the Confederates cautiously. He saw Shelby replace Marmaduke as rear guard, and form line after line of defense as the column moved away. Across the Little

Osage, the road forked. The west branch led to Fort Scott, twenty miles beyond. The east branch went back into Missouri. At the dividing of the ways Price formed for another stand. His legions appeared ragged and exhausted, standing there on the dreary plain under lowering storm clouds.

As Crawford watched, Blunt's column came in sight, but instead of stopping, the grim little commander marched along the Fort Scott road without turning his head toward the enemy — in plain sight only a half mile away. Behind Blunt, Crawford saw Pleasanton's guidons, the headquarters flag of the commanding general, a long file of prisoners, and the ten captured guns. This column, too, followed the Fort Scott road, oblivious to Price's entire army standing miserable as wet sheep on the eastern sky line.

The gubernatorial candidate galloped back up the road hunting Curtis. He was sure that a final display of force would win the surrender of Price's entire army. Only one thing needed to be done now: Order Blunt and Pleasanton to wheel and surround him. Curtis listened to Crawford's description of the situation and from his ambulance dispatched a courier to overtake the generals with an order to turn and fight. Rain had begun to fall as this rider reached the columns. Both generals refused to obey and splashed on toward Fort Scott. Their men had been fighting almost continually for three days with little food. Tired troopers, drenched to the skin, nodded in their saddles. Pleasanton sent back a surgeon's certificate declaring his men physically unable to remain in the field. Four hours later, when they arrived at Fort Scott and unsaddled, the men toppled, sound asleep, on the wet ground beside their gear. Pleasanton, however, was sufficiently awake to telegraph the press that he had captured Marmaduke, thus giving credit for the victory to himself and Rosecrans.

Curtis arrived at the fort in a huff. He insisted that the prisoners, captured in his department, be sent to Leavenworth. Pleasanton wanted them sent to St. Louis. The two commanders quarreled. Volunteer soldiers, resting and drying their clothes in the mud, complained that the generals were more concerned about the bushwhacker than they were about the comfort of their own men. The quarrel over prisoners soon extended itself into mutual accusations of negligence for bypassing Price's army — censures that would last for years. Certainly the Confederates had been on the edge of collapse, for the poetic Shelby reported officially:

The fight was to be made now, and General Price, with the pilot's wary eye, saw the storm-cloud sweep down, growing larger and larger and darker and darker. . . . The fate of the Army hung upon the result, and our very existence tottered and tossed in the smoke of strife. The red sun looked down upon the scene, and the redder clouds floated away with angry sullen glare. Slowly, slowly my old brigade was melting away.

When the disintegrating brigade was left to itself by the retreating Federals, Price ordered four hundred of his wagons burned. Then he exploded all excess ammunition and, in a drizzling rain, started on a sixty-one-mile forced march. The road behind him was strewn with guns and clothing. Men deserted by battalions. Exhausted survivors bivouacked the second night in the fields around friendly Carthage. A few of them remembered driving Sigel from this village in the sizzling July days of 1861. The villagers still hated the "Dutch" as much as ever. "I don't know that a longer march graces history," one trooper scrawled in his journal, "a fatal day for horse flesh." Another wrote: "No bread for 6 days."

The Kansas militia, after pursuing Price so bravely, returned home from Fort Scott and adjacent encampments to vote. Kansas elected Samuel Crawford governor, with a legislature pledged to return Lane to the Senate. Abraham Lincoln was the state's choice for President. Crawford went back to Topeka, hung up his sword, and told fellow citizens: "General Price, like Napoleon from Moscow, faced the November storms and jogged along southward, wrapped in thoughts of the wreckage occasioned by his indiscretion."

General Curtis, freed at last from political soldiers, became himself again. Always at his best on the march, he overtook Price at Newtonia, Missouri. Here Old Pap held back the Federal Army for three hours. During the fighting Blunt noticed a great cloud of dust south of town. Suspecting the Confederates to be retreating, he galloped around to flank them but found himself cut off by Shelby and barely fought his way out to a relief unit from Pleasanton's column. Those Iron Horsemen were a match even for Blunt's Coloradoans. In the confusion Wild Bill Hickok, who had been spying in Price's lines during the entire raid, slipped into the Federal lines.

Marching on down the wire road, the Union boys gloated as they swung past the battlefield of Pea Ridge — covered now with a skiff of snow. Elk Horn Tavern had burned. Here was the scene of Curtis's great triumph. No other commander west of the Missouri had won a comparable battle. Here rolled the fields below the bristling ridge. Here Curtis had smelled horse sweat and saddle soap as he watched the enemy's lines dissolve. "Victory, victory," he had shouted, forgetting himself. Sight of the battlefield revived another forgotten memory. The great triumph had been tempered by news of the fatal illness of his "dear Sadie."

South of Pea Ridge, Curtis's army marched through Cross Hollows. His other army of victorious soldiers had feasted here on captured Louisiana game chickens. Great times then and now! At Fayetteville the Federal garrison reported that Price's army had circled the town without stopping to fight, and was still streaming westward on the wire road, less than ten miles away. Following them through the rich farming country toward the battleground of Prairie Grove, the Federals foraged and feasted, as they had always done, on apples, beef, pork, and sorghum.

Price's men also foraged and rested for a day at Cane Hill. Confederate soldiers wrote in their journals that they received the first corn here for horse and man since leaving Independence, the first issue of salt, also. Price's Arkansas conscripts refused to march out of the state into Indian Territory and deserted by regiments. Told that the pursuing Federals would kill them on sight, they disappeared into the Boston Mountains rather than remain longer in ranks.

General Curtis feared that Price might strike at Fort Smith as he retreated, for the Confederate still had a formidable army, but Old Pap did not even dare cut south across the Federal line of communications between Fort Smith and Little Rock. His one idea was escape. At the Arkansas River, in Indian Territory, friendly red men supplied bear grease for him to calk boats and cross the stream. Curtis followed to the riverbank and called a halt. Beyond stretched the interminable plains, dreary now under tawny grass. To construct new boats would consume enough time for Price to reach Texas or the enemy lines in Arkansas. The exultant Federals fired a parting salute of twenty-four shots at the great plains beyond and turned their faces north.

Price's desolate journey across the Indian country proved to be the worst experience his men had yet suffered. Hundreds of them perished. One soldier reported marching three days without food. Another wrote that his troop ate nothing but acorns for four. A fat pony was devoured with relish by a third company. "G-- d--- old Price" became a constant ejaculation. "We have endured more than is recorded of any soldiers in the annals of History and yet half is not felt nor told," Private J. H. P. Baker complained in his journal. Three days later he wrote that the army reminded him of the children of Israel traveling through the wilderness. "But alas! We have no cloud by day nor pillar of fire by night." Instead, the retreating Confederates heard the maniac laughter of coyotes on the inky ridges. Men who dropped out asked to have enough sticks piled over them to keep off these little wolves.

Only six thousand men survived the circle west through Indian Territory and back into the Confederate lines at Laynesport, Arkansas, where the column arrived on December 2, 1864. Price could report optimistically that he had marched fourteen hundred and fifty-four miles, fought forty-three battles, and captured great quantities of Federal supplies. He did not say that he had lost five thousand stand of arms, all his cannon, and the greater part of his army. "Governor" Reynolds released to the press a scathing criticism, accusing Price of "glaring mismanagement and distressing mental and physical military incapacity."

General Curtis rode back to Fort Leavenworth in his ambulance. On the way he learned that Rosecrans had been superseded by Grenville M. Dodge, the Iowa colonel who had fought so doggedly at Pea Ridge. Wounded in that battle, Dodge had continued to distinguish himself, fighting in the deep South until wounded again under Sherman before Atlanta. Recuperating on a visit to Grant's headquarters at City Point, Virginia, he had traveled up to Washington as Lincoln's guest, discussed with him the great ambition of his life — a transcontinental railroad — and now was assigned this western department on the edge of the plains where he hoped some day to lay the first rails.

Curtis wrote to congratulate Dodge, warning him that both of them would have trouble with horse thieves since the Missouri River had frozen. His own spare troops must be sent to re-establish the mail line to Denver. Then he learned that the people of that city had taken a drastic step to quell the plains Indians themselves. Colonel J. M. Chivington, commander of the district, had marched nine hundred volunteers across the winter plains to an Indian encampment on Sand Creek. Seven hundred Cheyenne and Arapaho had congregated forty miles below Fort Lyon — named for the martyr general. They claimed to be peaceful and denied participation in last summer's raids on the mail and stage lines. Denver settlers were not so sure. They knew that the Confederates had been contriving since 1861 to incite the plains Indians against Northern whites. George Bent, son of fur trader William Bent and the Cheyenne Owl Woman, was in the Sand Creek encampment. He was an intelligent mixblood, educated at Westport and at an academy in St. Louis. His father, a friend of Frank Blair's, had remained loyal to the North, but George had fought in the Confederate Army at Wilson's Creek and Pea Ridge. Recently he had "gone native" and fought with his mother's people against the whites on the plains. He had great influence with the "horse Indians" and his loyalty to the Union was questionable.

Colonel Chivington surprised this Indian encampment on the morning of November 29, 1864, by opening fire without warning. Several hundred men, women, and children were shot. Scores of others escaped, some to die of exposure on the plains, others to dedicate the remainder of their lives to killing white men for revenge. General Curtis's policing of the mail line thus became a major Indian war. As he prepared for the frigid midwinter expedition, newspapers printed glowing accounts of Sherman's victorious march to the sea. The nation went wild with joy. General Curtis was taken aback by the popular adulation and wrote his brother, "Sherman's success was glorious but in justice to myself not equal to my pursuit of Price in that I had a less force against a larger, won several victories and had to go as far *through a desolate country*."

In the face of such lack of appreciation of his services, elderly General Curtis asked to be relieved from the hardships of the midwinter campaign, and Lincoln complied with his request. The President did not fill his place but, instead, extended Dodge's department to include Kansas, Nebraska, and Utah — the plains country Dodge knew so well.

The reorganization of the border departments and the disintegration of Price's army had been watched from the Missouri "bresh" by Charles Quantrill, who had noted with grim satisfaction the violent deaths of his hated rivals Todd and Anderson. In spite of these dead men's boasting about Centralia, his sacking of Lawrence remained the outstanding bushwhacker victory of the war. Quantrill had a plan now to eclipse that glowing achievement. He would ride to Washington and assassinate the President. With thirty followers, disguised in blue uniforms as the Fourth Missouri Cavalry, and with forged papers of identification in his pocket, Quantrill mounted his horse Charley and rode east.

X X X I I

Epilogue

Price's retreat in 1864 ended organized Confederate resistance west of the Missouri, but bushwhacking continued almost as vigorously as ever until the end of the war. Then some of the freebooters enlisted in the Federal Army to escape prosecution. Others emigrated to the Western frontier, where they used the old pattern of riding and robbing, in new surroundings. Back in Missouri, the last of them disappeared when Jesse James was killed in St. Joseph on April 3, 1882. In the same year, his brother Frank gave himself up to Governor Thomas Crittenden, who as a colonel had led the charge up the hollow from Byram's Ford. Frank handed his gun and his belt to the governor, saying that he had taken it in fair fight at Centralia and had never since been parted from it.

Quantrill's march east to assassinate Lincoln ended in his own death. The guerrillas succeeded remarkably in their disguise as Federal cavalry. They were entertained at farmhouses, and Quantrill wrote sentimental stanzas in the memory book of at least one admiring damsel. In April 1865, news of Lincoln's assassination obliged them to abandon their mission. The thwarted guerrillas celebrated with a drinking spree: "Here's to the death of Abraham Lincoln, hoping his bones may serve in hell as a gridiron to fry Yankees on." Shortly thereafter, Quantrill's horse, Charley, was injured while being shod. His master pronounced the mishap a bad omen and, true to his premonition, Quantrill was fatally wounded on May 10, in a skirmish with Federals in Spencer County, Kentucky, fifty miles southeast of Louisville. For twenty days he tossed on a hospital bed, babbling about women. Kate Clarke inherited his property of about $500 in gold. With this she opened a fancy house in St. Louis.

General VanDorn did not survive the war. An outraged husband called on the general at his headquarters near Spring Hill, Tennessee, on May 8, 1863. In a solitary interview he shot the commander without alarming the sentry outside the building and escaped to the Union Army.

The surrender of Robert E. Lee at Appomattox on April 9, 1865, was protested by the Western forces. They cheered news of Lincoln's assassination, as Quantrill's men had done, and urged undefeated partisans to join them and continue the war on the plains. The official Confederate guard with the bullion train, accompanying Jeff Davis's retreat from Richmond, planned to enlist with E. Kirby-Smith in Texas.

The last Confederate force in the East was surrendered on May 4 in Mississippi by General Richard Taylor — son of President Zachary Taylor. On May 9 Brigadier General M. Jeff Thompson surrendered what was left of his brigade after Price's retreat. The Swamp Fox and his men had reverted to the bayous during the late winter of 1864–1865. They hid what arms and horses they had saved, and relinquished to the government three or four hundred dugout canoes.

E. Kirby-Smith and a few other ranking officers arranged to meet on May 13 with the governors of Arkansas, Louisiana, Missouri, and Texas, at Marshall, Texas, to draw up provisions for capitulation. The governor of Arkansas was too ill to attend personally. "Governor" Reynolds was too angry to sign the terms agreed upon. Shelby and a few division and brigade commanders learned about the plan of surrender and threatened to arrest Kirby-Smith unless he promised to continue the war. Kirby-Smith relinquished his command to Simon Bolivar Buckner, defender of Vicksburg, but the change did not help the recalcitrant Westerners. On May 26, 1865, Buckner went to New Orleans and surrendered the entire command "on paper" to Major General Peter J. Osterhaus, the Missouri volunteer who had shouted commands in German on the way to Wilson's Creek only four years ago.

The next problem was to force the scattered units to come in and lay down their arms. Stand Watie, Shelby, Price, Hindman, and other leaders still commanded Confederate forces. Stand Watie and a third of his nation were outlawed by his own people who had renewed their allegiance to the United States and appropriated the Confederate faction's plantations and cattle. Watie's dispossessed mixbloods — men, women, and children — had congregated along the Texas border. From here, when groceries ran low, they had been able to take a slave to town and trade him for a wagonland of supplies, but with war's end this purchasing medium became worthless. Desperate and disconsolate, Stand Watie surrendered to the United States on June 23, 1865 — probably the last Confederate to submit.

When Shelby learned of Stand Watie's surrender and Buckner's betrayal, he offered his Iron Brigade service in the Mexican civil war — although he had not consulted either of the belligerents. Five hundred of Shelby's soldiers elected to remain with him, so the commander asked them to vote for the side they wished to support — the monarchy under Maximilian or the democratic form of government under Benito Juárez. Believing in race superiority, sympathetic with slaveholding, and hating the democratic "Dutch," they voted to support the monarchy. After this decision, Shelby sold the last of his cannon to the Juárez republicans, then — before crossing the border to join the monarchists — he assembled his men on the Rio Grande near Eagle Pass on July 4, 1865, for a farewell ceremony dedicated to his unconquered battle flag. To this ritual came Generals Price and Hindman, John B. Magruder, and Missouri's Trusten Polk, who had been expelled from the Senate in 1862 as a rebel. With ruffling drums, and bugles' thrilling blasts, Shelby's tattered battle flag was lowered into the muddy water.

The recalcitrant Confederates marched to Monterrey, Mexico, where they separated — some going to Sonora, some to California, others to British Honduras and Brazil. Maximilian refused to enlist Shelby's brigade as a unit, but he did set aside a plot of land where Confederates might homestead. The veterans tried to farm, for a season, but they dreamed always of past battles and read in imported newspapers the accounts of reconstruction in their native states.

Within a year Hindman was back in Arkansas. The girl-wife he had taken from the convent school insisted on rearing her children in the United States. At his old home, a personal enemy shot him one night from outside a window. Realizing that the wound was fatal, Hindman limped on his high-heeled boot to the front gallery, delivered a speech to the crowd congregating below, forgave his enemies, and asked forgiveness for his own sins. Staggering back into the house, he kissed his wife and four small children, then sank into a chair and died. The fashionable little egotist was master of his destiny to the end — almost.

Pap Price also returned to the United States within a year. An old man now at fifty-five, broken in spirit and health, he died shortly after his return. Shelby followed him to Missouri, living quietly near his old home until the Democrats became respectable under President Cleveland in 1893. Then he was appointed United States marshal for the western district of Missouri. People looked at the quiet little gray-haired man and marveled that he had ever been a border fireball.

During the first summer after the war, Wild Bill Hickok performed a daring feat which, with the McCanles gang killing, established him as a notorious Western gunman. In southwest Missouri, he quarreled with his old friend Dave Tutt, who threatened to shoot him at sight when next he came to Springfield. Wild Bill's position in the community demanded that he accept this challenge. Soon afterward, while walking from the livery barn along one side of the courthouse square, where Lyon had ridden his gray stallion and Zagoni had mustered the survivors of his Balaclava charge, Bill spied Tutt coming toward him. Citizens edged back out of the line of fire. Wild Bill and Tutt both shot. Tutt pitched forward on his face. Hickok gave himself up to the sheriff and, in his trial, was successfully defended by the prominent congressman, general, and Civil War governor of Arkansas, John S. Phelps.

The end of the war brought the end of Thomas Ewing's residence on the Western border. Rock-bound Republican Kansas promised him little. Back in Ohio his father's name was magic. But in the years to come, reactionary Democrats could never forgive young Ewing for Order Number Eleven. Radical Republicans deemed him guilty by association for defending, before a military commission in Washington, Samuel Mudd — the doctor who set fugitive John Wilkes Booth's broken leg. Eventually Ewing was elected to Congress from Ohio, but he failed in a gubernatorial campaign, and he never achieved his ambition to be United States senator.

The notorious Milt McGee, who had openly associated with the most radical proslavery groups during the Kansas territorial days, became mayor of Kansas City — where someone probably helped him with his spelling. Dr. James Blunt never returned to the practice of medicine. With advancing age he became more belligerent and independent — so much so that he was eventually confined in an asylum for the mentally ill. Preston Plumb, the Good Bishop, became a United States senator, being elected three times to that office from Kansas. Bottle-nosed Totten was dismissed from the army during Grant's administration for excessive drinking. The old artilleryman wrote Grant that, of all men, he should overlook such an offense.

Dan Anthony continued his violent journalistic career into his late seventies. To the end, he prided himself on doing and saying what his conscience dictated. He advocated the impeachment of Andrew Johnson and made the telegraph wires smoke with the heat of his imprecations against Kansas politicians who would vote for acquittal. In 1875 he was shot by W. W. Embry of the *Leavenworth Appeal*. Seven doctors, including two from Fort Leavenworth, treated his wound. His sister, Susan B. Anthony, now embarked on her reform crusade, came to nurse him. For over a month it was necessary for someone to hold a finger on the artery over his collarbone to regulate the proper flow of blood. Susan took her place with the others in this delicate performance, and Dan Anthony's life was saved. Veteran newspapermen in Leavenworth remembered how the convalescent tetrarch ordered a Salvation Army band away from the front of his office building. When the musicians moved only a few doors down the street, the old man strode out from his editorial desk, kicked a hole in the bass drum, and limped back minus a boot. His missing footgear had stuck in the punctured drumhead. On his deathbed, in 1904, the eighty-year-old Dan Anthony was asked if he would lead a different life, could he live it again. "Yes," the bearded patriarch replied from his pillows. "Next time I'd be more positive."

Ex-Senator David Rice Atchison, the self-styled Kickapoo Ranger, spent the war years namelessly in Texas. After the surrender he came back to his Missouri plantation a disillusioned man. The phantom world of great slave owners, rural aristocrats, and bombastic hustings oratory at Lige Green's country tavern had disappeared forever. Atchison took no more part in politics, nor would he discuss Kansas affairs with callers. When his pillared mansion burned down in 1870, he replaced it with — of all things — a New England farmhouse. Kate Chase, the fading beauty of a faded era, came to his farm for a story which, in her straitened circumstances, she hoped to sell. Elderly David Atchison was hoeing his garden. Flushed and a little breathless from the exertion, he came in the house. Kate reported him drunk as usual — a pale ghost's last scratch at a specter, to attract an audience that no longer cared.

Jim Lane, most picturesque of all the vivid characters in the border war, survived the peace only a little more than a year. After a lifetime of demagoguery, the Grim Chieftain insisted on supporting Andrew Johnson's veto of the radicals' Civil Rights bill. Thus the rabble rouser aligned himself with the moderates in reconstruction. Perhaps he had been with them always except in his wild talk. But when he came back to Kansas, he failed to interest the mob in his temperate program, and the radical political machine turned against him. Lane's day had passed, a limit had come to the demigod's fleeting period of power. The Grim Chieftain lost self-confidence, lapsed into despondency, and shot himself in the head. For ten days he survived this wound, but on July 11, 1866, he died. His fellow Kansan, Noble Prentis, wrote: "The scheming brain worked and suffered no more; there was an end of plots and plans; a last farewell to all that men strive for to find ruin in the gaining."

Notes

The order for which the references are given for each page or group of pages is determined by the first use of each reference work in that particular section of the text.

A Challenge Accepted

3–4   Frederick Trevor Hill, *Lincoln the Lawyer*, p. 264. *History of Buchanan County, Missouri*, pp. 234–238. *Chicago Tribune*, February 1, 1887. George Fort Milton, *The Eve of Conflict*, p. 102. Mrs. Archibald Dixon, *The True History of the Missouri Compromise*, p. 458.

5–6   Charles F. Horner, *The Life of James Redpath*, p. 74. John Bach McMaster, *A History of the People of the United States*, VIII, pp. 201, 215. St. Louis *Daily Missouri Republican*, May 10, 1853. *St. Joseph Weekly Commercial Cycle*, March 24, April 14, 1854. Daniel W. Wilder, *The Annals of Kansas* (1886 edition), p. 47. *St. Louis Reveille*, May 26, 1848. Many societies are listed by William H. Carruth, "The New England Emigrant Aid Company as an Investment Society," p. 96. See also Edward Everett Hale, *Kansas and Nebraska*, p. 230. Franklin P. Rice, "The Life of Eli Thayer" (Ms.), XXII, pp. 11, 14. Frank W. Blackmar, *The Life of Charles Robinson*, p. 102.

7   Rice, "Life of Eli Thayer," XIV, p. 6. Samuel A. Johnson, "The Genesis of the New England Emigrant Aid Company," p. 95. Albert D. Richardson, *Garnered Sheaves*, p. 138. *St. Joseph Gazette*, July 5, 1854. *Report of the Special Committee Appointed to Investigate the Troubles in Kansas*, p. 3. Benjamin H. Hibbard, *A History of the Public Land Policies*, p. 208. Richard Walsh, *The Making of Buffalo Bill*, pp. 27–28. Daniel Leasure, "Personal Observations," p. 143. *Report of the Special Committee*, p. 355. Interview with Mrs

John Brown in Atchison. [John McNamara], *Three Years on the Kansas Border*, p. 138. Kansas City was first called City of Kansas.

8–9 Elijah Milton McGee, autobiography (Ms.). *Daily Kansas City Journal of Commerce*, February 11, 1873. William H. Miller, *History of Kansas City*, p. 51. *Westport Border Times*, April 5, 1856. Wilbur Cortez Abbott, "Political Warfare in Early Kansas," p. 628. Louise Barry, "The Emigrant Aid Company Parties of 1854," p. 118. Lawrence *Herald of Freedom*, February 28, 1857. Elizabeth Cady Stanton, *Eighty Years and More*, p. 158. Charles Robinson, *The Kansas Conflict*, p. 69. Rice, "The Life of Eli Thayer," IX, p. 19; XII, p. 3. *St. Joseph Gazette*, April 26, 1854. *St. Joseph Weekly Commercial Cycle*, January 20, February 10, 1854.

10–12 *Boston Advertiser*, September 16, in Kansas Territory, Clippings, I, p. 16. [Hanna Anderson Ropes] *Six Months in Kansas*, p. 145. Frank W. Blackmar, "The Annals of an Historic Town," p. 485. Eli Thayer, *A History of the Kansas Crusade*, p. 165. Barry, "Emigrant Aid Company Parties," p. 128. On p. 116, Barry corrects an earlier statement in Leverett W. Spring, *Kansas: the Prelude to the War for the Union*, p. 32, that five companies came, totaling 750. Elmer LeRoy Craik, "Southern Interest in Territorial Kansas, 1854–1858," p. 388.

13 *United States Biographical Dictionary*, Kansas Volume, p. 621. Spring, *Kansas*, p. 37. Roy F. Nichols, *Franklin Pierce*, p. 407. [Ropes], *Six Months in Kansas*, p. 54. Henry Shindler, "The First Capital of Kansas," p. 333. Blackmar, *Life of Robinson*, p. 125. Charles Robinson, "Address," p. 117. George W. Martin, "The First Two Years of Kansas," p. 128.

14 Charles Sumner, *Kansas Affairs*, p. 12. *Report of Special Committee*, p. 8. Blackmar, *Life of Robinson*, p. 125. Spring, *Kansas*, pp. 27, 41. William E. Connelley, "First Homicide of the Territorial Troubles in Kansas" (Ms.). John J. Ingalls, "First Homicide" (Ms.). Hugh Fisher, *The Gun and the Gospel*, p. 30. Martin, "First Two Years," p. 129. John Speer, *Life of James H. Lane*, p. 14. [McNamara], *Three Years*, pp. 32–35. *St. Joseph Gazette*, September 20, 1854. Daniel R. Goodloe, "Is it Expedient to Introduce Slavery into Kansas." Benjamin F. Stringfellow, *Negro-Slavery, No Evil, passim*.

15 R. H. Williams, *With the Border Ruffians*, pp. 65, 69–70. Richardson, *Garnered Sheaves*, p. 139. *New York Tribune*, July 3, 1855.

Blackmar, "Annals," p. 490, and *Life of Robinson*, p. 103. Carruth, "New England Emigrant Aid Company," p. 94. Oliver Johnson, *The Abolitionists Vindicated*, p. 15. Samuel A. Johnson, "The Genesis of the New England Emigrant Aid Company," p. 95. Sumner, *Kansas Affairs*, p. 19. Rice, "Life of Eli Thayer," XIII, p. 11.

CHAPTER II

It Looks Very Much Like War: 1855

16–17   Roy P. Basler, ed., *The Collected Works of Abraham Lincoln*, IV, p. 131. William H. Miller, *History of Kansas City*, p. 55. St. Louis *Daily Missouri Republican*, May 10, 1855. William A. Phillips, "Kansas History," p. 355. William Lawrence, *Life of Amos A. Lawrence*, pp. 89–91. R. G. Elliott, "The Twenty-first of May," p. 523 fn. *Report of the Special Committee Appointed to Investigate the Troubles in Kansas*, p. 836.

18–19   Leverett W. Spring, *Kansas*, pp. 24, 44. George W. Martin, "First Two Years of Kansas," pp. 126, 127, 133. John H. Gihon, *Geary and Kansas*, p. 34. James C. Malin, "The Proslavery Background of the Kansas Struggle," p. 300. Charles H. Ambler, ed., *Correspondence of Robert M. T. Hunter*, p. 161. Richard Walsh, *Making of Buffalo Bill*, p. 34. David Y. Thomas, *Arkansas in War and Reconstruction*, p. 196. Charles Robinson, "Address," p. 118. William P. Borland, "General Jo. O. Shelby," p. 18. *Report of Special Committee*, pp. 10, 13, 140, 178. Mortimer R. Flint, "The War on the Border," p. 401. Thomas Shackelford, "Early Recollections of Missouri," p. 3. Frank W. Blackmar, "Annals of an Historic Town," p. 128.

20   *Report of Special Committee*, p. 186. Frank W. Blackmar, *Life of Charles Robinson*, pp. 132, 146. Martin, "First Two Years," p. 131. William A. Phillips, *The Conquest of Kansas*, p. 87. *Daily Missouri Republican*, May 9, 1855. George W. Martin, "Early Days in Kansas," p. 137. William E. Connelley, *The Life of Preston B. Plumb*, p. 23, quotes Marcus Parrott as saying that eighteen of the nineteen districts were overrun. The *Report of the Special Committee* cites obvious frauds in all districts except 9, 10, 12, and 17. William H. Smith, *A Political History of Slavery*, p. 187. Spring, *Kansas*, p. 45. Robinson, "Address," p. 118.

21   W. H. Isley, "Sharps Rifle Episode in Kansas History," pp. 554–555. Winston O. Smith, *The Sharps Rifle*, pp. 11–12. Spring, *Kansas*, pp. 40, 60. *Daily Missouri Republican*, July 3, 1855, gives details

of the encounter. John McNamara, *Three Years on the Kansas Border*, p. 138, scoffs at the idea of B. F. Stringfellow's fighting. James R. Mead, "The Saline River Country in 1859," p. 10. Roy F. Nichols, *Franklin Pierce*, pp. 402–405.

22–24   *Washington Sentinel*, May 29, 1855. Lawrence *Herald of Freedom*, July 28, 1855. *Report of Special Committee*, p. 899. Nichols, *Pierce*, pp. 400, 415. Charles F. Horner, *The Life of James Redpath*, p. 106. Leverett W. Spring, "The Career of a Kansas Politician," p. 80. Noble L. Prentis, *Kansas Miscellanies*, pp. 108, 110. Kansas Scrapbook, Biography, IV, p. 302.

25–26   Lawrence *Herald of Freedom*, July 21, 1855. Thomas L. Snead, *The Fight for Missouri*, p. 121. Lemuel Knapp, "Kansas Experiences," p. 207. Spring, *Kansas*, p. 62. George W. Martin, "The Territorial and Military Combine at Fort Riley," p. 368. Washington, D.C., *National Intelligencer*, July 31, 1856. *Jefferson Examiner*, November 15, 1856. Kansas Scrapbook, Biography, IV, p. 92. Court records of the divorce complaint were printed in the *Lecompton Union*, August 30, 1856. "Governor Reeder's Administration," p. 191.

27   Smith, *Political History*, p. 187. *Daily Missouri Republican*, October 15, 1855. *New York Times*, August 11, 1855. Martin, "Territorial and Military," p. 371. Henry Shindler, "The First Capital of Kansas," p. 333. Theodore Weichselbaum, "Statement," p. 568. Percival G. Lowe, *Five Years a Dragoon*, p. 188, states that the first man died of cholera toward the end of the month, so this disease may have had little effect on the hasty removal of the capital. William A. Hammond, *Personal Recollections of General Nathaniel Lyon*, p. 191. Blackmar, *Life of Robinson*, p. 133. Spring, *Kansas*, p. 62. R. G. Elliott, "The Big Springs Convention," p. 365. Blackmar, *Life of Robinson*, pp. 134–135. *Report of Special Committee*, p. 140.

28–30   Shalor W. Eldridge, "Recollections," p. 33, 40. Phillips, *Conquest*, p. 17. Lawrence, *Life of Amos A. Lawrence*, pp. 92, 95. Nichols, *Pierce*, p. 418. *The Border Ruffian Code in Kansas*. Smith, *Political History*, pp. 187–188. Blackmar, *Life of Robinson*, pp. 133, 367.

31   *Daily Missouri Republican*, December 11, 1855. Blackmar, *Life of Robinson*, p. 276. William E. Connelley, *James Henry Lane*, p. 50. Spring, "Career," p. 83. Allan Nevins, *Ordeal of the Union*, II,

p. 390. Smith, *Political History*, p. 190. George D. Brewerton, *The War in Kansas*, p. 135. [Hanna A. Ropes], *Six Months in Kansas*, p. 140. Spring, *Kansas*, p. 82. "Documentary History of Kansas," p. 234.

32–33   Albert G. Brackett, *History of the United States Cavalry*, p. 168. Elliott, "Big Springs Convention," p. 375. Lawrence, *Life of Amos A. Lawrence*, p. 100. Connelley, *James Henry Lane*, p. 59. John Speer, *Life of James H. Lane*, p. 47. George W. Martin, "A Chapter from the Archives," p. 362, summarizes the issuance of Topeka scrip. *White Cloud Chief*, September 8, 1864. Charles Robinson, "Topeka and Her Constitution," p. 296, and *The Kansas Conflict*, pp. 177–179. Wendell H. Stephenson, *The Political Career of General James H. Lane*, p. 52 fn.

CHAPTER III

The Wakarusa War

34   John Speer, *Life of James H. Lane*, p. 48. Leverett W. Spring, *Kansas*, pp. 70, 83. The proceedings of the constitutional convention were printed in *Report of the Special Committee*, pp. 608–640. *New York Herald*, January 21, 1856. *Leavenworth Herald*, October 25, 1855, quoted by George W. Martin in "The First Two Years of Kansas," p. 135. Frank W. Blackmar, *Life of Charles Robinson*, p. 138. William H. Smith, *A Political History of Slavery*, p. 190.

35–36   Walter L. Fleming, "The Buford Expedition to Kansas," pp. 39–40. *Washington Sentinel*, November 10, 1855. John G. Haskell, "The Passing of Slavery in Western Missouri," p. 37 fn. *Fort Smith New Era*, February 4, 1856. Kansas Territory, Clippings, I, p. 294. Spring, *Kansas*, p. 85. *Report of Special Committee*, pp. 1040–1121. Blackmar, *Life of Robinson*, p. 139. Richard J. Hinton, "Pens That Made Kansas Free," p. 375.

37–38   George D. Brewerton, *The War in Kansas*, p. 159. John H. Gihon, *Geary and Kansas*, p. 90. Spring, *Kansas*, p. 91, states that fifty men responded. Brewerton, *War in Kansas*, p. 162, states that Shannon estimated two to three hundred answered the call. Evidently the governor considered the Missourians legitimate Kansans. "Documentary History of Kansas," p. 243. Galusha Anderson, *The Story of a Border City*, p. 124. Moses Harris, "The Old Army," p. 336.

R. S. Bevier, *History of the First and Second Missouri Confederate Brigades,* p. 278. St. Louis *Daily Missouri Republican,* July 18, 1885. Susan A. A. McCausland, "The Battle of Lexington as Seen by a Woman," p. 128. James C. Malin, "Proslavery Background of the Kansas Struggle," p. 300.

39–40   *Atlas & Daily Bee,* October 2 and 24, 1859, in Webb Scrapbook. Spring, *Kansas,* p. 92. [Hanna Anderson Ropes], *Six Months in Kansas,* p. 131. Speer, *Life of Lane,* p. 53. George W. Brown, *Reminiscences of Gov. R. J. Walker,* p. 7. Charles L. Chandler, ed., "Two Letters from Kansas, 1855–1856," pp. 77–78. Sara Robinson, "The Wakarusa War," p. 469. Charles Howard Dickson, "The 'Boy's' Story," p. 84. Leverett W. Spring, "Career of a Kansas Politician," p. 86.

41–42   Spring, *Kansas,* pp. 96, 97. Bevier, *History of the First and Second Missouri,* p. 278. *Report of Special Committee,* p. 1123. Brewerton, *War in Kansas,* pp. 135, 142. [Ropes], *Six Months,* p. 135. *Daily Missouri Republican,* December 6, 1855. William R. Bernard, "Westport and the Santa Fe Trade," p. 565. Sara Robinson, "Wakarusa War," pp. 468–469. Charles Robinson, "Address," pp. 119–120.

43   Speer, *Life of Lane,* pp. 62–64, 66. [Ropes], *Six Months,* p. 140. Spring, *Kansas,* pp. 71, 101. James C. Malin, *John Brown and the Legend of Fifty-Six,* p. 15. *Atlas & Daily Bee,* October 2, 1859, in Webb Scrapbook. Charles Sumner, *Kansas Affairs,* p. 10.

CHAPTER IV

The Crime Against Kansas

45   Don E. E. Braman, *Braman's Information about Texas,* p. 69. James R. Mead, "The Saline River Country in 1859," p. 10. William A. Hammond, *Personal Recollections of General Nathaniel Lyon,* p. 14. Percival G. Lowe, *Five Years a Dragoon,* p. 222. Samuel A. Drake, "The Old Army in Kansas," p. 149. Moses Harris, "The Old Army," p. 337.

47   George D. Brewerton, *War in Kansas,* p. 391. G. Raymond Gaeddert, "First Newspapers in Kansas Counties," pp. 4–10. Noble L. Prentis, "Kansas Journalism — the Men of '57," pp. 93–98. Shalor W. Eldridge, "Recollections of Early Days," p. 51. George W. Martin, "First Two Years of Kansas," p. 136. John Speer, *Life of James H.*

Lane, p. 73. Leverett W. Spring, *Kansas,* p. 72. Charles Sumner also referred to this in *Kansas Affairs.* Blackmar, *Life of Charles Robinson,* p. 194. Roy F. Nichols, *Franklin Pierce,* p. 444.

48   Amos Townsend, "With the Kansas Congressional Committee of 1856," pp. 490, 492. John Sherman, *Recollections,* I, p. 126.

49   William H. Miller, *History of Kansas City,* pp. 60–61. Evangeline Thomas, *Nativism in the Old Northwest,* pp. 154–155. Theo. S. Case, ed., *History of Kansas City,* p. 54. *Westport Border Times,* April 5, 12, 1856. Eldridge, "Recollections," p. 33. Walter L. Fleming, "Buford Expedition to Kansas," pp. 39, 42. Harold E. Briggs, "Lawlessness in Cairo, Illinois," p. 72. John G. Haskell, "Passing of Slavery in Western Missouri," p. 37.

50   *Wheeling Daily Times,* April 25, 1856, in Webb Scrapbook, XI, p. 163. Spring, *Kansas,* pp. 40, 115. *Westport Border Times,* April 5, 1856. Fleming, "Buford Expedition," p. 44. William E. Connelley, *Life of Preston B. Plumb,* p. 32. Lawrence *Herald of Freedom,* April 12, 1856. Sherman, *Recollections,* I, p. 129.

51–52   Blackmar, *Life of Robinson,* p. 202. Spring, *Kansas,* pp. 109, 111, 116. Eldridge, "Recollections," p. 35. *Kansas in 1856. An Authentic Account,* pp. 1, 3. Andrew H. Reeder, "Governor Reeder's Escape," p. 207. Speer, *Life of Lane,* pp. 78–79. Kansas Scrapbook, Biography, III, May 4, 1863. R. G. Elliott, "The Twenty-first of May," p. 528, lists another man who may have fired the shot. "Governor Geary's Administration," p. 392. Sherman, *Recollections,* p. 130.

53–54   Reeder, "Governor Reeder's Escape," p. 209. Martin, "First Two Years," p. 139. Eldridge, "Recollections," p. 39. *Chicago Tribune,* May 22, 1856. Nichols, *Pierce,* p. 465. George Fort Milton, *Eve of Conflict,* p. 232. Sumner, *Kansas Affairs,* pp. 8–11. Edward L. Pierce, *Memoir and Letters of Charles Sumner,* III, p. 446.

55–56   Milton, *Eve of Conflict,* p. 234. Pierce, *Memoir,* III, pp. 453, 471. Charles Robinson, "Address," p. 121. *Herald of Freedom,* May 12, 1857. Eldridge, "Recollections," p. 50. "Governor Geary's Administration," p. 415. *Kansas in 1856,* p. 8. Spring, *Kansas,* pp. 121–122.

57–59   [A. T. Andreas], *History of the State of Kansas,* p. 129. Eldridge, "Recollections," pp. 49, 52–55. "Governor Geary's Administration," p. 400. *Herald of Freedom,* November 14, 1857. Frank W. Blackmar, *Kansas: A Cyclopedia*, II, p. 89. Case, *History of Kansas City*, pp. 52–53. Richard L. Douglas, "History of Manufactures in the Kansas District," p. 93 fn. Walter B. Stevens, *Missouri, the Center State*, I, p. 889. Fleming, "Buford Expedition," pp. 44–45. *Kansas in 1856*, pp. 8, 9. Elliott, "Twenty-first of May," p. 529 fn. Webb Scrapbook, XIII, pp. 91, 200. Thomas H. Gladstone, *The Englishman in Kansas*, p. 39. "Governor Geary's Administration," p. 399.

CHAPTER V

I Went to Take Old Brown and Old Brown Took Me

60–61   Daniel Geary, "Looking Backward," p. 224. James C. Malin, *John Brown*, p. 60. Shalor W. Eldridge, "Recollections," pp. 41–42. Andrew H. Reeder, "Escape from Kansas," p. 219. Francis M. I. Morehouse, *The Life of Jesse W. Fell*, p. 55. *Report of the Select Committee . . . to Inquire into the Late Invasion . . . at Harper's Ferry*, p. 76. *Kansas in 1856*, p. 11. Franklin Benjamin Sanborn, *The Life and Letters of John Brown*, p. 268.

62   Leverett W. Spring, *Kansas*, p. 143. August Bondi, "With John Brown in Kansas," p. 280. Malin, *John Brown*, p. 27. George W. Martin, "First Two Years of Kansas," pp. 140–141. Hill P. Wilson, *John Brown*, p. 99.

63   Spring, *Kansas*, pp. 139, 152–154. Huntsville, Missouri, *Randolph Citizen*, November 20, 1856. William P. Tomlinson, *Kansas in Eighteen Fifty-Eight*, p. 23. "Governor Geary's Administration," p. 387. Malin, *John Brown*, p. 589. Henry H. Crittenden, *Memoirs*, p. 240. Bondi, "With John Brown," p. 288. Lloyd Lewis, "Propaganda and the Kansas-Missouri War," p. 17.

64   *Leavenworth Daily Tribune*, June 7, 1879. [A. T. Andreas], *History of the State of Kansas*, p. 141. "Correspondence of Governor Shannon," p. 388. Spring, *Kansas*, pp. 158, 161, 180. "Correspondence of Governor Geary," pp. 442–443. Crittenden, *Memoirs*, p. 240. Walter L. Fleming, "Buford Expedition to Kansas," p. 47. G. W. E. Griffith, "The Battle of Black Jack," p. 525.

65–66   *Chicago Daily Democratic Press*, July 3, 1856. Webb Scrapbook, XIII, p. 216. William E. Connelley, *Life of Preston B. Plumb*, pp. 25, 27, 30, 37. Elmer LeRoy Craik, "Southern Interest in Territorial Kansas," p. 360. Winston O. Smith, *The Sharps Rifle*, p. 15. Interview with Mrs. J. H. Stallard, St. Joseph, Mo. R. H. Williams, *With the Border Ruffians,* pp. 73, 83, 84. Cyrus K. Holliday, "The Presidential Campaign of 1856," p. 50. Robert Morrow, "Emigration to Kansas in 1856," p. 304 fn. Washington, D.C., *National Intelligencer,* July 17, 1856. John H. Gihon, *Geary,* p. 181. Charles Robinson, "Address," p. 122. Frank W. Blackmar, *Life of Charles Robinson,* p. 324.

67–68   *Chicago Tribune,* July 15, 1856. Webb Scrapbook, XV, p. 2. Franklin G. Adams, "The Capitals of Kansas," p. 346. fn.

CHAPTER VI
Lane's Army of the North

69–70   *Chicago Daily Democratic Press,* June 2, 1856. William E. Connelley, "Daniel W. Wilder," p. 14. [A. T. Andreas], *History of the State of Kansas,* p. 136. John Speer, *Life of James H. Lane,* pp. 105, 106.

71   *The Border Ruffian Code in Kansas. New York Times,* July 4, 1856. James R. Mead, "The Saline River Country in 1859," p. 9. Leverett W. Spring, *Kansas,* pp. 165, 169. Speer, *Life of Lane,* p. 102. Washington, D.C., *National Intelligencer,* August 9, 1856. [Andreas], *History of the State of Kansas,* p. 141. William E. Connelley, "Col. Richard J. Hinton," p. 489. St. Louis *Daily Missouri Republican,* July 26, 1856. William E. Connelley, *Life of Preston B. Plumb,* p. 39.

72–74   Connelley, *Life of Plumb,* pp. 38, 39. Charles S. Gleed, "Samuel Walker," pp. 260, 266–268. *Kansas City Journal,* September 7, 1879. *United States Biographical Dictionary,* Kansas Volume, pp. 183–184. Albert D. Richardson, *Beyond the Mississippi,* pp. 44, 46, 49. Spring, *Kansas,* pp. 170, 179, 181. *Kansas City Journal,* September 7, 1879. V. E. Gibbons, ed., "Letters on the War," p. 374. James C. Malin, "Colonel Harvey," p. 59. Speer, *Life of Lane,* p. 114.

75–76   Gibbons, "Letters," pp. 374, 375. George R. Gibson, *Journal of a Soldier,* p. 351. Susan A. A. McCausland, "Battle of Lexington," p. 128. Connelley, *Life of Plumb.* p. 38. Richard B. Foster, "Statement," p. 227. Malin, "Colonel Harvey," pp. 60, 61 fn. Frank W. Blackmar, *Life of Charles Robinson,* pp. 324, 369. Spring, *Kansas,* p. 182. "Capture of Col. Titus," p. 228. Speer, *Life of Lane,* p. 115.

77   "Capture of Titus," p. 228. Gibbons, "Letters," pp. 376–377. Connelley, *Life of Plumb,* p. 40. Gleed, "Samuel Walker," pp. 270, 272. Spring, *Kansas,* pp. 183, 184. Malin, "Colonel Harvey," p. 61. Foster, "Statement," pp. 226–227.

78–79   "Capture of Titus," p. 228. Spring, *Kansas,* pp. 186, 188. "Correspondence of Governor Geary," pp. 403, 471. *Chicago Tribune,* August 20, September 19, 1856. Connelley, *Life of Plumb,* p. 41. Washington, D.C., *Daily National Era,* October 9, 1856. Charles Robinson, "Address," p. 123.

80   Roy F. Nichols, *Franklin Pierce,* pp. 479–480. W. Z. Hickman, *History of Jackson County,* p. 168. William H. Miller, *History of Kansas City,* p. 61. William M. Johnson Papers. Theo. S. Case, ed., *History of Kansas City,* p. 66. Lawrence *Kansas Daily Tribune,* June 7, 1879. Connelley, *Life of Plumb,* pp. 41, 83.

81–82   Spring, *Kansas,* pp. 238, 241. *Kansas City Star,* August 8, 1945. The number of casualties at Osawatomie is uncertain. Note Spring, *Kansas,* p. 190, and J. F. Snyder, "Battle of Osawatomie," p. 84. William E. Connelley, *Wild Bill and His Era,* p. 17. Gibbons, "Letters," p. 378.

83–84   Speer, *Life of Lane,* pp. 115, 121. Connelley, *Wild Bill,* p. 17. Gleed, "Samuel Walker," p. 274. "Correspondence of Geary," p. 487. Spring, *Kansas,* p. 192. Gibbons, "Letters," p. 378.

CHAPTER VII

Geary Takes Command

85   "Correspondence of Governor Geary," p. 486. Charles Robinson, "Address," p. 123. Leverett W. Spring, *Kansas,* pp. 188, 197. Charles Robinson, *Kansas Conflict,* p. 321. Robinson, "Address," p. 123. Extract from *Geary City Era,* August 1, 1857, in *Kansas Historical Quarterly,* VI, No. 2 (May 1937), p. 200. Percival G. Lowe, *Five Years a Dragoon,* p. 239.

86   James C. Malin, "Colonel Harvey and His Forty Thieves," p. 65. Frank W. Blackmar, *Life of Charles Robinson,* p. 207. "Executive Minutes of Governor John W. Geary," pp. 522, 526, 559, 565. Spring, *Kansas,* p. 195. Elmer LeRoy Craik, "Southern Interest in Territorial Kansas," p. 424. Spring, *Kansas,* p. 208. Robinson, "Address," p. 124.

87   Brinton W. Woodward, "Reminiscences of September 14, 1856,"
            p. 79. Spring, *Kansas,* p. 199. John Speer, *Life of James H. Lane,*
            p. 125. Charles S. Gleed, "Samuel Walker," p. 273. "Governor
            Geary's Administration," p. 479. Woodward, " Reminiscences," p. 78.
            St. Louis *Daily Missouri Republican,* July 3, 1856.

88–89   Blackmar, *Life of Robinson,* p. 207. George W. Martin, "First
            Two Years of Kansas," p. 144. "Executive Minutes," p. 533. [A. T.
            Andreas], *History of the State of Kansas,* pp. 151. Spring, *Kansas,*
            p. 201. John H. Gihon, *Geary and Kansas,* p. 167.

90   Blackmar, *Life of Robinson,* p. 329. Malin, "Colonel Harvey,"
            p. 69. *Chicago Tribune,* October 7, 1856. St. Louis *Daily Missouri
            Republican,* October 14, 1856. *New York Tribune,* September 22, 23,
            October 7, 1856. Mary T. Higginson, ed., *Letters and Journals of
            Thomas Wentworth Higginson,* p. 144. Speer, *Life of Lane,* p. 129.
            Leverett W. Spring, "Career of a Kansas Politician," p. 89.

91–92   Spring, "Career," p. 89. William E. Connelley, "Col. Richard J.
            Hinton," p. 489. Oswald Garrison Villard, *John Brown, 1800–1859,*
            p. 679. Albion W. Tourgée, *The Story of a Thousand,* p. 33. *Chi-
            cago Tribune,* September 5, 1856. "Executive Minutes," p. 562. Hig-
            ginson, *Letters and Journals,* p. 141. William E. Connelley, *Life of
            Preston B. Plumb,* p. 43.

93   Frank W. Blackmar, *Kansas: A Cyclopedia,* II, p. 809. "Executive
            Minutes," p. 601. William E. Connelley, *John Brown,* p. 306.
            James S. Pike, *First Blows of the Civil War,* p. 349. Roy F. Nichols,
            Franklin Pierce, p. 452. Lawrence *Herald of Freedom,* December 6,
            1856. *Cincinnati Gazette,* February 10, 1857. Nathan Parker, *Kansas
            and Nebraska Handbook,* pp. 109–110. Noble L. Prentis, *Kansas
            Miscellanies,* p. 83. Albert D. Richardson, *Beyond the Mississippi,*
            p. 53. Richardson, *Garnered Sheaves,* p. 145. George A. Root, ed.,
            "Extracts from Diary of Captain Wolf," p. 204. Samuel A. Drake,
            "The Old Army," p. 141. Extract from Doniphan *Kansas Crusader
            of Freedom in Kansas Historical Quarterly,* VI, No. 2 (May 1927),
            p. 201.

94–95   Letter from Thomas Ewing, Jr., to "Dearest Ellen," November 13,
            1856, Ewing Papers. Springfield *Illinois State Journal,* April 23,
            June 6, 1857. Craik, "Southern Interest," p. 392. William H. Miller,
            History of Kansas City, p. 108. Blackmar, *Life of Robinson,* pp. 213,
            215. Robinson, "Address," pp. 124–126. Richardson, *Garnered
            Sheaves,* p. 141.

CHAPTER VIII

Buchanan Tries His Hand

96–97 Jay Monaghan, *Diplomat in Carpet Slippers*, p. 290. Leverett W. Spring, *Kansas*, p. 211. H. Donaldson Jordan, "A Politician of Expansion: Robert J. Walker," p. 378. Frank W. Blackmar, *Life of Charles Robinson*, p. 230. "Governor Walker's Administration," p. 391. William E. Connelley, *James Henry Lane*, p. 104.

98 Spring, *Kansas*, pp. 218, 220. Albert D. Richardson, *Beyond the Mississippi*, p. 101. John Speer, *Life of James H. Lane*, p. 141. Lawrence *Herald of Freedom*, October 24, 1857. William E. Connelley, *Life of Preston B. Plumb*, p. 76.

99 James S. Green, *Speech . . . on the Constitution of Kansas*. Spring, *Kansas*, p. 223. Roy F. Nichols, *The Disruption of American Democracy*, p. 122. Allan Nevins, *The Emergence of Lincoln*, I, p. 234. Blackmar, *Life of Robinson*, pp. 232, 254. Leverett W. Spring, "Career of a Kansas Politician," p. 91. Connelley, *Life of Plumb*, p. 76.

100–101 James H. Lane, "Report on Trouble in Bourbon County," *Kansas Territorial Legislature, House Journal, Extra Session, 1858*, pp. 84–85. Connelley, *Life of Plumb*, pp. 55, 69, 84, 86. Charles Robinson, *Kansas Conflict*, p. 379. Noble L. Prentis, *Kansas Miscellanies*, p. 85. G. Raymond Gaeddert, "First Newspapers in Kansas Counties," p. 10. Charles W. Goodlander, *Memoirs and Recollections*, p. 61. Spring, *Kansas*, pp. 228, 243. Lawrence *Herald of Freedom*, December 26, 1857. Speer, *Life of Lane*, p. 175. Spring, "Career," p. 92.

102 Connelley, *Life of Plumb*, pp. 73–76. Springfield *Illinois State Journal*, February 19, May 7, 1858. Stephen A. Douglas, *Report . . . on the Kansas-Lecompton Constitution*, p. 98.

103 Goodlander, *Memoirs*, p. 62. W. A. Mitchell, "Historic Linn," pp. 642–643, 645. Joel Moody, "Marais des Cygnes Massacre," p. 209. William P. Tomlinson, *Kansas in Eighteen Fifty-Eight*, pp. 62–63. Ed. R. Smith, "Marais des Cygnes Tragedy," p. 368. William E. Connelley, *John Brown*, p. 323. Data on Marais des Cygnes marker, *Kansas Historical Quarterly*, X, No. 4 (November 1941), p. 356.

104   Moody, "Marais des Cygnes Massacre," p. 215. Smith, "Marais des
       Cygnes Tragedy," p. 369. Spring, *Kansas*, p. 249. Mitchell, "Historic
       Linn," p. 646. Franklin B. Sanborn, "Some Notes," p. 261. A. H.
       Tannar, "Early Days in Kansas," p. 229. Tomlinson, *Kansas in
       Eighteen Fifty-Eight*, pp. 63, 77, 84. *Leavenworth Times*, May 29,
       1858.

105–106 Kansas City *Western Journal of Commerce*, May 29, 1858. Rich-
       ardson, *Beyond the Mississippi*, p. 125. Blackmar, *Life of Robinson*,
       p. 324. August Bondi, "With John Brown in Kansas," p. 276 fn.
       Correspondence between John Brown and George Stearns, Brown
       Papers. Hildegarde R. Herklotz, "Jayhawkers in Missouri, 1858–
       1863," p. 279. *Leavenworth Times*, September 4, 11, 18, October 9,
       1858, February 19, 1859.

CHAPTER IX

He'll Trouble Them More When His Coffin's Nailed Down

107–108 Albert D. Richardson, *Beyond the Mississippi*, pp. 113–114. John
       Speer, *Life of James H. Lane*, pp. 208, 214, 215. *Leavenworth Times*,
       July 23, 1858. Hugh Fisher, *The Gun and the Gospel*, p. 36. Lev-
       erett W. Spring, "Career of a Kansas Politician," p. 95.

109   Jacob Stringfellow, "Jim Lane," p. 767. Kansas Scrapbook, Biog-
       raphy, IV, p. 183a. Letter from Thomas Ewing, Jr., to Ellen, Jan-
       uary 30 [1859], Ewing Papers. LeRoy Hafen, *Pike's Peak Gold
       Rush Guidebooks of 1859*.

110   A. H. Tannar, "Early Days in Kansas," pp. 230–231. William E.
       Connelley, *John Brown*, p. 326. George W. Martin, "The First Two
       Years of Kansas," p. 142. Leverett W. Spring, *Kansas*, pp. 252–256.
       Frank W. Blackmar, *Life of Charles Robinson*, p. 324. *Leavenworth
       Times*, January 22, 1859.

111–112 *Leavenworth Times*, January 29, February 12, 1859, January 4,
       1860. Jim Beckwourth came thus in 1860, *Leavenworth Times*,
       March 6, 1860. G. Raymond Gaeddert, *Birth of Kansas*, p. 13. Elvid
       Hunt, *History of Fort Leavenworth 1827–1927*, pp. 97–98.

113–114 Blackmar, *Life of Robinson*, p. 248 fn. *Martin, "First Two Years,"*
       p. 145. Richardson, *Beyond the Mississippi*, pp. 152–153. Oswald
       Garrison Villard, *John Brown*, p. 459. Richard J. Hinton, *John*

Brown and His Men, p. 324. Winston O. Smith, *The Sharps Rifle*, p. 15.

115–116 *Chicago Press and Tribune*, October 29, 1859. James S. Pike, *First Blows of the Civil War*, p. 449. *Daily Kansas City Journal of Commerce*, February 11, 1873. St. Joseph *Weekly West*, January 7, 1860. Westport *Border Star*, December 31, 1858. Kansas City *Western Journal of Commerce*, December 17, 1859. *New York Herald*, December 6, 1859. *Transactions of the Missouri Lodge of Research*, III, pp. 67, 82. *New York Tribune*, May 16, 1859. Charles J. Kappler, "Indian Treaties and Councils Affecting Kansas," p. 765. St. Joseph *Weekly West*, November 19, 1859, January 7, 28, April 7, 1860. *Leavenworth Times*, March 2, 20, 1862. Villard, *John Brown*, pp. 571–575. Franklin B. Sanborn, "Some Notes," p. 261. Letter from James McCool to John F. Snyder, n.d., Snyder Papers. The poem appears in the Reader diary in May 1860.

CHAPTER X

The Election of Abraham Lincoln

117 *Leavenworth Times*, March 23, April 14, 1860. St. Joseph *Weekly West*, April 7, 1860. Kansas Territory, Clippings, II, p. 275. *White Cloud Chief*, June 7, 1858. Franklin B. Sanborn, "Some Notes," pp. 261–265.

118 Letters dated June 11, 15, 1860, in John F. Snyder Papers. "Echoes of the Republican Convention," p. 151. Virgil C. Blum, "Political and Military Activities of the German Element in St. Louis," p. 103. Ernest D. Kargan, "Missouri's German Immigration," p. 23. Jay Monaghan, *The Great Rascal*, pp. 195–203.

119 George S. Grover, "Civil War in Missouri," p. 8. Charles M. Harvey, "Missouri from 1849 to 1861," p. 35. James Peckham, *Gen. Nathaniel Lyon and Missouri in 1861*, pp. xiv, xvii. Letters, June 26, 28, 1860, in Snyder Papers. Also clipping from Chillicothe *Chronicle*, July 19, 1860. Blum, "Political and Military Activities," p. 111. Raymond D. Thomas, "A Study in Missouri Politics," p. 167. McCoy Scrapbook, II, p. 62. *History of Jackson County*, p. 466. *Leavenworth Times*, February 15, 1860. Robert J. Rombauer, *The Union Cause*, p. 108. Thomas L. Snead, *The Fight for Missouri*, p. iii.

120 Snead, *Fight for Missouri*, p. 31. An account of the duel between Reynolds and Gratz Brown was also printed in the *Kansas City*

Star, November 21, 1938. S. M. Fox, *The Seventh Kansas Cavalry,* p. 8. Kansas Scrapbook, Biography, IV, p. 269. Letter from McCool to Snyder, November 29, 1860, Snyder Papers. Kansas City *Western Journal of Commerce,* November 29, December 6, 1860. Hildegarde R. Herklotz, "Jayhawkers in Missouri," p. 506. San Francisco *Alta California,* December 15, 1860. Clarksville *Standard,* December 22, 1860. *Van Buren Press,* December 21, 1860. *The Supreme Council, 33°,* p. 201.

121–122 *New York Tribune,* March 27, 1862. Jay Monaghan, *Great Rascal,* p. 99. Susan B. Riley, "Life and Works of Albert Pike" (Ph.D. thesis). *Supreme Council, 33°,* p. 240. Kansas City *Western Journal of Commerce,* November 22, December 13, 20, 27, 1860. Sanborn, "Some Notes," pp. 261–265. William E. Connelley, *Quantrill and the Border Wars,* pp. 140 ff. John J. Lutz, "Quantrill and the Morgan Walker Tragedy," pp. 324–331. William A. Johnson, "Early Life of Quantrill," p. 213. F. P. Blair Papers.

123 Letter from Lane to Lincoln, January 2, 1861, Lincoln Papers. John Speer, *Life of James H. Lane,* p. 234. Captains George Hazzard and John Pope also accompanied Lincoln to Washington.

124 Buel Leopard and Floyd C. Shoemaker, eds., *The Messages and Proclamations of the Governors of the State of Missouri,* III, pp. 333–334. Letter from John Snyder, July 4, 1860, Snyder Papers. William E. Smith, *The Francis Preston Blair Family,* pp. 22, 34. Rombauer, *The Union Cause,* p. 128. *Los Angeles Star,* June 7, 1861. Jessie Benton Frémont, *The Story of the Guard,* p. 46. L. G. Bennett and Wm. M. Haight, *History of the Thirty-Sixth . . . Illinois,* p. 84. George Alfred Townsend, *Campaigns of a Non-combatant,* p. 232. Otto C. Lademann, "The Capture of 'Camp Jackson,'" p. 438.

125 Snead, *Fight for Missouri,* pp. 53–57, 59, 124. Lademann, "Capture of 'Camp Jackson,'" p. 70. Rombauer, *The Union Cause,* p. 146. M. Jeff. Thompson, "Autobiography" (Ms.), pp. 10 ff.

126 James O. Broadhead, "Early Events of War in Missouri," p. 2. James F. How, "Frank P. Blair in 1861," p. 386. H. C. McDougal, "A Decade of Missouri Politics," p. 128. Thomas Shackelford, "Early Recollections of Missouri," p. 10. Lawrence *Herald of Freedom,* January 2, 1858. *Leavenworth Times,* July 2, 9, 1859, March 16, April 13, 24, 1860. *White Cloud Chief,* October 27, 1864.

127 Wendell H. Stephenson, *The Political Career of General James H. Lane,* p. 101. Jacob Stringfellow, "Jim Lane," pp. 272, 274. Abridged from *St. Joseph Morning Herald,* February 1889, in Kansas Territory, Clippings, I, p. 252. Hugh H. Fisher, *The Gun and the Gospel,* p. 33.

128 William E. Connelley, *James Henry Lane,* p. 112. Speer, *Life of Lane,* pp. 233, 238. Leverett W. Spring, *Kansas,* p. 273. G. Raymond Gaeddert, *Birth of Kansas,* p. 145. "The Frontier Guard," pp. 419–420.

CHAPTER XI
Lyon Shows Missouri

129–130 William E. Smith, *The Francis Preston Blair Family,* II, p. 36. William F. Switzler, *Illustrated History of Missouri,* p. 347. G. Raymond Gaeddert, *Birth of Kansas,* p. 141. Virgil C. Blum, "Political and Military Activities of the German Element in St. Louis," pp. 122, 124. M. Jeff. Thompson, "Autobiography" (Ms.), p. 13. Floyd C. Shoemaker, "The Story of the Civil War in Northeast Missouri," p. 74. *Chicago Tribune,* April 29, 1861. James Peckham, *Gen. Nathaniel Lyon,* p. 137.

131 Robert J. Rombauer, *The Union Cause in St. Louis,* pp. 225–226, 231. Switzler, *Illustrated History,* p. 349. Otto C. Lademann, "Capture of 'Camp Jackson,'" p. 71. Peckham, *Gen. Nathaniel Lyon,* p. 150. E. B. Long, ed., *Personal Memoirs of U. S. Grant,* p. 119.

132 Rombauer, *The Union Cause,* pp. 230, 234. Mortimer R. Flint, "The War on the Border," p. 404. Switzler, *Illustrated History,* p. 354. Lloyd Lewis, *Sherman, Fighting Prophet,* p. 159. William T. Sherman, *Memoirs,* I, p. 174. Jay Monaghan, *The Great Rascal,* p. 202. Peckham, *Gen. Lyon,* pp. 157, 165. *St. Joseph Morning Herald,* October 10, 1862.

133 Switzler, *Illustrated History,* p. 316. Thompson, "Autobiography," p. 15. John McElroy, *The Struggle for Missouri,* picture, p. 32. Thomas L. Snead, "The First Year of the War in Missouri," p. 264. *Reminiscences of the Women of Missouri,* p. 45.

134 Documents on the Harvey-Jackson agreement are printed in

Switzler, *Illustrated History,* p. 358. William Hemstreet, "Little Things about Big Generals," p. 159.

135   Rombauer, *The Union Cause,* p. 262. Thomas L. Snead, *Fight for Missouri,* p. 200. Switzler, *Illustrated History,* p. 361. Oliver W. Nixon, "Reminiscences of the First Year of the War," p. 417. Snead, "First Year of the War," p. 267. William H. Tunnard, *A Southern Record,* p. 64.

136–138   Milo M. Quaife, ed., *Absalom Grimes,* pp. 4, 17. Long, *Personal Memoirs,* p. 127. Samuel L. Clemens, "The Private History of a Campaign that Failed," pp. 235–264.

CHAPTER XII

Jefferson City, Boonville, and the Happy Land of Canaan

139–140   Kenneth P. Williams, *Lincoln Finds a General,* III, p. 413. Robert J. Rombauer, *The Union Cause in St. Louis,* pp. 266, 270. John F. Lee, "John Sappington Marmaduke," p. 27. Thomas L. Snead, "The Conquest of Arkansas," picture, p. 446.

141–142   William F. Switzler, *Illustrated History of Missouri,* p. 363. Eugene F. Ware, *The Lyon Campaign in Missouri,* p. 128. St. Louis *Daily Missouri Democrat,* June 26, 1861. R. I. Holcombe and F. W. Adams, *An Account of the Battle of Wilson's Creek,* p. 60.

143–144   Ware, *Lyon Campaign,* pp. 79, 137, 147, 151, 155, 260, 339. Franc Bangs Wilkie, *Pen and Powder,* pp. 29, 60. John M. Schofield, *Forty-six Years in the Army,* p. 37. Rombauer, *The Union Cause,* picture, p. 320. William E. Woodruff, *With the Light Guns,* p. 47.

145–146   Ware, *Lyon Campaign,* pp. 113–114, 175, 183. Kansas, *Report of Adjutant General,* p. 4. George A. Root, ed., "Extracts from Diary of Captain Lambert Bowman Wolf," p. 209. Wilkie, *Pen and Powder,* p. 60. *New York Times,* December 7, 1861. Samuel J. Crawford, *Kansas in the Sixties,* p. 35. James A. McGonigle, "First Kansas Infantry," p. 292. Seymour D. Thompson, *Recollections with the Third Iowa,* p. 161.

147–148   W. A. Mitchell, "Historic Linn," p. 634. Kansas, *Report of Adjutant General,* p. 76. Ware, *Lyon Campaign,* pp. 105, 195.

CHAPTER XIII

Battle of Carthage

149   Otto C. Lademann, "Battle of Carthage," p. 134. Eugene F. Ware, *The Lyon Campaign*, p. 336. Thomas W. Sweeney Papers. Samuel C. Reid, Jr., *The Scouting Expeditions of McCulloch's Texas Rangers*. David Y. Thomas, *Arkansas in War and Reconstruction*, p. 108. *New York Times*, December 7, 1861.

150   Letter, Day Elmoore at Rolla, n.d. L. G. Bennett and Wm. M. Haight, *History of the Thirty-Sixth Illinois*, pp. 68–69. Samuel Phillips Day, *Down South*, II, p. 171. *Harper's Weekly*, November 30, 1861. William E. Connelley, *Wild Bill*, p. 82. Wiley Britton, *The Civil War on the Border*, p. 51. Thomas L. Snead, *The Fight for Missouri*, p. 235. St. Louis *Daily Missouri Republican*, July 18, 1861. Claib Jackson's letters of April were published in the *New York Times* during the second half of July.

151–152   Britton, *Civil War*, pp. 52–53. Snead, *The Fight for Missouri*, p. 218. On p. 237, Snead states that 137 men were captured at Neosho. Lademann, "Battle of Carthage," p. 131. John N. Edwards, *Shelby and His Men*, p. 30. Susan A. A. McCausland, "Battle of Lexington as Seen by a Woman," p. 128. W. L. Webb, *Battles and Biographies of Missourians*, p. 320.

153   Snead, *The Fight for Missouri*, pp. 216–217. Robert J. Rombauer, *The Union Cause in St. Louis*, p. 279. Lademann, "Battle of Carthage," p. 134. William M. Wherry, *The Campaign in Missouri*, p. 4.

154–155   Lademann, "Battle of Carthage," pp. 134, 139. Snead, *The Fight for Missouri*, pp. 225, 227. James Peckham, *Gen. Nathaniel Lyon*, p. 295. Joseph A. Mudd, "What I Saw at Wilson's Creek," p. 101. William F. Switzler, *Illustrated History of Missouri*, p. 366. E. S. S. Rouse, *The Bugle Blast*, p. 73. *O. R.*, I, III, p. 18. Wiley Britton, *Civil War*, p. 55. It is noticeable that Lademann does not mention the sunken-road incident.

156   *Los Angeles Semi-Weekly Southern News*, August 7, 1861. Eli G. Foster, *The Civil War by Campaigns*, p. 58. Rouse, *Bugle Blast*, p. 76. *Daily Missouri Republican*, July 18, 1861. Snead, *The Fight for Missouri*, p. 238.

157   *Sacramento Daily Transcript,* September 9, 1850. *Cincinnati Commercial,* March 18, 1862. William H. Tunnard, *A Southern Record,* p. 47. Harvey S. Ford, "Van Dorn," p. 223. W. J. Hardee, *Rifle and Light Infantry Tactics,* I, p. 64. Mudd, "What I Saw," p. 95.

158   *Fort Smith Times and Herald,* July 15, 1861. A Clarksville *Standard* news note from the Richmond *Enquirer,* on August 17, 1861, states that "game cock Governor" Jackson and Atchison had arrived. M. Jeff. Thompson, "Autobiography" (Ms.), pp. 25, 28. *Daily Missouri Republican,* July 15, 29, August 26, 1861.

CHAPTER XIV
Born Among the Rocks

159–160   Eugene F. Ware, *The Lyon Campaign,* pp. 212, 270. Benjamin D. Dean, *Recollections of the 26th Missouri,* pp. 213–214. James Peckham, *Gen. Nathaniel Lyon,* p. 301. John B. Sanborn, "Reminiscences," p. 238.

161   R. I. Holcombe and F. W. Adams, comps., *An Account of the Battle of Wilson's Creek,* p. 12. Ware, *Lyon Campaign,* pp. 171, 244, 270, 284. Frank Moore, *Anecdotes, Poetry and Incidents of the War,* p. 409.

162   William H. Tunnard, *A Southern Record,* pp. 45, 65. New York *World,* August 12, 1861. Ware, *Lyon Campaign,* pp. 278, 296. Robert J. Rombauer, *The Union Cause,* p. 309. William M. Wherry, *The Campaign in Missouri,* p. 8. Letter from Frémont to Lincoln, August 6, 1861, Lincoln Papers. St. Louis *Daily Missouri Republican,* August 7, 1861. William M. Wherry, "General Nathaniel Lyon," p. 82. N. B. Pearce, "Price's Campaign of 1861," p. 338, gives an eyewitness account of the Price-McCulloch agreement.

163   L. E. Meador, *History of the Battle of Wilson Creek,* p. [15]. Rombauer, *The Union Cause,* pp. 316, 317. There is some question about Sweeney's presence at Lyon's council. Thomas L. Snead, *The Fight for Missouri,* p. 258. *Daily Missouri Republican,* August 12, 15, 1861. *Cincinnati Commercial,* August 17, 1861. James A. McGonigle, "First Kansas Infantry," p. 293. *New York Herald,* August 19, 1861.

164   *New York Tribune,* August 18, 1861. Peckham, *Gen. Lyon,* p. 327. Wiley Britton, *The Civil War on the Border,* p. 85. Ware, *Lyon*

Campaign, pp. 296, 303–304, 306. Snead, *The Fight for Missouri,* p. 266. The New York *World,* August 19, 1861, reported the Confederate muster roll as containing twenty thousand. It probably numbered about ten thousand effectives.

165 John M. Schofield, *Forty-six Years in the Army,* p. 42. Ware, *Lyon Campaign,* pp. 310–311. Noble L. Prentis, *Kansas Miscellanies,* p. 60. Otto C. Lademann, "Battle of Wilson's Creek," p. 438.

166 *Van Buren Press,* August 28, 1861. William E. Woodruff, *With the Light Guns,* p. 14. Peckham, *Gen. Lyon,* pp. 249–350. Ware, *Lyon Campaign,* p. 314. *New York Tribune,* August 18, 1861. Albert R. Greene, "On the Battle of Wilson Creek," p. 118. Holcombe and Adams, *Account of the Battle of Wilson's Creek,* p. 9.

167 Fred Steele diary, August 10, 1865. Addison A. Stuart, *Iowa Colonels and Regiments,* p. 179. Franc Bangs Wilkie, *Pen and Powder,* p. 210. *New York Herald,* August 19, 1861. Ware, *Lyon Campaign,* p. 315. Holcombe and Adams, *Account of the Battle of Wilson's Creek,* p. 85.

168–169 *New York Herald,* August 19, 1861. Rombauer, *The Union Cause,* p. 317. Peckham, *Gen. Lyon,* p. 330. *Cincinnati Commercial,* August 22, 1861. William E. Connelley, *Wild Bill,* p. 88. William E. Connelley, *Quantrill and the Border Wars,* p. 198. Interview with Schofield, reported in *New York Tribune,* February 18, 1883. William A. Hammond, *Personal Recollections of General Nathaniel Lyon,* p. 12. Greene, "On the Battle of Wilson Creek," p. 120. Franc B. Wilkie, "Battle of Wilson's Creek," pp. 291–310, tells about Lyon's marching out on August 9, oversleeping, and marching back to come out again the next night. This story cannot be credited in the face of various diaries and the account in the *Daily Missouri Republican,* September 3, 1861.

CHAPTER XV

The Battle of Wilson's Creek

170–171 *New York Herald,* August 19, 1861. *New York Tribune,* August 25, 1861. L. E. Meador, *History of the Battle of Wilson Creek,* p. [18]. *O. R.,* I, III, p. 100. Thomas L. Snead, *The Fight for Missouri,* pp. 271–272. San Francisco *Alta California,* January 11, 1862. Robert J. Rombauer, *The Union Cause in St. Louis,* p. 313. Richard Hubbell, "Reminiscences" (Ms.), p. 8. Wiley Britton, *The Civil*

War on the Border, I, p. 93. St. Louis *Daily Missouri Republican,* December 7, 1861.

172–173   *New York Herald,* August 23, 1861. Samuel B. Barron, *The Lone Star Defenders,* p. 39. William Baxter, *Pea Ridge and Prairie Grove,* p. 39. Snead, *The Fight for Missouri,* p. 299. *New York Times,* December 7, 1861. Albert R. Greene, "On the Battle of Wilson Creek," p. 122. Eugene F. Ware, *The Lyon Campaign,* p. 318. Eldredge Collection. *Van Buren Press,* January 2, 1862.

174   Ware, *Lyon Campaign,* pp. 317, 335. William E. Connelley, *Wild Bill,* p. 218. H. H. Crittenden, *Memoirs,* p. 346. *New York Tribune,* August 18, 1861. James Peckham, *Gen. Nathaniel Lyon,* p. 380. William H. Tunnard, *A Southern Record,* p. 52. William Watson, *Life in the Confederate Army,* p. 215. *Van Buren Press,* January 2, 1862. R. I. Holcombe and F. W. Adams, *An Account of the Battle of Wilson's Creek,* p. 93.

175   *New York Herald,* August 19, 1861. Snead, *The Fight for Missouri,* pp. 275, 282. Watson, *Life in the Confederate Army,* p. 229. Holcombe and Adams, *Account of the Battle,* pp. 92–93. W. L. Webb, *Battles and Biographies,* p. 318. Kansas, *Public Documents,* p. 76.

176   *New York Herald,* August 19, 23, 1861. *New York Tribune,* August 18, 23, 1861. James A. McGonigle, "First Kansas Infantry," p. 295. Kansas, *Public Documents,* pp. 73, 75. Kansas, *Report of the Adjutant General,* p. 12. St. Louis *Daily Missouri Republican,* September 10, 1861. Samuel J. Crawford, *Kansas in the Sixties,* pp. 32, 34. Joseph A. Mudd, "What I Saw at Wilson's Creek," p. 101. Philadelphia *Weekly Times,* August 4, 1877. Barron, *Lone Star Defenders,* pp. 34, 46. St. Louis *Daily Missouri Republican,* September 10, 1861. Greene, "On the Battle," p. 123.

177   Britton, *Civil War on the Border,* p. 93. David Y. Thomas, *Arkansas in War and Reconstruction,* p. 113. Letter, T. J. Churchill, August 10, 1861, MoSHi. Peckham, *Gen. Lyon,* pp. 357–358. Eldredge Collection. Meador, *History of the Battle,* p. 33. Franz Sigel, "The Flanking Column at Wilson's Creek," p. 305.

178   Noble L. Prentis, *Kansas Miscellanies,* p. 55. New York *World,* August 24, 1861. *Van Buren Press,* October 31, 1861. *Daily Missouri*

Republican, August 15, December 12, 1885. N. B. Pearce, "Arkansas Troops in the Battle of Wilson's Creek," p. 302. John N. Edwards, *Shelby and His Men,* p. 35. N. B. Pearce, "Price's Campaign of 1861," p. 337. *New York Tribune,* August 30, 1861. Mudd, "What I Saw," p. 95. William E. Woodruff, *With the Light Guns,* p. 47. Letter, Gratiot to Eakin, August 12, 1861, MoSHi.

179 John M. Schofield, *Forty-six Years in the Army,* pp. 45, 67. Holcombe and Adams, *Account of the Battle,* p. 46. *Los Angeles Star,* September 21, 1861. John B. Sanborn, "Reminiscences," p. 239. Pearce, "Price's Campaign," p. 345, states that Mitchell, in a Springfield hospital, said that he helped Lyon from his horse and was wounded himself shortly thereafter. This agrees with the account by Wherry in *Campaign in Missouri,* p. 295. Captain F. J. Herron, of Dubuque, claimed to have seen Lyon fall about twenty yards from him, according to George Alfred Townsend, "Annals of the War," p. 282.

180 Holcombe and Adams, *Account of the Battle,* p. 97. Wherry, *Campaign in Missouri,* p. 15. Lyon died about 8 or 9 A.M. according to the New York *World,* August 20, 1861, and the Philadelphia *Weekly Times,* August 4, 1877. *New York Tribune,* August 18, 1861. Peckham, *Gen. Lyon,* p. 381. Letter, Churchill, August 10, 1861, MoSHi. Britton, *Civil War on the Border,* p. 96. Meador, *History of the Battle,* p. [24].

181 *Van Buren Press,* August 28, 1861. Peckham, *Gen. Lyon,* pp. 335, 355, 391. McGonigle, "First Kansas Infantry," p. 295. Snead, *The Fight for Missouri,* p. 291. Thomas, *Arkansas,* p. 119; compare these casualty figures with William Fox, *Regimental Losses,* pp. 29, 36. *New York Tribune,* August 19, 23, 1861. Ware, *Lyon Campaign,* pp. 329, 331, 340. New York *World,* August 29, 1861. Meador, *History of the Battle,* pp. [29–31], analyzes the losses and summarizes the percentages with a difference from the 23 per cent in the text.

CHAPTER XVI

The Fall of Lexington

182 *O. R.,* I, Sup., LIII, p. 720. Jessie Benton Frémont, *Story of the Guard,* p. 115. Thomas Snead, *The Fight for Missouri,* p. 301. William H. Tunnard, *A Southern Record,* p. 78. *Lawrence Republican,* November 7, 1861. St. Louis *Daily Missouri Republican,* August 7, 1861.

183 George W. Herr, comp., *Episodes of the Civil War*, p. 34. Allan Nevins, *Frémont*, II, pp. 532–533. William F. Switzler, *Illustrated History*, p. 370. *Cincinnati Commercial*, August 20, October 14, 1861. Charles C. Nott, "The Tale of a Goblin Horse," pp. 150, 162–163. Franc Bangs Wilkie, *Pen and Powder*, p. 50. *Daily Missouri Republican*, August 27, 1861. Letter from Frémont to Lincoln, August 8, 17, 1861, Lincoln Papers. M. F. Force, *From Fort Henry to Corinth*, p. 385. Floyd C. Shoemaker, "The Story of the Civil War in Northeast Missouri," pp. 75, 115. William and Ophia Smith, *Colonel A. W. Gilbert*, p. 56 fn. Seymour D. Thompson, *Recollections with the Third Iowa*, p. 145.

184 Nevins, *Frémont*, p. 555. Wilkie, *Pen and Powder*, p. 50. John M. Schofield, *Forty-six Years in the Army*, p. 48. Hugh D. Fisher, *The Gun and the Gospel*, p. 149. Leverett W. Spring, *Kansas*, p. 274.

185 Richard Hubbell, "Reminiscences" (Ms.), p. 11. *O. R.*, I, III, pp. 466–467. Eli G. Foster, *The Civil War by Campaigns*, p. 62. Nevins, *Frémont*, p. 564. Roy P. Basler, ed., *Collected Works of Abraham Lincoln*, IV, p. 506. M. Jeff. Thompson, "Autobiography" (Ms.), pp. 35, 36. Oliver W. Nixon, "Reminiscences . . . of the War in Missouri," p. 418. John B. Sanborn, "Reminiscences of the War in . . . Missouri," p. 230. Switzler, *Illustrated History*, p. 392. Wiley Britton, *The Civil War on the Border*, p. 144.

186 Fisher, *Gun and Gospel*, p. 149. Charles W. Goodlander, *Memoirs and Recollections*, p. 69. Lincoln Papers, September 8, 1861. *O. R.*, I, III, p. 500. G. Raymond Gaeddert, *Birth of Kansas*, p. 143. Wilkie, *Pen and Powder*, p. 45.

187 *Chicago Daily Democratic Press*, July 3, 1856. Susan A. A. McCausland, "Battle of Lexington," p. 129. Little Rock *Daily State Journal*, November 27, 1861. Switzler, *Illustrated History*, p. 395. *Battle of Lexington*, pp. 5–6. James A. Mulligan, "The Siege of Lexington, Mo.," pp. 307, 313 fn. *Daily Missouri Republican*, September 16, 19, 1861. Nevins, *Frémont*, pp. 594–595.

188–189 *Battle of Lexington*, pp. 10, 24, 28. Mulligan, "Siege of Lexington," pp. 308, 313 fn. *Daily Missouri Republican*, July 18, 1885. Samuel Phillips Day, *Down South*, II, p. 183. Frank Moore, *Anecdotes, Poetry and Incidents of the War*, p. 416. McCausland, "Battle of Lexington," p. 130. Albert R. Greene, "On the Battle of Wilson Creek," p. 122.

190–191   McCausland, "Battle of Lexington," p. 131. Switzler, *Illustrated History*, pp. 395–396. *Battle of Lexington*, pp. 32, 56–57. Charles Morton, "Early War Days in Missouri," p. 156, gives credit to the Thirteenth Missouri, Companies B and E, for the charge on the hospital.

192   *Battle of Lexington*, pp. 8, 20, 57. Nixon, "Reminiscences," p. 420. The Negro's dialect has been edited. *Daily Missouri Republican*, September 25, 1861. Smith, *Colonel Gilbert*, p. 60. *Los Angeles Star*, December 7, 12, 1861. R. S. Bevier, *History of the First and Second Missouri*, p. 307.

193   Milo M. Quaife, ed., *Absalom Grimes*, p. 23. *Battle of Lexington*, pp. 14, 16, 33. Morton, "Early War Days," p. 156.

194   *Battle of Lexington*, p. 26. Britton, *Civil War on the Border*, p. 143. Day, *Down South*, p. 188. Van Horn Papers. Quaife, *Absalom Grimes*, p. 25. Wilkie, *Pen and Powder*, p. 47. Nevins, *Frémont*, p. 593. *Daily Missouri Republican*, September 25, 1861.

CHAPTER XVII

Osceola, Zagoni, and Frémont's Recall

195   Kansas Scrapbook, Biography, IV, p. 269. Frank W. Blackmar, *Life of Charles Robinson*, p. 279. Leverett W. Spring, *Kansas*, pp. 275–276. *O. R.*, I, III, p. 490. Annie Heloise Abel, *The American Indian as Participant in the Civil War*, p. 53. James G. Blunt, "Account of . . . Civil War Experiences," p. 214. William E. Connelley, *Life of Preston B. Plumb*, p. 90. San Francisco *Alta California*, October 12, 1861.

196   *Cincinnati Commercial*, October 7, 11, 31, 1861. Henry E. Palmer, "The Border War," pp. 176–177, and "The Soldiers of Kansas," p. 457. *Lawrence Republican*, October 3, 1861. Spring, *Kansas*, p. 276. *Alta California*, January 4, 1861. William E. and Ophia D. Smith, *Colonel A. W. Gilbert*, p. 65. *O. R.*, I, III, p. 517. Wiley Britton, *The Civil War on the Border*, p. 181. Blackmar, *Life of Robinson*, p. 277.

197   *Chicago Tribune*, October 22, 1861. *Leavenworth Times*, November 10, 1861. *Harper's Weekly*, November 23, 1861. *O. R.*, I, III, p. 529. Abel, *American Indian as Participant*, p. 57. Spring, *Kansas*, p. 278. Lane's speech in Leavenworth is reported in the *Cincinnati*

Commercial, October 11, 16, 1861. Note also the *Chicago Tribune,* October 31, 1861, the *Lawrence Republican,* October 24, 1861, the *New York Times,* November 7, 8, 1861. Smith, *Colonel Gilbert,* p. 61. Seymour D. Thompson, *Recollections with the Third Iowa,* pp. 160–161. *New York Times,* November 9, 1861. James F. Rusling, *Across America,* pp. 29–31. *Lawrence Republican,* September 30, 1861. St. Louis *Daily Missouri Republican,* October 16, 1861.

198–199   John N. Edwards, *Shelby and His Men,* p. 51. Milo M. Quaife, ed., *Absalom Grimes,* p. 25. *Daily Missouri Republican,* October 9, 1861. Floyd C. Shoemaker, "Story of the Civil War in Northeast Missouri," p. 115. James Peckham, *Gen. Nathaniel Lyon,* p. 268. *Alta California,* Sup., March 1, 1862. *Cincinnati Commercial,* October 2, 4, 1861. Francis Brown, *Raymond of the Times,* p. 219. *O. R.,* I, III, pp. 184–185. *Battle of Lexington,* p. 20. Allan Nevins, *Frémont,* II, pp. 601, 603. William F. Switzler, *Illustrated History,* p. 399.

200–201   Britton, *Civil War on the Border,* pp. 149–150, 160. Switzler, *Illustrated History,* p. 402. Nevins, *Frémont,* pp. 606–607. James L. Foley, "With Frémont in Missouri," pp. 502, 519. Jessie Benton Frémont, *Story of the Guard,* pp. 112, 122. *Junction City Union,* August 11, 1883. George W. Herr, comp., *Episodes of the Civil War,* p. 35. Charles Treichel, "Major Zagoni's Horse Guard," p. 241. Charles H. Lothrop, *History of the First Regiment,* pp. 25–26.

202   *Cincinnati Commercial,* October 31, 1861. Britton, *Civil War on the Border,* p. 154. Foley, "With Frémont," p. 513. Lothrop, *History of the First Regiment,* pp. 33–34. Frank Moore, *Anecdotes, Poetry and Incidents of the War,* p. 443. "Frémont's Hundred Days," p. 253. Frémont, *Story of the Guard,* p. 146. Of several maps the best is in Foley, "With Frémont," p. 517.

203   Treichel, "Major Zagoni's Horse Guard," p. 244. Frémont, *Story of the Guard,* pp. 139–140, 144. Moore, *Anecdotes,* p. 445. E. S. S. Rouse, *The Bugle Blast,* p. 92. *Cincinnati Commercial,* November 9, 1862. *O. R.,* I, III, p. 251. Foley, "With Frémont," p. 519.

204   Frémont, *Story of the Guard,* pp. 154, 181. Lothrop, *History of the First Regiment,* p. 36. *Cincinnati Commercial,* November 13, 1861. *New York Herald,* November 3, 4, 8, 1861. *Junction City Union,* August 11, 1883. *Alta California,* December 28, 1861, Sup., March 1, 1862. New Orleans *Picayune,* December 3, 1861. *Daily*

Missouri Republican, October 22, 1861. Britton, *Civil War on the Border*, pp. 153, 158, 201. Switzler, *Illustrated History*, p. 319.

205   Nevins, *Frémont*, p. 614. *Daily Missouri Republican*, October 2, November 9, 1861. Smith, *Colonel Gilbert*, p. 68 fn. Letter, Day Elmoore, November 12, 1861. *Van Buren Press*, November 21, 1861. Gustave Koerner, *Memoirs*, II, p. 190. *Military History . . . Thirteenth . . . Illinois*, p. 85. Frémont, *Story of the Guard*, p. 196.

206   *Los Angeles Star*, December 14, 1861. *Alta California*, January 4, 1862. *Van Buren Press*, November 28, 1861. *Harper's Weekly*, November 23, 1861, p. 738. *Junction City Union*, August 11, 1883. Smith, *Colonel Gilbert*, p. 69 fn. Hunter's testimony on the retreat appears in *Report of the Joint Committee on the Conduct of the War*, III, pp. 234–248. Franz Sigel, "Military Operations in Missouri," p. 367.

207–208   Benjamin D. Dean, *Recollections of the 26th Missouri Infantry*, p. 217. Rouse, *Bugle Blast*, p. 278. *Lawrence Republican*, November 7, 21, 1861. *Van Buren Press*, November 28, 1861. The quotation from Hugh D. Fisher, *The Gun and the Gospel*, p. 149, has been edited. *Daily Missouri Democrat*, February 1, 1862. Smith, *Colonel Gilbert*, p. 71 fn. *Alta California*, January 4, 1862. *Harper's Weekly*, December 28, 1861. Lloyd Lewis, *Sherman, Fighting Prophet*, pp. 199–200. Smith, *Colonel Gilbert*, p. 74. *Daily Missouri Republican*, December 27, 1861. Letter, Benjamin, in CSmH.

CHAPTER XVIII

The Five Nations Secede

209–210   Cherokee Register of Claims, N. 8, p. 22. Carolyn T. Foreman, *Park Hill*, pp. 30–31. *Cincinnati Commercial*, October 4, 1861. Albert D. Richardson, *Beyond the Mississippi*, pp. 222, 224. "Indian-Pioneer History" (Ms.), I, pp. 292, 300. Annie Heloise Abel, "The Indians in the Civil War," p. 289. Emmet Starr, *History of the Cherokee Indians*, p. 497. Morris L. Wardell, *A Political History of the Cherokee Nation*, p. 122.

211   *Chicago Tribune*, November 29, December 4, 1863. United States Indian Office, *Report of the Commissioner . . . 1864*, p. 307. Annie Heloise Abel, *The American Indian as Slaveholder and Secessionist*, p. 135 fn. Abel, "Indians in the Civil War," p. 289. Rachel Caroline

Eaton, *John Ross and the Cherokee Indians,* p. 175. Letter of John R. Ridge to Major Ridge, March 10, 1835, Phillips Collection.

212   E. E. Dale and Gaston Litton, *Cherokee Cavaliers,* pp. xviii, 136. Affidavit of H. J. Wheeler, January 27, 1846, Tx. Pencil note by Emmet Starr in OkHi. *Washington Telegraph,* November 16, 1864. Cherokee Register of Claims, Case 13. Letters of John Ogden to Stand Watie, July 19, 1852, and J. W. Washburne to Stand Watie, September 21, 1849, both Tx.

213   Phillips Collection Correspondence. Abel, "Indians in the Civil War," p. 282. Clarksville *Standard,* July 13, 1861. *Van Buren Press,* June 19, 1861. Little Rock *Arkansas Gazette,* April 2, 1893. *New York Tribune,* March 27, 1862. Fred W. Allsop, *Albert Pike,* pp. 108, 131–132. Horace Van Deventer, *Albert Pike,* pp. 7–10, outlines Pike's Eastern school experience and reprints many of his poems. See also *Supreme Council, 33°,* p. 209. Letter, John Cox to William P. Dole, March 18, 1864. United States Indian Office, letters received and *Report of Commissioner . . . 1864,* p. 39. Abel, "Indians in the Civil War," p. 283. *Little Rock Times and Herald,* July 8, 1861.

214   Pencil note by Emmet Starr, n.d., OkHi. Letter, Ben McCulloch to John Ross, June 12, 1861, Phillips Collection, requests organization of such a company. Wardell, *Political History of Cherokee Nation,* p. 130. *Van Buren Press,* February 8, 1861. Clarksville *Standard,* May 18, July 20, 1861. Abel, "Indians in the Civil War," p. 285. Wiley Britton, *The Union Indian Brigade,* pp. 21–22, 31.

215   Clarksville *Standard,* July 20, 1861. Kiowa Agency, Letter Press Book. Wichita and Affiliated Tribes *vs* United States, in Court of Claims, No. E — 542. United States Indian Office, *Report of Commissioner . . . 1864,* p. 304. Will C. Barnes, "The Chisholm Trail — For Whom Was It Named?" p. 3. Carl Coke Rister, *Border Captives,* p. 128. T. U. Taylor, *Jesse Chisholm,* pp. 20, 83. Carl Coke Rister, *Southern Plainsmen,* p. 95.

216   Kiowa Agency, ledger of Shirley Trading House. Letter, Mathew Leeper to Pike, October 21, 1861, Phillips Collection. United States Office Indian Affairs, "Confederate Papers" (Ms.). Clarksville *Standard,* August 10, 1861. Letter, Mathew Leeper to Elias Rector, December 12, 1861, Tx. United States Indian Office, *Report of Com-*

missioner . . . *1864,* p. iii. Letter, Leeper to Pike, April 13, 1862. United States Office Indian Affairs, "Confederate Papers" (Ms.). "Indian-Pioneer History" (Ms.), pp. 268–270. Pencil note by Emmet Starr in OkHi. Cyrus Byington, diary (Ms.), September 5, 1861.

217   Letter, John Ross to I. R. Kannaday, May 17, 1861, Tx. *Fort Smith Times and Herald,* August 16, 24, 1861. Abel, "Indians in the Civil War," p. 288. *O. R.,* I, III, p. 673. United States Indian Office, *Report of Commissioner* . . . *1864,* p. 326. Letter, John Ross to A. Lincoln, September 7, 1862, Lincoln Papers. Abel, *The American Indian as Slaveholder,* p. 227. Pencil note by Emmet Starr in OkHi. O. O. Howard, *My Life* . . . *among Our Hostile Indians,* p. 100.

218   Clarksville *Standard,* October 26, November 23, 1861. *Fort Smith Times and Herald,* August 24, October 5, 1861. *Van Buren Press,* August 28, November 7, 1861. United States Indian Office, *Report of Commissioner* . . . *1864,* pp. 326, 354, 355. Abel, *American Indian as Slaveholder,* p. 137 fn. Letter of W. R. Brodgate to Stand Watie, September 20, 1861, Phillips Collection. *Supreme Council, 33°,* p. 209. Wardell, *Political History of Cherokee Nation,* pp. 139–141. R. S. Cate, of Norman, Oklahoma, has a copy of the letter of October 7, 1861, in which the offer is made, with Jim Ned excepted.

CHAPTER XIX

Slaveholding Indians Declare War

219   United States Indian Office, *Report of the Commissioner* . . . *1864,* p. 356. *New York Tribune,* January 6, 1862. Letter, signed with Opothleyoholo's mark, to Barent DuBois, February 1, 1849, in possession of R. S. Cate, Norman, Oklahoma. John B. Meserve, "The MacIntoshes," pp. 313, 322.

220   Creek Nation, Council Book. "Indian-Pioneer History" (Ms.), MCI, p. 316, LXXVI, pp. 76, 128. Clarksville *Standard,* November 16, 1861. William A. Tunnard, *A Southern Record,* p. 102. Note by Emmet Starr at OkHi. United States Indian Office, *Report of Commissioner* . . . *1864,* p. 351. Annie Heloise Abel, *The American Indian as Participant,* pp. 62 fn, 64 fn, 69–70. *O. R.,* I, III, p. 530. Abel, *The American Indian as Slaveholder,* p. 248. Abel, *American Indian as Participant,* pp. 66, 74. *Fort Smith Times and Herald,* October 9, 1861. *Van Buren Press,* October 9, 16, 31, November 21,

1861. Wiley Britton, *The Civil War on the Border*, p. 165. G. W. Grayson, "Red Paths and White" (Ms.), p. 67.

221   Interview with R. S. Cate, Norman, Oklahoma. Angie Debo, "The Site of the Battle of Round Mountain," p. 206. Clarksville *Standard,* November 23, 1861. *Van Buren Press,* November 21, 1861. Creek Nation, Council Book. Cooper countermanded McIntosh's promise to confiscate property of the Union-supporting Creeks. Leavenworth *Daily Conservative,* January 28, 1862. *Van Buren Press,* November 7, 1861. Britton, *Civil War on the Border,* p. 164.

222   Typed description of refugee camp in OkHi. "Indian-Pioneer History" (Ms.), CVIII, p. 201. Debo, "Site of the Battle," p. 200.

223   "Indian-Pioneer History" (Ms.), XLIV, p. 29, CVII, p. 361, CIX, pp. 175–183. *Van Buren Press,* November 14, December 5, 1861. Debo, "Site of the Battle," pp. 201–202. Britton, *Civil War on the Border,* pp. 164, 167. United States Office Indian Affairs, letters received, Choctaw, C-676-11868, enclosure, "Statement relative to the Exodus of Ho-poith-la-yo-ho-la." Little Rock *Daily State Journal,* December 5, 12, 1861. Letter, Samuel R. Curtis to brother, February 20, 1864, Curtis Papers, CSmH.

224   Letter, Jacob V. Carter to Hon. H. Price, October 30, 1883, Sac and Fox Agency, Letter Press Book. Kiowa Agency, Letter Press Book, p. 12. United States Indian Office, *Report of Commissioner . . . 1864,* pp. 41, 259, 536. "Indian-Pioneer History" (Ms.), CIX, p. 183. Homer Croy, *Our Will Rogers,* p. 10. *O. R.,* I, VIII, p. 8. Britton, *Civil War on the Border,* p. 168. The number deserting Drew's regiment was between four and five hundred, according to a letter from Col. Garrett to David Hubbard, December 16, 1861. United States Office Indian Affairs, letters received, and United States Indian Office, *Report of Commissioner . . . 1864,* pp. 285, 323, 334.

225–226 Little Rock *Daily State Journal,* December 17, 24, 1861. San Francisco *Alta California,* February 22, 1862. *"Indian-Pioneer History"* (Ms.), CV, pp. 268–270, CIX, p. 178. United States Office Indian Affairs, "Statement." *O. R.,* I, VIII, pp. 11, 22–24. Abel, *American Indian as Participant,* p. 19. *Van Buren Press,* January 9, 1862.

227   "Indian-Pioneer History" (Ms.), XXVI, p. 254, CVII, pp. 69, 361, CVIII, p. 201. *O. R.,* I, VIII, pp. 32, 690. Little Rock *Daily State*

Journal, December 1, 7, 1861, January 7, 1862. *Chicago Tribune,*
December 5, 1863. Abel, *American Indian as Slaveholder,* p. 79.
Abel, *American Indian as Participant,* pp. 20, 76 fn. Letters, Pike
to Elias Rector, December 29, 1861; Mathew Leeper to Rector and
to Chisholm, Buffalo Hump to John Jumper, all December 1861;
H. P. Jones to Pike, May 8, 1862; all Tx. Mathew Leeper to Pike,
October 21, 1861, United States Office Indian Affairs, "Confederate
Papers" (Ms.). George Bent to George Hyde, April 7, 1905, Bent
Correspondence. Letter dated December 15, 1861, Tx.

CHAPTER XX

I Must Have St. Louis — Then Huzza!

228   Letter, Curtis, January 30, 1861, Curtis Papers, CSmH. Nathan C.
Harwood, "The Pea Ridge Campaign," p. 112.

229   Jay Monaghan, *The Great Rascal,* p. 198. John W. Noble, "Battle
of Pea Ridge," p. 239. Letter, Curtis to brother, December 16, 1861,
Curtis Papers, CSmH. William E. Connelley, *Wild Bill,* p. 51.
Harvey S. Ford, "Van Dorn and the Pea Ridge Campaign," p. 226.
Wiley Britton, *Civil War on the Border,* I, p. 204. Addison A.
Stuart, *Iowa Colonels,* p. 111. *Military History . . . of the Thir-
teenth . . . Illinois,* p. 128.

230   Stuart, *Iowa Colonels,* p. 115. Franz Sigel, "The Pea Ridge Campaign," p. 316. New Orleans *Picayune,* March 2, 1862. Price was
later exchanged, and he resigned from the Confederate Army to
return home, *St. Joseph Morning Herald,* October 28, 1862.

231   Milo M. Quaife, ed., *Absalom Grimes,* p. 38. Letter, George
Waley, n.d., MoSHi. L. G. Bennett and Wm. M. Haight, *History of
the Thirty-Sixth . . . Illinois,* p. 113. Grenville M. Dodge, *Battle of
Atlanta,* p. 36. Stuart, *Iowa Colonels,* pp. 111, 113. David Lathrop,
History of Fifty-Ninth . . . Illinois, pp. 73, 75, 78. Britton, *Civil
War on the Border,* p. 205. David Y. Thomas, *Arkansas,* p. 124. St.
Louis *Daily Missouri Republican,* December 12, 1885. Charles H.
Lothrop, *History of First . . . Iowa Cavalry,* p. 74. *Military History
. . . of Thirteenth . . . Illinois,* p. 170. Sigel, "Pea Ridge Cam-
paign," p. 317.

232   *Daily Missouri Republican,* December 12, 1885. Britton, *Civil War
on the Border,* pp. 207, 209. Letter, Curtis to brother, February 25,
1862, Curtis Papers, CSmH. *Winona Weekly Republican,* March 9,

1887. Lathrop, *History of Fifty-Ninth*, p. 81. A. W. Bishop, *Loyalty on the Frontier*, pp. 141–143.

233   Letter, Curtis to brother, February 25, 1862, Curtis Papers, CSmH. *Daily Missouri Republican*, December 12, 1885. Letter, Col. W. T. Freeman, February 3, 1862, Snyder Papers. Little Rock *Daily State Journal*, January 15, 16, 18, 1862. Annie Heloise Abel, *American Indian as Participant*, pp. 21, 25. Ford, "Van Dorn and Pea Ridge," pp. 222–223. Eldredge Collection. George W. Herr, *Episodes of the Civil War*, p. 86. [E. Van Dorn Miller], *A Soldier's Honor*, p. 63.

234   Herr, *Episodes*, p. 65. Britton, *Civil War on the Border*, pp. 214, 259–260. John N. Edwards, *Shelby and His Men*, p. 49. San Francisco *Alta California*, May 10, 1862. *O. R.*, I, VIII, p. 196. Eli G. Foster, *The Civil War by Campaigns*, p. 63. Fred W. Allsop, *Albert Pike*, p. 207. A contradiction to this description of Pike's feathered costume may be found in *Supreme Council, 33°*, pp. 220–221 and Herr, *Episodes*, p. 83. It is presumed that Ross wore his usual costume. "Indian-Pioneer History" (Ms.), XXVII, p. 421.

235   John Bartlett Meserve, "The MacIntoshes," p. 316 fn. *Van Buren Press*, October 9, 1861. *Daily Missouri Republican*, December 12, 1885. Letter, Curtis, March 13, 1862, Curtis Papers, CSmH. Connelley, *Wild Bill*, p. 64. Ford, "Van Dorn and Pea Ridge," p. 229.

236   Noble L. Prentis, *Kansas Miscellanies*, p. 50. John D. Crabtree, "Recollections of the Pea Ridge Campaign," p. 217. William Baxter, *Pea Ridge and Prairie Grove*, p. 246. Herr, *Episodes*, p. 66. Sigel, "Pea Ridge Campaign," p. 331 fn, and Bishop, *Loyalty on the Frontier*, pp. 56, 60, disagree on Cox's presence at the tavern.

237–238   Britton, *Civil War on the Border*, p. 220. Edwards, *Shelby*, p. 49. Samuel B. Barron, *Lone Star Defenders*, p. 66. Ford, "Van Dorn and Pea Ridge," p. 231. Quaife, *Absalom Grimes*, pp. 30, 38.

CHAPTER XXI

The Battle of Pea Ridge

239   *O. R.*, I, VIII, p. 199. Wiley Britton, *Civil War on the Border*, p. 224. Harvey S. Ford, "Van Dorn and the Pea Ridge Campaign," p. 232. George W. Herr, *Episodes of the Civil War*, p. 76. David Y. Thomas, *Arkansas*, p. 128. *Winona Weekly Republican*, March 9, 1887. [E. Van Dorn Miller], *A Soldier's Honor*, pp. 74, 291.

240–241   L. G. Bennett, *History of the Thirty-Sixth . . . Illinois*, pp. 146, 154, 157. R. S. Bevier, *History of the First and Second Missouri*, p. 316. Grenville M. Dodge, *Battle of Atlanta*, p. 35. Herr, *Episodes*, pp. 69–70. William Baxter, *Pea Ridge and Prairie Grove*, p. 39. John D. Crabtree, "Recollections of the Pea Ridge Campaign," p. 218. "Indian-Pioneer History" (Ms.), IX, p. 288. Annie Heloise Abel, *The American Indian as Participant in the Civil War*, p. 31. Samuel B. Barron, *Lone Star Defenders*, p. 68. John W. Noble, "Battle of Pea Ridge," pp. 227, 228. *O. R.*, I, VIII, p. 288. United States Indian Office, *Report of the Commissioner . . . 1861*, p. 323. Sam H. M. Byers, *Iowa in War Times*, p. 115. William Watson, *Life in the Confederate Army*, p. 294.

242   *O. R.*, I, VIII, p. 218. Abel, *American Indian as Participant*, p. 31. Baxter, *Pea Ridge*, p. 102. John N. Edwards, *Shelby and His Men*, p. 49. Wiley Britton, "Union and Confederate Indians," p. 336. Annie Heloise Abel, "Indians in the Civil War," p. 289. Byers, *Iowa in War Times*, p. 115. Frank Moore, *Anecdotes, Poetry and Incidents*, p. 120. In *Supreme Council, 33°*, p. 220, the scalping story is not given the horrendous dimensions other propagandists gave it.

243–244   Crabtree, "Recollections," p. 219. Dodge, *Battle of Atlanta*, p. 27. Noble, "Battle of Pea Ridge," p. 234. William E. Connelley, *Wild Bill*, p. 64. Frank J. Wilstach, *Wild Bill Hickok*, p. 8. The presence of the tavern owner is contradicted by A. E. Bishop, *Loyalty on the Frontier*, pp. 56, 60, and by Franz Sigel, "Pea Ridge Campaign," p. 331 fn. Edward A. Blodgett, "The Army of the Southwest," p. 307. Britton, *Civil War*, pp. 257–261. Samuel P. Curtis, "The Army of the South-West," p. 144. Noble L. Prentis, *Kansas Miscellanies*, p. 51. William Clark Kennerly, *Persimmon Hill*, p. 242.

245   Curtis reported the incident more mildly in *O. R.*, I, VIII, p. 201, than he did in his personal correspondence. Noble, "Battle of Pea Ridge," p. 238. Bennett, *History of the Thirty-Sixth*, p. 161, cites Sigel as being confident of victory, but Curtis, in a letter to his brother, April 16, 1862, tells a different story. Curtis may have been supercritical of the German on account of the undue credit given him in the press. David Lathrop, *History of the Fifty-Ninth . . . Illinois*, pp. 96–97.

246   Curtis, "Army of the South-West," p. 153. Moore, *Anecdotes*, p. 119. Lathrop, *History of the Fifty-Ninth*, p. 96. Britton, *Civil*

War, pp. 261, 264. Abel, *American Indian as Participant,* p. 31.
Bennett, *History of the Thirty-Sixth,* pp. 163–165. Kennerly, *Persimmon Hill,* pp. 242–243. *O. R.,* I, VIII, p. 285. Edwards, *Shelby,*
p. 51.

247   Curtis, "Army of the South-West," p. 143. Kennerly, *Persimmon
Hill,* p. 243. Letter, Curtis to brother, March 13, 1862, Curtis Papers,
CSmH. St. Louis *Daily Missouri Republican,* July 18, 1885. Ben-
nett, *History of the Thirty-Sixth,* p. 167. Britton, *Civil War,* p. 264.
Herr, *Episodes,* pp. 74–75.

248   Britton, *Civil War,* pp. 270, 275. Thomas, *Arkansas,* p. 133. Curtis,
"Army of the South-West," pp. 144, 146, 174. Noble, "Battle of Pea
Ridge," pp. 232–233. Bennett, *History of the Thirty-Sixth,* pp. 151,
170, 173. Herr, *Episodes,* pp. 79–80. Milo M. Quaife, ed., *Absalom
Grimes,* pp. 38, 43. *St. Joseph Morning Herald,* September 10, 1862.

249   Homer Field reprint from *History of Pottawattamie County.* Ad-
dison A. Stuart, *Iowa Colonels,* p. 114. Eugene F. Ware, *The In-
dian War of 1864,* p. 4. *O. R.,* I, VIII, p. 206. Sigel, "Pea Ridge
Campaign," p. 333. Dodge, *Battle of Atlanta,* p. 30. Prentis, *Kansas
Miscellanies,* p. 51. Letter, Curtis to brother, March 13, 1862, Curtis
Papers, CSmH.

250   Letter, Curtis to brother, April 16, 1862, Curtis Papers, CSmH.
Curtis, "Army of the South-West," pp. 147, 158. Wilfred R. Hollister
and Harry Norman, *Five Famous Missourians,* p. 352. *Military His-
tory . . . of the Thirteenth . . . Illinois,* p. 164. O. R., I, VIII, p. 195.
"Indian-Pioneer History" (Ms.), XXVI, p. 277. Abel, *American
Indian as Participant,* p. 33.

251   Baxter, *Pea Ridge,* pp. 85, 94–95, 101, 124, 152. *St. Joseph Morning Herald,* October 10, 31, 1862. Richard H. Benton, "Reminiscences" (Ms.). Britton, *Civil War,* p. 313. Eli G. Foster, *Civil War
by Campaigns,* p. 64. Edward A. Davenport, ed., *History of the
Ninth . . . Illinois Cavalry,* p. 43. San Francisco *Alta California,*
October 18, 1862. Charles E. Nash, *Biographical Sketches,* p. 65.
Thomas L. Snead, "The Conquest of Arkansas," p. 444. New Orleans *Picayune,* April 20, 1862.

CHAPTER XXII

The Bloodstained Kansas Banner

252   St. Louis *Daily Missouri Republican,* August 13, 1861. Wiley
Britton, *Union Indian Brigade,* pp. 62–63. Annie Heloise Abel,

American Indian as Participant, pp. 115 fn, 126, 251. United States Indian Office, *Loyal Creek Claim: Hearings*, p. 29, and *Report of the Commissioner . . . 1865*, p. 39.

253   Abel, *American Indian as Participant*, p. 121. Wiley Britton, *Civil War on the Border*, pp. 299, 306, and *Union Indian Brigade*, p. 74. Albert R. Greene, "Campaigning in the Army of the Frontier," p. 287. *O. R.*, I, XIII, pp. 162, 521. Annie Heloise Abel, *American Indian as Slaveholder*, pp. 138 fn, 139 fn. United States Indian Office, *Report of the Commissioner . . . 1865*, pp. 38, 323. *National Cyclopaedia of American Biography*, VIII, p. 257. Abel, *American Indian as Participant*, pp. 139–142.

254   Harrison Hannahs, "General Thomas Ewing, Jr.," p. 276. John Speer, *Life of James H. Lane*, pp. 333, 353. Leverett W. Spring, *Kansas*, p. 282. Interview with Mrs. Daniel C. Johnson, Kansas City, Missouri. Noble L. Prentis, *Kansas Miscellanies*, p. 110.

255   San Francisco *Alta California*, January 21, 1863. *St. Joseph Morning Herald*, August 15, September 2, October 3, 1862. *O. R.*, I, XXIII, pp. 235–239, and III, II, pp. 802–805. Some Negroes were supplied with regulation uniforms, according to Benjamin Quarles, *The Negro in the Civil War*, p. 114. Britton, *Civil War*, p. 316. Abel, *American Indian as Participant*, p. 205. William E. Connelley, *Quantrill*, pp. 260–267, 269. Leavenworth *Daily Conservative*, September 29, 1862. Edward A. Davenport, ed., *History of the Ninth . . . Illinois*, p. 43.

256   John N. Edwards, *Shelby and His Men*, pp. 77, 106. Charles E. Nash, *Biographical Sketches*, p. 77. Thomas L. Snead, "Conquest of Arkansas," p. 444. David Y. Thomas, *Arkansas*, p. 352. Letter, Pike to Elias Rector, January 28, 1862, Tx. *Washington Telegraph*, September 17, 1862. *O. R.*, I, XIII, pp. 869–871. Fred W. Allsop, *Albert Pike*, p. 200. Abel, *American Indian as Participant*, pp. 181, 198.

257   Watie, as chief, printed proclamation of Hindman's calling all loyal Cherokee to their homes under his protection, GEU. Edwards, *Shelby*, p. 77. Snead, "Conquest of Arkansas," p. 447. *Fort Smith New Era*, November 5, 1864. *White Cloud Chief*, June 9, 1864. Abel, "Indians in Civil War," p. 293. *O. R.*, I, XXII, pt. 1, p. 43. Addison A. Stuart, *Iowa Colonels*, p. 361.

258–259   "Diary of Unknown Soldier" (Ms.), November 26, 1862. Connelley, *Quantrill*, p. 281. Edwards, *Shelby*, pp. 94, 100, 102. Britton, *Civil War*, pp. 388, 393. Thomas, *Arkansas*, p. 157.

260   *O. R.*, I, XXII, pt. 1, pp. 42, 46. Wilfred R. Hollister and Harry Norman, *Five Famous Missourians*, p. 256. Britton, *Civil War*, p. 386. William E. Connelley, *Life of Preston B. Plumb*, p. 113, 126. Samuel J. Crawford, *Kansas in the Sixties*, p. 72. Edward Bumgardner, *Life of Edmund G. Ross*, p. 46. John F. Lee, "John Sappington Marmaduke," p. 29.

CHAPTER XXIII
The Battle of Prairie Grove

261   Wiley Britton, *Civil War on the Border*, p. 397. "Diary of Unknown Soldier" (Ms.), November 4, 1862. A. W. Bishop, *Loyalty on the Frontier*, p. 68. Henry E. Palmer, "An Outing in Arkansas," p. 221.

262–263   William Baxter, *Pea Ridge and Prairie Grove*, p. 179. Britton, *Civil War*, p. 396. Noble L. Prentis, *Kansas Miscellanies*, pp. 17, 19. John N. Edwards, *Shelby and His Men*, pp. 110–111, 113. Frank Moore, *Anecdotes, Poetry and Incidents*, p. 506.

264–265   W. W. Denison, "Battle of Prairie Grove," pp. 589–590. Edwards, *Shelby*, p. 116. William E. Connelley, *Life of Preston B. Plumb*, p. 120. H. H. Crittenden, *Memoirs*, pp. 213–239, 345. Baxter, *Pea Ridge*, p. 181. "Diary of Unknown Soldier" (Ms.), December 7, 1862. David Y. Thomas, *Arkansas*, p. 164.

266–267   *O. R.*, I, XXII, pt. 1, pp. 94, 102 ff. Bishop, *Loyalty*, p. 69. Edwards, *Shelby*, pp. 118, 122–124. Wilfred R. Hollister and Harry Norman, *Five Famous Missourians*, pp. 359–360. Prentis, *Kansas Miscellanies*, pp. 13, 18–22. Britton, *Civil War*, p. 412. Thomas, *Arkansas*, p. 170.

268–269   Samuel J. Crawford, *Kansas in the Sixties*, pp. 77–78. Prentis, *Kansas Miscellanies*, pp. 24, 29, 32. Denison, "Battle of Prairie Grove," p. 587. Connelley, *Life of Plumb*, pp. 123, 125–126. *White Cloud Chief*, June 9, 1864.

270   Edwards, *Shelby*, pp. 125–126, 128. James G. Blunt, "Account of Civil War Experiences," p. 233. Prentis, *Kansas Miscellanies*, p. 29.

Richard H. Benton, "Reminiscences" (Ms.), p. 6. *Fort Smith New Era,* December 12, 1862. *O. R.,* I, XXII, pt. 1, p. 69.

271   Britton, *Civil War,* pp. 430, 436, 440. Prentis, *Kansas Miscellanies,* p. 29. Edwards, *Shelby,* p. 127. *O. R.,* I, XXII, pt. 2, p. 6. Annie Heloise Abel, *American Indian as Participant,* p. 219 fn. Henry C. Adams, "Battle of Prairie Grove," p. 462. Connelley, *Life of Plumb,* pp. 26, 131. Letter, Rector to Johnson, January 29, 1863, Tx. United States Indian Office, *Report of the Commissioner . . . 1865,* p. 285. Blunt, "Account of Experiences," p. 236.

272–273   Crawford, *Kansas in the Sixties,* p. 95. Thomas, *Arkansas,* p. 196. C. B. Holland, report of battle (Ms.). *St. Joseph Morning Herald,* January 13, 18, 22, 1863. Little Rock *Arkansas True Democrat,* January 28, 1863. Eli G. Foster, *Civil War by Campaigns,* p. 66. Hollister and Norman, *Five Famous Missourians,* p. 361.

CHAPTER XXIV

Quantrill Redresses Gettysburg

274   William E. Connelley, *Quantrill and the Border Wars,* p. 281, suggests that Price may have conferred the colonelcy. Annie Heloise Abel, *American Indian as Participant,* p. 251. R. J. Bell, diary (Ms.), August 12, 1863. Letter, Rector to Johnson, January 29, 1863, Tx. *O. R.,* I, XXII, pt. 2, p. 411. Samuel H. Chester, *Pioneer Days,* p. 53.

275   *Daily Kansas City Journal of Commerce,* June 17, 1865. *Soldier's Letter* (newspaper), I, No. 4. Henry H. Crittenden, *Memoirs,* p. 347. Letter, Ross to W. P. Dole, April 2, 1863, Tx. Cherokee Nation, Minute-book, February 18, November 16, 1863. United States Indian Office, *Report of the Commissioner . . . 1865,* p. 36. Abel, *American Indian as Participant,* pp. 256, 258, 267, 271. *O. R.,* I, XXII, pt. 1, p. 34, pt. 2, pp. 1049–1053. Warner Lewis, "Massacre of Confederates by the Osages," p. 49.

276   Clarksville *Standard,* June 16, 1863. Description of marker in *Kansas Quarterly,* No. 4 (November 1941), p. 357. *O. R.,* I, XXII, pt. 2, p. 286, lists nineteen as killed. Abel, *American Indian as Participant,* p. 237 fn. W. L. Bartles, "Massacre of Confederates," pp. 62–66. Wiley Britton, *Civil War on the Border,* II, p. 228. Warner Lewis, "Civil War Reminiscences," p. 229.

277   *Chicago Times*, June 13, 1863. Roy P. Basler, ed., *Collected Works of Abraham Lincoln*, VI, p. 234. John M. Schofield, *Forty-six Years in the Army*, p. 90.

278   William E. Connelley, *Life of Preston B. Plumb*, p. 142. Kansas City *Western Journal of Commerce*, July 11, August 15, 1863. Connelley, *Life of Plumb*, p. 153. Eli G. Foster, *Civil War by Campaigns*, p. 66. Wilfred R. Hollister and Harry Norman, *Five Famous Missourians*, p. 363.

279–280 Clarksville *Standard*, September 12, October 10, 1863. *O. R.*, I, XX, pt. 2, pp. 457–461, I, XXII, pt. 1, pp. 448, 457–461, pt. 2, p. 961. Britton, *Civil War*, p. 123. E. E. Dale and G. Litton, *Cherokee Cavaliers*, p. 136. Charles R. Freeman, "Battle of Honey Springs," pp. 154–168. Kansas Scrapbook, IV, p. 269. Connelley, *Life of Plumb*, pp. 146–149, 151. Connelley, *Quantrill*, p. 300.

281   Interview with Hannah Oliver in Lawrence, Kansas. Connelley, *Quantrill*, pp. 314, 384–385. John C. Shea, *Reminiscences of Quantrell's Raid*, p. 20. The raid's destination was disclosed to the men at 8 P.M., according to Henry E. Palmer, "Lawrence Raid," p. 318. Estimates of the number of Quantrill's raiders vary from three to six hundred. Note Connelley, *Life of Plumb*, p. 154. Albert R. Greene, "What I Saw of the Quantrill Raid," p. 433. Palmer, "Lawrence Raid," p. 317.

282–283 Connelley, *Life of Plumb*, pp. 156, 158. Leverett W. Spring, *Kansas*, p. 290. Hugh D. Fisher, *The Gun and the Gospel*, pp. 174, 176, 185. Gregg is quoted by Connelley, *Quantrill*, p. 467, as saying that Quantrill rode a lighter-colored horse than his brown Charlie. Shea, *Reminiscences*, pp. 20, 25.

284–285 Connelley, *Quantrill*, p. 344. George W. E. Griffith, "My Experiences in the Quantrill Raid" (Ms.). Fisher, *Gun and Gospel*, pp. 188–190. Hannah Oliver interview. Kansas City *Western Journal of Commerce*, August 29, 1863. Connelley, *Life of Plumb*, p. 157. Letter, Thomas Ewing, Jr., to father, August 28, 1863, Ewing Papers.

286   Daniel Geary, "War Incidents," p. 284. Greene, "What I Saw," p. 436. Shea, *Reminiscences*, pp. 6, 24. *Western Journal of Commerce*, August 29, 1863. Connelley, *Life of Plumb*, p. 159. Connelley, *Quantrill*, p. 430. Spring, *Kansas*, pp. 287, 292, 296. John N. Edwards, *Shelby and His Men*, p. 400. John Speer, *Life of James H.*

Lane, p. 315. Theophilus F. Rodenbough, *From Everglade to Cañon,* p. 22.

287   Shea, *Reminiscences,* pp. 8, 9. *O. R.,* I, XXII, pt. 1, p. 592. Palmer, "Lawrence Raid," p. 194. *Western Journal of Commerce,* August 29, 1863. The recorded account has been put in direct vernacular quotation.

288   Connelley, *Life of Plumb,* p. 165. *Western Journal of Commerce,* August 29, 1863. Greene, "What I Saw," p. 439. Ewing reported in *O. R.,* I, XXII, pt. 1, p. 579.

289   Greene, "What I Saw," p. 447. *Los Angeles Star,* December 19, 1863. St. Louis *Daily Missouri Republican,* September 16, 1863. *St. Joseph Morning Herald,* September 1, 1863. *Western Journal of Commerce,* September 5, 12, 1863. *Chicago Tribune,* June 5, 8, 1863. New York *World,* June 9, 1863. Caroline Abbot Stanley, *Order No. 11, A Tale of the Border,* demonstrates this sentiment in fiction after a reaction had occurred. Thomas Ewing, Jr., to father, August 28, September 22, 1863, Ewing Papers.

CHAPTER XXV
Baxter Springs

290   *O. R.,* I, XXII, pt. 2, p. 411. Letter, Phillips to Ewing, September 1, 1863, Tx. Letter, Blunt to Lincoln, September 24, 1863, Lincoln Papers. *O. R.,* I, XXII, pt. 2, p. 411. Annie Heloise Abel, *American Indian as Participant,* p. 295. James G. Blunt, "Account of Civil War Experiences," p. 247. Samuel J. Crawford, *Kansas in the Sixties,* pp. 97, 99. United States Indian Office, *Report of the Commissioner . . . 1865,* p. 322. David Y. Thomas, *Arkansas,* p. 225.

291–293   John G. Nicolay and John Hay, *Abraham Lincoln,* VIII, p. 215. Tyler Dennett, *Lincoln and the Civil War,* pp. 97, 108. Roy P. Basler, ed., *Collected Works of Abraham Lincoln,* VI, pp. 499–504. *Sacramento Union,* November 4, 1863, quoting St. Louis *Daily Missouri Republican,* October 14, 1863. Letter, Samuel Curtis to brother, February 20, 1864, Curtis Papers, CSmH. Blunt, "Account of Experiences," p. 248. Letter, Milo Gookins to W. P. Dole, March 8, 1864, DNA. Letter, Curtis to brother, February 20, 1864, Curtis Papers, CSmH.

294–295   William E. Connelley, *Quantrill,* pp. 425, 430. *O. R.,* I, XXII, pt. 2, pp. 595–597 and XLI, pt. 2, pp. 727–729. E. A. Calkins, "Wisconsin Cavalry Regiments," pp. 173–193. Letter, Ewing to Jennison, November 25, 1863, DLC. *Fort Smith New Era,* October 8, November 14, 1863. Basler, *Collected Works,* pp. 543–544. John M. Schofield, *Forty-six Years in the Army,* p. 105.

296–297   Thomas, *Arkansas,* p. 229. Schofield, *Forty-six Years,* p. 101. Cherokee Nation, Minute-book of Executive Department, October 24, November 3, 1863. E. E. Dale and G. Litton, *Cherokee Cavaliers,* pp. 144–145. Mollie Ross, *Life and Times of Hon. William P. Ross,* p. viii. *O. R.,* I, XXII, pt. 1, pp. 781–782, pt. 2, pp. 246, 722, 752, 1094; I, XXXIV, pt. 2, pp. 188, 928. *Chicago Tribune,* December 21, 22, 27, 1863. Letter from George Bent to Hyde, November 16, 1904, Bent Correspondence.

CHAPTER XXVI

Lincoln's Re-election Campaign on the Border

298   Harrison Hannahs, "General Thomas Ewing, Jr.," pp. 278–280. Letter, Thomas Ewing, Jr., to wife, April 10, 15, May 11, 1864, Ewing Papers.

299   David Y. Thomas, *Arkansas,* p. 254. Letter, W. G. Coffin to W. P. Dole, January 6, 1864, Tx. United States Indian Office, *Report of the Commissioner . . . 1865,* p. 317. *Emporia News,* May 14, 1864. *Fort Smith New Era,* May 21, June 11, 1864. Letter, W. L. G. Mills to Secretary of Interior, April 23, 1864, DNA.

300–301   Letter, Coffin to Dole, May 28, June 7, 16, 1864; Stanton to Usher, May 26, 1864; both Tx. United States Indian Office, *Report of the Commissioner . . . 1864,* pp. 31, 303. Letter, Coffin to Dole, June 7, 1864, Tx. United States Indian Office, *Report of the Commissioner . . . 1864,* pp. 38, 337, 340–342. Letter, Henry Smith to Dole, June 6, 1864, Tx. General Order No. 47, May 13, 1864, Phillips Collection.

302   G. W. Grayson, "Red Paths and White" (Ms.), pp. 99–108. *Fort Smith New Era,* June 18, 1864. *O. R.,* I, XXXIV, pt. 1, pp. 1011–1013, pt. 4, pp. 686–687; II, IV, pp. 417, 621. Samuel J. Crawford, *Kansas in the Sixties,* p. 137. Telegrams, Livingston to Dodge, February 9, 1864; Dodge, Sr., to Dodge, Jr., September 1, 1864; both in

Dodge Papers. *White Cloud Chief,* September 1, 1864. *Emporia News,* May 26, July 2, 23, 30, September 10, 1864. United States Indian Office, *Report of the Commissioner . . . 1864,* p. 1. William E. Connelley, *Life of Preston B. Plumb,* p. 193.

303   *White Cloud Chief,* June 4, 1863. Joe Medill to Washburne, February 12, 1864, Washburne Papers. *White Cloud Chief,* June 2, August 11, 1864. Other escapades with women are cited in the *Chief,* August 4, 1864.

304   Kansas Scrapbook, Biography, IV, p. 282. W. A. Stoddard, "Story of a Nomination," p. 272. Leverett W. Spring, "Career of a Kansas Politician," p. 103. *Fort Smith New Era,* July 23, 1864. *White Cloud Chief,* June 9, 1864.

305   Report of Brigadier General Thayer, August 10, 1864, Tx. *Emporia News,* August 6, September 3, 1864. Leavenworth *Daily Conservative,* November 8, 1864. *White Cloud Chief,* October 13, 1864. United States Indian Office, *Report of the Commissioner . . . 1864,* p. 33. *Leavenworth Times,* August 25, September 14, 1864. *Emporia News,* September 10, 1864. St. Louis *Daily Missouri Republican,* September 4, 1864. *White Cloud Chief,* August 18, September 22, 1864. Letter, Smith Christie to John Ross, August 19, 1864, Phillips Collection.

306   *Fort Smith New Era,* November 5, 1864. Crawford, *Kansas in the Sixties,* p. 200. *White Cloud Chief,* September 22, 1864. *Leavenworth Times,* September 4, 1864. Letters, Thomas Ewing, Jr., to wife, August 21, 28, September 22, 1864, Ewing Papers. Letter, Lanigan to Col. Johnson, June 17, 1864, MoSHi. *Cincinnati Commercial,* October 28, 1864. Thomas C. Fletcher, "Battle of Pilot Knob," p. 30. John B. Sanborn, "Campaign in Missouri," p. 138.

CHAPTER XXVII

Cabin Creek and Pilot Knob

307   *O. R.,* I, XLI, pt. 1, p. 781. G. W. Grayson, "Red Paths and White" (Ms.), pp. 109–114, 116–119. Clarksville *Standard,* September 3, 1864. Watie's accomplishments are listed in *O. R.,* I, XLI, pt. 1, p. 792.

308 Grayson, "Red Paths," pp. 118, 143. Clarksville *Standard,* October 15, 1864. Watie reported eighty-five prisoners, in *O. R.,* I, XLI, pt. 1, pp. 766–769. See also I, XLI, pt. 1, pp. 785–786.

309 "Indian-Pioneer History" (Ms.), LXXXI, pp. [81], 429; C, pp. 427–431. Grayson, "Red Paths," pp. 123, 126. Clarksville *Standard,* October 15, 1864. Letter, Peck to Haines, September 23, 1864, Dodge Papers. Clarksville *Standard,* October 8, 1864. *Fort Smith New Era,* October 1, 1864. Watie's, Gano's, and Hopkins's reports are printed in *O. R.,* I, XLI, pt. 1, pp. 766–769, 784–791. United States Indian Office, *Report of the Commissioner . . . 1865,* p. 276.

310 Grayson, "Red Paths," p. 129. Telegram, Fuller to Dole, n.d., Tx. Telegram, Cutter to Dole, October 13, 1864, Tx. Wilfred R. Hollister and Harry Norman, *Five Famous Missourians,* p. 367. H. H. Crittenden, *Battle of Westport,* p. 34.

311 Grayson, "Red Paths," pp. 265–266. Hollister and Norman, *Five Famous Missourians,* p. 367. Samuel J. Crawford, *Kansas in the Sixties,* p. 136. David Y. Thomas, *Arkansas,* p. 286. St. Louis *Daily Missouri Republican,* September 27, 28, 1864. Annie Heloise Abel, *American Indian as Participant,* p. 332. Thomas, *Arkansas,* p. 287. *Cincinnati Commercial,* October 28, 1864. Clarksville *Standard,* June 16, 1862. New Orleans *Picayune,* December 3, 1861. Leavenworth *Democratic Standard,* October 12, 1883. *O. R.,* I, XLI, pt. 1, p. 446, pt. 3, p. 683. Thomas C. Fletcher, "Battle of Pilot Knob," p. 34. *Soldier's Letter* (newspaper), I, No. 16, September 27, 1864.

312 Harrison Hannahs, "General Thomas Ewing, Jr.," picture, p. 153. *St. Louis Globe-Democrat,* May 14, September 4, 1882. Albert D. Richardson, *Garnered Sheaves,* p. 153. David Murphy, "My Recollections of Pilot Knob" (Ms.). Fletcher, "Battle of Pilot Knob," p. 39, edited. *New York Herald,* February 2, 1896.

313 Letter, William G. Hazen to brother, 1864. St. Louis *Daily Missouri Democrat,* October 3, 1864. *White Cloud Chief,* October 6, 1864.

314–315 *O. R.,* I, XLI, pt. 1, p. 448. *Soldier's Letter* (newspaper), I, Nos. 16, 17. *New York Herald,* February 2, 1896. Letter, Hazen to brother, 1864. *Cincinnati Commercial,* October 28, 1864. *St. Louis*

Globe-Democrat, April 4, 1897. Letter, "Ellen" to Thomas Ewing, Jr., October 7, 1864, Ewing Papers. Hannahs, "General Ewing, Jr.," p. 280.

CHAPTER XXVIII

Centralia

316–317 *Kansas City Journal,* October 26, 1902. Wilfred R. Hollister and Harry Norman, *Five Famous Missourians,* pp. 367, 396. St. Louis *Daily Missouri Republican,* November 5, 1864. William E. Connelley, *Quantrill,* p. 449. Cloyd Bryner, *Bugle Echoes,* p. 148. H. H. Crittenden, *Memoirs,* p. 345. Mary G. C. Gordon, diary (Ms.), October 7, 1864. John N. Edwards, *Shelby and His Men,* p. 434.

318 Kansas City *Western Journal of Commerce,* October 8, 1864. W. A. Neal, *Illustrated History of the Missouri Engineer,* p. 150. Gordon, diary (Ms.), October 7, 1864.

319 Charles H. Lothrop, *History of the First Regiment Iowa Cavalry,* pp. 193–194, states that Jesse was not present. Frank James, an eyewitness, states that he was. Crittenden, *Memoirs,* pp. 336, 339, 345. Connelley, *Quantrill,* p. 453.

CHAPTER XXIX

The Eve of Austerlitz

320 *O. R.,* I, XLI, pt. 1, p. 654. Interview with Thompson's daughter, Marcie Bailey, St. Joseph. Little Rock *Arkansas Patriot,* August 11, 1863. St. Louis *Daily Missouri Republican,* August 27, 1863. *Fort Smith New Era,* November 28, 1863. *St. Joseph Morning Herald,* February 5, August 27, 30, 1863. *Cincinnati Commercial,* October 28, 1864. John B. Sanborn, "Campaign in Missouri," pp. 146–147, 157. Cloyd Bryner, *Bugle Echoes,* p. 146. Richard Walsh, *Making of Buffalo Bill,* p. 85.

321 Mary G. C. Gordon, diary (Ms.), October 7, 1864. J. H. P. Baker, diary (Ms.), October 4, 5, 1864. Sanborn, "Campaign in Missouri," p. 157. Eli G. Foster, *Civil War by Campaigns,* p. 66. Wilfred R. Hollister and Harry Norman, *Five Famous Missourians,* p. 365.

322 *St. Louis Globe-Democrat,* April 4, 1897. Henry E. Palmer, "Soldiers of Kansas," pp. 433, 437. Gordon, diary (Ms.), October 9, 20,

25, 1864. *O. R.,* I, XLI, pt. 1, p. 655. David Y. Thomas, *Arkansas,* p. 287. John N. Edwards, *Shelby and His Men,* p. 398. On p. 471, Edwards prints Governor Reynolds's account. Charles H. Lothrop, *History of First . . . Iowa Cavalry,* p. 194. *Cincinnati Commercial,* October 28, 1864. St. Louis *Daily Missouri Democrat,* October 10, 1864. Frank Moore, *Anecdotes, Poetry and Incidents,* p. 180.

323   Gordon, diary (Ms.), October 19, 1864. *Boonville Weekly Advertiser,* November 17, 1899. *Centralia Fireside Guard,* April 16, 1915, reprints article on Anderson's life from its April 15, 1871, issue. *Fort Smith New Era,* November 26, 1864. Kansas City *Western Journal of Commerce,* November 3, 1864. *Kansas City Journal,* October 17, 26, 1901. John Speer, *Life of James H. Lane,* pp. 286, 292, 333. Leverett W. Spring, *Kansas,* p. 298. Baker, diary (Ms.), October 14, 1864. *St. Louis Globe-Democrat,* April 4, 1897. [Richard J. Hinton], *Rebel Invasion of Missouri,* pp. 65–68. *O. R.,* I, XLI, pt. 4, p. 117. *White Cloud Chief,* August 11, 1864. Letter, John N. Moulton to Elizabeth Jane Martin, September 20, 1864, MoSHi. Kansas Scrapbook, Biography, IV, p. 62.

324   Speer, *Life of Lane,* pp. 285–287, 292–294. *White Cloud Chief,* October 6, 1864. William E. Connelley, *Life of Preston B. Plumb,* p. 181. Baker, diary (Ms.), October 18, 19, 1864. *St. Louis Globe-Democrat,* April 4, 1897. *Soldier's Letter* (newspaper), I, No. 20. *Western Journal of Commerce,* December 31, 1864. *O. R.,* I, XLI, pt. 1, p. 656. "Campaign against Sterling Price," Philadelphia *Weekly Times,* August 7, 1881.

325–326   Sanborn, "Campaign in Missouri," pp. 151, 171. *Western Journal of Commerce,* November 3, 1864. [Hinton], *Rebel Invasion,* p. 105. Baker, diary (Ms.), October 20, 21, 1864. Clad Hamilton, "A Colonel of Kansas," p. 286. John F. Phillips, "Diary," October 20–21, 1864. Leavenworth *Daily Conservative,* November 27, 1864. *Soldier's Letter* (newspaper), I, No. 27. Paul B. Jenkins, *Battle of Westport,* p. 73. W. L. Webb, *Battles and Biographies of Missourians,* p. 342. William H. Schrader, "Reminiscences" (Ms.), p. 24.

327–328   *Western Journal of Commerce,* December 31, 1864. *O. R.,* I, XLI, pt. 1, p. 313. *Soldier's Letter* (newspaper), I, No. 42. *Battle of the Blue of the Second Regiment, K.S.M. Kansas City Journal,* October 17, 1901. *Kansas City Star,* May 19, 1888. H. H. Crittenden, *Battle of Westport,* p. 35. Phillips, "Diary," October 23, 1864.

CHAPTER XXX

The Battle of Westport

329–330   William E. Connelley, *Life of Preston B. Plumb,* pp. 187–189. H. H. Crittenden, *Battle of Westport,* p. 38. John Speer, *Life of James H. Lane,* p. 288. Richard J. Hinton, "Pens That Made Kansas Free," p. 374. Samuel J. Reader, diary (Ms.), October 13–21, 1864. *St. Louis Globe-Democrat,* April 4, 1897. Samuel J. Crawford, *Kansas in the Sixties,* p. 148.

331–333   Crawford, *Kansas in the Sixties,* p. 149. Letter, William G. Hazen to brother, 1864. Paul B. Jenkins, *Battle of Westport,* p. 82. Crittenden, *Battle of Westport,* pp. 38–40. John F. Phillips, "Diary," October 23, 1864.

334–335   Crittenden, *Battle of Westport,* pp. 45–46. Jenkins, *Battle of Westport,* pp. 95, 104, 127. *O. R.,* I, XLI, pt. 1 — Reports, p. 486. *St. Louis Globe-Democrat,* April 4, 1899. Stephen H. Ragan, "Battle of Westport," p. 263.

336   Crittenden, *Battle of Westport,* pp. 45, 60. [R. J. Hinton], *Rebel Invasion of Missouri,* p. 161. *O. R.,* I, XLI, pt. 1, p. 659. *Kansas City Star,* June 19, 1932, January 23, 1938. *Kansas City Post,* August 2, 1925. Wilfred R. Hollister and Harry Norman, *Five Famous Missourians,* p. 370. Ragan, "Battle of Westport," p. 265. John B. Sanborn, "Campaign in Missouri," p. 184. Kansas City Native Sons Scrapbook, II, p. 81. Ewing Papers, October 24, 1864.

CHAPTER XXXI

Retreat from Moscow

337   John B. Sanborn, "Campaign in Missouri," p. 185. John Speer, *Life of James H. Lane,* p. 298. *St. Louis Globe-Democrat,* April 4, 1897. Kansas City *Western Journal of Commerce,* December 31, 1864. *Soldier's Letter* (newspaper), I, No. 42.

338   J. H. P. Baker, diary (Ms.), October 24, 1864. Sanborn, "Campaign in Missouri," pp. 186, 193–194. Samuel J. Crawford, *Kansas in the Sixties,* pp. 158, 160. *Topeka Mail,* March 3, 1899. Eli G. Foster, *Civil War by Campaigns,* p. 66. *St. Louis Globe-Democrat,* April 4,

1897. David Y. Thomas, *Arkansas*, p. 289. John F. Phillips, "Diary," October 25, 1864.

339   Letter, J. S. Williams to W. Stevens, April 4, 1921, MoSHi. *O. R.*, I, XLI, pt. 1, pp. 335, 636–637. Phillips, "Diary," October 25, 1864. *Forth Smith New Era*, November 26, 1864. *Western Journal of Commerce*, November 3, 1864. Leavenworth *Conservative*, November 27, 1864. *Soldier's Letter* (newspaper), I, No. 31. Thomas C. Fletcher, "Battle of Pilot Knob," p. 242.

340   *St. Louis Globe-Democrat*, April 4, 1897. *Soldier's Letter* (newspaper), I, No. 31. Letter, Samuel Curtis to brother, December 12, 1864, Curtis Papers, CSmH. *Western Journal of Commerce*, November 3, 1864. Letter, Hawkins Taylor to Grenville M. Dodge, December 19, 1864, Dodge Papers. Crawford, *Kansas in the Sixties*, p. 175.

341   *O. R.*, I, XLI, pt. 1, p. 66, pt. 4, pp. 1013–1014. Letter, William G. Hazen to brother, 1864. *Western Journal of Commerce*, November 3, 1864. Baker, diary (Ms.), October 25, 26, 1864. R. L. Brown and A. T. Irwine, "Army Journal" (Ms.), October 26, 1864. *Fort Smith New Era*, November 12, 1864. Crawford, *Kansas in the Sixties*, pp. 171, 202. Speer, *Life of Lane*, pp. 290, 299. Letter of D. C. Nettleton in *Annals of Kansas City*, I, No. 3, pp. 272–273. *Soldier's Letter* (newspaper), I, Nos. 32, 34, 42. Sanborn, "Campaign in Missouri," pp. 171, 200.

342   Letter, Samuel Curtis to brother, December 12, 1864, Curtis Papers, CSmH. *Soldier's Letter* (newspaper), I, No. 40. Letter, Hazen to brother, 1864. Brown, "Army Journal" (Ms.), November 1, 5, 1864. Letter of Nettleton in *Annals*, pp. 272–273.

343   Brown and Irwine, "Army Journal" (Ms.), November 10, 17, 1864. Letter, Hazen to brother, 1864. Sanborn, "Campaign in Missouri," p. 201. Baker, diary (Ms.), October 31, November 3–4, 1864. John N. Edwards, *Shelby and His Men*, p. 467. Thomas, *Arkansas*, p. 291. Letter, Samuel Curtis to Grenville M. Dodge, December 14, 1864, IaDH.

344–345   George Hyde, "Life of George Bent" (Ms.), Chap. V. pp. 6–9, CoD. Letter, Samuel Curtis, dated January 7, 1864, Curtis Papers,

CsmH. J. T. Granger, *Brief Biographical Sketch of . . . Major-General Grenville M. Dodge,* p. 20. William E. Connelley, *Quantrill,* p. 457.

CHAPTER XXXII

Epilogue

346   Kansas City *Western Journal of Commerce,* January 7, March 25, 1865. Roy P. Basler, ed., *Collected Works of Abraham Lincoln,* VIII, p. 308. Jay Monaghan, *Legend of Tom Horn,* p. 49. H. H. Crittenden, *Memoirs,* p. 260. William E. Connelley, *Quantrill,* pp. 465, 475. *St. Louis Post-Dispatch,* February 9, 1930.

347   Little Rock *Arkansas Patriot,* June 30, 1863. John N. Edwards, *Shelby and His Men,* p. 538. William W. Heartsill, *Fourteen Hundred and 91 Days,* p. 24. Richmond *Southern Opinion,* September 7, 1867. David Y. Thomas, *Arkansas,* pp. 310, 314. *Western Journal of Commerce,* June 13, 1865.

348–349   Letter, D. H. Cooper to Stand Watie, April 21, 1865, Phillips Collection. "Indian-Pioneer History" (Ms.), CXII, p. 180, OkU. United States Indian Office, *Report of the Commissioner . . . 1865,* p. 245. Edwards, *Shelby,* pp. 545–550. Charles Edward Nash, *Biographical Sketches,* p. 218. William E. Connelley, *Wild Bill and His Era,* p. 82.

350–351   William E. Woodruff, *With the Light Guns,* p. 47. *Leavenworth Times,* May 13, June 10, July 11, 1875. *United States Biographical Dictionary,* Kansas Volume, pp. 61–63. Interview with J. M. Mickey, who wrote editorials for Anthony. Noble L. Prentis, *Kansas Miscellanies,* p. 116.

Sources

BOOKS AND ARTICLES

Abbott, Wilbur Cortez, "Political Warfare in Early Kansas," *Journal of American History*, III, pp. 627–635.

Abel, Annie Heloise, *The American Indian as Participant in the Civil War* (Cleveland, 1919).

Abel, Annie Heloise, *The American Indian as Slaveholder and Secessionist* (Cleveland, 1915).

Abel, Annie Heloise, *The American Indian under Reconstruction* (Cleveland, 1925).

Abel, Annie Heloise, "Indian Reservations in Kansas and the Extinguishment of their Titles," *Transactions of the Kansas State Historical Society*, VIII, pp. 72–109.

Abel, Annie Heloise, "The Indians in the Civil War," *American Historical Review*, XV, No. 2 (Jan. 1910), pp. 281–296.

"Ad Interim Report on Site of the Battle of Round Mountain," *Chronicles of Oklahoma*, XXVIII, No. 4 (Winter 1950–1951), pp. 492–495.

Adams, Franklin G., "The Capitals of Kansas," *Transactions of the Kansas State Historical Society*, pp. 331–351.

Adams, Henry C., "Battle of Prairie Grove," *War Papers . . . Indiana Commandery, Military Order of the Loyal Legion* (Indianapolis, 1898), pp. 451–464.

Address of the Committee from the State of Missouri to President Lincoln (n.p., n.d.).

Address to the People of the United States, together with the Proceedings and Resolutions of the Pro-Slavery Convention of Missouri held in Lexington, July, 1855 (St. Louis, 1855).

"Administration of Governor Shannon," *Transactions of the Kansas State Historical Society*, V, pp. 234–241.

Allsop, Fred W., *Albert Pike, A Biography* (Little Rock, Ark., 1928).

Ambler, Charles Henry, ed., *Correspondence of Robert M. T. Hunter, 1826–1876 (Annual Report of the American Historical Association, II, 1916).*

American Annual Cyclopaedia and Register of Important Events (New York, 1862).

Anderson, Ephraim McD., *Memoirs: Historical and Personal, Including Campaigns of the First Missouri Confederate Brigade* (St. Louis, 1868).

Anderson, Galusha, *The Story of a Border City during the Civil War* (Boston, 1908).

Anderson, Mabel Washbourne, *Life of General Stand Watie* (Pryor, Okla., 1915).

[Andreas, A. T.], *History of the State of Kansas* (Chicago, 1883).

Asbury, Ai Edgar, *My Experiences in the War 1861 to 1865; or, A Little Autobiography, written in 1892* (Kansas City, 1894).

Barnes, Will C., "The Chisholm Trail — For Whom Was It Named?" *The Producer: The National Live Stock Monthly,* X, Nos. 8, 9 (Jan. and Feb. 1929).

Barron, Samuel B., *The Lone Star Defenders; A Chronicle of the Third Texas Cavalry, Ross' Brigade* (New York, 1908).

Barry, Louise, "The Emigrant Aid Company Parties of 1854," *Kansas Historical Quarterly,* XII, No. 2 (May, 1943), pp. 115–155.

Bartles, W. L., "Massacre of Confederates by Osage Indians," *Transactions of the Kansas State Historical Society,* VIII, pp. 62–66.

Basler, Roy P., ed., *The Collected Works of Abraham Lincoln* (New Brunswick, N.J., 1953).

The Battle of Lexington Fought in and around the City of Lexington, Missouri, on September 18th, 19th and 20th, 1861 (Lexington, 1903).

"The Battle of Springfield. August 10th, 1861," *Public Documents of the State of Kansas for the Year 1862* (Lawrence, Kan., 1862).

The Battle of the Blue of the Second Regiment, K.S.M., October 22, 1864. The Fight, the Captivity, the Escape, as Remembered by Survivors and Commemorated by the Gage Monument at Topeka, Kansas (Chicago, n.d.).

Baxter, William, *Pea Ridge and Prairie Grove; or, Scenes and Incidents of the War in Arkansas* (Cincinnati, 1864).

Bay, William Van Ness, *Reminiscences of the Bench and Bar of Missouri* (St. Louis, 1878).

Bennett, L. G., and Wm. M. Haight, *History of the Thirty-Sixth Regiment Illinois Volunteers, during the War of the Rebellion* (Aurora, Ill., 1876).

Benton, Thomas Hart, *Nebraska and Kansas. Speech of Mr. Benton, of Missouri, in the House of Representatives, April 25, 1854* (Washington, 1854).

Bernard, William R., "Westport and the Santa Fe Trade," *Transactions of the Kansas State Historical Society,* IX, pp. 552–565.

Bevier, R. S., *History of the First and Second Missouri Confederate Brigades, 1861–1865* (St. Louis, 1879).

Bishop, Albert Webb, *Loyalty on the Frontier, or, Sketches of Union Men of the South-west* (St. Louis, 1863).

Blackmar, Frank W., "The Annals of an Historic Town," *Annual Report of the American Historical Association for the Year 1893*, pp. 481–499.

Blackmar, Frank W., "A Chapter in the Life of Charles Robinson, the First Governor of Kansas," *Annual Report of the American Historical Association for the Year 1894*, pp. 213–226.

Blackmar, Frank W., *Kansas: A Cyclopedia of State History* (Chicago, 1912).

Blackmar, Frank W., *The Life of Charles Robinson, the First State Governor of Kansas* (Topeka, 1902).

Blair, Francis Preston, *Frémont's Hundred Days in Missouri* (Speech in House of Representatives, March 7, 1862).

Blodgett, Edward A., "The Army of the Southwest and the Battle of Pea Ridge," *Military Essays and Recollections . . . Illinois Military Order of the Loyal Legion*, II (Chicago, 1894), pp. 289–312.

Blum, Virgil C., "The Political and Military Activities of the German Element in St. Louis, 1859–1861," *Missouri Historical Review*, XLII, No. 2 (Jan. 1948), pp. 103–129.

Blunt, James G., "General Blunt's Account of his Civil War Experiences," *Kansas Historical Quarterly*, I, No. 3 (May 1932), pp. 211–265.

Bondi, August, "With John Brown in Kansas," *Transactions of the Kansas State Historical Society*, VIII, 275–289.

The Border Ruffian Code in Kansas (New York, 1856).

Borland, William P., "General Jo. O. Shelby," *Missouri Historical Review*, VII, No. 1 (Oct. 1912), pp. 10–19.

Boyden, William L., "The Character of Albert Pike as Gleaned from his Correspondence," *New Age Magazine* (March 1915).

Brackett, Albert G., *History of the United States Cavalry* (New York, 1865).

Braman, Don E. E., *Braman's Information about Texas* (Philadelphia, 1857).

Brant, Randolph C., *Campaign of Gen. Lyon in Missouri. War Paper No. 3, Oregon . . . Military Order of the Loyal Legion* (Portland, 1895).

Brewerton, George Douglas, *The War in Kansas. A Rough Trip to the Border, among New Horses and a Strange People* (New York, 1856). A later edition is titled *Wars of the Western Border*.

Brewster, S. W., *Incidents of Quantrill's Raid on Lawrence, August 21, 1863. The Remarkable and Heretofore Unpublished Personal Experiences of Hon. Henry S. Clarke* (Lawrence, Kan., 1898).

Briggs, Harold E., "Lawlessness in Cairo, Illinois, 1848–1858," *Mid-America, An Historical Review*, XXX, New Series, XX, No. 2 (April 1951), pp. 67–88.

Brinkerhoff, Fred W., "The Kansas Tour of Lincoln the Candidate," *Kansas Historical Quarterly*, XIII, No. 5 (Feb. 1945), pp. 294–307.

Britton, Wiley, *The Civil War on the Border* (New York, 1891).

Britton, Wiley, *Memoirs of the Rebellion on the Border, 1863* (Chicago, 1882).

Britton, Wiley, "Resume of Military Operations in Missouri and Arkansas, 1864–65," *Battles and Leaders of the Civil War*, IV, pp. 364–377.

Britton, Wiley, "Some Reminiscences of the Cherokee People," *Chronicles of Oklahoma*, VI, No. 2 (June 1928), pp. 163–177.

Britton, Wiley, "Union and Confederate Indians in the Civil War," *Battles and Leaders of the Civil War*, I, pp. 335–336.

Britton, Wiley, *The Union Indian Brigade in the Civil War* (Kansas City, 1922).

Broadhead, James O., "Early Events of War in Missouri," *War Papers and Personal Reminiscences, 1861–1865 . . . Missouri Military Order of the Loyal Legion*, I (St. Louis, 1892), pp. 1–28.

Brockett, Linius Pierpont, *Scouts, Spies, and Heroes of the Great Civil War* (Jersey City, 1892).

Bronaugh, Warren C., *The Youngers' Fight for Freedom* (Columbia, Mo., 1906).

Brotherhead, William, *General Frémont and the Injustice Done Him by Politicians and Envious Military Men* (Philadelphia, 1862).

Brown, Francis, *Raymond of the Times* (New York, 1951).

Brown, George W., *False Claims of Kansas Historians Truthfully Corrected* (Rockford, Ill., 1902).

Brown, George W., *Reminiscences of Gov. R. J. Walker; with the True Story of the Rescue of Kansas from Slavery* (Rockford, Ill., 1902).

Brown, George W., *Reminiscences of Old John Brown* (Rockford, Ill., 1880).

Bryner, Cloyd, *Bugle Echoes: The Story of Illinois 47th* (Springfield, Ill., 1905).

Bumgardner, Edward, *The Life of Edmund G. Ross: The Man Whose Vote Saved a President* (Kansas City, 1949).

Bundy, M. L., "Missouri in '61," *War Papers . . . Indiana Commandery, Military Order of the Loyal Legion* (Indianapolis, 1898), pp. 207–211.

Burch, John P., *Charles W. Quantrell, A True History of the Guerilla Warfare, etc.* (Vega, Texas, 1923).

Burdette, Robert J., *The Drums of the 47th* (Indianapolis, 1914).

Byers, Sam H. M., *Iowa in War Times* (Des Moines, 1888).

Calkins, E. A., "The Wisconsin Cavalry Regiments," *War Papers . . . Wisconsin Military Order of the Loyal Legion*, II (Milwaukee, 1896), pp. 173–193.

"Capture of Col. Titus — The Treaty — The Exchange," *Transactions of the Kansas State Historical Society*, I and II, pp. 228–230.

Carr, Lucien, *Missouri: A Bone of Contention* (Boston, 1888).

Carruth, William H., "The New England Emigrant Aid Company as an Investment Society," *Transactions of the Kansas State Historical Society*, VI, pp. 90–96.

Caruthers, Samuel, *Speech of Hon. S. Caruthers, of Missouri, on the Nebraska and Kansas Bill. Delivered in the House of Representatives, April 7, 1854* (Washington, 1854).

Case, Theo. S., ed., *History of Kansas City, Missouri, with Illustrations and Biographical Sketches of Some of its Prominent Men and Pioneers* (Syracuse, N.Y., 1888).

Chandler, Charles L., ed., "Two Letters from Kansas, 1855–1856," *Mississippi Valley Historical Review*, XXIX, No. 1 (June 1942), pp. 77–79.

Cherokee Almanac (Park Hill, Okla., 1851–1861).

"The Cherokee Question," *Chronicles of Oklahoma*, II, No. 2 (June 1924), pp. 141–242.

Chester, Samuel H., *Pioneer Days in Arkansas* (Richmond, Va., 1927).

Clark, J. S., "General Lyon and the Fight for Missouri," *War Sketches and Incidents . . . Iowa Commandery, Military Order of the Loyal Legion*, II (Des Moines, 1898), p. 274.

Clay-Clopton, Virginia, *A Belle of the Fifties, Memoirs of Mrs. Clay of Alabama, covering Social and Political Life in Washington and the South, 1853–66* (New York, 1905).

Clemens, Samuel L., "The Private History of a Campaign that Failed," *The American Claimant and Other Stories and Sketches*, pp. 235–264 of Vol. XXI of *The Writings of Mark Twain* (New York, 1907–1918).

Cole, Arthur Charles, *The Irrepressible Conflict, 1850–1865* (New York, 1934).

Collins, L. W., "The Expedition against the Sioux Indians in 1863, under General Henry H. Sibley," *Glimpses of the Nation's Struggle, Second Series . . . Minnesota Commandery of the Military Order of the Loyal Legion* (St. Paul, 1890), pp. 173–203.

Commager, Henry Steele, ed., *The Blue and the Gray* (Indianapolis, 1950).

"Communication from the Payne County Historical Society Concerning the Site of the First Battle of the Civil War in Indian Territory," *Chronicles of Oklahoma*, XXVIII (1950–1951), pp. 210–211.

Connelley, William Elsey, *An Appeal to the Record, Refuting "False Claims" & Other Things* (Topeka, 1903).

Connelley, William Elsey, "Col. Richard J. Hinton," *Transactions of Kansas State Historical Society*, VII, pp. 486–493.

Connelley, William Elsey, "Daniel W. Wilder, the Father of Kansas History and Literature," *Collections of the Kansas State Historical Society*, XVI, pp. 1–21.

Connelley, William Elsey, *Doniphan's Expedition and the Conquest of New Mexico and California* (Topeka, 1907).

Connelley, William Elsey, *James Henry Lane, The "Grim Chieftain" of Kansas* (Topeka, 1899).

Connelley, William Elsey, *John Brown* (Topeka, 1900).

Connelley, William Elsey, "The Lane Trail," *Collections of the Kansas State Historical Society*, XIII, pp. 268–279.

Connelley, William Elsey, *The Life of Preston B. Plumb, 1837–1891* (Chicago, 1913).

Connelley, William Elsey, *The Old Pawnee Capitol* (Topeka, 1928).

Connelley, William Elsey, *The Provisional Government of Nebraska Territory and the Journals of William Walker* (Lincoln, Neb., 1899).

Connelley, William Elsey, *Quantrill and the Border Wars* (Cedar Rapids, 1910).

Connelley, William Elsey, *A Standard History of Kansas and Kansans* (Chicago, 1918).

Connelley, William Elsey, "Visit to Kansas in 1857," *Mississippi Valley Historical Review*, XIII, No. 4 (March 1927), pp. 541–544.

Connelley, William Elsey, *Wild Bill and His Era* (New York, 1933).

Connolly, Alonzo, *A Thrilling Narrative of the Minnesota Massacre and the Sioux War of 1862–63* (Chicago, 1896).

Cordley, Richard, *Pioneer Days in Kansas* (Boston, 1903).

"Correspondence of Governor Geary," *Transactions of the Kansas State Historical Society*, IV, pp. 403–519.

"Correspondence of Governor Wilson Shannon," *Transactions of the Kansas State Historical Society*, IV, pp. 385–403.

Crabtree, John D., "Recollections of the Pea Ridge Campaign," *Military Essays and Recollections . . . Illinois Military Order of the Loyal Legion*, III (Chicago, 1899), pp. 211–226.

Craik, Elmer LeRoy, "Southern Interest in Territorial Kansas, 1854–1858," *Collections of the Kansas State Historical Society*, XV, pp. 334–450.

Craven, Avery O., *The Growth of Southern Nationalism* (Baton Rouge, 1953).

Crawford, Samuel J., *Kansas in the Sixties* (Chicago, 1911).

Crittenden, Henry H., *The Battle of Westport and National Memorial Park* (Kansas City, 1938).

Crittenden, Henry H., *The Crittenden Memoirs* (New York, 1936).

Croy, Homer, *Our Will Rogers* (New York, 1953).

Crutchfield, William, "The Capture of Titus, August 16, 1856," *Transactions of the Kansas State Historical Society*, VII, pp. 532–534.

Curtis, Samuel Prentis, "The Army of the South-West, and the First Campaign in Arkansas," *Annals of Iowa*, VI, No. 1 (Jan. 1868), pp. 1–12; No. 2 (April 1868), pp. 69–84; continued in later issues.

Dacus, J. A., *Life and Adventures of Frank and Jesse James* (St. Louis, 1880).

Dale, Edward Everett, "Additional Letters of General Stand Watie," *Chronicles of Oklahoma,* I, No. 2 (Oct. 1921), pp. 131–149.

Dale, Edward Everett, and Gaston Litton, *Cherokee Cavaliers . . . Correspondence of the Ridge-Watie-Boudinet Family* (Norman, 1940).

Dalton, Kit, *Under the Black Flag* (Memphis, 1914).

Davenport, Edward A., ed., *History of the Ninth Regiment Illinois Cavalry Volunteers* (Chicago, 1888).

Davis, Nicholas A., *The Campaign from Texas to Maryland* (Richmond, 1863).

Dawson, Francis W., *Reminiscences of Confederate Service 1861–1865* (Charleston, S.C., 1882).

Day, Samuel Phillips, *Down South; or, An Englishman's Experience at the Seat of the American War* (London, 1862).

Dean, Benjamin Devor, *Recollections of the 26th Missouri Infantry, in the War for the Union* (Lamar, Mo., 1892).

Debo, Angie, "The Site of the Battle of Round Mountain, 1861," *Chronicles of Oklahoma,* XXVII, No. 2 (Summer 1949), pp. 187–206.

Denison, W. W., "Battle of Prairie Grove," *Collections of the Kansas State Historical Society,* XVI, pp. 586–590.

Dennett, Tyler, *Lincoln and the Civil War in the Diaries and Letters of John Hay* (New York, 1939).

Denslow, Van Buren, *Frémont and McClellan, their Political and Military Careers Reviewed* (Yonkers, N.Y., 1862).

Dickson, Charles Howard, "The 'Boy's' Story: Reminiscences of 1855," *Transactions of the Kansas State Historical Society,* V, pp. 76–87.

Dickson, Charles Howard, "The True History of the Branson Rescue," *Collections of the Kansas State Historical Society,* XIII, pp. 280–289.

Dixon, Mrs. Archibald, *The True History of the Missouri Compromise and Its Repeal* (Cincinnati, 1899).

"Documentary History of Kansas," *Transactions of the Kansas State Historical Society,* V, pp. 156–633.

"Documents Accompanying Special Messages of Governor in Reference to Border Troubles," *House Journal, 20th Missouri General Assembly,* 1858–1859, *Appendix,* pp. 78–80.

Dodge, Grenville M., *The Battle of Atlanta and other Campaigns,* etc. (Council Bluffs, 1910).

Douglas, Richard L., "History of Manufactures in the Kansas District," *Collections of the Kansas State Historical Society,* XI, pp. 81–215.

Douglas, Stephen A., *Report of Senator Douglas, of Illinois, on the Kansas-Lecompton Constitution* (Washington, 1858).

Drake, Samuel Adams, "The Old Army in Kansas," *Civil War Papers . . .*

Massachusetts Military Order of the Loyal Legion, I (Boston, 1900), pp. 141–152.

Drought, E. S. W., "James Montgomery," *Transactions of the Kansas State Historical Society,* VI, pp. 342–343.

[Dupré, Louis J.], *Fagots from the Camp Fire* (Washington, 1881).

Eaton, Rachel Caroline, *John Ross and the Cherokee Indians* (Menasha, Wis., 1914).

"Echoes of the Republican Convention in Chicago in 1860 when Seward and Lincoln were the Leading Candidates and Kansas Supported Seward," *Kansas Historical Quarterly,* XIII, No. 2 (May 1944), p. 151.

Edwards, Jennie, *John N. Edwards, Biography, Memoirs, Reminiscences and Recollections* (Kansas City, 1889).

Edwards, John N., *Noted Guerrillas, or the Warfare of the Border* (St. Louis, 1877).

Edwards, John N., *Shelby and His Men: or, The War in the West* (Cincinnati, 1867).

Eisele, Wilbert E., *The Real Wild Bill Hickok* (Denver, 1931).

Eldridge, Shalor Winchell, "Recollections of Early Days in Kansas," *Publications of the Kansas State Historical Society,* II (Topeka, 1920), pp. 1–178.

Elliott, E. N., *Cotton Is King, and Pro-slavery Arguments: Comprising the Writings of Hammond, Harper, Christy, Stringfellow, Hodge, Bledsoe, and Cartwright* (Augusta, Ga., 1860).

Elliott, Isaac H., *History of the Thirty-Third Regiment Illinois Veteran Volunteer Infantry* (Gibson City, Ill., 1902).

Elliott, R. G., "The Big Springs Convention," *Transactions of the Kansas State Historical Society,* VIII, pp. 362–377.

Elliott, R. G., "The Quantrell Raid as Seen from the Eldridge House," *Publications of the Kansas State Historical Society,* II (1920), pp. 179–196.

Elliott, R. G., "The Twenty-first of May," *Transactions of the Kansas State Historical Society,* VII, pp. 521–530.

Ellis, James Fernando, *The Influence of Environment on the Settlement of Missouri* (St. Louis, 1929).

Encyclopedia of the History of St. Louis (New York, 1899).

Escott, George B., *History of Springfield* (Springfield, Mo., 1878).

Ewing, Thomas, *The Struggle for Freedom in Kansas.* Reprinted from the *Cosmopolitan Magazine* of May 1894.

"Executive Minutes of Governor John W. Geary," *Transactions of the Kansas State Historical Society,* IV, pp. 520–742.

Fahrney, Ralph Ray, *Horace Greeley and the Tribune in the Civil War* (Cedar Rapids, 1936).

Farlow, Joyce, and Louise Barry, "Vincent B. Osborne's Civil War Experiences," *Kansas Historical Quarterly,* XX, No. 2 (May 1952), pp. 108–133; No. 3 (Aug. 1952), pp. 187–223.

Field, Homer H., Reprint of untitled article on Grenville M. Dodge from *History of Pottawattamie County, Iowa* (Chicago, 1902).

Fisher, Hugh Dunn, *The Gun and the Gospel: Early Kansas and Chaplain Fisher* (Chicago, 1896).

Fleming, Walter L., "The Buford Expedition to Kansas," *American Historical Review,* VI, No. 1 (Oct. 1900), pp. 38–48.

Fletcher, Thomas C., "The Battle of Pilot Knob, and the Retreat to Leasburg," *War Papers and Personal Reminiscences, 1861–1865 . . . Missouri Military Order of the Loyal Legion,* I (St. Louis, 1892), pp. 29–53.

Flint, Mortimer R., "The War on the Border," *Glimpses of the Nation's Struggle. Fifth Series . . . Minnesota Commandery of the Military Order of the Loyal Legion* (St. Paul, 1903), pp. 396–416.

Foley, James L., "With Frémont in Missouri," *Sketches of War History, 1861–1865 . . . Ohio Military Order of the Loyal Legion,* V (Cincinnati, 1903), pp. 484–521.

Foote, Henry S., *The Bench and Bar of the South and Southwest* (St. Louis, 1876).

Force, Manning F., *From Fort Henry to Corinth* (New York, 1881).

Force, Manning F., "John Pope, Major-General, U.S.A." *Sketches of War History, 1861–1865 . . . Ohio Commandery of the Military Order of the Loyal Legion,* IV (Cincinnati, 1896), pp. 355–362.

Ford, Harvey S., "Van Dorn and the Pea Ridge Campaign," *Journal of the American Military Institute,* III, No. 4 (Winter 1939), pp. 222–236.

[Ford, Worthington Chauncey, ed.], *War Letters, 1862–1865, of John Chapman Gray and John Codman Ropes* (Boston, 1927).

Foreman, Carolyn Thomas, "Augusta Robertson Moore; A Sketch of Her Life and Times," *Chronicles of Oklahoma,* XIII, No. 4 (Dec. 1935), pp. 399–420.

Foreman, Carolyn Thomas, *Park Hill* (Muskogee, Okla., 1948).

Foreman, Grant, *The Five Civilized Tribes* (Norman, Okla., 1934).

Foreman, Grant, *Fort Gibson; A Brief History* (Oklahoma City, 1936).

Forney, John W., *Anecdotes of Public Men* (New York, 1873).

Foster, Eli G., *The Civil War by Campaigns* (Topeka, 1899).

Foster, Richard B., "Richard B. Foster's Statement," *Transactions of the Kansas State Historical Society,* I and II, pp. 226–228.

Fox, Simeon M., "The Early History of the Seventh Kansas Cavalry." Reprinted from *Collections of the Kansas State Historical Society,* XI, pp. 238–253.

Fox, Simeon M., *The Seventh Kansas Cavalry: Its Service in the Civil War* (Topeka, 1908).

Fox, William F., *Regimental Losses in the American Civil War, 1861–1865* (Albany, 1889).

Frank Pierce and His Abolition Allies (n.p., 1852).

Freeman, Charles R., "The Battle of Honey Springs," *Chronicles of Oklahoma,* XIII, No. 2 (June 1935), pp. 154–168.

Frémont, Jessie Benton, *The Story of the Guard: A Chronicle of the War* (Boston, 1863).

Frémont, John C., "In Command in Missouri," *Battles and Leaders of the Civil War,* I, pp. 278–288.

"Frémont's Hundred Days in Missouri," *Atlantic Monthly,* IX, No. 51 (Jan. 1862), pp. 115–125; 247–258; 372–386.

"The Frontier Guard," *Transactions of the Kansas State Historical Society,* X, pp. 418–421.

Gaeddert, G. Raymond, *The Birth of Kansas* (Topeka, 1940).

Gaeddert, G. Raymond, "First Newspapers in Kansas Counties," *The Kansas Historical Quarterly,* X, No. 1 (Feb. 1941), pp. 3–33.

[Gage, G. G.], *The Battle of the Blue of the Second Regiment, K. S. M.* (Chicago, 1896).

Gardner, Theodore, "The First Kansas Battery," *Collections of the Kansas State Historical Society,* XIV, pp. 235–282.

Gates, Paul Wallace, "A Fragment of Kansas Land History: The Disposal of the Christian Indian Land Tract," *Kansas Historical Quarterly,* VI, No. 3 (Aug. 1937), pp. 227–240.

Gause, Isaac, *Four Years with Five Armies* (New York, 1908).

Geary, Daniel, "Looking Backward," *Missouri Valley Historical Society Publication: Annals of Kansas City,* I, No. 2 (Dec. 1922), pp. 224–235.

Geary, Daniel, "War Incidents at Kansas City," *Collections of the Kansas State Historical Society,* XI, pp. 282–291.

Gibbons, V. E., ed., "Letters on the War in Kansas in 1856," *Kansas Historical Quarterly,* X, No. 4 (Nov. 1941), pp. 369–379.

Gibson, George R., *Journal of a Soldier under Kearny and Doniphan* (Glendale, Calif., 1935).

Gihon, John H., *Geary and Kansas: Governor Geary's Administration in Kansas* (Philadelphia, 1857).

Gladstone, Thomas H., *The Englishman in Kansas; or, Squatter Life and Border Warfare* (New York, 1857).

Gleed, Charles S., *The Kansas Memorial, a Report of the Old Settlers' Meeting Held at Bismark Grove, Kansas, Sept. 15th and 16th, 1879* (Kansas City, 1880).

Gleed, Charles S., "Samuel Walker," *Transactions of the Kansas State Historical Society,* VI, pp. 249–274.

Goodlander, Charles W., *Memoirs and Recollections* (Fort Scott, Kan., 1900).

Goodloe, Daniel R., "Is It Expedient to Introduce Slavery into Kansas," *Two Tracts for the Times* (Boston, 1855), pp. 39–55.

"Governor Denver's Administration," *Transactions of the Kansas State Historical Society*, V, pp. 464–561.

"Governor Geary's Administration," *Transactions of the Kansas State Historical Society*, IV, pp. 373–520; V, pp. 264–289.

"Governor Reeder's Administration," *Transactions of the Kansas State Historical Society*, V, pp. 163–234.

"Governor Walker's Administration," *Transactions of the Kansas State Historical Society*, V, pp. 290–464.

Grand Entertainment by the Union Veterans . . . of the Battle of Pilot Knob, Mo., at Concordia Park, Sunday, September 28th, 1890 (n.p., 1890).

Granger, J. T., *A Brief Biographical Sketch of the Life of Major-General Grenville M. Dodge* (New York, 1893).

Green, Charles Ransley, *Early Days in Kansas* (Olathe, Kan., 1912).

Green, James S., *Speech . . . on the Constitution of Kansas* (Washington, 1857).

Greene, Albert Robinson, "Campaigning in the Army of the Frontier," *Collections of the Kansas State Historical Society*, XIV, pp. 283–310.

Greene, Albert Robinson, "On the Battle of Wilson Creek," *Transactions of the Kansas State Historical Society*, V, pp. 116–127.

Greene, Albert Robinson, "What I Saw of the Quantrill Raid," *Collections of the Kansas State Historical Society*, XIII, pp. 430–451.

Greene, Max, *The Kansas Region: . . . Directions as to Routes, Outfit for the Pioneer, and Sketches of Desirable Localities for Present Settlement* (New York, 1856).

Gregg, Thomas, *History of Hancock County, Illinois* (Chicago, 1880).

Griffith, G. W. E., "The Battle of Black Jack," *Collections of the Kansas State Historical Society*, XVI, pp. 524–528.

Grover, George S., "Civil War in Missouri," *Missouri Historical Review*, VIII, No. 1 (Oct. 1913), pp. 1–28.

Grover, George S., "The Price Campaign of 1864," *Missouri Historical Review*, VI, No. 4 (July 1912), pp. 167–181.

Grover, George S., "The Shelby Raid, 1863," *Missouri Historical Review*, VI, No. 3 (April 1912), pp. 107–126.

Hafen, LeRoy, *Pike's Peak Gold Rush Guidebooks of 1859* (Glendale, Calif., 1941).

Hale, Edward Everett, *Kansas and Nebraska . . . an Account of the Emigrant Aid Companies, and Directions to Emigrants* (Boston, 1854).

Hallum, John, *Biographical and Pictorial History of Arkansas* (Albany, N.Y., 1887).

Hamilton, Clad, "A Colonel of Kansas," *Collections of the Kansas State Historical Society*, XII, pp. 282–292.

Hammond, John Martin, *Quaint and Historic Forts of North America* (Philadelphia, 1915).

Hammond, William A., *Personal Recollections of General Nathaniel Lyon. War Papers No. 33. Military Order of the Loyal Legion . . . District of Columbia* (Washington, 1900). Also printed in *Magazine of American History*, XIII, p. 237.

Hannahs, Harrison, "General Thomas Ewing, Jr.," *Collections of the Kansas State Historical Society*, XII, pp. 276–282.

Hardee, William Joseph, *Rifle and Light Infantry Tactics* (Philadelphia, 1855).

Harlan, Edgar Rubey, *A Narrative History of the People of Iowa* (Chicago, 1931).

Harris, Moses, "The Old Army," *War Papers . . . Wisconsin Military Order of the Loyal Legion*, II (Milwaukee, 1896), pp. 331–344.

Harsha, David A., *The Life of Charles Sumner* (New York, 1856).

Harvey, Charles M., "Missouri from 1849 to 1861," *Missouri Historical Review*, II, No. 1 (Oct. 1907), pp. 23–40.

Harwood, Nathan C., "The Pea Ridge Campaign," *Civil War Sketches and Incidents . . . Nebraska Military Order of the Loyal Legion*, I (Omaha, 1902) pp. 110–121.

Haskell, John G., "The Passing of Slavery in Western Missouri," *Transactions of the Kansas State Historical Society*, VII, pp. 28–39.

Heartsill, William Williston, *Fourteen Hundred and 91 Days in the Confederate Army* (Marshall, Texas, 1876).

Hemstreet, William, "Little Things about Big Generals," *Personal Recollections of the War of the Rebellion . . . New York Military Order of the Loyal Legion*, III (New York, 1907), pp. 148–166.

Herklotz, Hildegarde Rose, "Jayhawkers in Missouri, 1858–1863," *Missouri Historical Review*, XVII, No. 3 (April 1923), pp. 266–284; No. 4 (July 1923), pp. 505–513; XVIII, No. 1 (Oct. 1923), pp. 64–101.

Herndon, William H., and Jesse W. Weik, *Herndon's Life of Lincoln* (New York, 1936).

Herr, George W., comp., *Episodes of the Civil War: Nine Campaigns in Nine States . . . History of the 59th Regiment, Illinois Veteran Volunteer Infantry* (San Francisco, 1890).

Herriott, F. I., "James W. Grimes versus the Southrons," *Annals of Iowa*, XV, No. 6, third series (July and Oct. 1925), pp. 323–357, 403–432.

Hibbard, Benjamin H., *A History of the Public Land Policies* (New York, 1939).

Hickman, Russell K., "Speculative Activities of the Emigrant Aid Company," *Kansas Historical Quarterly*, IV, No. 3 (Aug. 1935), pp. 235–267.

Hickman, W. Z., *History of Jackson County, Missouri* (Topeka, 1920).

Higginson, Mary Thacher, ed., *Letters and Journals of Thomas Wentworth Higginson, 1846–1906* (Boston, 1921).

Higginson, Thomas Wentworth, *Cheerful Yesterdays* (Boston, 1898). Also published serially in *Atlantic Monthly* beginning Nov. 1896.

Higginson, Thomas Wentworth, *A Ride Through Kansas* (New York? 1856?).

Hill, Alfred J., *History of Co. E of the Sixth Minnesota Regiment of Volunteer Infantry* (St. Paul, 1899).

Hill, Frederick Trevor, *Lincoln the Lawyer* (New York, 1906).

Hindman, Thomas C., *Report of Major General Hindman on the Operations in the Trans-Mississippi District* (Richmond, Va., 1864).

Hinton, Richard J., *John Brown and His Men* (New York, 1894).

Hinton, Richard J., "The Nationalization of Freedom, and the Historical Place of Kansas Therein," *Transactions of the Kansas State Historical Society,* VI, pp. 175–186.

Hinton, Richard J., "Pens That Made Kansas Free," *Transactions of the Kansas State Historical Society,* VI, pp. 371–382.

[Hinton, Richard J.], *Rebel Invasion of Missouri and Kansas and the Campaign of the Border, against General Sterling-Price* (Chicago, 1865).

History of Buchanan County, Missouri (St. Joseph, 1881).

History of Clay and Platte Counties, Missouri (St. Louis, 1885).

The History of Jackson County, Missouri, etc. (Kansas City, 1881),

Hodder, Frank Heywood, "The Genesis of the Kansas-Nebraska Act," *Proceedings of the State Historical Society of Wisconsin at its Sixtieth Annual Meeting Held October 24, 1912* (Madison, 1913), pp. 69–86.

Hodder, Frank Heywood, "The Railroad Background of the Kansas-Nebraska Act," *Mississippi Valley Historical Review,* XII, No. 1 (June 1925), pp. 3–22.

Hodge, David M., *Argument before the Committee on Indian Affairs of the U.S. Senate, Mch. 10, 1880, in support of Senate Bill No. 1145, providing for the payment of awards made to the Creek Indians who enlisted in the Federal Army, loyal refugees, and freedmen* (Washington, 1880).

Hodge, David M., *Is-ha-he-char, and Co-we Harjo. To the Committee on Indian Affairs of the House of Representatives of the 51st Congress in the matter of the claims of the loyal Creeks for losses sustained during the late rebellion* (Washington, 1891).

Holcombe, R. I., and F. W. Adams, comps., *An Account of the Battle of Wilson's Creek, or Oak Hills* (Springfield, Mo., 1883).

Holliday, Cyrus K., "The Presidential Campaign of 1856 — The Frémont Campaign," *Transactions of the Kansas State Historical Society,* V, pp. 48–60.

Hollister, Wilfred R., and Harry Norman, *Five Famous Missourians* (Kansas City, 1900).

Holloway, John N., *History of Kansas: From the First Exploration of the Mississippi Valley, to its Admission into the Union* (Lafayette, Ind., 1868).

Horn, Stanley F., *The Army of Tennessee* (Norman, Okla., 1953).

Horner, Charles F., *The Life of James Redpath and the Development of the Modern Lyceum* (New York, 1926).

Horton, James C., "Two Pioneer Merchants," *Transactions of the Kansas State Historical Society*, X, pp. 589–621.

Houck, Louis, *A History of Missouri* (Chicago, 1908).

How, James F., "Frank P. Blair in 1861," *War Papers and Personal Reminiscences, 1861–1865 . . . Missouri Military Order of the Loyal Legion*, I (St. Louis, 1892), pp. 382–395.

Howard, John R., "Frémont in the Civil War," *Personal Recollections of the War of the Rebellion . . . New York Military Order of the Loyal Legion*, III (New York, 1907), pp. 177–195.

Howard, John R., *Remembrance of Things Past* (New York, 1925).

Howard, Oliver Otis, *My Life and Experiences among Our Hostile Indians* (Hartford, Conn., 1907).

Humphrey, Seth K., *The Indian Dispossessed* (Boston, 1906).

Hunt, Elvid, *History of Fort Leavenworth 1827–1927* (Fort Leavenworth, 1926).

Hunter, Martha T., *A Memoir of Robert M. T. Hunter* (Washington, 1903).

Hunter, Moses H., ed., *Report of the Military Services of General David Hunter, U.S.A., during the War of the Rebellion* (New York, 1873).

"In Memoriam — Lieutenant-General John M. Schofield, U.S.A.," *Personal Recollections of the War of the Rebellion . . . New York Military Order of the Loyal Legion*, III (New York, 1907), pp. 438–447.

Ingalls, John James, *A Collection of the Writings of John James Ingalls* (Kansas City, 1902).

Ingalls, John James, "Last of the Jayhawkers," *Kansas Magazine*, I (1872), p. 356.

Isely, Jeter Allen, *Horace Greeley and the Republican Party, 1853–1861, a Study of the New York Tribune* (Princeton, 1947).

Isley, W. H., "Sharps Rifle Episode in Kansas History," *American Historical Review*, XII, No. 3 (April 1907), pp. 546–566.

Jenkins, Paul B., *The Battle of Westport* (Kansas City, 1906). Also printed in *Annals of Kansas City*, I, No. 3 (Dec. 1923), pp. 243–255.

Johnson, Allen, *Stephen A. Douglas; A Study in American Politics* (New York, 1908).

Johnson, Harry, *A History of Anderson County* (Garnett, Kan., 1936).

Johnson, Oliver, *The Abolitionists Vindicated in a Review of Eli Thayer's*

Paper on the New England Emigrant Aid Company (Worcester, Mass., 1887).

Johnson, Samuel A., "The Emigrant Aid Company in the Kansas Conflict," *Kansas Historical Quarterly*, VI, No. 1 (Feb. 1937), pp. 21–33.

Johnson, Samuel A., "The Genesis of the New England Emigrant Aid Company," *New England Quarterly*, III, No. 1 (1930), pp. 95–122.

Johnson, William Alexander, "Early Life of Quantrill in Kansas," *Transactions of the Kansas State Historical Society*, VII, pp. 212–229.

Jordan, H. Donaldson, "A Politician of Expansion: Robert J. Walker," *Mississippi Valley Historical Review*, XIX, No. 3 (Dec. 1932), pp. 362–381.

Kansas, *Public Documents of the State of Kansas* (Topeka, 1862).

Kansas, *Report of the Adjutant General of the State of Kansas, 1861–65* (Topeka, 1896).

Kansas in 1856. An Authentic Account of the Outrages in Kansas, since the Appointment of the Kansas Investigating Committee, and not Embraced in Their Report to the House of Representatives (Washington, 1856).

The Kansas Question (n.p. [1856]).

Kappler, Charles J., "Indian Treaties and Councils Affecting Kansas," *Collections of the Kansas State Historical Society*, XVI, pp. 746–772.

Kargan, Ernest D., "Missouri's German Immigration," *Missouri Historical Society Collections*, II, pp. 23–34.

Kelso, Isaac, *The Stars and Bars; or, the Reign of Terror in Missouri* (Boston, 1863).

Kennedy, O. P., "Capture of Fort Saunders, August 15, 1856," *Transactions of the Kansas State Historical Society*, VII, pp. 530–531.

Kennerly, William Clark, *Persimmon Hill: A Narrative of Old St. Louis and the Far West* (Norman, Okla., 1948).

Knapp, Lemuel, "Kansas Experiences of Lemuel Knapp," *Transactions of Kansas State Historical Society*, I and II, pp. 206–208.

Koerner, Gustave, *Memoirs of Gustave Koerner, 1809–1896* (Cedar Rapids, Iowa, 1909).

Lademann, Otto C., "The Battle of Carthage, Mo., Friday, July 5th, 1861," *War Papers . . . Wisconsin Military Order of the Loyal Legion*, IV (Milwaukee, 1914), pp. 131–139.

Lademann, Otto C., "The Battle of Wilson's Creek," *War Papers . . . Wisconsin Military Order of the Loyal Legion*, IV (Milwaukee, 1914), pp. 433–438.

Lademann, Otto C., "The Capture of 'Camp Jackson,' St. Louis, Mo., Friday, May 10th, 1861," *War Papers . . . Wisconsin Military Order of the Loyal Legion*, IV (Milwaukee, 1941), pp. 69–75.

Lane, James Henry, *The People's Choice. Speech of Hon. James H. Lane . . . at the Cooper Institute, New York, March 30, 1864* (n.p., n.d.).

Lane, James Henry, "Report on Trouble in Bourbon County in 1857," *Kansas Territorial Legislature, House Journal, Extra Session, 1858,* pp. 84–85.

Langsdorf, Edgar, "Jim Lane and the Frontier Guard," *Kansas Historical Quarterly,* IX, No. 1 (Feb. 1940), pp. 13–25.

The Last Political Writings of Gen. Nathaniel Lyon, U.S.A., with a Sketch of His Life and Military Service (New York, 1861).

Lathrop, David, *The History of Fifty-Ninth Regiment Illinois Volunteers* (Indianapolis, 1865).

Laughlin, Sceva Bright, *Missouri Politics during the Civil War* (Salem, Ore., 1930).

Lawrence, William, *Life of Amos A. Lawrence with Extracts from His Diary and Correspondence* (Boston, 1899).

Lawrence, William Richards, *Extracts from the Diary and Correspondence of the Late Amos Lawrence; wih a Brief Account of Some Incidents in His Life* (Boston, 1856).

Leake, Joseph B., "Campaign of the Army of the Frontier," *Military Essays and Recollections . . . Illinois Military Order of the Loyal Legion,* II (Chicago, 1894), pp. 269–287.

Leasure, Daniel, "Personal Observations and Experiences in the Pope Campaign in Virginia," *Glimpses of the Nation's Struggle,* First Series (St. Paul, Minn., 1887).

Lee, John F., "John Sappington Marmaduke," *Missouri Historical Society Collections,* II, No. 6 (July 1906), pp. 26–40.

Leopard, Buel, and Floyd C. Shoemaker, eds., *The Messages and Proclamations of the Governors of the State of Missouri* (Columbia, Mo., 1922–1951).

Letters to the Great Democratic Anti-Lecompton Meeting, against the Lecompton Fraud, held at Philadelphia, Pennsylvania, February 8, 1858 (Washington, 1858).

Lewis, Lloyd, "The Man the Historians Forgot," *Kansas Historical Quarterly,* VIII, No. 1 (Feb. 1939), pp. 85–103.

Lewis, Lloyd, "Propaganda and the Kansas-Missouri War," *Missouri Historical Review,* XXXIV, No. 1 (Oct. 1939), pp. 3–17.

Lewis, Lloyd, *Sherman, Fighting Prophet* (New York, 1932).

Lewis, Sinclair, and Lloyd Lewis, *The Jayhawker, a Play in Two Acts* (New York, 1934).

Lewis, Warner, "Civil War Reminiscences," *Missouri Historical Review,* II, No. 3 (April 1908), pp. 221–232.

Lewis, Warner, "Massacre of Confederates by the Osages," *Osage Magazine,* I, Feb. and May 1910, pp. 49–52 and 68–70.

Lewis, Warner, "The Only Survivor's Story of Massacre on Rebel Creek, 1863," Indian Depredations & Battles, Clippings, I, pp. 15–21. KHi.

Lewis, Warner, "Thrilling Story of Indian Massacre in Kansas in 1863 Told by Warner Lewis," Indian Depredations & Battles, Clippings, III, p. 25. KHi.

Long, E. B., ed., *Personal Memoirs of U. S. Grant* (Cleveland, 1952).

Lothrop, Charles H., *A History of the First Regiment Iowa Cavalry Veteran Volunteers* (Lyons, Iowa, 1890).

Love, Robertus, *The Rise and Fall of Jesse James* (New York, 1926).

Love, William De Loss, *Wisconsin in the War of the Rebellion* (Chicago, 1866).

Lowe, Percival G., *Five Years a Dragoon ('49 to '54) and Other Adventures on the Great Plains* (Kansas City, 1906).

Lutz, John J., "Quantrill and the Morgan Walker Tragedy," *Transactions of the Kansas State Historical Society,* VIII, pp. 324–331.

Lynch, William Orlando, *Population Movements in Relation to the Struggle for Kansas* (Bloomington, Ind., 1926).

McAllaster, Octavius W., "My Experience in the Lawrence Raid," *Collections of the Kansas State Historical Society,* XII, pp. 401–404.

McCausland, Susan A. Arnold, "The Battle of Lexington as Seen by a Woman," *Missouri Historical Review,* VI, No. 3 (April 1912), pp. 127–135.

McCorkle, John, *Three Years with Quantrell; a True Story, told by His Scout John McCorkle* (Armstrong, Mo., 1914).

McCormick, Andrew W., "Battles and Campaigns in Arkansas," *Sketches of War History, 1861–1865 . . . Ohio Military Order of the Loyal Legion,* VI (Cincinnati, 1908), pp. 2–13.

McCulloch, Ben, "Report of Engagement at Oak Hill, on the 10th August, with United States Troops, Ben McCulloch, Brigadier General Commanding," *Official Reports of Generals Johnston and Beauregard,* etc. (Richmond, Va., 1862).

McDougal, H. C., "A Decade of Missouri Politics, 1860 to 1870," *Missouri Historical Review,* III, No. 2 (Jan. 1909), pp. 126–153.

McElroy, John, *The Struggle for Missouri* (Washington, 1913).

McGonigle, James A., "First Kansas Infantry in the Battle of Wilson's Creek," *Collections of the Kansas State Historical Society,* XII, pp. 292–295.

McMaster, John Bach, *A History of the People of the United States during Lincoln's Administration* (New York, 1927).

McMaster, John Bach, *A History of the People of the United States, from the Revolution to the Civil War,* XIII (New York, 1918).

[McNamara, John], *Three Years on the Kansas Border. By a Clergyman of the Episcopal Church* (New York, 1856).

Magers, Roy V., "The Raid on the Parkville Industrial Luminary," *Missouri Historical Review,* XXX, No. 1 (Oct. 1935), pp. 39–46.

Malin, James Claude, "Colonel Harvey and His Forty Thieves," *Mississippi Valley Historical Review,* XIX, No. 1 (June 1932), pp. 57–76.

Malin, James Claude, "Identification of the Stranger at the Pottawatomie Massacre," *Kansas Historical Quarterly*, IX, No. 1 (Feb. 1940), pp. 3–12.

Malin, James Claude, *John Brown and the Legend of Fifty-Six* (Philadelphia, 1942).

Malin, James Claude, "The Proslavery Background of the Kansas Struggle," *Mississippi Valley Historical Review*, X, No. 3 (Dec. 1923), pp. 285–305.

Manning, E. C., "In at the Birth, And—" *Transactions of the Kansas State Historical Society*, VII, pp. 202–205.

Martin, George W., "A Chapter from the Archives," *Collections of the Kansas State Historical Society*, XII, pp. 359–375.

Martin, George W., "Early Days in Kansas," *Transactions of the Kansas State Historical Society*, IX, pp. 126–143.

Martin, George W., "The First Two Years of Kansas," *Transactions of the Kansas State Historical Society*, X, pp. 120–148. Also published as a pamphlet.

Martin, George W., "The Territorial and Military Combine at Fort Riley," *Transactions of the Kansas State Historical Society*, VII, pp. 361–390.

Martin, John A., "Kansas in the War," *War Talks . . . Kansas Commandery of the Military Order of the Loyal Legion* (Kansas City, 1906), pp. 371–377.

Mead, James R., "The Saline River Country in 1859," *Transactions of the Kansas State Historical Society*, IX, pp. 8–19.

Meador, L. E., *History of the Battle of Wilson Creek* (Springfield, Mo., 1938).

Meigs, M. C., *Outline Description of United States Military Posts and Stations* (Washington, 1871).

Merrill, O. N., *A True History of the Kansas Wars* (Cincinnati, 1856). Reprinted in *Magazine of History with Notes and Queries*, Extra No. 178, Vol. 45, No. 2.

Meserve, John Bartlett, "The MacIntoshes," *Chronicles of Oklahoma*, X, No. 3 (Sept. 1932), pp. 310–325.

Military History of Kansas Regiments during the War for the Suppression of the Great Rebellion (Leavenworth, 1870).

Military History and Reminiscences of the Thirteenth Regiment of Illinois Volunteer Infantry (Chicago, 1892).

[Miller, E. Van Dorn], *A Soldier's Honor: With Reminiscences of Major-General Earl Van Dorn* (New York, 1902).

Miller, George, *Missouri's Memorable Decade, 1860–1870* (Columbia, Mo., 1898).

Miller, William H., "History of Kansas City," *The History of Jackson County, Missouri* (Kansas City, 1881). Also published as a separate.

Milton, George Fort, *The Eve of Conflict: Stephen A. Douglas and the Needless War* (Boston, 1934).

Missouri, "Report of the Committee on Federal Relations . . . ," *House Journal*, 20th Missouri General Assembly, 1858–1859, *Appendix*, pp. 107–112.

Mitchell, W. A., "Historic Linn," *Collections of the Kansas State Historical Society*, XVI, pp. 607–657.

Monaghan, Jay, *Diplomat in Carpet Slippers: Abraham Lincoln Deals with Foreign Affairs* (Indianapolis, 1945).

Monaghan, Jay, *The Great Rascal: The Life and Adventures of Ned Buntline* (Boston, 1952).

Monaghan, Jay, *The Legend of Tom Horn: Last of the Bad Men* (Indianapolis, 1946).

Monks, William, *A History of Southern Missouri and Northern Arkansas* (West Plains, Mo., 1907).

Montgomery, James, Letter to George L. Stearns, May 8, 1861, *Transactions of the Kansas State Historical Society*, I and II, pp. 232–233.

Moody, Joel, "The Marais des Cygnes Massacre," *Collections of the Kansas State Historical Society*, XIV, pp. 208–223.

Moore, Frank, *Anecdotes, Poetry and Incidents of the War: North and South* (New York, 1866). Published in 1889 as *The Civil War in Song and Story*.

Moore, Frank, *The Portrait Gallery of the War, Civil, Military, and Naval* (New York, 1865).

Moore, Frank, ed., *The Rebellion Record: A Diary of American Events, with Documents, Narratives, Illustrative Incidents, Poetry*, etc., XII (New York, 1867).

Moore, Frank, *Women of the War; Their Heroism and Self-Sacrifice* (Chicago, 1866).

Moore, Henry Miles, *Early History of Leavenworth, City and County* (Leavenworth, Kan., 1906).

Moore, John C., *Missouri*, Vol. IX of *Confederate Military History* (Atlanta, 1899).

Morehouse, Frances Milton I., *The Life of Jesse W. Fell* (Urbana, Ill., 1916).

Morrow, Robert, "Emigration to Kansas in 1856," *Transactions of the Kansas State Historical Society*, VIII, pp. 302–315.

Morton, Charles, "Early War Days in Missouri," *War Papers . . . Wisconsin Military Order of the Loyal Legion*, II (Milwaukee, 1896), pp. 145–158.

Mudd, Joseph Aloysius, "What I Saw at Wilson's Creek," *Missouri Historical Review*, VII, No. 2 (Jan. 1913), pp. 89–105.

Mudd, Joseph Aloysius, *With Porter in North Missouri* (Washington, 1909).

Mulligan, James A., "The Siege of Lexington, Mo.," *Battles and Leaders of the Civil War*, I, pp. 307–313.

Nash, Charles Edward, *Biographical Sketches of Gen. Pat Cleburne and Gen. T. C. Hindman* (Little Rock, 1898).

The National Cyclopaedia of American Biography (New York, 1900).

Neal, W. A., *An Illustrated History of the Missouri Engineer and the 25th Infantry Regiments* (Chicago, 1889).

Nettleton, D. C., Letter to sister in *Annals of Kansas City*, I, No. 3 (Dec. 1923), pp. 272–273.

Nevins, Allan, *The Emergence of Lincoln* (New York, 1950).

Nevins, Allan, *Frémont, the West's Greatest Adventurer* (New York, 1928).

Nevins, Allan, *Ordeal of the Union* (New York, 1947).

Nichols, Roy F., *The Disruption of American Democracy* (New York, 1948).

Nichols, Roy F., *Franklin Pierce, Young Hickory of the Granite Hills* (Philadelphia, 1931).

Nicolay, John G., and John Hay, *Abraham Lincoln: A History* (New York, 1890).

Nixon, Oliver W., "Reminiscences of the First Year of the War in Missouri," *Military Essays and Recollections . . . Illinois Military Order of the Loyal Legion*, III (Chicago, 1899), pp. 413–436.

Noble, John W., "Battle of Pea Ridge, or Elk Horn Tavern," *War Papers and Personal Reminiscences, 1861–1865 . . . Missouri Military Order of the Loyal Legion*, I (St. Louis, 1892), pp. 211–242.

Nott, Charles C., "The Tale of a Goblin Horse," *Stories of the Army* (New York, 1893).

O.R. (*Official Records*); see *The War of the Rebellion*.

Oberholzer, Emil, "The Legal Aspects of Slavery in Missouri," *Bulletin of the Missouri Historical Society*, VI, No. 4 (July 1950), pp. 540–545.

Official Reports of Battles (Richmond, 1862).

O'Flaherty, Daniel, *General Jo Shelby: Undefeated Rebel* (Chapel Hill, 1954).

Oliver, Mordecai, *Nebraska and Kansas, Speech of Hon. M. Oliver, of Missouri, in the House of Representatives, May 17, 1854* (Washington, 1854).

Our Border in Danger (n.p., n.d.). Broadside at KHi.

[Painter, Henry M.], *Brief Narrative of Incidents in the War in Missouri* (Boston, 1863).

Palmer, Henry E., "The Border War — When — Where," *Civil War Sketches and Incidents . . . Nebraska Military Order of the Loyal Legion*, I (Omaha, 1902), pp. 173–189.

Palmer, Henry E., "Company A, Eleventh Kansas Regiment in the Price Raid," *Transactions of the Kansas State Historical Society*, IX, pp. 431–443.

Palmer, Henry E., "The Lawrence Raid," *Civil War Sketches and Incidents . . . Nebraska Military Order of the Loyal Legion*, I (Omaha, 1902), pp. 190–204.

Palmer, Henry E., "The Lawrence Raid," *Transactions of the Kansas State Historical Society*, VI, pp. 317–325.

Palmer, Henry E., "An Outing in Arkansas, or, Forty Days and a Week in the Wilderness," *Civil War Sketches and Incidents . . . Nebraska Military Order of the Loyal Legion,* I (Omaha, 1902), pp. 213–225.

Palmer, Henry E., "The Soldiers of Kansas," *Transactions of the Kansas State Historical Society,* IX, pp. 431–466.

Paris, Louis Philippe Albert d'Orléans, Count of, *History of the Civil War in America* (Philadelphia, 1875–1888).

Parker, Nathan, *The Kansas and Nebraska Handbook for 1857–8 with a New and Accurate Map* (Boston, 1857).

Parker, Thomas V., *The Cherokee Indians, with Special Reference to Their Relations with the United States Government* (New York, 1907).

Paxton, W. M., *Annals of Platte County, Missouri* (Kansas City, 1897).

Peak, June, "Civil War Repeated in Indian Territory," Dallas *Morning News,* July 1, 1923. Reprinted in J. B. Thoburn and Muriel H. Wright, *Oklahoma, A History of the State and its People,* II (New York, 1929), p. 836.

Pearce, N. Bartlett, "Arkansas Troops in the Battle of Wilson's Creek," *Battles and Leaders of the Civil War,* I, pp. 298–303.

Pearce, N. Bartlett, "Price's Campaign of 1861," *Publications of the Arkansas Historical Association,* IV, pp. 333–351.

Peckham, James, *Gen. Nathaniel Lyon and Missouri in 1861* (New York, 1866).

"People and Places Mentioned in the Bogus Statutes," *Collections of the Kansas State Historical Society,* XVI, pp. 612–618.

Peterson, Cyrus A., and Joseph M. Hanson, *Pilot Knob, The Thermopylae of the West* (New York, 1914).

Phillips, John F., "Diary of Acting Brig. Genl. Jno. F. Phillips," *The Annals of Kansas City, Missouri,* I, No. 3 (Dec. 1923), pp. 267–274.

Phillips, John F., "Hamilton Rowan Gamble and the Provisional Government of Missouri," *Missouri Historical Review,* V, No. 1 (Oct. 1910), pp. 1–14.

Phillips, William Addison, *The Conquest of Kansas by Missouri and Her Allies* (Boston, 1856).

Phillips, William Addison, "Kansas History," *Transactions of the Kansas State Historical Society,* IV, pp. 351–359.

Pierce, Edward L., *Memoir and Letters of Charles Sumner,* III (Boston, 1893).

Pike, James S., *First Blows of the Civil War: The Ten Years of Preliminary Conflict in the United States from 1850 to 1860* (New York, 1879).

Portrait and Biographical Record of Leavenworth, Douglas and Franklin Counties, Kansas (Chicago, 1899).

Prentis, Noble Lovely, *History of Kansas* (Winfield, Kan., 1899).

Prentis, Noble Lovely, "Kansas Journalism — the Men of '57," *American Journalist,* I, No. 4 (Dec. 1883), pp. 93–98.

Prentis, Noble Lovely, *Kansas Miscellanies* (Topeka, 1889).

Prince, Ezra M., ed., "Convention of May 29, 1856," *Transactions of the McLean County Historical Society, Bloomington, Illinois,* III.

Proctor, Addison C., "Slave Holding Indians at Time of Civil War," printed in Barstow A. Ulrick, *Abraham Lincoln and New Constitutional Governments: Third Part* (Chicago, 1921), pp. 233–245.

Quaife, Milo M., ed., *Absalom Grimes: Confederate Mail Runner* (New Haven, 1926).

Quarles, Benjamin, *The Negro in the Civil War* (Boston, 1953).

Ragan, Stephen H., "The Battle of Westport," *Annals of Kansas City,* I, No. 3 (Dec. 1923), pp. 259–266.

Randall, James G., *The Civil War and Reconstruction* (Boston, 1937).

Ray, P. Orman, "The Genesis of the Kansas-Nebraska Act," *Annual Report of the American Historical Association for the Year 1914* (Washington, 1916), pp. 259–289.

Ray, P. Orman, *The Repeal of the Missouri Compromise: Its Origin and Authorship* (Cleveland, 1909).

Redpath, James, "Dispersion of the Topeka Legislature," Webb Scrapbook, XV, p. 2. KHi.

Redpath, James, *Public Life of John Brown with an Autobiography of His Childhood and Youth* (Boston, 1860).

Redpath, James, *The Roving Editor: or, Talks with Slaves in the Southern States* (New York, 1859).

Redpath, James, "Whereabouts or Fate of the Leading Border Ruffians and Free State Men of Kansas," Kansas Scrapbook, Biography, I, p. 283. KHi.

Reeder, Andrew H., "Governor Reeder's Escape from Kansas," *Transactions of the Kansas State Historical Society,* III, pp. 205–223.

Reid, Samuel C., Jr., *The Scouting Expeditions of McCulloch's Texas Rangers* (Philadelphia, 1847).

Reid, Whitelaw, *Ohio in the War: Her Statesmen, Her Generals, and Soldiers* (Cincinnati, 1868).

Reminiscences of the Women of Missouri during the Sixties (Jefferson City, n.d.).

Report of the Joint Committee on the Conduct of the War (Washington, 1863).

Report of the Select Committee of the Senate Appointed to Inquire into the Late Invasion and Seizure of the Public Property at Harper's Ferry (Washington, 1860).

"Report of the Secretary of War," *Transactions of the Kansas State Historical Society,* IV, pp. 424–519.

Report of the Special Committee Appointed to Investigate the Troubles in Kansas (Washington, 1856).

Rhodes, James Ford, *History of the United States from the Compromise of 1850,* II (New York, 1920).

Richards, Oscar G., "Kansas Experiences," *Transactions of the Kansas State Historical Society,* IX, pp. 545–548.

Richardson, Albert D., *Beyond the Mississippi* (Hartford, 1867).

Richardson, Albert D., *Garnered Sheaves from the Writings of Albert D. Richardson, Collected and Arranged by his Wife* (Hartford, Conn., 1871).

Rister, Carl Coke, *Border Captives* (Norman, Okla., 1940).

Rister, Carl Coke, "Outlaws and Vigilantes of the Southern Plains," *Mississippi Valley Historical Review,* XIX, No. 4 (March 1933), pp. 537–554.

Rister, Carl Coke, *Southern Plainsmen* (Norman, Okla., 1938).

Roberts, O. F., "The Lane Family," *Collections of the Kansas State Historical Society,* XVI, pp. 29–32.

Robinson, Charles, "Address of Governor Robinson," *Transactions of the Kansas State Historical Society,* I and II, pp. 115–130.

Robinson, Charles, *The Kansas Conflict* (New York, 1892).

Robinson, Charles, "Topeka and Her Constitution," *Transactions of the Kansas State Historical Society,* VI, pp. 291–305.

Robinson, Sara, *Kansas; Its Interior and Exterior Life* (Boston, 1856).

Robinson, Sara, "The Wakarusa War," *Transactions of the Kansas State Historical Society,* X, pp. 457–471.

Rodenbough, Theophilus Francis, *From Everglade to Cañon with the Second Dragoons* (New York, 1875).

Rogers, James B., *War Pictures. Experiences and Observations of a Chaplain in the U.S. Army, in the War of the Southern Rebellion* (Chicago, 1863).

Rombauer, Robert J., *The Union Cause in St. Louis in 1861* (St. Louis, 1909).

Root, George A., ed., "Extracts from Diary of Captain Lambert Bowman Wolf," *Kansas Historical Quarterly,* I, No. 3 (May 1932), pp. 195–210.

Root, George A., "Ferries in Kansas," *Kansas Historical Quarterly,* VI, No. 1 (Feb. 1937), pp. 14–20.

[Ropes, Hanna Anderson], *Six Months in Kansas* (Boston, 1856).

Rose, Victor M., *The Life and Services of Gen. Ben McCulloch* (Philadelphia, 1888).

Rose, Victor M., *Ross' Texas Brigade. Being a Narrative of Events Connected with its Service in the Late War between the States* (Louisville, 1881).

Rosengarten, Joseph George, *The German Soldiers in the Wars of the United States* (Philadelphia, 1886).

Ross, Mollie, *The Life and Times of Hon. William P. Ross* (Fort Smith, Ark., 1893).

Roster and Record of Iowa Soldiers in the War of the Rebellion (Des Moines, 1908).

Rouse, E. S. S., *The Bugle Blast; or, Spirit of the Conflict* (Philadelphia, 1864).

Royce, Charles C., "The Cherokee Nation of Indians," *Fifth Annual Report of American Bureau of Ethnology* (Washington, 1887), pp. 121–378.

Royce, Josiah, "The Squatter Riot of '50 in Sacramento," *Overland Monthly,* VI, 2nd Ser. (Sept. 1885), pp. 224–246.

Rusling, James F., *Across America: or, The Great West and the Pacific Coast* (New York, 1874).

Sanborn, Franklin Benjamin, "J. G. Whittier as Politician," Kansas Scrapbook, Miscellaneous Speeches, I. KHi.

Sanborn, Franklin Benjamin, *The Life and Letters of John Brown* (Boston, 1885).

Sanborn, Franklin Benjamin, *Recollections of Seventy Years* (Boston, 1909).

Sanborn, Franklin Benjamin, "Some Notes on the Territorial History of Kansas," *Collections of the Kansas State Historical Society,* XIII, pp. 249–265.

Sanborn, John B., "The Campaign in Missouri in September and October, 1864," *Glimpses of the Nation's Struggle. Third Series . . . Minnesota Commandery of the Military Order of the Loyal Legion* (New York, 1893), pp. 135–204.

Sanborn, John B., "Reminiscences of the War in the Department of the Missouri," *Glimpses of the Nation's Struggle . . . Minnesota Commandery of the Military Order of the Loyal Legion* (St. Paul, 1887), pp. 224–257.

Sandburg, Carl, *Abraham Lincoln: The War Years* (New York, 1939).

Sandburg, Carl, *Lincoln Collector: The Story of Oliver R. Barrett's Great Private Collection* (New York, 1950).

Scharf, John Thomas, *History of Saint Louis City and County,* etc. (Philadelphia, 1883).

Schofield, John M., *Forty-six Years in the Army* (New York, 1897).

Scott, William Forse, "The Last Fight for Missouri," *Personal Recollections of the War of the Rebellion . . . New York Military Order of the Loyal Legion,* III (New York, 1907), pp. 292–328.

Scott, William Forse, *The Story of a Cavalry Regiment. The Career of the Fourth Iowa Veteran Volunteers from Kansas to Georgia, 1861–1865* (New York, 1893).

Scroggs, William Oscar, *Filibusters and Financiers, the Story of William Walker and his Associates* (New York, 1916).

Seabrook, S. L., "Expedition of Col. E. V. Sumner against the Cheyenne Indians, 1857," *Collections of the Kansas State Historical Society,* XVI, pp. 306–315.

Shackelford, Thomas, "Early Recollections of Missouri," *Missouri Historical Society Collections,* II, No. 2 (April 1903), pp. 1–19.

Shannon, Fred Albert, "The Civil War Letters of Sergeant Onley Andrus," *Illinois Studies in Social Science,* XXVIII, No. 4 (Urbana, 1947).

Shannon, Fred Albert, *The Organization and Administration of the Union Army, 1861–1865* (Cleveland, 1928).

Shea, John C., *Reminiscences of Quantrell's Raid upon the City of Lawrence, Kas.* (Kansas City, 1879).

[Sheahan, James W.], *The Life of Stephen A. Douglas* (New York, 1860).

Sheridan, Philip H., *Personal Memoirs* (New York, 1888).

Sherman, John, *John Sherman's Recollections of Forty Years in the House, Senate and Cabinet* (Chicago, 1895).

Sherman, William Tecumseh, *Memoirs* (New York, 1875).

Shimmons, J. H., "Reply to Hon. Eli Thayer," Lawrence *Kansas Daily Tribune,* June 7, 1879.

Shindler, Henry, "The First Capital of Kansas," *Collections of the Kansas State Historical Society,* XII, pp. 331–337.

Shoemaker, Floyd C., *Missouri and Missourians, Land of Contrasts and People of Achievements* (Chicago, 1943).

Shoemaker, Floyd C., "The Story of the Civil War in Northeast Missouri," *Missouri Historical Review,* VII, No. 2 (Jan. 1913), pp. 63–75; No. 3 (April 1913), pp. 113–131.

Sigel, Franz, "The Flanking Column at Wilson's Creek," *Battles and Leaders of the Civil War,* I, pp. 304–306.

Sigel, Franz, "The Military Operations in Missouri in the Summer and Autumn of 1861," *Missouri Historical Review,* XXVI, No. 4 (July 1932), pp. 354–367.

Sigel, Franz, "The Pea Ridge Campaign," *Battles and Leaders of the Civil War,* I, pp. 314–334.

Simons, W. C., "Lawrence Newspapers in Territorial Days," *Collections of the Kansas State Historical Society,* XVII, pp. 325–338.

A Sketch of the Early Life and of the Civil and Military Services of Maj. Gen. John W. Geary (Philadelphia, 1866).

Smith, Charles W., "Battle of Hickory Point, September 13, 1856," *Transactions of the Kansas State Historical Society,* VII, pp. 534–536.

Smith, Ed. R., "Marais des Cygnes Tragedy," *Transactions of the Kansas State Historical Society,* VI, pp. 365–370.

Smith, George Gardner, ed., *Spencer Kellogg Brown, his Life in Kansas and his Death as a Spy, 1842–1863, as Disclosed in his Diary* (New York, 1903).

Smith, William E., and Ophia D., *Colonel A. W. Gilbert, Citizen-Soldier of Cincinnati* (Cincinnati, 1934).

Smith, William E., *The Francis Preston Blair Family in Politics* (New York, 1933).

Smith, William Henry, *The History of the State of Indiana* (Indianapolis 1897).

Smith, William Henry, *A Political History of Slavery* (New York, 1903).

Smith, Winston O., *The Sharps Rifle, Its History, Development and Operation* (New York, 1943).

Snead, Thomas L., "The Conquest of Arkansas," *Battles and Leaders of the Civil War*, III, pp. 441–461.

Snead, Thomas L., *The Fight for Missouri from the Election of Lincoln to the Death of Lyon* (New York, 1886).

Snead, Thomas L., "The First Year of the War in Missouri," *Battles and Leaders of the Civil War*, I, pp. 262–277.

Snow, Francis Huntington, "The Beginnings of the University of Kansas," *Transactions of the Kansas State Historical Society*, VI, pp. 70–75.

Snyder, J. F., "Battle of Osawatomie," *Missouri Historical Review*, VI, No. 2 (Jan. 1912), pp. 82–85.

Sosey, Frank H., *Robert Devoy: A Tale of the Palmyra Massacre* (Palmyra, Mo., 1903).

Spear, Stephen Jackson, "Reminiscences of the Early Settlement of Dragoon Creek, Wabaunsee County," *Collections of the Kansas State Historical Society*, XIII, pp. 345–363.

Speer, John, "Accuracy in History," *Transactions of the Kansas State Historical Society*, VI, pp. 60–69.

Speer, John, *Life of James H. Lane, "the Liberator of Kansas"; with Corroborative Incidents of Pioneer History* (Garden City, Kan., 1897).

Spring, Leverett W., "The Career of a Kansas Politician," *American Historical Review*, IV, No. 1 (Oct. 1898), pp. 80–104.

Spring, Leverett W., *Kansas: the Prelude to the War for the Union* (Boston, 1885).

Stanley, Caroline Abbot, *Order No. 11, A Tale of the Border* (New York, 1904).

Stanton, Elizabeth Cady, *Eighty Years and More (1815–1897); Reminiscences of Elizabeth Cady Stanton* (London, 1898).

Stanton, Henry B., *Random Recollections* (Johnstown, N.Y., 1885).

Starr, Emmet, *History of the Cherokee Indians* (Oklahoma City, 1921).

Stephenson, Wendell Holmes, "Amos Lane, Advocate of Western Democracy," *Indiana Magazine of History*, XXVI, No. 3 (Sept. 1930), pp. 177–217.

Stephenson, Wendell Holmes, *The Political Career of General James H. Lane (Publications of the Kansas State Historical Society*, III, 1930).

Stephenson, Wendell Holmes, "The Transitional Period in the Career of General James H. Lane," *Indiana Magazine of History*, XXV, No. 2 (June 1929), pp. 75–91.

Sterling, Ada, *A Belle of the Fifties* (New York, 1905).

Stevens, Walter Barlow, "Lincoln and Missouri," *Missouri Historical Review*, X, No. 2 (Jan. 1916), pp. 63–119.

Stevens, Walter Barlow, *Missouri, the Center State, 1821–1915* (St. Louis, 1915).

Stevens, Walter Barlow, *St. Louis, the Fourth City, 1764–1909* (St. Louis, 1909).

Stewart, Faye L., "Battle of Pea Ridge," *Missouri Historical Review*, XXII, No. 2 (Jan. 1928), pp. 187–192.

Stillwell, Leander, *The Story of a Common Soldier of Army Life in the Civil War 1861–1865* (n.p., 1920).

Stoddard, W. A., "Story of a Nomination," *North American Review*, No. 328 (1884), pp. 263–273.

Stringfellow, Benjamin F., *Negro-Slavery, No Evil; or, the North and the South* (St. Louis, 1854). Also printed in *Two Tracts for the Times* (1855).

Stringfellow, Benjamin F., *Slavery in Kansas; Letter in Reply to One Addressed to Him by the Hon. P. S. Brooks, T. L. Clingman, Wm. Smith, and John McQueen* (Washington, 1855).

Stringfellow, Jacob, "Jim Lane," *Lippincott's Magazine of Literature, Science and Education* (March 1870), pp. 260–278.

Stuart, Addison A., *Iowa Colonels and Regiments: Being a History of Iowa Regiments in the War of the Rebellion* (Des Moines, 1865).

Sumner, Charles, *The Crime Against Kansas* (Washington, 1856).

Sumner, Charles, *Kansas Affairs: Speech of Hon. Charles Sumner of Massachusetts in the Senate of the United States, May 19, 1856* (n.p., n.d.).

The Supreme Council, 33°. Mother Council of the World Ancient and Accepted Scottish Rite of Freemasonry, Southern Jurisdiction, U.S.A. (Louisville, Ky., 1931).

Switzler, William F., *Switzler's Illustrated History of Missouri from 1541 to 1877* (St. Louis, 1879).

Tannar, A. H., "Early Days in Kansas. The Marais des Cygnes Massacre and the Rescue of Ben Rice," *Collections of the Kansas State Historical Society*, XIV, pp. 224–234.

Taylor, T. U., *Jesse Chisholm* (Baudera, Texas, 1939).

Thayer, Eli, *A History of the Kansas Crusade* (New York, 1889).

Thayer, Eli, *The New England Emigrant Aid Company and Its Influence, through the Kansas Contest, upon National History* (Worcester, Mass., 1887).

Thoburn, Joseph B., "The Cherokee Question," *Chronicles of Oklahoma*, II, No. 2 (June 1924), pp. 140–242.

Thomas, David Y., *Arkansas in War and Reconstruction, 1861–1874* (Little Rock, 1926).

Thomas, Evangeline, *Nativism in the Old Northwest* (Washington, 1936).

Thomas, John L., "Some Historical Lines of Missouri," *Missouri Historical Review*, III, No. 1 (Oct. 1908), pp. 5–33.

Thomas, Raymond D., "A Study in Missouri Politics, 1840–1870," *Missouri Historical Review*, XXI, No. 2 (Jan. 1927), pp. 166–184; No. 3 (April 1927), pp. 438–454.

Thompson, S. D., *Recollections with the Third Iowa* (Cincinnati, 1864).

Tomlinson, William P., *Kansas in Eighteen Fifty-Eight, Being Chiefly a History of the Recent Troubles in the Territory* (New York, 1859).

Tourgée, Albion Winegar, *The Story of a Thousand* (Buffalo, 1896).

Townsend, Amos, "With the Kansas Congressional Committee of 1856," *Magazine of Western History*, VII, No. 5 (March 1888), pp. 487–505.

Townsend, George Alfred, "Annals of the War," Philadelphia *Weekly Times*, Aug. 4, 1877, printed in *Switzler's Illustrated History of Missouri* (St. Louis, 1879), p. 382.

Townsend, George Alfred, *Campaigns of a Non-combatant* (New York, 1866).

Transactions of the Missouri Lodge of Research (privately printed, 1945).

Treichel, Charles, "Major Zagoni's Horse Guard," *Personal Recollections of the War of the Rebellion . . . New York Military Order of the Loyal Legion*, III (New York, 1907), pp. 240–246.

The Trial of Frank James for Murder (Kansas City, n.d.).

Tunnard, William H., *A Southern Record. The History of the Third Regiment Louisiana Infantry* (Baton Rouge, 1866).

United States Biographical Dictionary, Kansas Volume (Chicago, 1879).

United States Indian Office, *Executive Documents*, House of Representatives, 37th to 39th Congresses, containing correspondence to the Indian Office.

United States Indian Office, *Loyal Creek Claim: Hearings before a Subcommittee of the Committee on Indian Affairs of the House of Representatives on H. R. 9326* (Washington, 1916).

United States Indian Office, *Report of the Commissioner of Indian Affairs, 1859 to 1865.*

United States Record and Pension Office, *Organization and Status of Missouri Troops (Union and Confederate) in Service during the Civil War* (Washington, 1902).

United States War Department, *The Report of the Secretary of War, 1861* (Washington, 1862).

United States War Department, *A Report on Barracks and Hospitals, with Descriptions of Military Posts* (Washington, 1870).

Upton, Lucile Morris, *Battle of Wilson's Creek: Reprinted from Articles by Lucile Morris Upton in the Springfield News and Leader* (Springfield, Mo., 1950).

Van Deusen, Glyndon Garlock, *Horace Greeley, Nineteenth-Century Crusader* (Philadelphia, 1953).

Van Deventer, Horace, *Albert Pike: A Biographical Sketch* (Knoxville, Tenn., 1910).

Victor, Orville J., *Incidents and Anecdotes of the War: Together with Life Sketches of Eminent Leaders, and Narratives of the Most Memorable Battles for the Union* (New York, 1862).

Viles, Jonas, ed., "Documents Illustrating the Troubles on the Border, 1858, 1859, 1860," *Missouri Historical Review*, I, No. 3 (April 1907), pp. 198–215; No. 4 (July 1907), pp. 293–306; II, No. 1 (Oct. 1907), pp. 61–77.

Villard, Henry, *Memoirs of Henry Villard, Journalist and Financier, 1835–1900* (Boston, 1904).

Villard, Oswald Garrison, *John Brown, 1800–1859: A Biography Fifty Years After* (Boston, 1910).

Violette, Eugene Morrow, "Battle of Kirksville, Aug. 6, 1862," *Missouri Historical Review*, V, No. 2 (Jan. 1911), pp. 94–112.

Violette, Eugene Morrow, *History of Missouri* (Boston, 1918).

Vocke, William, "Our German Soldiers," *Military Essays and Recollections . . . Illinois Military Order of the Loyal Legion*, III (Chicago, 1899), pp. 341–371.

"Wakarusa War Papers," *Transactions of the Kansas State Historical Society, 1889–'96*, V, pp. 242–250.

Walker, William, *The War in Nicaragua* (Mobile, 1860).

Wallace, William A., *Speeches and Writings* (Kansas City, 1914).

Walsh, Richard, *The Making of Buffalo Bill* (Indianapolis, 1928).

The War of the Rebellion: A Compilation of the Official Records of the Union and Confederate Armies (Washington, 1880–1901).

Wardell, Morris L., *A Political History of the Cherokee Nation, 1838–1907* (Norman, Okla., 1938).

Ware, Eugene Fitch, *The Indian War of 1864* (Topeka, 1911).

Ware, Eugene Fitch, *The Lyon Campaign in Missouri: Being a History of the First Iowa Infantry* (Topeka, 1907).

Watson, William, *Life in the Confederate Army, Being the Observations and Experiences of an Alien in the South during the American Civil War* (London, 1887).

Webb, W. L., *Battles and Biographies of Missourians, or, the Civil War Period of our State* (Kansas City, 1900).

Weichselbaum, Theodore, "Statement of Theodore Weichselbaum, of Ogden, Riley County, July 17, 1908," *Collections of the Kansas State Historical Society*, XL, pp. 561–571.

Weisberger, Bernard A., *Reporters for the Union* (Boston, 1953).

Wherry, William M., *The Campaign in Missouri and the Battle of Wilson's Creek, 1861. A Paper Read before the Missouri Historical Society of St. Louis, March, 1880* (St. Louis, 1880).

Wherry, William M., "General Nathaniel Lyon and his Campaign in Missouri in 1861," *Sketches of War History, 1861–1865 . . . Ohio Commandery of the Loyal Legion,* IV (Cincinnati, 1896), pp. 68–86.

Wherry, William M., "In Memoriam — Lieutenant-General John M. Schofield, U.S.A.," *Personal Recollections of the War of the Rebellion . . . New York Military Order of the Loyal Legion,* III (New York, 1907), pp. 446–471.

Wherry, William M., "Wilson's Creek, and the Death of Lyon," *Battles and Leaders of the Civil War,* I, pp. 289–297.

Wilder, Daniel Webster, *The Annals of Kansas* (Topeka, 1875).

Wilder, Daniel Webster, *The Annals of Kansas* (Topeka, 1886). A different book from the preceding.

Wilder, Daniel Webster, "The Story of Kansas," *Transactions of the Kansas State Historical Society,* VI, pp. 342–343.

Wilkie, Franc Bangs, "The Battle of Wilson's Creek," *Palimpsest,* IX, No. 8 (Aug. 1928), pp. 291–310.

Wilkie, Franc Bangs, *The Iowa First; Letters from the War* (Dubuque, 1861).

Wilkie, Franc Bangs, *Pen and Powder* (Boston, 1888).

Williams, Ellen, *Three Years and a Half in the Army; or, History of the Second Colorados* (New York, 1885).

Williams, Kenneth P., *Lincoln Finds a General: A Military Study of the Civil War* (New York, 1952).

Williams, R. H., *With the Border Ruffians: Memories of the Far West, 1852–1868,* ed. by E. W. Williams (New York, 1907).

Williams, T. Harry, "Frémont and the Politicians," *Journal of the American Military History Foundation,* II, pp. 179–191.

Williams, T. Harry, *Lincoln and His Generals* (New York, 1952).

Wilson, Hill P., *John Brown, Soldier of Fortune: A Critique* (Lawrence, 1913).

Wilstach, Frank J., *Wild Bill Hickok: Prince of Pistoleers* (New York, 1926).

Woodhull, Alfred A., "Kansas in 1861," *War Talks in Kansas . . . Kansas Commandery of the Military Order of the Loyal Legion* (Kansas City, 1906), pp. 10–23.

Woodruff, William Edward, *With the Light Guns in '61–'65. Reminiscences of Eleven Arkansas, Missouri and Texas Light Batteries, in the Civil War* (Little Rock, 1903).

Woodward, Ashbel, *Life of General Nathaniel Lyon* (Hartford, Conn., 1862).

Woodward, Brinton W., "Reminiscences of September 14, 1856; Invasion of the 2700," *Transactions of the Kansas State Historical Society,* VI, pp. 77–83.

Wright, Marcus J., *General Officers of the Confederate Army* (New York, 1911).

Wyman, Walker D., "Kansas City, Mo., a Famous Freighter Capital," *Kansas Historical Quarterly,* VI, No. 1 (Feb. 1937), pp. 3–13.

Zornow, William F., "The Missouri Radicals and the Election of 1864," *Missouri Historical Review*, XLV, No. 4 (July 1951), pp. 354–370.

NEWSPAPERS

Boonville [Missouri] *Weekly Advertiser*
Camp Register of the Thirty-Seventh Reg't. Ill's. Vol's.
Centralia [Missouri] *Fireside Guard*
Chicago Daily Democratic Press
Chicago Times
Chicago Tribune
Cincinnati Commercial
Cincinnati Gazette
Clarksville, Texas, *Standard*
Doniphan *Kansas Crusader of Freedom*
Emporia [Kansas] *News*
Fort Smith [Arkansas] *New Era*
Fort Smith Times and Herald
Huntsville, Missouri, *Randolph Citizen*
Jefferson [City, Missouri] *Examiner*
Jefferson [City, Missouri] *Weekly Inquirer*
Junction City, Kansas, *Smoky Hill and Republican Union*
Junction City Union
Kansas City Journal
Daily Kansas City Journal of Commerce
Kansas City Post
Kansas City Star
Kansas City Times
Kansas City *Western Journal of Commerce*
Lawrence Daily Journal-World
Lawrence *Herald of Freedom*
Lawrence *Kansas Daily Tribune*
Lawrence *Kansas Free State*
Lawrence Republican
Leavenworth *Daily Conservative*
Leavenworth *Daily Tribune*
Leavenworth *Democratic Standard*
Leavenworth Herald
Leavenworth Times
Lecompton [Kansas] *Union*
Little Rock *Arkansas Gazette*

Little Rock *Arkansas Patriot*
Little Rock *Arkansas True Democrat*
Little Rock *Daily State Journal*
Los Angeles Semi-Weekly Southern News
Los Angeles Star
New Orleans *Picayune*
New York Herald
New York Times
New York Tribune
New York *World*
Philadelphia *Weekly Times*
Richmond, Virginia, *Southern Opinion*
Sacramento Daily Transcript
Sacramento Union
St. Joseph Gazette
St. Joseph Morning Herald
St. Joseph Weekly Commercial Cycle
St. Joseph *Weekly West*
St. Louis *Daily Missouri Democrat*
St. Louis *Daily Missouri Republican*
St. Louis Globe-Democrat
St. Louis Post-Dispatch
St. Louis Reveille
San Francisco *Alta California*
Soldier's Letter (regimental newspaper of the Second Colorado)
Springfield *Illinois State Journal*
Topeka Mail
Tulsa Daily World
Van Buren [Arkansas] *Press*
Washington [Arkansas] *Telegraph*
Washington, D.C., *Daily National Era*
Washington, D.C., *National Intelligencer*
Washington [D.C.] *Sentinel*
Westport, Missouri, *Border Star*
Westport Border Times
White Cloud [Kansas]*Chief*
Winona [Minnesota] *Weekly Republican*

SCRAPBOOKS

Anderson, James, History of Westport, Clippings, Native Sons of Kansas City Archives, Kansas City.

Kansas City Native Sons Scrapbook.

Kansas Indian Depredations & Battles, Clippings, KHi.

Kansas Scrapbook, Biography, KHi.

Kansas Scrapbook, Miscellaneous Speeches, KHi.

Kansas Territory, Clippings, KHi.

McCoy Scrapbook, Native Sons of Kansas City Archives, Kansas City.

Webb, Thomas H., Scrapbook, KHi.

MANUSCRIPTS

Baker, J. H. P., diary, MoHi.

Bell, R. J., diary, MoSHi.

Bent, George, correspondence, CtY.

Benton, Richard H., "Reminiscences," typescript, MoHi.

Blair Papers, DLC.

Broadhead Papers, MoSHi.

Brown, John, Papers, DLC.

Brown, R. L., and A. T. Irwine, "Army Journal, 1864," MoSHi.

Byington, Cyrus, typed copy of diary, OkHi.

Cherokee Nation, Minute-book of Executive Department, OkHi.

Cherokee Register of Claims, Phillips Collection, OkU.

Cherokee Tribal File, Indian Archives Division, OkHi.

Choctaw Nation Council, Acts and Minutes, OkHi.

Connelley, William E., "First Homicide of the Territorial Troubles in Kansas," typescript, KHi.

Creek Nation, Council Book, OkHi.

Curtis, Samuel Ryan, Papers, CSmH and IaDH.

Davis, Jefferson, Papers, DLC.

"Diary of Unknown Soldier," MoSHi.

Dodge Papers, IaDH.

Eldredge Collection, Colton Greene folder, Box 38, CSmH.

Elmoore, Day, letters in possession of Mrs. Hall Mosher, Memphis, Tenn.

Ewing Papers, DLC.

Gordon, Mary Gentry Clark, typed copy of diary-letter to sister, MoHi.

Grabill, Lee R., "A Long Story," typescript, MoHi.

Grayson, G. W., "Red Paths and White," typed autobiography, Phillips Collection, OkU.

Griffith, George W. E., "My Experiences in the Quantrill Raid," typed copy from Lawrence, Kan., *Daily Journal World,* Aug. 21, 1924, DLC.

Gunn, Jack Winton, "Life of Ben McCulloch" (M.A. thesis, University of Texas).

Hand, George O., photostat of diary, Aug. 19, 1861 to May 19, 1864, DLC.

Hazen, William G., typed copy of letter to brother Alex, n.d., 1864, MoHi.

Holland, C. B., typed report of Battle of Springfield, MoHi.

Hubbell, Richard, "Reminiscences," typescript, MoHi.

Hyde, George, "Life of George Bent," CoD.

"Indian-Pioneer History," typed interviews, Phillips Collection, OkU.

Ingalls, John James, "First Homicide," typescript, KHi.

Johnson, Charles B., Papers, ICN.

Johnson, William M., Papers, Native Sons Library, Kansas City.

Kimmel, C. T., diary, MoHi.

Kiowa Agency, copy of Letter Press Book, Phillips Collection, OkU.

Kiowa Agency, copy of Shirley Trading House ledger, Phillips Collection, OkU.

Langston, Bernadyn Haradon, "The South and the Kansas-Nebraska Bill" (M.A. thesis, University of Texas).

Lincoln Papers, DLC.

Lowman, Hovey E., "Narrative of the Lawrence Massacre," typed copy, KHi.

McGee, Elijah Milton, autobiography, Native Sons Library, Kansas City.

Morgan, J. L., copy of letter to brother, 1864, MoHi.

Murphy, David, "My Recollections of Pilot Knob," MoSHi.

Neely, McGinley M., Papers, DLC.

Phillips Collection, Correspondence, Miscellaneous Papers, OkU.

Pike, Albert, Papers, DLC and Scottish Rite Temple, Washington, D.C.

"Proceedings of the [Lafayette] County Board which convened on the order of the Military Department to investigate the murder of loyal citizens," minutes from Aug. 14 to Oct. 2, 1862, MoSHi.

Quesenberry, John T., diary, MoSHi.

Reader, Samuel J., diary, KHi.

Reynolds, Thomas C., "General Sterling Price and the Confederacy," typescript, St. Louis Public Library.

Rice, Franklin P., "The Life of Eli Thayer," typescript, MWA.

Riley, Susan B., "The Life and Works of Albert Pike to 1860" (Ph.D. thesis, Peabody College).

Rombauer, Robert, "Biographical Notes," MoSHi.

Ryle, Walter H., "Missouri: Union or Secession" (Ph.D. thesis, Peabody College).

Sac and Fox Agency, Letter Press Book, OkHi.

Schrader, William H., "Reminiscences," MoHi.

Smith, George Winston, "Generative Forces of Union Propaganda: A Study of Civil War Pressure Groups" (Ph.D. thesis, University of Wisconsin).

Snyder, John F., Papers, MoSHi.

Sweeney, Thomas William, Papers, Heintzelman Collection, CSmH.

Tasher, Lucy Lucile, "The *Missouri Democrat* and the Civil War" (Ph.D. thesis, University of Chicago).

Thayer, Eli, Papers, RPB.

Thompson, M. Jeff., "Autobiography," in Jay Monaghan's possession.

Treat, Samuel, Papers, MoSHi.

United States Office Indian Affairs, "Confederate Papers," DNA.

United States Office Indian Affairs, correspondence relating to Texas, Tx.

United States Office Indian Affairs, letters received, DNA.

United States Office Indian Affairs, "Statement relative to the Exodus of Hopoith-la-yo-ho-la and his followers from the Creek and Cherokee Country in the fall and winter of 1861-'62," letters received, Choctaw C-676-11868, DNA.

Van Horn Papers, MoSHi.

Venable, Robert Cross, "The Kansas Frontier, 1861–1875" (M.A. thesis, University of Oklahoma).

Washburne Papers, DLC.

Watie, Stand, File on Finances, Phillips Collection, OkU; Papers, Tx.

Westover, John Glendower, ed., "The Civil War Experiences of General M. Jeff. Thompson in 1861" (M.A. thesis, University of Missouri).

Wichita and Affiliated Tribes *vs* United States, Court of Claims No. E — 542, DNA.

Acknowledgments

I AM INDEBTED to the American Philosophical Society for a grant in aid which gave me the opportunity to study the civilized Indian nations. At the University of Oklahoma, E. E. Dale, Morris Wardell, Gaston Litton, and R. S. Cate helped immeasurably with my research in the Phillips Collection, as did Charles Evans, Muriel Wright, and Rella Looney at the Oklahoma State Historical Society, and Professor C. C. Rister at Texas Technological College. Winnie Allen, Lorena Baker, and N. A. Cleveland were unstinting in their aid at the University of Texas. Ruth Lapham Butler, of the Ayer Collection at the Newberry Library, Chicago, and Richard G. Wood, of the National Archives in Washington, provided valuable documents for my consideration. Many thanks are due James Anderson, historian of the Native Sons of Kansas City, for the use of a splendid library and for taking me over the battlefields of Independence and Westport.

A fellowship at the Henry E. Huntington Library enabled me to work in that institution's vast Civil War collection of manuscripts and printed sources, with the Misses Norma Cuthbert, Mary Isabelle Fry, Haydee Noya, and Phyllis Rigney ever on the alert to provide pertinent material. I also want to express my gratitude to Donald C. Davidson, whose long-range vision has made the Wyles library of Lincolniana, University of California at Santa Barbara, an outstanding collection in the Civil War field.

Nyle Miller and Helen McFarland, of the Kansas State Historical Society, have been indefatigable in their search for helpful items in the large repository at Topeka. Floyd Shoemaker and Sarah Guitar, of the Missouri State Historical Society, have supplied important data from the fine sources in Columbia. At the Jefferson Memorial Library in St. Louis, Francis Biese was resourceful and untiring in my behalf. David C. Mearns and Roy P. Basler, in the Library of Congress, have aided me far beyond the call of duty. I am especially indebted to Claude R. Cooke, Department of History and Archives at Des Moines, for photostats of important documents. Historians Bell I. Wiley and Richard Harwell, of Emory University, shared with me their knowledge of rare books and letters. To David Lavander, of Ojai, California, I owe the material on George Bent. Harry E. Pratt and Margaret Flint, of the Illinois State Historical Library, Don Russell, military analyst in Chicago, and Elmer Gertz, enthusiastic Civil War scholar, have always answered inquiries with alacrity. Mrs. Kathryn C. Merriam has typed this manuscript with speed and skill.

As in previous books, my greatest obligation is to Mildred, my wife. She has been a Florence Nightingale, alleviating the blood and tears on all the battle-fields of this book. Together we have traveled up and down the Western border and through the long, dusty pages of manuscript. Her skillful editorial eye, literary judgment, and sweet indulgence for a guerrilla husband — who is apt to shoot and run — truly makes this OUR book.

J. M.

Index

ADAMS, BOSTON, 328
Alabama, 100, 312
Alligator (Indian), 220, 227
Alma, battle of, 181
Alton, Illinois, 16
American Hotel, 28, 53, 60, 107
American Party, 132. *See also* Know-Nothing Party
American Revolution, 221, 323
Anderson, William ("Bloody Bill"), 254, 274, 281, 316, 322; sisters imprisoned, 280; at Centralia, 317; killed, 323, 344
"Andersonville or hell," 261
Andrews, George L., 166
Anthony, Dan, characterized, 9–11; early days in Kansas, 9, 110, 111, 128; newspaperman, 94, 126, 289; acquitted of murder, 182; cattle trader, 305; death, 350
Anthony, Susan B., 10, 350
Antietam, 314
Anti-Nebraska Party, 16
Anzeiger des Westens, 118, 132
Apache Indians, 227
Appomattox, 347
Arapaho Indians, 227, 275, 302, 344
Arkansas, in early war days, 135, 146, 149, 151, 162; regiments, 156, 172, 177, 178, 180, 242; newspapers, 214; state Democratic convention, 214; young men addressed by Van Dorn, 234; Sigel in northwest, 236; conscripts, 265, 267, 279, 342; Price starts to, 328; surrenders, 347
Arkansas College, 232
Arkansas River, 225, 308, 310, 342
Armstrong Academy, 297
Army of the North. *See* Lane, James Henry
Army of the Potomac, 253
Arnold, Benedict, 127
Asboth, Alexander S., under Frémont, 183,

199, 200, 205; under Curtis, 232, 236, 237, 244; wounded, 245
Ash Hollow, 32
Atchison, Kansas, 9, 18, 111, 323
Atchison, David Rice, in Senate, 4, 6, 54; returns to Missouri, 7, 8; and his constituents, 11, 12, 15, 20, 78; relations with Pierce, 11, 21, 22; at Kansas elections, 13, 17; political machine, 28, 46, 47, 64, 65, 98; with Missouri invaders, 38, 86, 88, 89; at sack of Lawrence, 57–59, 80–82; Benton's opponent, 66, 120, 183; Lane proposes duel, 90; endorses Lecompton, 99; Denver's friend, 101; retirement from politics, 106, 119, 125; joins Jackson column, 150, 153, 156–158; old age, 350–351
Atlanta, Georgia, 302, 306
Aubry, Kansas, 281
Austerlitz, 259, 328

BAKER, J. H. P., 343
Balaclava, battle of, 181, 201, 349
Baldwin City, Kansas, 108, 287, 304
Ball's Bluff, battle of, 204
Baltimore, Maryland, convention of 1864, 303
Banks, Nathaniel, Jr., 48, 50, 298
Baptist Church, 219, 220
Barber, Thomas, 41–44, 56, 57
Bates, Edward, 118
Batesville, Missouri, 272
Baxter Springs, 293
Bear Creek, 152, 154
Beauregard, Pierre Gustave, 130, 183
Belch, Seth, 103
Bell, Casper, 326
Bell, John, 119
Belleville, Illinois, 131

"A damaged post-war city and two damaged post-war hearts collide in Rachel McMillan's latest gripping romantic drama. Ex-codebreaker Sophie Villier... ...e, are thrown... ...relic, and ju... ...wine beauti... ...—an enchar...

"Vienn... deft, ch... meticu... throug... —Su... T... ...LING ...ODE ...with ...lan's ...hine ...R OF ...SPY

"Rach... trigu... fictio... ible S... and l... feels... kept... rom... a ris... ...t in... ...ical ...ess- ...nna ...on ...rt, ...us ...1 is ...OR ...ES

"Sw... writ... ...lly ...ND ...HE

"Beautifully lush and atmospheric, *The Mozart Code* is a novel full of nuances and brimming with danger, romance, and intrigue. Simon and Sophie are wonderfully complicated, both in personalities and in their interactions. I lived for the moments Simon and Sophie were on page together and I delighted in the ending Rachel McMillan penned for them."

—JENNI L. WALSH, AUTHOR OF *BECOMING BONNIE* AND *THE CALL OF THE WRENS*

"Equal parts heart-fluttering romance and heart-pounding mystery, *The Mozart Code* left me breathless as the strike of an eighth note or a move on a chess board propelled steadfast Simon and whip-smart Sophie through the seedy streets of post–World War II Vienna and Prague seeking not only the answers to the clues set before them, but also the missing notes concealed from the concerto of their hearts."

—JOY CALLAWAY, INTERNATIONAL BESTSELLING AUTHOR OF *THE FIFTH AVENUE ARTISTS SOCIETY* AND *THE GREENBRIER RESORT*

"With sumptuous storytelling and impeccable attention to historical detail, the cities of Vienna and Prague hang like lovers from each arm as McMillan leads readers along the streets of her imagined post-war world of intrigue and romance in *The Mozart Code*. Before they know it, they're far from their armchairs and deeply in love with Simon and Sophie. Rife with secret codes, haunting melodies, betrayal and sacrifice, at its heart this is a story about the courage it takes to love and be loved. Long after I finished reading, a sweet and hopeful refrain lingers. Highly recommended!"

—KIMBERLY BROCK, AUTHOR OF *THE LOST BOOK OF ELEANOR DARE*

"*The Mozart Code* is a dashing, elegant, and occasionally heartbreaking adventure that takes us to post-war Vienna in all its beauty and despair."

—DIANA BILLER, AUTHOR OF *THE WIDOW OF ROSE HOUSE*

"A well-researched and engrossing tale richly woven with intrigue, mystery, and romance. *The Mozart Code* takes readers on a gripping journey through post-war Vienna and Prague, with its hero and heroine forced to navigate the perils of both treachery and trust. Yet amid a world built on duplicity and deception, Simon and Sophie discover an unexpected truth of their own—that an extraordinary friendship can become the most extraordinary love."

—KELLY BOWEN, AUTHOR OF *THE PARIS APARTMENT*

"A seamless blend of history, romance, and suspense, *The Mozart Code* perfectly encapsulates the essence of a beautiful city steeped in intrigue and a relationship filled with both deep trust and poignant uncertainty. Vivid historical detail, moments taut with secrets and danger, and McMillan's luminous prose make this an absolute gem of a book. I was invested in every moment of Simon and Sophie's story!"

—ASHLEY WEAVER, AUTHOR THE AMORY AMES
MYSTERIES AND THE ELECTRA MCDONNELL SERIES

"*The Mozart Code* is a gorgeous novel reminiscent of classic film noir with atmospheric storytelling and a tightly woven plot. This is a simmering love story set amidst danger and espionage that historical fiction readers will love."

—HARPER ST. GEORGE

"Electricity crackles across the pages of *The Mozart Code* as Rachel McMillan puts her characters on the high stakes chessboard of postwar Vienna and sets them loose, each move bringing them closer to uncovering secrets concealed by the shadow of WWII. The suspense is only heightened by the will-they-won't-they dynamic of the main characters, the twists and turns of their personal and professional lives keeping me reading late into the night."

—BRYN TURNBULL, BESTSELLING AUTHOR
OF *THE WOMAN BEFORE WALLIS*

"By turns elegantly intellectual and bewitchingly romantic, *The Mozart Code* is a stand-out, set against the lavishly textured backdrops of Prague and Vienna. Stretched to the breaking point in a world fraught with secrets, subterfuge, and spies, the indelible connection between Simon and Sophie sparkles like sun on snow. An absolute pleasure."

—STEPHANIE GRAVES, AUTHOR OF THE
OLIVE BRIGHT MYSTERY SERIES

"With its elegant prose and beautifully nuanced characters, *The Mozart Code* is a joy to read. As luminous as Vienna after the rain and as lyrical as a piece of classical music, it takes the reader not only through a captivating tale of espionage but also deep into the experience of love. Historical romance fans will swoon over Simon and Sophie and their journey towards peace."

—INDIA HOLTON, NATIONAL BESTSELLING AUTHOR OF
THE WISTERIA SOCIETY OF LADY SCOUNDRELS

"Deftly traversing the lushness of Vienna and Prague and upper-crust England, *The Mozart Code* brings to life the glories and devastation and intrigue of postwar Europe. Shady characters and cryptic codes and mixed motives and double-crosses make for a pulse-pounding read. And oh, the romance! Simon and Sophie's story is one for the ages, crackling with electricity and witty banter and buried hurts and guarded emotions. Rachel McMillan's beautiful writing encourages you to read slowly, to savor the lines and ponder the clues—but the story propels you to flip pages faster than a Mozart arpeggio! Enjoy the journey."

—SARAH SUNDIN, BESTSELLING AND AWARD-WINNING AUTHOR
OF *UNTIL LEAVES FALL IN PARIS* AND *WHEN TWILIGHT BREAKS*